Pidgin and Creole Linguistics

DEREK BICKERTON, *University of Hawaii*
ROBERT CHAUDENSON, *Centre Universitaire de la Réunion*
DENNIS R. CRAIG, *University of the West Indies, Jamaica*
CHARLES E. DEBOSE, *California State University, Fresno*
DAVID DECAMP, *University of Texas, Austin, and the Center for
Applied Linguistics*
CHARLES A. FERGUSON, *Stanford University*
IAN F. HANCOCK, *University of Texas, Austin*
ROBERT LE PAGE, *University of York*
GABRIEL MANESSY, *Université de Nice*
GUUS MEIJER, *University of Amsterdam*
PIETER MUYSKEN, *University of Amsterdam*
JOHN R. RICKFORD, *University of Guyana*
ELIZABETH CLOSS TRAUGOTT, *Stanford University*
ALBERT VALDMAN, *Indiana University*
KEITH WHINNOM, *University of Exeter*
STEPHEN A. WURM, *Australian National University*

Pidgin and Creole Linguistics

Edited by

ALBERT VALDMAN

NORTHWEST COMMUNITY
COLLEGE

INDIANA UNIVERSITY PRESS
BLOOMINGTON & LONDON

Published in Canada by Fitzhenry & Whiteside Limited, Don Mills, Ontario
Manufactured in the United States of America

Library of Congress Cataloging in Publication Data
Main entry under title:
Pidgin and creole linguistics.
   Bibliography
   Includes index.
   1. Pidgin languages—Addresses, essays, lectures.
2. Creole dialects—Addresses, essays, lectures.
3. Sociolinguistics—Addresses, essays, lectures.
I. Valdman, Albert.
PM7802.P48   301.2'1   76-48496
ISBN 0-253-34495-6   1 2 3 4 5 81 80 79 78 77

Contents

Foreword

The writing of this foreword has fallen to me, not because I can add anything theoretical to the book, but because I am probably the only survivor of the persons who were writing on pidgins and creoles in the 1930s, such as Carlo Tagliavini, László Gáldi, Jules Faine, Suzanne Comhaire-Sylvain, George S. Lane, Alfredo German, Louis Hjelmslev, Melville and Frances Herskovits, T. E. Pardoe, Lorenzo D. Turner, Harry Sawyerr, Melville Jacobs, Malcolm Guthrie, É. de Boeck and other missionaries in the Belgian Congo.[1] In a way I am a link with the earlier period analyzed by Muysken and Meijer in this volume, for I exchanged a few letters with the aged Hesseling.

Creole studies, if we begin with J. M. Magens's *Grammatica over det Creolske sprog* (1770), have passed their bicentennial. Chronologically speaking, they were by no means in their infancy forty-five years ago. A number of reasonably full descriptions of particular languages had appeared before Schuchardt's time. Beginning with Greenfield's surprisingly sophisticated defense (1830) of the Surinam Negro-English Testament against its detractors and Van Name's survey of eight West Indian creoles (1870), we can detect a movement toward the comparative study of creoles of European lexical base. Linguists and to some extent the general public were aware of pidgins and creoles. Besides Schuchardt's influence we must count that of Jespersen's widely read *Language* (1922), a book at once scholarly and popular, which devoted a chapter to "Pidgins and Congeners." Even though most of the writing about these languages was confined to description, many of the problems that concern creolists today had been stated or at least adumbrated.

But if no longer in their infancy, creole studies in the 1930s had not passed their adolescence either quantitatively or qualitatively. (Have they outgrown it in 1976? Reading the pages of respectful argument devoted to some of the more dogmatic and extreme forms of what is called the monogenetic theory, I sometimes wonder.)[2] For the most part, creole studies were peripheral to the main theoretical concerns of linguistics; they were a field cultivated mainly by amateur or semi-amateur aficionados. Reflecting this distance from the subtler problems of linguistics and a general lack of sophistication, writing on pidgins and creoles was mostly in such untechnical language that a layman like myself could understand it without much difficulty. The amount of information on any one pidgin or creole ranged from bare mention to two or three tolerably adequate sketches of it. (For all but a few such languages this statement is equally true in the present tense.) Except for a few glances at Chinook Jargon, creole studies were Eurocentric, concerned with languages of European lexicon and especially with that classic area of plantation creoles, the Caribbean. (For the most part they still are.) Descriptions of African-based and other non-European pidgins/creoles were scarcely considered part of creole studies. (Although the situation is now changing, as evidenced among other writings by Manessy's article in this volume, theoretical treatment of pidgins and creoles is still overwhelmingly based on those of European lexicon.) Creole studies were compartmentalized: Guthrie and Jacobs and Sawyerr, for instance, might almost have been writing on three different planets for aught each knew and cared about the others' work. The inaccessibility of much of the writing, unpublished theses in particular, hindered the development of a wide perspective among creolists. (And still does, although the situation is improving.)[3]

Now, but chiefly since the Mona conference of 1959—as pointed out by DeCamp in this volume and Bickerton (1976)—creole studies have won a place as a distinctive, respectable area of linguistics. In Traugott's words, instead of being the special and the marginal case, "pidginization and creolization have become central to linguistic theory." Every year the literature expands: more than a hundred synopses of papers were submitted for the Honolulu conference of 1975 alone. Every year some new linguistic problem is tied in with creole studies. Every year the writing becomes more nuanced, wide-ranging, and thorough. For the time being, 'creolistics' flourishes as a more or less autonomous area. One asks: For how long will this state of things continue? Certainly, from now on, the problems of pidginization, creolization, and decreolization will continue to be treated with respect. But will there continue to be 'creolists' per se? I leave the answer to more competent persons than I, and, at the risk of emphasizing the obvious, call attention to two respects in which creole studies still fall short of maturity and therefore are not of maximum usefulness to the student.

First, the material we have to work with is very inadequate and unevenly distributed. Think of the languages on which nothing has yet been written, such as Sadari (in Bihar and Orissa), or for which we depend on a single paper or article, such as the creole Portuguese of Senegal (Chataigner 1963). What would we know about the extinct pidgin of the Japanese ports if Atkinson (1879) had not published 31 pages in a spirit of tomfoolery (see Howell 1976)? Or about the extinct Russenorsk if Broch had not devoted two articles (1927, 1930) to it? Billions of dollars were poured into the Vietnam war; not a cent was spent to record whatever incipient pidgin(s) was/were spoken between the Vietnamese and American and other foreign soldiers.

I am strongly of the opinion—based, I admit, only on a hunch—that theoretical treatment of pidginization and creolization will remain seriously incomplete as long as it is based almost wholly on languages of European lexicon. But only a few non-European-based pidgins and creoles have been described with anything approaching adequacy, and those few are seldom drawn upon for comparative purposes. To cite a few examples: Ki-Nubi, a language of Uganda derived from pidgin Arabic of the southern Sudan, was creolized about eighty years ago, but there is only one short paper on it (Nhial 1975). Pidgin Assamese, the lingua franca of the Nagaland legislature, which also has a history running back to the turn of the century, was first described by Sreedhar in 1974. The first writing on Bazaar Malay is nearly two centuries old, but available descriptions still do not give a clear answer to the question whether any of its varieties are or were full-fledged pidgins.

Second, notwithstanding their increasingly high quality, descriptions of pidgins and creoles are likely to be limited in scope: a researcher, typically striking out on his own, works with and sometimes generalizes from a single idiolect or at best a few, so that the great variety of actual speech does not appear in the resulting description. Take as an example Harrison's admirable thesis—still, alas, unpublished—on Norfolk Island creole English (1972). Since it is confined to 'Broad' Norfolk, mainly as spoken

by one family, and does not treat of formal 'Modified' Norfolk
and of whatever it is that Norfolk creoles speak to Australians, we
get only a partial, though valuable, picture of *The language of
Norfolk Island.* The revolution in description made possible by
cheap tape recording is only beginning to get under way. Whether
or not Bickerton's explanation of language acquisition as presented in this volume is accepted, he has certainly provided models of
broadly based recording in Guyana (1975) and Hawaii (Bickerton
and Odo 1976). Obviously, the greater the range of speech we
have at hand for analysis, the more comprehensive and rich in
insights the analysis should be, especially if the recording is
coupled with what Chaudenson dubs a "pluridisciplinary approach"–careful and detailed attention to all relevant historical
data. Not only theoretical linguistics but also what we may call
'applied creolistics', as exemplified by Craig's and Wurm's contributions to this volume, cannot but profit.

JOHN E. REINECKE

NOTES

1. For pre-1973 writers mentioned in the Foreword see the index to
J. E. Reinecke et al., *A Bibliography of Pidgin and Creole Languages.*

2. The 'monogenetic' theory does not touch many pidgins and
creoles; at best it would account only for a number of European-lexicon
languages and (quoting Walter F. Edwards 1976, p. 27) "even this involves
the acceptance of a dizzying concatenation of events with little in the way of
concrete evidence to support plausibility."

3. *The Carrier Pidgin*, a quarterly newsletter founded in 1973 and
currently issued at the University of Hawaii, lists many obscure publications,
theses, and papers. The semiannual *Journal of Creole Studies* and a
forthcoming bulletin of French creole studies also will doubtless call
attention to much obscure material. But getting this material into the hands
of creolists at a reasonable cost remains a problem.

REFERENCES

Bickerton, Derek. 1975. *Dynamics of a creole system*. Cambridge: Cambridge University Press.

———. 1976. Pidgin and creole studies. *Annual Review of Anthropology 5*.

———, and Odo, Carol. 1976. *Change and variation in Hawaiian English*. Vol. I. *General phonology and pidgin syntax*. Honolulu, SSLI, University of Hawaii.

Edwards, Walter F. 1975. Sociolinguistic behaviour in rural and urban circumstances in Guyana. Unpub. Ph.D. diss., University of York.

Howell, Richard W. 1976. Linguistic reflections of sociocultural differences in the pidgins of Japan and Hawaii. Paper read at symposium on Language, Thought, and Culture, University of Hawaii, Hilo, August 14, 1976.

Nhial, Abdon Agaw Jok. 1975. Ki-Nubi and Juba Arabic: the relationship between a creole and a pidgin of the Arabic language. Paper presented in absentia at 1975 International Conference on Pidgins and Creoles, Honolulu, University of Hawaii.

Sreedhar, M. V. 1974. *Naga Pidgin: A sociolinguistic study of inter-lingual communication pattern in Nagaland*. Mysore: Central Institute of Indian Languages.

Preface

This collective volume is intended as a basic reader for the fast developing field of pidgin and creole linguistics. It is designed to acquaint linguists, anthropologists, language planners, educators, and other interested readers with the most provocative current theoretical issues in the field, to bring them abreast of recent research, and to put basic information and research tools at their disposal. It differs from the few available introductory surveys of pidgin and creole languages by its focus on research problems and by virtue of its being fully up to date.

With one exception—Keith Whinnom's paper on *Lingua Franca*, which is the modified version of a paper originally delivered at a specialized European colloquium—the volume consists entirely of papers commissioned especially for the project and appearing here in print for the first time. Each contributor has attempted to treat one of a finite set of assigned topics and to provide for that topic a broad survey rather than a narrowly focussed statement about his or her own research. The goal was a set of papers that would complement one another while overlapping minimally, and that, taken all together, would afford a comprehensive view of the field of pidgin and creole linguistics as it exists today and suggest the fruitfulness of the field for researchers interested in a variety of issues in general linguistic theory.

Pidgin and Creole Linguistics is organized in five sections. In Section I, DeCamp surveys the development of the field, with emphasis on the activities that followed the First International Conference in Creole Language Studies organized by Robert Le Page at the University of the West Indies, Jamaica, in 1959. Unless the early history of a field of scholarly endeavor is well documented and the documentation readily available, there is the risk that present workers will repeat the errors of their forebears or rediscover the well-charted and the well-described. Meijer and Muysken have examined closely the works of the two pioneers of pidgin and creole studies, the Dutchman Hesseling and the German Schuchardt, who wrote primarily in their native languages. As the authors point out in their summary of the theoretical positions held by these two early creolists, modern workers who started from oversimplified statements of Schuchardt's views have been unaware of their complexity and of how closely they reflected some current theoretical positions.

Section II deals both with the relationship between pidgin and creole studies and general linguistics and the issue of the genesis and development of pidgin and creole languages, or—put in a more contemporary frame of reference—the processes of pidginization and creolization. To account for features shared by plantation creoles, Bickerton proposes that they have their source in universal processes of language acquisition, and he defines pidginization and creolization as special types of second- and first-language learning, respectively. Pidgins and creoles, by their extreme variability, offer a challenge to models of language change as well as to linguistic theory generally. Traugott discusses the implications of pidginization and creolization for three models of linguistic change: the genetic, the acquisitional, and the dynamic wave theory, and she points out, particularly with regard to the last-mentioned model, that these two sets of processes are fundamental to the very conception of linguistic theories. Ferguson and DeBose adopt an interactive rather than an innatist stance on pidginization, although they too relate that process to those of second language acquisition. They see pidginization as the transformation of normal language input into a reduced, hybridized, and unstable variety that may become foreigner talk, broken talk (approximative systems), or pidgin, depending on external circumstances.

The contributions of Section III exemplify the three stages of the life cycle of pidgins. Manessy shows that simplification of surface structure and reduction of inner form also characterize the vehicular varieties of indigenous languages in Africa, thus providing support both for the current emphasis on processes rather than reified stages in pidgin and creole linguistics and for appeal to universal strategies of language learning rather than linguistic transfer to account for the salient features of these languages.

Valdman deals with the relationship between syntactic and phonological features in the development of more elaborated determiner systems in Caribbean Creole French dialects. He points out how extensive morphophonemic alternations resulting from elaboration serve to differentiate regional dialects and to provide speakers with a broad stylistic range. An issue that is the subject of much recent controversy is the creole origin of American Black English. Rickford attempts to answer three fundamental questions that this issue raises: the nature of the pidgin life-cycle; whether sociohistorical conditions in the United States were propitious for pidginization, creolization, and decreolization; the type of evidence that must be brought forward to prove prior creolization. He then proceeds to examine the key phonological, morpho-syntactic, and lexical features of Black English that have been attributed to the influence of an antecedent creole stage. Le Page's article serves to bring together the threads woven in the other three contributions of Section III. However, his emphasis is on the identification of the psychological and sociolinguistic factors that lead to the various phases of the pidgin cycle: pidginization, creolization, and decreolization (post-creolization).

The papers in Section IV are concerned with the reconstruction of the sociohistorical matrix in which pidgin and creole languages emerge and the problem of the documentation of early stages or progenitors of these languages. Chaudenson studies the history of the settlement of Bourbon Island in the Indian Ocean to evaluate the plausibility of the relexification hypothesis for the development of Creole French varieties. He argues that the reconstruction of the sociocultural setting of plantation colonies is the preliminary step in accounting for the genesis of European-based creoles. Given the scant samples available of early stages of pidgins and creoles, Hancock suggests that historical rather than linguistic evidence must provide the principal leads in historical comparative studies. Basing his theories on attested mentions of contact languages, he claims that Lingua Franca (Sabir) arose much earlier than is generally recognized and had its origin in a contact language in use in the Western part of the Roman Empire; he concludes with the tantalizing suggestion that Yiddish might be an offspring of this trade vernacular. In his attempt to date the emergence of Lingua Franca, Whinnom is both more cautious in his use of historical evidence and more exacting in his definition of the term pidgin. He makes a useful distinction between contact strategies in which communication is attained by mutual accommodation and the elaboration of a crystallized pidgin. The latter requires a particular social setting, including multilingual contacts, for which he finds conclusive evidence only in the Barbary states of the sixteenth century.

Section V is devoted to the role that pidgins and creoles play in developing nations and the particular problems their existence poses in basic education, communication, and community development. Craig weighs the educational alternatives—transitional, monoliterate, partial, or full bilingualism—available to policy makers in creole-speaking areas such as Jamaica or Haiti, in light of the linguistic and sociolinguistic relationship between the creole and the official language, particularly the presence or absence of a decreolization continuum. He also considers such central educational issues as the effect of the choice of classroom language on the communicative behavior of children, the preparation of materials, and the implementation of curricula. Among pidgins and creoles, only Melanesian Pidgin English (Tok Pisin) has attained high status; it is the main language for deliberations in the national legislature of Papua-New Guinea and its functional domains are being rapidly expanded in that state as well as in the New Hebrides and the Solomons. Wurm charts the development of Tok Pisin from major lingua franca to semiofficial language and outlines a program of standardization and instrumentalization that must be undertaken if that language is to assume its new functions efficiently.

The reference apparatus of the volume comprises a list of languages recognized generally as pidgins or creoles, accompanied by maps showing their geographical location, prepared by Ian F. Hancock; a summary bibliography; and an index to the works cited and the languages mentioned in the individual contributions. Full bibliographical references appear in each of the end-of-article lists.

Pidgin and Creole Linguistics should enable persons unfamiliar with the field to follow current debates, to evaluate existing descriptions of individual pidgin and creole languages, and to identify research problems and topics. It may also serve as a basic textbook in courses in the area of sociolinguistics, bilingualism, and language contact as well as in ethno- or anthropological linguistics that center on language variation and its cultural and social implications.

i.

The Field of
Pidgin and Creole Studies

The Development of
Pidgin and Creole Studies

David DeCamp

Whenever anyone refers to a group of languages by its family name (e.g., Germanic or Romance), by its geographical location (e.g., Amerindian or Siberian), or by some structural characteristic (e.g., tone languages), there is unlikely to be much disagreement about the definition of the group or about the list of its members. Linguists may disagree on whether there really is a Sino-Tibetan or a Ural-Altaic language family, but they would generally agree on the definition and membership of these alleged family groups and would debate only whether the proposed concept of a Ural-Altaic group is meaningful or useful.

There is no such agreement on the definition of the group of languages called pidgins and creoles. Linguists all agree that there is such a group, that it includes many languages and large numbers of speakers, and that pidgin-creole studies have now become an important field within linguistics. Yet even the authors of this book would not agree among themselves on a definition of these languages. Some definitions are based on function, the role these languages play in the community: e.g., a pidgin is an auxiliary trade language. Some are based on historical origins and development: e.g., a pidgin may be spontaneously generated; a creole is a language that has evolved from a pidgin. Some definitions include formal characteristics: restricted vocabulary; absence of gender, true tenses, inflectional morphology, or relative clauses, etc. Some linguists combine these different kinds of criteria and include additional restrictions in their definitions. To a creolist, almost everyone else's definition of a creole sounds absurd and arbitrary; yet creolists communicate and collaborate with their colleagues just as Slavicists and Amerindianists do.

Because there is no agreement on the definition of the pidgin-creole group, there is also no agreement on its membership. Ian Hancock has provided for this book an excellent and helpful list of pidgin and creole languages, but the other authors would not all exactly agree on this list. Some would reject some of his nominations for membership in this language group, and some would propose additional candidates of their own. Is Yiddish a creole? Is the language sometimes used by Italian immigrants in the United States a true pidgin? Were Middle English and Old French once creoles? Both at their professional meetings and in their publications, linguists debate such questions.

This does not mean that the study of pidgin and creole languages is disorganized and unproductive. It is simply that the structures, functions, origins, and historical processes involved in these definitions are very complex. Sorting them out and trying to define the group are intimately tied up with the search for answers to the most basic questions in linguistics: What are languages? How can they be meaningfully described? How do they originate and how do they change? How do people learn them? What roles do they play in society? Pidgin-creole studies have already made substantial contributions toward finding answers to these questions and have helped shake up the entire epistemology of linguistics. This book will provide no simple and unassailable definition of pidgin and creole, but the reader may obtain from it a working knowledge of what these languages are and why they are important. The authors hope that he or she will gain from this some new insights into what language is and how it works.

At this point, therefore, let us use clear-cut examples rather than formal definitions. Everyone would agree that the Juba Arabic spoken in the southern Sudan is a pidgin. In most communities it is not the native language of any of its speakers but functions as an auxiliary interlingua for communication between speakers of the many mutually unintelligible languages spoken in that region. It is a new language, only about a hundred years old. It has a small vocabulary, limited to the needs of trade and other interlingual communication, but this restricted vocabulary is supplemented, whenever the need arises, by using words from the various native languages or from normal Arabic. It has a very simple phonology with few morphophonemic processes. The complicated morphological system of Arabic (which includes, for example, suffixes on the verb to indicate tense, negation, and the person, number, and gender of both the subject and the direct and indirect objects) has been almost entirely eliminated. Such grammatical information is indicated by word order, by separate uninflected pronouns or auxiliaries, or else is simply missing. Yet Juba Arabic is a relatively stable language in its own right, with its own structure, not just half-learned or baby-talk Arabic. It is easier for an Arabic speaker to learn than for an English speaker, but the Arabic speaker still must learn it as a foreign language; he cannot simply improvise it.

Similarly everyone agrees that the vernacular-language of Haiti is a creole. It is the native language of nearly all Haitians, though standard French is also spoken by some people and is the official language, and one also hears many varieties intermediate between the standard and the creole. Historically it probably evolved from pidginized varieties of French at the time when these began to be acquired as a native language. Because it is a native language and must perform a wide range of communicative and expressive functions, it has an extensive vocabulary and complex grammatical system comparable to that of a so-called normal language. In fact, scholars disagree on whether there are any formal characteristics by which we could identify Haitian as a creole if we did not know its history. Although its vocabulary is largely French, the phonology and syntax are so different that most varieties are mutually unintelligible with standard French. In some ways its grammatical structure is more similar to creole Portuguese, creole Spanish, and even to creole English than to standard French, and most creolists object to calling it a dialect of French.

These are clear-cut examples, but there are many border-line cases. Yiddish, usually classified either as a Germanic language or as a dialect of German, shares some characteristics with Haitian Creole: its vocabulary, though mostly German, includes many Hebrew words, and at one time it was widely used for interlingual communication between Jews speaking different native languages. Some scholars therefore argue that Yiddish is a creole, but others insist that it lacks structural and functional characteristics that they would require of a creole. Italian immigrants in the United States and Canada sometimes speak a simplified mixture of Italian and English, and a similar mixture of Italian and Spanish is heard in Buenos Aires. Because such mixtures are not native tongues used in the home, but auxiliary interlinguas, like Juba Arabic, used for communication not only with English speakers but between speakers of different Italian dialects, Di Pietro (forthcoming) would call them pidgins. Other scholars (e.g., Whinnom 1971) doubt that these mixtures have sufficiently stable structures to be called pidgins, insisting that a pidgin must be a real language, as Juba is, not just an interlingual improvisation newly created for each conversation.

When a Japanese businessman talks with an Egyptian client using the limited English they both learned in school (perhaps including a number of elements from Japanese and Arabic), are they speaking a pidgin? No, because the structure would not be stable and predictable, and because English does function as the native language of many millions of people. On the other hand, many pidgins, including Juba Arabic, are in the process of creolizing. As speakers of many different Sudanese languages move from their villages into the city of Juba, they use the pidgin Arabic for intercommunication, but their children now are growing up speaking it as a native language. Thus they are speaking it as a creole, with much larger vocabulary and greater structural complexity than the pidgin variety spoken by their own parents. Therefore the existence of a related mutually intelligible language with native speakers does not necessarily disqualify a pidgin.

The origins of the two terms are also complex and confusing. Many scholars believe that the word *pidgin* was first used for Chinese pidgin English (in which *pidgin* is the word for "business") and was later generalized to mean any language of this type. In the Far East today one can still hear, and occasionally read, the expression "That's my pigeon" (meaning "That's my own private affair"). A *creole* originally meant a white colonist born in the tropics. Later it was extended to include African slaves and other residents of tropical colonies, still later to include languages (and foods) used by creoles, and finally to any language of this type. But as we have just seen, it is not easy to define what is meant by a 'language of this type'.

Depending on which list is consulted, creoles are the native languages of between ten and seventeen million persons today, located all over the world but predominantly in tropical and subtropical regions. About seven million speak creole French, mostly in and around the Caribbean but in other parts of the world too, including the islands of Mauritius and Réunion in the Indian Ocean. Creole English is second in number of speakers, mostly in West Africa and the Caribbean, though the current creolization of pidgin English in the Pacific islands is rapidly increasing the creole-speaking population there. If Afrikaans is recognized as a creole, then creole Dutch ranks third, followed by creole Portuguese and Spanish. The number of pidgin speakers is even more elusive, for in some communities not everyone knows the pidgin. A trader, for example, may use pidgin every day but his wife and children at home may never use it, for he speaks only the native language in the home. Furthermore a pidgin is relatively easy to learn and so can spread rapidly through an area when a need for interlingual communication arises. The establishment of a new industrial plant or a foreign military base or the development of a new trade route can result in thousands of new pidgin speakers within only weeks. Until recently, pidgin speakers were never identified in surveys and censuses, and competent estimates range from six to twelve million.

Creole languages are thus an important group of languages, perhaps comparable to Persian in number of native speakers. Pidgins are not only numerically important but are so essential to commerce, government, and education in many countries that their significance to national development planning may be greater than that of native languages with even greater numbers of speakers. In some highly multilingual areas like the southern Sudan and the western Pacific islands, where no single native language is spoken by more than a small fraction of the population, a pidgin is often the only medium of communication.

Furthermore, the feedback from pidgin-creole studies to sociolinguistics and to theoretical and descriptive linguistics has been so productive that the number of linguists working with these languages has increased geometrically from about a dozen in the 1950s to nearly a thousand today. The appearance of books, articles, and university courses on the subject has increased at the same pace. A recent annotated bibliography of the field (Reinecke et al. 1975) lists about eight thousand items, of which approximately half are serious academic studies focussing on pidgin and creole languages, and the list is far from complete.

Until the 1950s, however, there was no recognized field of pidgin-creole studies. Only a few of the individual languages had been reliably and objectively studied, and most educated people were totally unaware of them or did not consider them to be real languages. Pidgins and creoles are spoken in places where two or more cultures have come in contact, with one group of people usually dominating the others economically, socially, or militarily. Slavery, colonialism, military occupation, migration from villages to the city, new trade relations—each can produce an intercultural contact in which one group has the upper hand, and it is the dominated who are associated with the pidgin or creole that is often used in such a community. If the dominant people speak it, it is usually either condescendingly—talking down to the natives—or else, if they begin to use it among themselves, they somehow lose status. Eighteenth-century accounts were filled with criticisms of the speech of the children of European colonists growing up in tropical colonies and learning the 'barbarous dialect' of slaves and other natives (e.g., Cassidy 1961: 21-23). Even today a language or dialect spoken primarily by the poor and uneducated is too often thought of as the cause, or as the inevitable result, of that poverty and ignorance. A creole is a fully developed language that has evolved from a pidgin and has as much potential for communication and expression as any other native language, but until recently it was a universal that creoles had low prestige, even among linguists.

Furthermore, a pidgin quite naturally takes its vocabulary from the various languages involved in the cultural contact, with the dominant group contributing the most. When the pidgin acquires native speakers and the process of creolization occurs, some of the added vocabulary and grammatical structures may be indigenous creations (e.g., by compounding: *eye-water* 'tears', or by reduplication: *chip-chip*, the plural 'chips'), but most are drawn from the language of the dominant group. Thus pidgin English is not English but shares many features with English, and creole English often becomes even more similar to English. Because it is similar yet different, and because it has low prestige, it has generally been considered not as a language but simply as careless and ungrammatical English or, at best, as a bad dialect of English. Even George Philip Krapp (1925: 1.252), the foremost historian of American English, described Gullah (a creole still spoken in coastal Georgia and South Carolina) as "merely a debased dialect of English learned by the negroes from the whites." French scholars were equally uncharitable toward creole French, Spanish scholars toward creole Spanish, etc. Although Sudanese authorities are gradually accepting the necessity of dealing with Juba Arabic in the southern provinces, there is great reluctance to view it as anything but corrupt Arabic.

Little is known of pidgin-creole history before the nineteenth century. Most creolists today believe that the pidgin that developed into the Caribbean creoles was brought to the New

World by slaves who learned it in Africa or on shipboard, and even the dissenters agree that it must have been formed shortly after the slaves' arrival here. Some scholars would trace its history all the way back to the most famous of all pidgins: Sabir (also called Lingua Franca, from which we got the common noun *lingua franca*). This was a Mediterranean trade language, now extinct, which in the fifteenth and sixteenth centuries was spread by the Portuguese and other explorers down the west coast of Africa and from there to Asia and the New World. But most of the early history is conjecture, based on fragmentary evidence.

Beginning in 1770, there were a few careful and objective descriptions of creole languages. Until about a century ago, however, most accounts had been nothing more than fragmentary quotations, parodies portraying creole speakers as ignorant fools, and travelers' reports of crude, corrupt, barbarous Portuguese, French, English, etc., being spoken in colonies and trading posts. The literary traditions of Tarzan and Tonto have exalted the noble savage, but the implications of their linguistic inferiority to Jane and the Lone Ranger are still in the spirit of those early reports of pidgins and creoles. It may well be, as Whinnom (1965) suggested, that the early ships brought to the New World yet another language in addition to the well-known colonial tongues English, Spanish, French, Portuguese, Dutch, etc., but if so, the event was not recorded and the language, until recently, seldom written down or even acknowledged to be a language.

Although he was not the first to write about creole languages, the undisputed father of pidgin-creole studies was Hugo Schuchardt (1842-1927). This great Romance philologist, who was also a pioneer in the study of Basque, was a rebel against the 'neo-grammarian' school of Leipzig, whose theories of genetic descent of languages into family-tree groups then dominated linguistics. He saw in pidgins and creoles the evidence that language relationships and linguistic change were not so simple as most scholars believed. At one time he was warned by a senior colleague that he should abandon this foolish study of funny dialects and work on Old French if he wished to further his academic career.[1]

Schuchardt nevertheless persevered. Although he is best known to creolists for his careful description of Mediterranean Lingua Franca (1909) made at the end of the nineteenth century, just before the spread of French in North Africa brought about the death of that famous pidgin, his contributions were much broader. He studied a great variety of pidgins and creoles, and his many publications included nine major monographs entitled *Kreolische Studien.*[2]

Most scholars then believed that any language, like any biological species, could be classified as a unique point on a genetic family tree. Schuchardt proved that if this were true, we would then have to say of creole languages that some have completely changed their genetic affiliation (e.g., from Portuguese to Dutch) and others are so mixed as to defy classification. In the course of evolution, whales have developed many characteristics similar to those of fish, but they are still clearly identifiable as mammals. Languages, especially creoles, do not necessarily preserve any essential classificatory features equivalent to the warm blood and mammary glands of the whale. Schuchardt's arguments were later reinforced by linguists studying the process of *decreolization.* If, for example, Jamaican Creole or Gullah is continuously exposed to influences from standard English, some varieties may merge with standard English. If, as some linguists believe, Jamaican Creole and Gullah originally evolved from the Portuguese-based Lingua Franca, then a rigidly genetic family-tree classification would force us to the absurd conclusion that some people are speaking a dialect of Portuguese even though it is trivially different, or even indistinguishable, from standard English.[3]

The other great and controversial creolist at the turn of the century was D. C. Hesseling, who published in 1899 the first edition of his *Het Afrikaans*, a book in which he argued that Afrikaans, the official language of South Africa, was not a dialect of Dutch but rather a creole that had developed (with many Dutch influences, of course) out of an earlier Malayo-Portuguese pidgin used on the trade route around the Cape of Good Hope. This theory, though now generally accepted, was repugnant to the ruling white Afrikaners because of the prejudice against creoles, for it was misinterpreted as implying that their beloved Afrikaans was a primitive language with an illegitimate ancestry (Valkhoff 1966). In 1905 Hesseling published a book on another Dutch-related creole, Negerhollands, now nearly extinct but once widely spoken in what are now the American Virgin Islands. Although Negerhollands also shares many features with Dutch, especially vocabulary, it is very different from Afrikaans and, many scholars believe, has a common origin with the English, French, and Portuguese creoles of the Caribbean.

The study of 'exotic' languages was vastly accelerated in

the twentieth century. The growth of descriptive linguistics and cultural anthropology as respected academic disciplines, the increased activity of missionary groups and Bible translators, and the development of modern military and foreign service language schools all resulted in detailed descriptions of hundreds of languages about which little or nothing had been known in Schuchardt's day. Yet pidgin and creole languages were largely neglected during the first half of the century. Scholarly books were published on dying Amerindian languages with fewer than a half dozen surviving speakers, but pidgin-creole studies lay almost dormant until well after World War II. Most linguists, like the general public, considered them not to be real languages or, at best, to be just funny dialects.

There were notable exceptions, of course. For example, Melville Jacobs published in 1932 some notes on the structure of Chinook Jargon, a pidgin still spoken by some American Indians in the Pacific Northwest. Throughout the 1930s Lorenzo D. Turner studied Gullah and established that it is indeed a creole. In 1934 John Reinecke and Aiko Tokimasa described the dialect system of Hawaii as a continuum or spectrum, with Standard English at one extreme and a creole at the other. But these were isolated studies whose importance was not recognized until much later. Turner's book was not published until 1949. Few people read the early Reinecke and Tokimasa article, and the great impact of John Reinecke on pidgin-creole studies was not felt until the 1960s and 70s.

The two pioneers in the rediscovery of pidgin-creole studies in the 1940s were Douglas Taylor and Robert A. Hall, Jr. Taylor contributed not only his useful structural descriptions of several Caribbean creoles but also his conception of creole as a general phenomenon. He insisted on studying creoles throughout the Caribbean, whether French, English, or Portuguese. Hall's conception of the field was even broader. Already well established as a leading scholar in both general and Romance linguistics, he turned in the 1940s to the study of both pidgins and creoles, and his interests included the Pacific as well as the Caribbean. He became the strongest champion of both the theory of spontaneous generation of pidgins (still hotly debated by scholars) and the life-cycle theory (now generally accepted), according to which the origin of creoles is an evolution out of earlier pidgins.

The establishment of pidgin-creole studies as a general academic field took place in the 1950s, when Robert B. Le Page organized a linguistic survey of the West Indies and established at the University College of the West Indies a research center for creolists. The scholars who came to work there included F. G. Cassidy, Jack Berry, David DeCamp, Alan S. C. Ross, and Beryl Loftman Bailey. The senior member of this group was Cassidy. He had previously done field research in Jamaica, resulting in the publication in 1961 of a lexical and ethnolinguistic description that has still not been equalled. In 1958 he returned to Jamaica to collaborate with Le Page on the *Dictionary of Jamaican English,* the first major dictionary of a creole. Le Page later returned to England and established at York the first major center in England for pidgin-creole studies. Berry, who had worked on both African and Caribbean creoles, later established at Northwestern University a similar center for the United States. Bailey, herself a Jamaican, began work on a project that culminated in the publication (1966) of the first transformational grammar of creole. Ross, who later (1964) also coauthored a book on Pitcairnese, the English creole spoken by the descendents of the Bounty mutineers, worked on the historical phonology of Jamaican creole. DeCamp concentrated on the study of linguistic variation within a creole society and, unaware of the earlier article by Reinecke and Tokimasa, independently developed the concept of a continuum of speech varieties as opposed to a discrete set of dialects.

In 1959 the Le Page group convened the First International Conference on Creole Language Studies. Virtually all the world's known pidgin-creole specialists were invited, and most of them did attend, including both Hall and Taylor. The total number of participants was only thirteen, however, and the conference sessions were held in one small room. In spite of the size of the group, never before had so many creolists, representing different continents and different languages, confronted each other face to face. The proceedings of that conference (Le Page 1961) formed the basis of much of the discussion and research of the following decade. As discussions of the applicability of such concepts as generative grammar, diglossia, continuum, and comparative-historical reconstruction progressed, the participants began to think of themselves more as 'creolists' than just as students of Haitian French or Jamaican English.

One of the most intriguing ideas to surface at that 1959 conference was the possibility of a monogenetic theory of the origin of most if not all of the world's pidgins and creoles. Sixty years earlier, Hesseling had suggested a Portuguese origin for New World creoles such as Negerhollands, but new evidence presented by Keith Whinnom (1957) and R. W. Thompson (1961) indicated that Pacific pidgin English and the Spanish creoles of the Philippines might have had a similar origin. The suggestion that many of the pidgins and creoles of both the Old and the New World were related as a language family with a common historical origin was very exciting in 1959, for it could explain the many striking similarities among creoles. If pidgins are spontaneously created whenever contact occurs between speakers of different languages, as Hall had claimed, then why are the French creoles, including those spoken in the Indian Ocean as well as in the Caribbean, so similar that they are usually mutually comprehensible? And why do French and English creoles share many basic features found in neither French nor English?

The case for monogenesis was stated most strongly by Whinnom (1965), who argued that Mediterranean Lingua Franca was the origin of all 'European-based' pidgins and creoles, i.e., those that share most of their vocabulary with one or more European languages. He suggested that a variety of Lingua Franca heavily influenced by Portuguese was carried by the explorers and traders of the fifteenth and sixteenth centuries both to the New World and also down the west coast of Africa and across the Indian Ocean to the Far East. Later, as the English, the Dutch, the French, and others took over the formerly Portuguese trade routes and trading ports, this pidgin differentiated into pidgin English, Dutch, French, etc., by adopting much of the vocabulary of these languages, a process known as *relexification.*

Some creolists, including Hall, strongly opposed the monogenetic theory, and during the 1960s this issue became part of one of the most widely and hotly debated controversies in sociolinguistics: the nature and origin of so-called Black English. Although some scholars, both black and white, vehemently insisted that there is no such thing as Black English, inasmuch as there are few if any features characteristic of the speech of all American blacks but of no whites, most linguists believed that there are at least some combinations of speech characteristics associated with black American culture. William Stewart (1968) and J. L. Dillard (1972), like Turner, were claiming an African-American cultural continuity for Black English. They saw the early slave-trade pidgin as an essential link in this history. This pidgin, or an already somewhat Anglicized version of it, was brought by African slaves to America, where it first 'creolized', i.e., expanded in vocabulary and structure as it became the native language of subsequent generations of speakers, and later 'decreolized', i.e., assimilated toward white speech, and lost many of its creole characteristics.

This involvement in the very topical issue of black speech undoubtedly helped popularize pidgin-creole studies in the 1960s. Other controversies also began to attract the attention of linguists. For example, William Labov and David DeCamp both saw the immense social, chronological, and stylistic variability characteristic of creoles as evidence of the inadequacy of the static theoretical models in vogue among most linguists of the 1960s. They believed that to attempt to describe anything as complex as Jamaican creole English in terms of a set of rules for one idiolect, i.e., the idealized competence of a single unvarying speaker, results in a picture as descriptively inadequate as a black and white snapshot of a circus. Their approaches, however, were quite different. Labov (1969) added variables to grammatical rules, indicating the probability as well as the possibility of a particular variant's occurring in a given context. DeCamp (1971) stressed the interdependence of variables along a continuum of usage and constructed hierarchies called implicational rules (or Guttman scales) to describe the variation.

While these and other issues in pidgin-creole studies were increasingly attracting the attention of general historical and descriptive linguists, the subject was also being taught more frequently to students of linguistics and anthropology. Although the University of the West Indies remained the principal center, at least through the 1960s, pidgin-creole courses were offered at more and more British and American universities. The first general textbook was published by Hall in 1966, and others have appeared since. Albert Valdman (1970) and David Dwyer (1967) prepared modern courses for students learning to speak creole languages. Both in Jamaica and in England, where many West Indian children were enrolled in schools, conferences were held and research undertaken on the educational problems encountered by creole-speaking children.

Recognizing the growing importance of this field, the Social Science Research Council in 1968 sponsored a second international conference, also held in Jamaica, chaired by the leading American ethnolinguist, Dell Hymes. The growth, both in scope and in sophistication, between 1959 and 1968 is evident in comparing the published proceedings of the two conferences (Le Page 1961, Hymes 1971). More than fifty creolists attended, including ten of the thirteen participants in the 1959 conference. Some of the new faces were already established linguists (e.g.,

William Labov, Charles Ferguson, Martin Joos, Edgar Polomé, and Henry Hoenigswald), who had only recently turned their attention to pidgin-creole studies. But there was also an entirely new generation: Mervyn Alleyne, who vigorously opposed Whinnom's theory of a Lingua Franca origin for creoles; Dennis Craig, the leading specialist in creole language problems in education; Derek Bickerton, who was to become the most important and most controversial of the linguistic theorists working on creoles.

As a result of the conference, John E. Reinecke returned to his active interest in creole studies, which had been in abeyance for thirty years, and organized a major basic research project in collaboration with Stanley Tsuzaki, David DeCamp, Ian F. Hancock, and Richard E. Wood: the preparation of an extensive annotated bibliography and research guide for pidgin and creole languages, which was published late in 1975. Prior to that conference, Dell Hymes had reprinted in a widely read anthology an important but hitherto little noticed article of Reinecke's, and Tsuzaki had encouraged him to prepare his 1935 thesis on Hawaiian English for publication as a book.

Since 1968, the growth of pidgin-creole studies has continuously accelerated. A conference held at Georgetown University in 1972 was attended by more than sixty creolists and resulted not only in the publication of a set of papers (DeCamp and Hancock 1974) but also in the launching of a quarterly newsletter, dubbed the *Carrier Pidgin* by its first editor, Barbara Robson.

Later in 1972, an international conference was held in Trinidad, at which a new professional organization, the Society for Caribbean Linguistics, was formed, with Cassidy as its first president. Until this meeting, all creole conferences had been dominated by American and European scholars who were themselves not native speakers of any creole. Only two out of the thirteen papers at the 1959 conference had been presented by creole speakers, and one of these, Cassidy, although he had been born in Jamaica, had lived nearly all his life in the United States. Only about a half dozen native speakers were represented on the program in 1968. By 1972, however, the fifteen years of training creole speakers in linguistics had had its effect. They no longer came just to listen to lectures by Americans and Englishmen. It was their program. In 1959, a creole speaker had been made available so that the conference participants could make tape recordings of his speech. In 1972, the creole speakers were presenting the results of their own research on their own languages. Several of the papers at the conference on Melanesian Pidgin, Boroko, Sept. 21-23, were presented in Tok Pisin by both Niuginians and foreign scholars.

The increase in the size, scope, frequency, and international participation of these creole language conferences is a good measure of the growth of pidgin-creole studies since 1959. It could also be described in terms of the ever-increasing number of books and articles appearing each year. Perhaps the best measure is the number of theoretical issues raised in this field and their relevance to general linguistics. The old debate between monogenesis and polygenesis is still not completely resolved, but it has already had considerable influence on general theories of language change. The search for typological characteristics and the disagreements over definitions are still with us, but these are now interrelated with the general linguistic search for language universals. For example, John Schumann has shown that second-language learners exhibit speech behavior typologically characteristic of pidgin when they are at that stage of language learning when the second language performs the same communicative function as a pidgin does, i.e., informational but not expressive communication. Gillian Sankoff has found that observations of creolization, i.e., the expansion of a pidgin into a creole, provide insights into the processes of language creation and evolution. Bickerton goes still further and claims (this volume) that the typological characteristics of pidgins and creoles are not only universal but were an essential stage in the origin of human language. Charles Ferguson (1971) has suggested that pidginization is a natural process of simplification, a suggestion strongly challenged by Whinnom, and this debate has made clear that simplicity in language is difficult to measure objectively and is largely a function of whatever theoretical model of language one uses.

The static idiolectal linguistics of the 1960s is rapidly waning, and most linguists now concede that variation must be accounted for in any adequate theory, but there is still no agreement on how to describe the variable speech behavior of even one speaker, let alone an entire community of speakers. Labov's variable rules have been very successful in describing statistically the mass speech behavior of groups of speakers, but they do not account well for the interrelationships between variables or for what goes on in the mind of the speaker. Building on DeCamp's concept of a structured, scalable continuum of variation, Charles-James Bailey (1973) and Derek Bickerton (1975) have constructed elaborate theories of language as a dynamic system, simultaneously variable along several dimensions, including time, place, and style. But these theories have so far been tested on only one set of data (Guyanese creole, recorded by Bickerton), and they are so incompatible with basic assumptions about language that linguists have long held that they are unlikely to be widely accepted without further empirical verification. Although these and other issues are still unresolved, there has been great progress since the 1940s, when many linguists still questioned whether pidgins and creoles had structures worth describing at all.

As pidgin-creole studies have developed into an established discipline, the pidgins and creoles themselves have been growing in respectability and significance. Until recently, children in most underdeveloped areas were educated, if at all, entirely in a 'colonial' language (English, Dutch, French, etc.) that was foreign to them. With the emergence of independent developing nations, there has been a movement toward education in the native language, at least during the first few years of school. As Craig points out in his section of this book, even the formerly despised creoles now have an important role in education, and creoles are even beginning to emerge as national languages. We have come a long way since the 1950s, when Le Page was savagely attacked by a Jamaican newspaper columnist merely for making a scholarly study of creole, an academic activity that, the columnist warned, could undermine all Jamaican education by encouraging teachers to tolerate the use of creole in the schools.

NOTES

1. History indeed repeats itself. When I myself began studying Jamaican Creole in 1957, I received from a colleague a similar warning that I should avoid such quasi-languages and should work on an American Indian or other 'real' language. And a number of other contemporary linguists (e.g., Labov, Sankoff, Bickerton, Hymes) have found in pidgins and creoles ammunition against the rigid structuralism of Saussurean and Chomskian theories.

2. The *Schuchardt Brevier*, edited by Leo Spitzer in 1928, is the most conveniently available sample of Schuchardt's work. For a detailed assessment of the contribution of Schuchardt and Hesseling to the develop-

ment of theories on the genesis and evolution of pidgins and creoles, see the contribution of Meijer and Muysken in this volume.

3. See also Whinnom (1971) and Weinreich (1958), who also use creole evidence in arguments against language classification based on metaphors from biology.

REFERENCES

Bailey, Beryl L. 1966. *Jamaican Creole Syntax: A Transformational Approach*. Cambridge: Cambridge University Press.

Bailey, Charles-James N. 1973. *Variation and Linguistic Theory*. Arlington: Center for Applied Linguistics.

Bickerton, Derek. 1975. *Dynamics of a Creole System*. New York: Cambridge University Press.

Cassidy, F. G. 1961. *Jamaica Talk: Three Hundred Years of the English Language in Jamaica*. London: Macmillan.

————, and Le Page, Robert B. 1967. *Dictionary of Jamaican English*. Cambridge: Cambridge University Press.

DeCamp, David. 1971. Toward a generative analysis of a post-creole speech continuum. In *Pidginization and Creolization of Languages*, Dell Hymes, ed., pp. 349-70.

————, and Hancock, Ian F., eds. 1974. *Pidgins and Creoles: Current Trends and Prospects*. Washington, D. C.: Georgetown University Press.

Di Pietro, Robert. (forthcoming). Language as a marker of Italian ethnicity. *International Migration Review*.

Dillard, J. L. 1972. *Black English*. New York: Random House.

Dwyer, David. 1967. *An Introduction to West African Pidgin English*. East Lansing: African Studies Center, Michigan State University.

Ferguson, Charles A. 1971. Absence of copula and the notion of simplicity: a study of normal speech, baby talk, foreigner talk, and pidgins. In *Pidginization and Creolization of Languages*, Dell Hymes, ed., pp. 141-50.

Hall, Robert A., Jr. 1966. *Pidgin and Creole Languages*. Ithaca: Cornell University Press.

Hesseling, Dirk Christiaan. 1905. *Het Negerhollands van de Deense Antillen; Bijdrage tot de geschiedenis der Nederlandse taal in Amerika*. Leiden: A. W. Sijthoff.

————. 1923. *Het Afrikaans; Bijdrage tot de geschiedenis der Nederlandse taal in Zuid-Afrika.* 2nd ed., Leiden: E. J. Brill.

Hymes, Dell, ed. 1971. *Pidginization and Creolization of Languages.* Cambridge: Cambridge University Press.

Jacobs, Melville. 1932. Notes on the structure of Chinook Jargon. *Language* 8:27-50.

Krapp, George Philip. 1925. *The English Language in America.* 2 vols. New York: Frederick Ungar.

Labov, William. 1969. Contraction, deletion, and inherent variability of the English copula. *Language* 45:715-62.

Le Page, Robert B., ed. 1961. *Proceedings of the Conference on Creole Language Studies (1959).* (Creole Language Studies 2). London: Macmillan.

Reinecke, John E., and Tokimasa, Aiko. 1934. The English dialect of Hawaii. *American Speech* 9:48-58, 122-31.

Reinecke, John E.; DeCamp, David; Hancock, Ian F.; Tsuzaki, Stanley M.; and Wood, Richard E. 1975. *A Bibliography of Pidgin and Creole Languages.* Honolulu: The University of Hawaii Press.

Ross, Alan S. C., and Moverley, A. W. 1964. *The Pitcairnese Language.* London: Deutsch.

Russell, Thomas. 1868. *The Etymology of Jamaican Grammar.* Kingston, Jamaica: DeCordova, MacDougall.

Schuchardt, Hugo. 1909. Die Lingua Franca. *Zeitschrift für romanische Philologie* 33:441-61.

————. 1928. *Schuchardt Brevier: Ein Vademecum der allgemeinen Sprachwissenschaft.* Leo Spitzer, ed. 2d ed. Halle: Niemeyer.

Stewart, William A. 1968. Continuity and change in American Negro dialects. *The Florida FL Reporter,* Vol. 6, No. 1. Reprinted in 1971 in *Black-White Speech Relationships,* Walt Wolfram and Nona H. Clarke, eds. Washington: Center for Applied Linguistics.

Thomas, J. J. 1869. *The Theory and Practice of Creole Grammar.* Port-of-Spain, Trinidad: The Chronicle Publishing Office. (New ed., 1969, London: New Beacon Books Ltd.).

Thompson, R. W. 1961. A note on some possible affinities between the creole dialects of the Old World and those of the New. In *Proceedings of the Conference on Creole Language Studies (1959),* Robert B. Le Page, ed., pp. 107-13.

Turner, Lorenzo Dow. 1949. *Africanisms in the Gullah Dialect.* Chicago: University of Chicago Press. Reprinted 1973 with a foreword by David DeCamp. Ann Arbor: University of Michigan Press.

Valdman, Albert, et al. 1970. *Basic Course in Haitian Creole.* The Hague: Mouton.

Valkhoff, Marius F. 1966. *Studies in Portuguese and Creole, with Special Reference to South Africa.* Johannesburg: Witwatersrand University Press.

Weinreich, Uriel. 1958. On the compatability of genetic relationship and convergent development. *Word* 14:374-79.

Whinnom, Keith. 1957. *Spanish Contact Vernaculars in the Philippine Islands.* London and Hong Kong: Hong Kong University Press.

———. 1965. The origin of the European-based creoles and pidgins. *Orbis* 14:509-27.

———. 1971. Linguistic hybridization and the 'special case' of pidgins and creoles. In *Pidginization and Creolization of Languages,* Dell Hymes, ed., pp. 91-115.

On the Beginnings of Pidgin and Creole Studies: Schuchardt and Hesseling

Guus Meijer and Pieter Muysken

The investigation of pidgins and creoles, now a major area of linguistic studies, began at the end of the nineteenth century as an offshoot of Romance Linguistics. Although only limited data were available on creoles, the early creolists were highly original in their thinking and extremely resourceful in their handling of the data. Most of the hypotheses about the genesis and development of creoles proposed today appeared then in embryonic form. A review of the early work on pidgins and creoles should prove illuminating in terms of providing a fresh perspective on the assumptions and motivations behind the various present-day hypotheses. Moreover, at least a few theoretical frameworks and hypotheses were suggested that have not yet been explored in detail, as will be shown here.

Undoubtedly, the most prominent and brilliant of the early creolists were Hugo Schuchardt and Derk Christiaan Hesseling, to whom the larger part of this essay will be devoted. But a review of the climate of ideas in which early work on pidgins and creoles took place is essential for a proper evaluation of the work of the pioneering scholars.

THE SOCIO-POLITICAL CONTEXT

Nineteenth-century views

Most of the nineteenth-century views on creoles were shaped by the same racism that characterized slavery. A typic' exponent of these views was Bertrand-Bocandé:

It is clear that people used to expressing themselves with a rather simple
language cannot easily elevate their intelligence to the genius of a
European language. When they were in contact with the Portuguese and
forced to communicate with them, speaking the same language, it was
necessary that the varied expressions acquired during so many centuries
of civilization dropped their perfection, to adapt to ideas being born
and to barbarous forms of language of half-savage peoples. (1849, p.
73)

Bertrand's theory contained the following tenets:
    (1) There is a direct correlation between the level of
civilization and the complexity of the language.
    (2) European languages contain too many morphological
distinctions and syntactic categories for simple black souls, so that
the languages have to be stripped of these in order to be usable by
Africans. The stripping process causes the emergence of a creole
language.
These generalizations were held sufficient to account for
most observable facts about creole, such as its sociolinguistic
position and the gradient of variation linking it to its base
language. 'Base language' or 'model language' is understood here to
be the language that provided most of the lexicon of a given
creole.
    The *Grand Dictionnaire Universel du XIXe Siècle,* edited
by Pierre Larousse (1869), provides the following definition of
creole:

> The creole language, in our colonies, in Louisiana and Haiti, is a
> corrupted French in which several Spanish and gallicized words are
> mixed. This language, often unintelligible in the mouth of an old
> African, is extremely sweet in the mouth of white creole speakers.

A creole was a language of slaves, a corrupted European language
spoken by Africans. Though being "une funeste habitude"
(Bertrand, 1849, p. 75) when spoken by blacks, it carried a nice
local flavor when spoken by whites.
    In other words, there existed a clear notion of differentia-
tion in the types of creole spoken. Three levels were commonly
distinguished:
    (1) A slightly modified European model with a "local"
intonation pattern and new words added to it.
    (2) A form used by whites to speak to their social
inferiors, in which verbal inflection had disappeared and syntax
had been slightly simplified. This was also the level at which some
blacks could talk with their masters.

(3) A "creolo rachado" (the Cape Verdian expression), i.e., the form that Africans would use when speaking to each other.

Thus the nineteenth-century European intellectuals possessed a notion of creole and also realized, quite rightly, that there existed a gradation of speech varieties between a creole and its base language. However, their view of this gradation was erroneous: they considered it a linguistic one, based on degrees of corruption of the model language, rather than a social one, expressing social stratification. Nineteenth-century historical linguistics and dialectology focussed on separate lexical items and at best on morphology, neglecting syntactic structure. This approach facilitated the view of creoles as corruptions of their models.

Portugal and Coelho

While travellers and missionaries had made observations on pidgin and creole languages during previous centuries, a systematic investigation of their character did not begin until the 1880s. As the historical context of this beginning is of considerable interest, we will sketch it briefly here.

The European powers had been present in Africa since the fifteenth century, but they had limited themselves to the establishment of trading posts at various points along the coast. "In 1879, . . . only a small portion of the African continent was under European rule" (Oliver and Page, 1966, p. 181). A sudden change in this situation was triggered by the territorial ambitions of the Belgian king, Leopold II, and the Hohenzollern emperors, and it led to the intensification of European dominance over Africa and the partition of Africa among the major European powers.

The oldest European power present in Africa was Portugal, but the importance and size of its holdings along the African coast diminished greatly after the zenith of Portuguese economic power in the fifteenth and sixteenth centuries. In any case, despite being a colonial power, Portugal was dependent upon Britain, which had gained complete control over the Portuguese economy by 1880, and had become a mere stopping-off point between England and its own colonies, a middleman and a distribution center for British industrial goods.

Around 1880 a group of liberal intellectuals and entrepreneurs in Lisbon grew increasingly dissatisfied with Portugal's subordinate position and turned their attention to Africa. In 1878

they founded the Geographical Society of Lisbon, which sponsored exploratory expeditions to the colonies. The Bulletin of this
learned society, the *Boletim da Sociedade de Geografía de Lisboa,*
contained reports on climatic conditions, agricultural potential,
etc. Also included were articles by Adolpho Coelho, one of its
members, who began studying the creoles spoken in Portuguese
Africa and published in several installments "Os Dialectos Romanicos ou Neo-Latinos na Africa, Asia e América" (The Romance or
Neo-Latin Dialects in Africa, Asia and America, 1880-82). In spite
of the ambitious title, the vast majority of the data presented
came from the Cape Verde Islands; other areas were represented
by short quotations, references to other authors, etc. Coelho
gathered data by correspondence. He sent general inquiries to
postmasters, native minor officials, foremen, and others. Apparently the very fact of an investigation of their native creole came
as such a surprise to the respondents, and their feelings were so
strong about it, that some of the replies are full of social criticism
(why wasn't creole taught in schools?). Thus the inquiry revealed
strong local dissatisfaction with the status of the Cape Verdian
Islands.

     But Coelho proceeded to treat the response material in the
usual philological manner: comparison of texts, listing of alternate
forms, accounting for creole forms by reference to Portuguese
forms, etc. Unaware of the social context within which the creole
existed as an oppressed language, Coelho did not realize the
difficulties involved in studying it. His data are unreliable, both
because they suggest something static, and because they point to a
form of creole much closer to the Portuguese than some of its
varieties might have been. Many creolists have followed Coelho in
uncritically adopting the descriptive techniques of dialect investigation. Nonetheless, Coelho may rightfully be regarded as a
pioneer of the systematic investigation of creoles.

Lucien Adam and Coelho on creolization

     The prominent motivation for studying creoles in the
nineteenth century came from the field of Romance Linguistics.
Traditionally, scholars engaged in this field had been preoccupied
with the question of how to explain the development of Latin into
a number of different, mutually unintelligible languages. Several
theories had been proposed, but none of them could be proved
conclusively. People began to look outside Europe to find
evidence for comparison, and in particular to see whether

substratum languages played a decisive part in the formation of creoles.

In his book *Les idiomes négro-aryen et maléo-aryen* (1882) the French linguist Lucien Adam in fact suggests that creole languages are nothing but non-European languages with European lexical items. He adduces numerous supposed calques to prove his point. Similarly, he would argue for the development of the Romance languages from a mixture of Latin and the substratal vernaculars.

Coelho takes the opposite point of view and argues that creoles represent the first stage in the acquisition of a foreign language by speakers of another or other languages. The processes by which they are formed are based on universal psychological laws, and substratum languages have no influence (1880, pp. 193-95). The lowest level of second language learning, which leads to a lingua franca, takes place in an emergency contact situation. Other forms are more advanced in their acquisition of the model language. The lower status groups, reacting more spontaneously and instinctively, are responsible for the formation of creoles through the selective modification of the speech of the higher status group. The latter group might develop a kind of foreigner talk that is similar to the creole.

In support of his universality hypothesis, Coelho mentions a number of characteristics common to different creoles:

(1) General aspectual particles:
   ta "durative aspect": in Ceylon, Curaçao, Cape Verde, Macao;
   lo "potential aspect": in Ceylon, Haiti;
   té "perfective aspect": in Louisiana, Haiti.
(2) A preference for stressed pronouns in subject position;
(3) A number of common lexical items, such as:
   papia "speak": in Ceylon, Curaçao, Cape Verde;
   misté "need": in Ceylon, Curaçao, Cape Verde, Macao;
   pamóde "because": in Macao, San Antao (C.V.).

Writing at a time when little research in pidgins and creoles had been undertaken, Coelho developed an attractive universalist hypothesis, involving principles of language learning. His analysis was not detailed enough, however, to warrant calling him a major precursor of modern creole studies.

SCHUCHARDT AND HESSELING: MOTIVATION
AND METHODOLOGICAL APPROACH

The colonial structure of creole studies

While Coelho initiated the systematic investigation of creoles, his self-imposed task passed over to Schuchardt in a peculiar way. The latter apparently saw Coelho's first publication and reacted enthusiastically to it, as Coelho wrote in the preface to the second installment of his article:

> Having awakened interest among linguists in our study, . . . we prepared to treat the matter in a way as complete as possible, when the erudite and perceptive professor of Romance Languages at the University of Graz, Mr. Hugo Schuchardt, demonstrated his intention to us to occupy himself with the creole dialects, a thing which we are happy to see in such good hands; therefore we decided to limit ourselves in publishing, in the form of simple notes, the collected materials for the special part of our study, . . . waiting for the publication of the illustrious German linguist before we treat again and in a more complete way the general question of the "Formation of the Creole Dialects", in relation to which we do not agree completely with Mr. Schuchardt. (1882, p. 451)

Coelho's own theoretical contribution, mentioned in the cited text, never appeared.

When Schuchardt took over from Coelho, the gap between the speakers of creole and those investigating it again became much wider. Creole studies published in journals like the *Zeitschrift für Romanische Philologie* were of course intended for the *Zeitschrift*'s erudite readers, and no thought was given to the lack of educational opportunities or any other matters of importance to creole speakers, as might have been the case in the Lisbon *Boletim*.

Creole data became a product in themselves, separated from the people to whose language they belonged. In publishing the raw data in the *Boletim* and leaving their processing to Schuchardt and his more sophisticated linguistic apparatus, Coelho was only acting out Portugal's role as a middleman in colonial export goods, as is underscored by Schuchardt's following remark:

> Several years ago a friend of mine expressed his wonder about the fact that I had the courage to work on dialects which I myself had never heard spoken, in all seriousness he recommended to me overseas trips for the benefit of my creole investigations. The matter is not serious enough however to warrant such frantic ("verzweifelten") mea-

sures. . . . Moreover, this difficulty can be solved within certain bounds; for in London, Paris, Lisbon there are plenty of speakers of creole from the colonies, on the one hand, and on the other, people who are able to fleece ("entläuschen") them about small details for our purpose. Among those there are numerous ones with a higher education, who would take an active part in furthering our interests. (KS VII, p. 199)

Clearly, the historical context within which creole research came into existence was crucial in determining the nature of its development for a long time. This development had three primary characteristics:

(1) the separation of creole language studies from the interests of creole speakers;

(2) the necessity to define creoles as structurally dependent upon and as reductions of their base languages;

(3) an international division of labor between those producing, those collecting, and those analyzing creole language data.

Schuchardt's work

A major source of the attraction that pidgins and creoles had, particularly for Schuchardt, was the irregularity of their development: phonological changes were subject to a variety of factors; different languages contributed items to them in highly unexpected ways; syntactic structure was the result of the interaction of different grammars under varying circumstances. Thus creoles provided Schuchardt with another case in support of his opposition against the Neogrammarians' law of the regularity of sound-change. Nonetheless, Schuchardt's main interest in creoles did not seem to be the search for evidence against the Junggrammatiker, but rather the interaction between different grammars, as expressed in KS IV and KS IX. For him, this grew to be an important theoretical problem in its own right, separate from the substratum problem in Romance Linguistics. On this point, Schuchardt's position was somewhere between that of Adam and that of Coelho. His views on creolization were subtle and complex, to say the least. There is an additional difficulty, however, in that his work is "remarkable both for its complete continuity and for its entirely fragmentary character" (Iordan & Orr, 1970, p. 50).

Reconstructing Schuchardt's vision from about forty scattered publications, varying in size from about half a page to over two hundred pages, is no easy task. We embark upon it in the belief that Schuchardt had the richest and most complete perception of creoles of any single scholar up to the present. He combined the passion of his time for historical development and classification with a pronounced Humboldtian mentalism. The points at which he failed should be of prime importance to us, sometimes indicating wide gaps that have yet to be filled.

His work on creoles can be divided into three parts: (1) his reviews of fellow creolists and of incidental relevant publications; (2) his systematic series of articles: the *Kreolische Studien* (9 parts), the *Beiträge zur Kenntnis des kreolischen Romanisch* (Contributions to the Study of Creole Romance, 6 parts), and the *Beiträge zur Kenntnis des englischen Kreolisch* (Contributions to the Study of English Creole, 3 parts); (3) his major articles on the Lingua Franca and on Saramaccan. While Schuchardt's period of concentrated attention to creoles was from 1881 to 1890, the articles under (3) were written in 1909 and 1914 respectively. In the thirty-year span his thinking changed on many issues, so that there is some divergence between his earlier and his later views.

The scope of his work, although much wider than that of Coelho and Adam, is different from that of modern creole research. The main Caribbean creoles such as Jamaican Creole, Papiamentu, Haitian Creole, and Sranan Tongo are referred to only rarely, while the Portuguese-based creoles and pidgins of Africa and Asia receive meticulous attention. This difference can be partly explained with reference to Schuchardt's Romance Linguistics background, partly by the sources available to him, and partly by his particular theoretical interests in language mixture.

A bibliography of Schuchardt's works and an analysis of his phonological theories can be found in Vennemann & Wilbur (1972), and an anthology of his work was edited by Leo Spitzer (1922).

Hesseling

Derk Christiaan Hesseling was educated as a classical philologist, but as a young scholar he turned to the study of Modern Greek, in which he held a chair at Leyden University from 1907 till 1929. He was interested in the formation of the Greek *koinê*: was it a direct development of the Attic dialect or the result of dialect mixture? Hesseling tried to find an answer to this question in the detailed study of a possibly similar development, the emergence of Afrikaans in the seventeenth century. He read Schuchardt's article on Malayo-Portuguese (K S IX) and was struck

by the many similarities between Afrikaans and this trade jargon
of the East Indies. Consequently he developed the hypothesis that
Afrikaans represents the first stage of creolization of a language
under the influence of foreign languages, the most important of
which was Malayo-Portuguese, spoken by the relatively large
numbers of slaves that arrived at the Cape between 1658 and
1685. Via his work on Afrikaans Hesseling entered the field of
creole studies, to which he would contribute until the end of his
life in 1941.

Hesseling wrote two books on Afrikaans and Negerhollands (1899 and 1905, respectively), both preceded by an article
in *De Gids*. After that, he repeatedly returned to the questions
posed in his first contributions to creole studies, and, in addition
to a revised version of "Het Afrikaans" (1923), he published
nearly twenty articles and short notes in which he either defended
his views on the origin of Afrikaans or presented new materials
relating to Negerhollands and Papiamentu. The scope of Hesseling's work, since it dealt almost exclusively with Afrikaans,
Negerhollands, and Papiamentu, is much more restricted than
Schuchardt's, both descriptively and theoretically.

Hesseling was a philologist with a keen interest in spoken
language and all kinds of vernacular speech, but—like Schuchardt—
he never gathered creole data on the spot; instead, he relied on
texts, grammatical notes, and personal communications. We have
to bear in mind, however, that the phenomena he dealt with were
mainly historical: the early history of Afrikaans and the nearly
extinct Dutch Creole of the Virgin Islands.

SCHUCHARDT'S VIEWS ON PIDGINS AND CREOLES

Language structure

The linguistic model at the basis of Schuchardt's views
stems from Humboldt, but is quite modern in appearance. It can
be represented as follows:

INNER FORM	sentence construction
	relation words
OUTER FORM	inflection
	lexicon

The boundary between sentence construction ("Satzfügung") and relation words ("Beziehungswörter") is far from sharp, however (MALAIO, pp. 202-204). The particular way in which Schuchardt applies this model is strongly reminiscent of Stratificational Grammar.

The pidgin-creole life cycle

The idea of the creole life cycle was clearly developed by 1909, when Schuchardt's article on the Lingua Franca appeared. The question of the modes of simplification involved in pidginization received careful attention, and the resulting opinion can certainly not be reduced to the "baby talk" theory, which is often attributed to Schuchardt. Although this theory constitutes an important element in his work on pidginization, alternative theories receive equal attention.

Pidginization. In a contact situation involving two groups speaking different languages, the simplified language used for communication (the "contact language") will be based on one of the two. The choice of language is dictated by external circumstances, not by any inherent characteristics of the languages themselves. Within the contact language variations attributable to the native language background of the individual speakers may occur. A contact language may thus be related to any native language as "a tree to its roots"(LF, pp. 442-47).

Often there are several different processes of simplification involved in the development of a contact language (LF, p. 445). Two forms of simplification should be distinguished: simplification only with reference to the model language (e.g., lack of number and case), and simplification with reference to two languages. When a certain distinction a/b exists, for instance, in the model, but not in the substratum language, then the resulting creole will have either a or b, or a and b in free variation (KS IV, pp. 130-42). In many cases the choice of the particular form that the simplification will take rests with the speaker of the model language. The speaker of the substrate language will imitate him (SAR IV).

Creolization. Creoles have developed from pidgins into full-fledged, complete languages because the slaves, belonging to many different nations, had no other language in common (LF, p. 443). While creoles are lexically based on one language, many lexical items may have been contributed to them from different African languages. These African elements did not exist in the original

contact language, but were added to it when the contact language became the native language of slave communities (SAR V).
Decreolization. One of the peculiar traits of creoles is the existence of numerous degrees of similarity of the creole to its model, although this does not imply that creole is "individual broken talk" ("individuelles Radebrechen"). Thus system and variation co-occur in creoles (KS IV, p. 113). When in a given area creolized English coexists with standard English, a number of stages emerge in-between, until finally the creole speakers do not speak creole any more, but rather a modified form of standard English. In the case of other European languages coexisting with creoles, decreolization tends to occur to a much lesser degree (SAR VIII).

The special position of English

One interesting feature of Schuchardt's work that has not been clearly described is his claim that English creoles occupy a special position because of the already creolized character of their model. Both in the phase of pidginization and in the phase of decreolization, this trait is of importance. Along the coast of Africa, English could easily replace the pidginized Portuguese spoken there, "because of its already creolized character" (BEITRAGE I, p. 243). English is morphologically much more similar to a creole than are, for example, the Romance languages, and therefore English-based creoles differ from Romance-based creoles in the way both diverge from their model languages, and in the way a continuum is formed with them (SAR IX).

Monogenesis and the role of Portuguese

Because of Schuchardt's intensive preoccupation with the Portuguese-based creoles as his basis for research, one is tempted to consider him to have taken the monogenetic position in explaining the origin of creoles. Actually, his position is ambiguous, probably because for him the issue was not monogenesis versus polygenesis, but rather the relative importance of the substratum. Contrary to Voorhoeve's (1973) monogenetic position, for instance, Schuchardt did not consider Sranan Tongo to be originally Portuguese-based. The most reasonable conclusion as to Schuchardt's position would seem to be that he realized the influence of the early Portuguese-based trade language on individual lexical items and expressions in later creoles, but did not consider this influence determinant in defining them. Furthermore, he assumed borrowing to be such a widespread phenomenon that he did not need a separate concept of relexification to account for the many similarities existing between the different Caribbean creoles.

The similarities between the creole languages are not due to a common ancestor, but to parallel development. They have been constructed out of dissimilar material, but with the same design and in the same style. The difference between the creoles spoken by African slaves and the Asian creoles is not due to African influence in the former group, but to different racial backgrounds, conditions, and experiences (SAR VII).

Schuchardt's account of Annobon creole suggests that relexification must have played some part in his conception of the genesis of creoles: when the Spanish took over Annobon from the Portuguese, the creole speakers did not start speaking Spanish, but rather a predominantly Spanish-based creole based on the earlier Lusitanian creole (ANNOBON 407).

The explanation offered for the complex Surinam creole situation is ingenious, but would nowadays be considered rather weak: originally there were two creoles in Surinam, the English-based Sranan Tongo, and the Portuguese-based Saramaccan. The first borrowed a number of infrequently used Portuguese words from Saramaccan, which in turn borrowed some frequently used English words from Sranan. Now both creoles are subdialects of the same variety. If we would express their components in a formula (N=Negro, H=Dutch, E=English, and P=Portuguese), Sranan has the composition NEP_1H, and Saramaccan NEP_5H (SAR VIII).

The influence of the substratum languages

This topic held Schuchardt's main interest, and he treated it rather extensively. The German creolist was of the opinion that there is a considerable difference between the amount of influence that the African languages exerted on the slave creoles, and the amount of influence exerted by Malay and Tagalog on the creoles in Asia. The latter constituted one single influence on the respective creoles to which they contributed, while the African languages, being numerous, neutralized rather than reinforced each other (CABO, p. 139).

The following list of examples of substratum influence in creoles excludes the Asian creoles, and is limited to the African influence in the slave creoles:

(1) Sequences such as V_i NP V_i ..., to indicate verb-focus (SAR V):

> Papiamentu: *ta lesa bo ta lesa e buki*
>   read you   read book
> "it's reading that you are ... the book"

(2) Serial verbs (SAR IV):

> Ashanti: *ko fa ba*
> Sranan: *go teki kom*
> English: "to fetch"

(3) Use of a verb where a European language would have a preposition (SAR IV):

> Ewe: *ephle so na-m*
> Sranan: *him bai hasi gi mi*
> English: "he bought horses for me"

(4) Post-posed elements where European languages would have preferred pre-posed elements (KS VII):

> Annobon: adj more than
> Portuguese: more adj than

(5) The distinction between an unmarked aorist and a marked durative (CABO, p. 138)

(6) Aversion for the /r/ and a preference for labials due to the prominently developed lips of Africans (CABO, p. 138)

(7) Numerous proverbs, folktales, and turns of speech (SAR VII).

Changes in the meaning of individual words, which in creole often vary in meaning from the model language, are due to differences in the cultural background of the new speakers or differences in the physical and cultural environment in which the creole emerges (KS IX, p. 185).

According to Schuchardt, the true criterion for classifying a "mixed" language is to be found in its inflection and its relation words, i.e., in the inner part of the "outer form" (MALAIO, pp. 202-204). Maybe modern linguistics would rate the "inner word" higher as a criterion for classifying languages.

General features of creoles

Starting with his review of Adam's work (NAMA), Schuchardt was always very careful to distinguish between those features of creoles due to substratum influence, and the features due to universal processes of creolization. His enumeration of the latter type of features is of considerable theoretical interest, although features arising in the stage of pidginization are not kept apart from creolization features as clearly as contemporary creole research would indicate (with the exception of the very interesting point (2):

(1) "Grammatical" morphemes are replaced as much as possible by lexemes (SAR IV):
pierre+s "stones" will become:
pierre pierre, or:
pierre MANY, or:
pierre THEY

(2) All verb forms are replaced by infinitives, except for the irregular verbs, where the 3sg form is used. In a later stage, when the complete creole verbal paradigms are formed, all 3sg forms are replaced by infinitives (LF, p. 445).

(3) Unstressed weak forms are replaced by stressed strong forms (KS I, p. 142): e.g., instead of the preposition *a* "to," *por* "by, through" is used; instead of the article, a demonstrative is used.

(4) All preverbal pronoun clitics are moved or deleted (NAMA, p. 237).

(5) Verbal aspect particles are used instead of tense/aspect inflection (LF, p. 445).

(6) Prepositions are deleted when the meaning of the verb disambiguates the V - NP relation (KS IX, p. 228).

(7) When in predicate position, nouns and adjectives are not as clearly distinguished as in European languages. Thus I AM FEAR is the same as I AM AFRAID, and I HUNGER is equivalent to I HUNGRY. In creoles, the basic semantic relation is what counts (KS IX, p. 203).

(8) European reflexive verbs appear in creole without the reflexive pronoun, but with identical meanings (KS IX, p. 213).

(9) Modifiers that occur in European languages with a pre-nominal and a post-nominal element occur in creoles only as a post-nominal element (NAMA, p. 235): e.g., *ce cheval-là* "that horse over there" becomes *cheval-là* "that horse."

(10) The use of forms like *tem* or *tin* for the equivalent of the Spanish *hay* or the Portuguese *ha* "there is, there are" (KS IX, p. 194).

(11) Items originally meaning "too much" are used instead of items meaning "much" (SAR IV).

(12) Extension in the use and meaning of Portuguese *mesmo* / creole *mes* (KS IX, p. 239).

(13) Reduplicated forms such as (CABO, p. 137):

    de bó + bossa = de bossa
    of you   your   of your

(14) The frequent usage of analogy in the process of word-formation (LF, p. 445).

(15) Concrete lexical items from European languages sometimes appear in creoles with generalized or abstract meanings (LF, p. 445).

(16) A preference for visual, vivid, and simple expressions (LF, p. 444, CABO, p. 137).

HESSELING'S VIEWS

Views in common with Schuchardt

Hesseling followed Schuchardt in many respects, not only in his Humboldtian conception of language and in his rejection of Neogrammarian thinking, but also in his general approach to creolization. Although he had more sympathy for Coelho's position that creoles represent the first stages of foreign language learning, than for Lucien Adam's substratum theories, Hesseling fully agrees with Schuchardt that the real problem is to assess the different factors and to indicate their operation in every case (NEHO 2, p. 54).

Other views that Hesseling explicitly adopted from Schuchardt are the importance of the West African Portuguese pidgin in the early formative stage of creole, the possibility that pidgins are multilevel generative systems (Silverstein, 1972), and the general mechanism underlying creolization. Finally, the early creolists concur that different levels of creole coexist in the same speech community, which can be divided into different social classes and ethnic groups.

Afrikaans and Malayo-Portuguese

An evaluation of Hesseling's contribution to creole studies would not be complete without a word about his notorious (at least in South Africa) "Malayo-Portuguese theory" of the origin of Afrikaans.

The language of the slaves that were brought in large numbers to the Cape after 1658 was either Malayo-Portuguese, i.e., the broken Portuguese with Malay elements that formed the lingua franca of the East Indies (the remnants of which were described by Schuchardt), or the very similar Portuguese jargon that was used in the West African slave trade (AFRI 1, p. 54; 2, p. 37). At the Cape this Portuguese-based pidgin came into contact with Dutch, and the special social circumstances of the sudden and intimate confrontation between the two languages caused the simplification of forms that characterizes Afrikaans in comparison with Dutch itself (AFRI 1, p. 27; 2, p. 40).

Although Malayo-Portuguese was not the only factor involved in the simplification process, it was clearly the main one (AFRI 1, p. 153; 2, p. 127). The influence of the languages of the indigenous peoples of South Africa, e.g., the Hottentots, was rather restricted (mainly lexical items plus a single grammatical form), because the contacts with these peoples were of quite a different nature.

The resulting language, Afrikaans, is not a creole, but a language that stopped halfway in the process of creolization because of changing social conditions and the conservative influence of newly arrived groups from Holland (AFRI 1, pp. 70, 155; 2, pp. 60, 128).

Among the grammatical differences between Afrikaans and Dutch that have to be attributed to the influence of Malayo-Portuguese, we find:

(1) the article *die* (a demonstrative in Dutch), presumably a relexification from MP *ackel,* derived from the Portuguese demonstative *aquel.*

(2) Possessive constructions of the form *Peter his son.*

(3) *Ons* as the first person plural pronoun—MP had one form for subject and object position, and *ons* is the Dutch object pronoun.

(4) Loss of inflection in the verb (AFRI 2, p. 116).

Creolization

Although he clearly distinguished between a trade jargon or pidgin as an auxiliary language and a creole as the native language of a speech community, Hesseling did not give much weight to the distinction between the processes of pidginization and creolization. His central concern was simplification of forms, which he saw both in the formation of a common Negro jargon on board the slave ships and in the subsequent origin of a creole during contact with white colonists (NEHO 2, p. 59).

The most striking theoretical difference between Hesseling and Schuchardt is to be found in the question of the source of the simplification: the latter considered it to be mostly the "foreigner talk" of model language speakers, while the former considered the speech of the learners to be the primary source for the simplification (ZOND, p. 485, AFRI 2, p. 125, KREO, SPA, p. 48). But even on this point Hesseling leaves room for the opposite point of view: the masters do partially adopt the broken language of their social inferiors to make themselves best understood. In theory it may be feasible to distinguish between adaptation (by the inferiors) and borrowing (by the speakers of the model language or by children learning their language from black nurses), but in practice the two processes interact and flow together (ZOND, p. 485).

One has to distinguish between (a) a mixed language or "gemischte Sprache," (b) a "Mischsprache" or "mengeltaal" (the Dutch phrase), and (c) a creole. The first term is almost trivial since every language is in some sense mixed. The second one is applicable if the lexicon contains a very high percentage of loan words or if the grammar is affected. A creole is a kind of "mengeltaal," the defining traits of which stem from its origin (MENG, p. 319). Two conditions, one social and one linguistic, are a *sine qua non* for creolization, namely, the clash between two languages and their dissimilarity. When one of these conditions does not obtain, something different from creolization (=simplification) occurs (NEHO 2, p. 58, AFRI 2, p. 10, MENG, p. 321). The language clash arises from a sudden need to communicate intensively in daily life; one of its most extreme manifestations prevailed in slavery (NEHO 2, p. 59, MENG, p. 315). The main part in the institutionalization of the simplified forms resulting from this language clash is played by children (AFRI 2, p. 115).

The selection of a certain form (e.g., the infinitive) in the contact language is governed by the frequency of its occurrence in the model language (KREO).

Monogenesis and the role of Portuguese

DeCamp (1971, p. 22) honors Hesseling as the first adherent to the monogenetic hypothesis for Asian and Caribbean creoles, assuming the Portuguese pidgin to be the common ancestor, and Voorhoeve (1973, p. 134) seems to imply the same. The present authors, however, could not find any passage in Hesseling's work that would warrant such a conclusion. It is true that Hesseling stressed the importance and distribution of Portuguese both in the East Indies (including the Cape) and in the West African slave trade. He even argued that Angolan and Guinese slaves who were brought to the Cape in 1658 (partly from an intercepted Portuguese slaver that was on its way from Angola to Brazil) had learned the Portuguese-based lingua franca in West Africa or on board the ship (AFRI 1, p. 53; 2, p. 39).

But in relation to Negerhollands Portuguese is only mentioned as the possible source of some lexical items: "Furthermore, in every creole dialect one can expect Portuguese words from the nautical and slave language that was widely distributed along the Gold and Slave Coasts" (NEHO 2, p. 68). Hesseling explained the creolization of Dutch in the Danish Antilles and of Spanish on Curaçao as resulting from contact with the *African* mother tongues of the slaves.

The similarities between Afrikaans and the varieties of Dutch that were once spoken in the East Indies and Ceylon can possibly be explained by the existence of a general Indo-Dutch, from which they are all derived; this Indo-Dutch already contained Malayo-Portuguese elements. Another possibility is that these similarities are due to general factors of creolization and similar circumstances of emergence (AFRI 1, p. 73; 2, p. 63; CEYL, p. 311).

The similarities between Afrikaans and Negerhollands must be attributed to the fact that both languages developed under the influence of substratum languages (NEHO 2, p. 122). The differences between the two are due to the fact that (a) the creolization of Afrikaans stopped half-way; (b) slightly different dialects of Dutch were involved; and most importantly, (c) the creolization of Negerhollands was caused by other languages than Malayo-Portuguese (NEHO 2, pp. 69, 122).

The similarities between Negerhollands and Papiamentu

can be accounted for by referring to similar substratum languages, general characteristics of creolization, and by the extensive borrowing that Negerhollands did from Papiamentu (PAP).

We may conclude that Hesseling cannot be considered to be the spiritual father of the monogenetic hypothesis. The only elements in his work that would fit within a monogenetic hypothesis are his discussion of the origin of Afrikaans and some general remarks about borrowing.

Substratum influence

According to Hesseling, creole languages do not represent the grammar of substratum languages. The syntax of African languages, their most characteristic part, differs too much from that of creole for this to be the case (e.g., the so-called nominal classifiers and serial verbs of the Bantu languages) (SPA, p. 50; NEHO 1, p. 303; 2, p. 56).

The multiplicity of African languages involved in the contact situation neutralized their influence rather than strengthening it, and what remains is their greatest common denominator (NEHO, p. 58).

Among cases of direct African substratum influence in Papiamentu and Negerhollands we find:

(1) The use of the third person plural pronoun as a plural suffix: -*sender* in NH, -*nan* in Pap. (NEHO 2, p. 94, PAP, p. 272).

(2) The use of aspect particles. In NH these are the following: (*le*) 'durative', *lo* 'near future/durative present', (*h*) *a* 'past', *sa*(*l*) 'future', *ka* 'perfect' (NEHO 2, p. 103).

(3) The placement of all particles immediately before the verb (NEHO, p. 118).

(4) A general tendency to use double and periphrastic forms (NEHO 2, p. 111).

If we compare Hesseling's listing of substratum influences with that of Schuchardt's, we notice immediately that Hesseling is considerably more cautious in postulating substratum influence, but also that (1) and (4) would be characterized by Schuchardt as general characteristics of creolization. Similarly, all the features which Hesseling postulates to be due to a Malayo-Portuguese substratum influence in Afrikaans, Schuchardt would consider to have come about in an autonomous process of creolization.

AN EVALUATION

By 1880 linguists had gone beyond the kind of racism that held that the "simplicity" of creoles was due to the limited mental capacity of Africans. Note that the conception of creole languages as "simple" stems from a conception of language as an inventory of items and of morphological distinctions. Starting from the premise that creoles were modified forms of European model languages, it was felt necessary to explain the simplification that had taken place as a concomitant of the learning situation: the "baby talk theory" and the imperfect learning theory were suggested, but not clearly kept apart.

Schuchardt developed both theories in his work, although he probably valued the first one more highly. One may assume that the reason he did not keep the different theories apart is that his primary interest was language mixture ("Sprachmischung"), not processes of simplification, which has become one of our main present concerns. It would be unfortunate if this difference in theoretical focus made Schuchardt's work irrelevant to present-day creole research, because the complex problems that Schuchardt raised have not been solved yet, and a careful review of some parts of Schuchardt's work might provide a usable theoretical framework to deal with the problem of calques, forms of borrowing and relexification.

While Schuchardt's views reached later scholars oversimplified and distorted, Hesseling's writing hardly influenced modern creole research at all. This is probably because it relates mostly to Negerhollands and Afrikaans, and because of the language in which Hesseling wrote, Dutch.

Nonetheless Hesseling's work constitutes a complete theory of creolization in its own right, and probably on many points a much less ambiguous one than Schuchardt's. Also, Hesseling avoids the baby talk theory altogether, a position appealing to most modern scholars. As was already seen, the two pioneers in creole research coincide on a great many points, particularly as regards the general characteristics of pidginization and creolization. In scope they differ considerably, however, and Schuchardt's grasp of the data was much better. A case in point is the serial verbs, which Hesseling did not recognize in creole (a reason why he may have underestimated the role of the African languages in the formation of creoles), but which Schuchardt discusses extensively.

The question of Afrikaans is the only part of Hesseling's

writing still currently under discussion. The present authors do not pretend to evaluate the different theories as to the origin of Afrikaans; Hesseling's position on this point has been taken up again by the creolist Marius Valkhof (1966), who adduces additional evidence to support Hesseling's original hypothesis and makes the premises involved more explicit. At the same time, however, Valkhof departs from his predecessor's theory in postulating two separate lingua francas at the base of modern Afrikaans.

Pidgins, creoles, and universals

Rousseau's dream of contemplating man in his natural form, stripped of all the trappings of civilization and history, reappears in the image of creole universals. Interestingly enough, Bertrand-Bocandé already assumed that the grammar of creoles was universal in corresponding to a minimal communication system, in which only the basic semantic relations could be expressed. Coelho had a similar idea, referring to the spontaneity and instincts of creole speakers. Of course, that same idea of the naturalness and universality of creoles is still with us.

Research in pidgin and creole languages has centered around three types of linguistic universals involved in the formation of creoles: (1) universals of simplification; (2) universals of elaboration or grammar formation; (3) universal characteristics of the interaction between the substratum languages and the model language.

On (1) significant progress has been made. Here Schuchardt's work is illuminating not in the conceptual frameworks it provides, but in that it makes an inventory of some of the processes playing a part in the stage of pidginization. Two of these processes are worth mentioning. First the behavioral principle later made explicit by Naro (1973, p. 447): "express each separately intuited element of meaning by a phonologically separate stress-bearing form." Second a perceptual strategy which may be formalized as follows:

$$x_1 \; Y \; (x_2) \longrightarrow \phi \; Y \; (x_2)$$

This strategy accounts for the deletion for preverbal clitics, the reflexive pronoun, and prenominal modifiers, and can easily be explained on general psychological grounds. Slobin's conclusions from comparative research of child language acquisition seem to point in the same direction (1972, p. 74).

Universals of type (2) only recently have become a focus of interest, but the initial results are promising. Here the early creolists have next to nothing to contribute, as they were limited by their view that creoles are no more than reductions of their models.

Work on universals of type (3) has barely started. It is precisely on this point that Schuchardt's writing could be of relevance, once the articles on Asian creoles have been reviewed and evaluated carefully. The distinction between "inner" and "outer" forms enabled Schuchardt to adopt a powerful theory of linguistic interaction for Malaysian Portuguese and Philippine Spanish (KS IV, KS IX). Their Asian inner forms would have been filled up by a Romance lexicon, and the result, also partly due to morphological simplification, is classified by Schuchardt as Romance.

While Schuchardt made this relexification theory quite explicit in the Asian case and provided an interesting formalism to describe it (KS IX), he did not apply it to the Caribbean creoles. In the case of Saramaccan, where it is characterized as "language chemistry" ("Sprachchemie"), it appears diluted and vague.

Schuchardt and Hesseling gathered a tremendous body of data on creoles, and particularly on the Portuguese- and Dutch-based ones, which until the present moment have remained little studied. Their views on the general processes of pidginization and creolization are widely held now. Thus, they created a new field of linguistic investigation and at the same time contributed more to it than anyone else. If their work appears unsatisfactory because clear conceptual distinctions (e.g., between pidgins and creoles) remain blurred, and too many possible answers are suggested to undefined questions, then we must realize that only a small part of modern creole research conforms to the standards that we would like to set for the early creolists.

REFERENCES

I. Early Writings on Creoles

Adam, Lucien. 1882. *Les idiomes négro-aryen et maléo-aryen*. Paris: Maissonneuve.

Bertrand-Bocandé, M. 1849. De la langue créole de la Guinée portugaise. *Bulletin de la Société de Géographie de Paris*, 3ᵉ série 12:57-93.

Coelho, Adolpho. 1880. Os Dialectos Romanicos ou Neo-Latinos na Africa, Asia, e América. *Lisboa* 2:129-96 (1880-81); 3:451-78 (1882); 6:705-55 (1886). Reprinted in Monais-Barbosa, Jorge, ed. 1967. *Estudos linguísticos criulos.* Lisbon: Academia Internacional de Cultura Portuguesa.

Larousse, Pierre, ed. 1869. *Grand Dictionnaire Universel du XIX Siècle.* Paris: Larousse.

II. Schuchardt's Work on Pidgins and Creoles

Lb = *Literaturblatt für germanische und romanische Philologie*
Sb = *Sitzungsberichte der Wienische Akademie von Wissenschaften*
ZR = *Zeitschrift für Romanische Philologie*

A. Reviews

1881. Of Coelho 1880. *ZR* 5. (COELHO 1)

1883. Of Adam 1882. *Lb* 4. (NAMA)

1883. Of Coelho 1882. *Lb* 4. (COELHO 2)

1887. Of *O creolo de Cabo Verde. Breves estudos sobre o creolo de Cabo Verde. Lb* 8. (CABO)

1893. Of Isidro Vila, *Elementos de la Gramática ambú o de Annobón*, and *Compendio de la Doctrina cristiana en castellano y Fa d'Ambú. Lb* 14. (ANNOBON)

B. Kreolische Studien

1882. Uber das Negerportugiesische von S. Thomé. *Sb* 101 (2):889-917. (KS I)

1882. Uber das Indoportugiesische von Cochim. *Sb* 102 (2):799-816. (KS II)

1883. Uber das Indoportugiesische von Diu. *Sb* 103 (1):3-17. (KS III)

1883. Uber das Malaiospanischen der Philippenen. *Sb* 105 (1):111-50. (KS IV)

1883. Uber das Melaneso-Englische. *Sb* 105 (1):131-61. (KS V)

1883. Uber das Indoportugiesische von Mangalore. *Sb* 105 (3):882-904. (KS VI)

1888. Uber das Indoportugiesische von Annobom. *Sb* 116 (1):193-226. (KS VII)

1888. Uber das Annamito-französische. *Sb* 116 (7):227-34. (KS VIII)

1890. Uber das Malaioportugiesische von Batavia und Tugu. *Sb* 122 (12):1-255. (KS IX)

C. Beiträge zur Kenntnis des Kreolischen Romanisch

1888. Allgemeineres über das Negerportugiesisch. *ZR* 12:242-54. (BEITRAGE I)

1888. Zum Negerportugiesischen Senegambiens. *ZR* 12:301-12. (BEITRAGE II)

1888. Zum Negerportugiesischen der Kapverden. *ZR* 12:312-22. (BEITRAGE III)

1889. Zum Negerportugiesischen der Ilha do Principe. *ZR* 13:463-75. (BEITRAGE IV)
1889. Allgemeineres über das Indoportugiesische. *ZR* 13:476-576. (BEITRAGE V)
1889. Zum Indoportugiesischen von Mahé und Cannamore. *ZR* 13:516-24. (BEITRAGE VI)
D. Beiträge zur Kenntnis des englischen Kreolisch
I (ENG I)
Melaneso-englisches. (ENG II)
Das Indo-englische. (ENG III)
E. Major articles
1909. Die Lingua Franca. *ZR* 33:441-61. (LF)
1914. Die Sprache der Saramakkaneger in Surinam. *Verhandelingen der Koninklijke Akademie van Wetenschappen te Amsterdam, Afdeling Letteren*, Letterkunde N.R. 14, no. 6. (SAR)

III. Hesseling's Publications Relating to Creoles (not exhaustive)
Tijd = *Tijdschrift voor Nederlandse Taal- en Letterkunde*
1897. Het Hollandsch in Zuid-Afrika. *De Gids* 60, I:138-62. (HOZA)
1899. *Het Afrikaansch. Bijdrage tot de Geschiedenis der Nederlandse Taal in Zuid-Afrika.* Leiden: E. J. Brill. (AFRI 1)
1905. Het Negerhollands der Deense Antillen. *De Gids* 69, I:283-306. (NEHO 1)
1905. *Het Negerhollands der Deense Antillen. Bijdrage tot de Geschiedenis der Nederlandse Taal in Amerika.* Leiden: A. W. Sijthoff. (NEHO 2)
1906. Is het Afrikaans de zuivere ontwikkeling van een Nederlands dialekt? *Taal en Letteren* 16:477-90. (ZOND)
1910. Overblijfsels van de Nederlandse taal op Ceylon. *Tijd* 29:303-12. (CEYL)
1923. Het Frans in Noord-Amerika en het Nederlands in Zuid-Afrika. *De Gids* 87, I:438-57. (FRANA)
1923. *Het Afrikaans. Bijdrage tot de Geschiedenis der Nederlandse Taal in Zuid-Afrika. Tweede herziene en vermeerderde uitgave.* Leiden: E. J. Brill. (AFRI 2)
1933. Een Spaand boek over het Papiaments. *Tijd* 52:40-57. (SPA)
1933. Hoe ontstond de eigenaardige vorm van het Kreools? *Neophilologus* 18:209-15. (KREO)
1933. Papiaments en Negerhollands. *Tijd* 52:265-88. (PAP)
1934. Gemengde taal, Mengeltaal, Kreools en Kreolisering. *Nieuwe Taalgids* 28:310-22. (MENG)

IV. Other References Cited
DeCamp, David. 1971. Introduction. In *Pidginization and Creolization of Languages*, D. Hymes, ed. London: Cambridge University Press.

Iordan, I., and Orr, J. 1970. *An Introduction to Romance Linguistics; Its Schools and Scholars.*

Naro, Anthony J. 1973. The origin of West African Pidgin. *CLS* 9:442-49.

Oliver and Page. 1966. *A Short History of Africa.* London.

Silverstein, Michael. 1972. Chinook Jargon: Language contact and the problem of multi-level generative systems. *Language* 48:378-406, 596-625.

Slobin, Dan. 1972. They learn the same way all around the world. *Psychology Today*, May 1972.

Spitzer, Leo, ed. 1922. *Hugo-Schuchardt Brevier. Ein Vademekum der allgemeinen Sprachwissenschaft.* Halle.

Valkhof, Marius. 1966. *Studies in Portuguese and Creole.* Johannesburg: University of Witwatersrand Press.

Vennemann, Theo. 1972. *Schuchardt, the Neogrammarians, and the Transformational Theory of Phonological Change.* Frankfurt/M.: Athenaum Verlag. Linguistische Forschungen 26.

Voorhoeve, Jan. 1973. Historical and linguistic evidence in favour of the relexification theory in the formation of creoles. *Language and Society*, II, 1:133-45.

ii.

Pidgins, Creoles, and Problems of
Language Acquisition
and Language Universals

Pidginization and Creolization: Language Acquisition and Language Universals

Derek Bickerton

Existing theories about the process of pidginization have all either implied or directly stated that it is a process somehow distinct from other processes of language acquisition, whether these involve a first or a second language. Theories of creolization, while much fewer and vaguer, have similarly suggested something unique about the process. Such theories have, of course, been extremely useful in the maintenance of pidgin and creole studies as a benighted backwater of linguistics. However, the present paper will suggest that there is nothing at all mysterious or unique about either process: that pidginization is second-language learning with restricted input, and that creolization is first-language learning with restricted input. For reasons that will become apparent, the issue of language universals will arise only in connection with the second process.

Several theories about pidginization have involved the assumption that speakers of the superstrate language deliberately simplified it in order to accommodate the 'ignorant natives'. Bloomfield (1933) seems to have popularized—though he did not originate—this assumption, which crops up, not always with acknowledgment to its source,[1] in, e.g., Hall 1966; Ferguson 1971; Naro 1971, 1975; etc. Writers vary in the extent to which they regard the resultant artifact as a culturally learned construct (involving, as Bloomfield suggested, "imitation" of the "natives'

mistakes"), or as a resource within the reach of any native speaker
at any time; the latter view is most explicitly presented in Kay and
Sankoff 1974, a paper that was seminal in its linking of language
universals with the pidgin-creole field, but profoundly misleading
in its conception of that linkage. It is misleading because of the
two following false assumptions: "shared surface structures are
likely . . . to be close to universal underlying structures," and
"those [shared] surface structures . . . will be the first and perhaps
the only structures that speaker-hearers learn to produce and
interpret correctly" (1974, pp. 67-68). The first is false because
any underlying structure both broad enough to be universal and
rich enough to escape the triviality of the 'all-languages-have-oral-
vowels' type of 'universality' must be extremely abstract, at least
abstract enough to reconcile English and Japanese (which have NO
'shared surface structures'!), and thus can have little in common
with the surface structures of the so-called natural languages, be
they ever so simple. The second is simply empirically false, as we
shall see when we examine data from Hawaiian pidgin. It may well
be true that social superordinates in contact situations 'simplify'
their language by avoiding complex structures, deleting inflections,
case-markers, etc., as Naro has abundantly evidenced from the
original period of Afro-Portuguese contact, but it is by no means
clear that this has any effect whatsoever on the finished article,
i.e., there is good reason to suppose that pidgins would turn out
the way they do irrespective of whether their speakers were offered
'simplified' or 'non-simplified' models.

   Opposed to 'simplification' models are 'diffusion' models,
proposed in only slightly varying forms by, e.g., Thompson 1961,
Stewart 1962, Whinnom 1965, etc. As a theory of pidginization,
the 'diffusionist', perhaps better known as the 'monogeneticist',
position suffers from the defect that it was derived not to account
for pidginization at all, but to explain the puzzling similarities that
exist in creoles of diverse genetic history in widely separated
regions of the world. It did so by positing an Ur-pidgin, reaching
back perhaps as far as the medieval Mediterranean lingua franca
and relexified as it was disseminated round the globe by sailors.
The inadequacy of monogenesis as an explanation of creoles has
been discussed in Bickerton 1974, so I shall here confine myself to
its inadequacy as a theory of pidginization—which, granted, it was
never intended to be; however, of its very nature it contains some
obnoxious entailments with regard to pidgins. Principal among
these is that pidgin *had to be taught*, i.e., could not be
spontaneously generated in a contact situation. This entailment, of

course, admirably fits the usual colonial stereotype of a one hundred percent active 'white man' and a one hundred percent passive 'native', while ignoring trivial facts such as (a) merchants and seamen had better things to do than go around propagating a language that wasn't even their own; (b) a high percentage of the 'natives' were multilingual autodidacts with well-developed strategies for acquiring second, third, and even nth languages, who weren't going to sit around passively waiting for the merchants and seamen to 'provide an adequate corpus' for them; and (c) language learning, whether first or second, is a creative and not an imitative process. These facts would have applied even if (as so many writers seem to have assumed) PL, a pidgin lexically based on a language L, were invariably a means of communication between speakers of L on the one hand, and speakers of non-L_i, non-L_{ii} and non-L_{iii}, etc., on the other; they apply *a fortiori* in the far commoner situation in which (as pointed out by Alleyne 1971, Whinnom 1971) PL is used by speakers of non-L_i, non-L_{ii}, etc. to talk to one another.

I shall spend no more time discussing prior theories of pidginization, since they are clearly refuted by the empirical data on Hawaiian pidgin. To the best of our present knowledge, language contact in Hawaii went through three phases, (1) 1778-1876, the period of *hapa-haole*, when with negligible exceptions the only residents of Hawaii were native speakers of either Hawaiian or English, (2) 1876-c.1900, the early plantation period, when the lingua franca of Hawaii's polyglot population was probably a simplified form of Hawaiian,[2] and (3) 1900- , when the decline in the Hawaiian language led to its replacement as a target by English. Central to our understanding of this process must be the realization that nowhere has any group of people sat down and said 'Let us produce a pidgin language'; people either struggle to communicate by any means in their power, without bothering what language they are speaking, or else, if they progress beyond this stage, they perceive themselves as learning some preexisting language. Thus, in the *hapa-haole* period, Hawaiians saw themselves as learning English, and indeed, insofar as its scarce attestations enable one to judge, *hapa-haole* was simply a cover term for a language learning continuum such as one finds in all dual-language contact situations (its literal meaning, 'half-white', is a singularly appropriate one). In the early plantation period, Hawaiian became the target language for an immigrant population that might (though by no means always) have received its orders in the field from native speakers of English,[3] but that had far more social contact, both on and off the job, with Hawaiians; here, surviving immigrants, and perhaps even more so the children of such immigrants born prior to 1900, will claim to have been speakers of 'Hawaiian', though doubtless of a variety of Hawaiian that bore about as much resemblance to native Hawaiian as *hapa-haole* bore to English. From 1900, the influence of Hawaiian declined as that of English rose: rather than a complete break between pidgin Hawaiian and pidgin English, there seems to have been an intervening macaronic period characterized by considerable instability in the lexicon, followed by a rapid increase in the English component. The result was now a true pidgin in the Whinnom sense, since by this period native speakers of Hawaiian and English together constituted a minority of the population, and pidgin was therefore overwhelmingly used for interaction between persons who had neither the native competence of English speakers nor the century of *hapa-haole* experience of the Hawaiians. We can therefore claim that Hawaiian Pidgin English only came into existence in the present century, and therefore all the phases of its development are available for empirical study.[4]

True understanding of those phases has thus far been inhibited by an outmoded form of thinking that treats 'pidgins' as *states* or *entities* rather than *processes*. To reify is to falsify, as may be shown by the following quotations:

> . . . it is easy to show that [pidgins] have regular, socially sanctioned grammars. . . . On the other hand, there are isolated individuals who never learn this social pattern, but work out their own form of cross-linguistic expression . . . a very ingenious and original mode of expression. . . . The particular devices used are usually very different from the rules of the pidgin grammar; they show that pidgins are not the automatic consequence of language mixture (Labov 1971, pp. 15-16).

It is easy to show that pidgins have regular grammars if you use the kind of evidence that people used for describing nonpidgin languages prior to Labov. If, on the other hand, you look at them long and carefully, you find that 'regularity' is even more of a myth for pidgins than it was for so-called standard languages. The main source of irregularity in Hawaiian pidgin is nearness to, versus distance from, the speaker's native language, and, contrary to Labov's suggestion that native-language-influenced variants are the 'original' creations of 'isolated individuals', there is abundant evidence—too abundant to be given here in full—that they represent a stage in the pidginization process in which some speakers may get stuck, but through which all have passed. Possibly the most striking single piece of evidence is that the same individual can pass through the various phases in the course of code-switching, as does M J6 6H :[5]

(1) *as kerosin, plaenteishan, wan mans, fo gaelan giv,* "The plantation gave us four gallons of kerosene a month."

(2) *aemerikan pipl mun preis go, mun preis fularaun, enikain kam hom, aeswai gad ga maed nattekara,* "The American people went to the moon, fooled around there and got back somehow, that's why God became angry" (explaining present-day deterioration in the climate).

(3) *sore kara kech shite kara pulap*
and after catch do+past after pull-up
"When I'd caught [the turtle] I pulled [it] in."

While (1) still shows the influence of Japanese SOV order, it is quite free of Japanese lexicon; (3), however, shows a predominantly Japanese lexicon with a correspondingly stronger Japanese syntactic influence. The only contextual variable, incidentally, is the speaker's degree of interest in the subject matter, which increases from (1) through (3). Probably because he has passed through all the stages, his phonology is much less Japanese-influenced than that of some more retarded speakers; one of these, for instance, has the form *buranteesu* instead of *plaenteishan,* as in (1). Filipino speakers, in contrast, retain little native lexicon and feel the need to explain it when they do:

(4) *ai it tokak. yu sabe tokak? pfrawg. gud, dae wan, da pfrawg,* "I eat *tokak.* You know what *tokak* means? Frog. Frogs are very good [to eat]" MF69H.

However, for Filipino speakers one still finds sporadic verb-first, subject-final sentence ordering, reflecting their (mainly Ilocano) background:

(5) *hi kam gro da paemili,* "The family was beginning to grow up" MF77H.

(6) *hi haelp da medisin,* "The medicine helps" MF77H.

One never finds sentences of the latter type spoken by Japanese pidgin speakers, any more than one finds SOV sentences spoken by Filipino pidgin speakers. One does find, for pidgin speakers of all groups, temporal expressions with *-time,* which Nagara (1972, pp. 110 ff.) has shown conclusively derive from Japanese; however, for non-Japanese speakers, such expressions are limited in number (*smaw-taim,* "when I was small," *hawai-kam-taim,* "when I came to Hawaii" are the most popular) and probably learned as individual lexical items, whereas for Japanese speakers they are numerous, quite complex and obviously productive:

(7) *sam pat dei dono andastaen, aeswai dei go kweschin tu mi, no, sambadi-stei-tawking-taim,* "Some parts they don't understand, when somebody is talking [Japanese], so they ask me about it" FJ66K. (Context: speaker's children do not speak very much Japanese and she has to interpret for them.)

From these, and countless similar examples, we can conclude that pidginization is a process that begins by the speaker using his native tongue and relexifying first only a few key words (note that all the grammatical items in (3) are Japanese); that, in the earliest stages, even the few superstrate words will be thoroughly rephonologized to accord with substrate sound system and phonotactics; that, subsequently, more superstrate lexicon will be acquired, but may still be rephonologized to varying degrees and will be, for the most part, slotted into syntactic surface structures drawn from the substrate;[6] that, even when relexification is complete down to grammatical items, substrate syntax will be partially retained, and will alternate, apparently unpredictably, with structures imported from the superstrate.

This picture differs markedly from both the generally accepted stereotype of the 'grammatically regular' pidgin and the Kay-Sankoff suggestion that pidgin speakers select 'common', 'simple', and/or 'universal' structures. However, it accords closely with the picture of Chinook Jargon as presented by Silverstein (1972)—the distinction that Traugott (this volume) tries to make between 'pidgins' and 'trade jargons' appears to be quite baseless. It probably also accords with the way in which speakers naturally acquire second languages that are not pidgins. The 'probably' is regrettably necessary because, as I pointed out elsewhere (Bickerton 1975a, ch. 5), the whole area of natural second-language acquisition—a process that annually affects countless millions of persons—remains a vast and grotesque lacuna in our knowledge of language. However, the scanty evidence discussed in my other work does indicate that second languages are naturally acquired via piecemeal relexification, productive calquing, and the utilization of mother-tongue surface syntax (much as in the case of Hawaiian Pidgin English), in the early stages at least. Since then, supporting evidence has come to light from several areas. For instance, Tsou (1975) has shown that Chinese-type prenominal relative clauses (e.g., *The live-down-the-street-lady*, "The lady who lives down the street," *He's make-shoes-man*, "He's a man who makes shoes," etc.) are retained by isolated Chinese speakers of English in California, despite their gross difference from English structures. Gilbert and Orlovic (1975) have found that the frequency of the definite article in the speech of *gastarbeiten* in Germany correlates with the presence or absence of a definite article in the speaker's native language, although there was no similar correlation with respect to article inflection (presumably because of the mismatch between inflectional patterns in, on the one hand, German, and, on the other, Greek, Italian, Spanish, and Portuguese, which prevents the establishment of one-to-one surface equivalents).

In fact, the difference between arriving at a pidgin and arriving at a reasonably accurate version of a standard language lies mainly in the availability of target models and the amount of interaction with speakers of the target language. If models of the latter are readily available, and if the speaker interacts only or mainly with those who speak it natively, he or she should eventually acquire a recognizably nonpidginized 'foreigner's version' of that language. If, however, target models are scarce, and if he or she speaks mainly to non-native speakers who suffer a similar restriction of access to the target, the end product will be a pidgin. Situations intermediate between these two will produce varieties of language intermediate between pidgin and 'good foreigner's version', e.g., the English of Fiji or the Philippines. But in general, no issue of language universals will arise.[7]

The suggestion that universals are involved in pidginization came about partly because pidgins are so often defined in purely negative terms, partly through mistaken concepts of what constitutes a universal of language. Pidgins are usually described as lacking inflections, lacking articles, lacking markers of tense and aspect, lacking sentence-embedding, nominalization, allomorphic variation, etc., etc., and people conclude from such definitions that all pidgins are more or less the same; it would, in fact, be as reasonable to suppose that a brick is the same as a cabbage because neither has legs, wings, fur, feathers, independent locomotion, etc., etc. Language universals are usually conceived of in a Greenbergian sense, i.e., as being features found in the surface structures of all languages, or at least implicationally distributed (if a language has X, it will also have Y). Since the most widely distributed features of language are usually the least complex, since the features pidgins lacked were often (though by no means always) the product of late rules, and since (as Kay and Sankoff correctly observed) pidgins have little transformational depth, i.e., relatively few differences between deep and surface structures, the possibility that pidgins were somehow closer to language universals looked a good bet to scholars who, for the most part, lacked any first-hand experience of early-stage pidgins.

Another source of confusion about pidgins lies in the failure (already referred to—but it cannot, apparently, be referred to often enough) to appreciate their true nature as ongoing processes. In a last-ditch effort to preserve entities, Todd (1974, p. 50) has distinguished between *pidgins* and *extended pidgins* (the latter equivalent, Robson [1975] claims, to her own category of an 'effable' pidgin, i.e., one in which anything can be said). However, Todd's and Robson's definitions simply split up what is not merely a continuous process, but one whose phases may occur concurrently as well as consecutively. One and the same pidgin, Hawaiian, Neo-Melanesian, or whatever, may at one and the same time be 'extended' and 'effable' for some of its speakers, 'restricted' and 'noneffable' for others, for it is simply untrue that a pidgin, like a native language, is equally well controlled by all who speak it. In the case of any given pidgin that persists over time, the number of speakers for whom it is 'effable' will tend to increase, just as a levelling process will tend to remove distinctive markers of individual first-language influence, thus causing the pidgin to approximate more closely (but never completely) the idealized 'regular' pidgin of linguistic myth. How long such a levelling process takes will probably depend on a variety of factors, such as that of syntactic distance between the various substrates; it has certainly never proceeded very far in Hawaii. However, if (as in New Guinea) all substrates have strong genetic and/or areal resemblances, superstrate models are rare and relatively inaccessible, and the period of use is sufficiently long, there may develop a language that is (for at least a large core of speakers) 'effable', that is noticeably more homogeneous than Hawaiian Pidgin, yet that is not (or at least was not, until relatively recently) the native tongue of any of its speakers.

It has been suggested both by Robson (in the paper cited) and Koefoed (1975) that, in Robson's words, "before a pidgin can become someone's native language, it must already have become effable," or in Koefoed's, that "before a pidgin can become the first language of a new generation, a considerable extension in use, and thus expansion in inner form and complication in outer form, must have taken place." No evidence in support of this strange assertion is offered by Koefoed, and Robson merely cites her experience of bilingual households in Turkey. In fact, there is abundant evidence to the contrary, both historical (Saramaccan must have come into existence some time between 1650 and 1670, far too short a period for any pidgin to become 'effable') and contemporary (since Hawaiian Pidgin is to this day not 'effable' for a majority of its surviving speakers, we may conclude that Hawaiian Creole derived from a 'noneffable' pidgin). One is forced to conclude that a pidgin can creolize at any stage of its development, and that the period at which this step takes place will be decided, not by any internal development in the pidgin, but by the communicational needs of children, i.e., whether the ancestral languages of their pidgin-speaking parents do or do not constitute adequate and feasible means of communication for them.

This communicational need is in turn a function of population displacement. Where a population remains stable, indigenous languages will survive and even flourish under considerable adverse pressure; where a population is abruptly transferred to a new terrain, languages will wither even in the face of positive efforts to keep them alive. On a purely historical basis, we can divide the pidgin-creole world into those areas where populations have been displaced (the Caribbean, the Bight of Benin islands, the Indian Ocean, Hawaii) and those where populations have remained in their original environment (West Africa, the China coast, Melanesia, the Pacific Northwest). In all of the former areas except Hawaii, all traces of any antecedent pidgin have long since been eliminated, and, including Hawaii, all are now creole or post-creole-speaking; in all of the latter, pidgins still exist, and have either never creolized or (in the case of, e.g., the Cameroons, New Guinea) are only now beginning to creolize. The former areas are, of course, precisely those areas for which we have direct or indirect evidence of early and rapid creolization. The latter areas are those in which pidgins, while still remaining such, have achieved quite high (in the case of Neo-Melanesian, perhaps optimal) levels of 'effability'.

Given two sets of historical and linguistic circumstance so distinct, one would expect that, from a strictly formal viewpoint, the products of the two would differ equally strikingly. Indeed, this is the case. West African Pidgin, Chinese Pidgin English, Neo-Melanesian, and Chinook Jargon differ markedly from one another in their grammatical structure. In contrast, the creole languages of Hawaii, Haiti, Jamaica, the lesser Antilles, Surinam, Guyana, São Thomé, Annobon, Mauritius, Rodrigues, and the Seychelles show grammatical similarities not far short of identity in several crucial areas. These areas include:

A. *Articles.* In all those creoles that formed after only a brief period of pidginization (hereinafter referred to as 'early-creolized' creoles) there are three and only three articles, which cover identical semantic areas in each language:

(i) A so-called definite article (*di* in most Anglo-Creoles, *da* in Hawaii, *a* in Surinam, *-la* in most Franco-Creoles), which in fact corresponds to the semantic category of 'existentially presupposed' NP (see Bickerton 1975b for details of 'existentially presupposed', 'asserted', and 'hypothesized' NP).

(ii) A so-called indefinite article (*wan* in all Anglo-Creoles, *youn* in Haitian Creole, etc.), which corresponds to the semantic category of 'existentially asserted' NP.

(iii) A 'generic' and/or 'non-specific' article (zero in all early-creolized creoles without exception), which corresponds to the semantic category of 'existentially hypothesized' NP.
These three categories may be illustrated by the following examples from Guyanese Creole:

(8) *mi bai di buk,* "I bought the [presupposed known to speaker] book."
(9) *mi bai wan buk,* "I bought a [presupposed not known to speaker] book."
(10) *mi go bai buk,* "I shall buy a book or books [even speaker does not know which]."

B. *Tense and aspect.* All early-creolized creoles share almost all, and many share all, of the following characteristics:

(i) The zero form of the verb marks 'simple past' for action verbs and 'nonpast' for state verbs (as explained at some length in Bickerton 1975a, 'simple past action' and 'nonpast state' would not be characterized as separate entities in a creole grammar, but form a single 'nonanterior' category).

(ii) A marker of anterior aspect (*bin* or some phonological variant—*ben, en, wen, min,* etc.—in all Anglo-Creoles, *té, t'* etc., in Franco-Creoles, etc.) indicates past-before-past for action verbs and simple past for state verbs.

(iii) A marker of irrealis aspect (*go* in many Anglo-Creoles, *sa* in Sranan and early Guyanese Creole, (*a*)*va* or *ke* in Franco-Creoles) indicates 'unreal time', i.e., future, conditional, subjunctive, etc., for all verbs.

(iv) A marker of nonpunctual aspect (*stei* in Hawaii, *de, e, da,* or *a* in most Anglo-Creoles, *ap*(*e*) or *ka* in Franco-Creoles, etc.) indicates both durative and iterative aspects (or better, a single 'nonpunctual' category) for all action verbs. This marker is indifferent to the past/nonpast (but not the anterior/nonanterior) distinction, and cannot co-occur with state verbs.

(v) All markers are in preverbal position (exception: Papiamento *lo,* the irrealis marker, which retains the clause-external position commonly occupied by tense-aspect markers in pidgins).

(vi) With the exception noted in (v), all markers can combine, but only in the following invariant ordering: 1. anterior; 2. irrealis; 3. nonpunctual.

(vii) The meaning of anterior + nonpunctual is "a durative action or a series of non-durative actions taking place either before some other event under discussion, or during a period of time understood to be definitely closed."

(viii) The meaning of irrealis + nonpunctual is "a nonpunctual action occurring in unreal time," e.g., a future progressive.

(ix) The meaning of anterior + irrealis is "an unrealized condition in the past."[8]

(x) The meaning of anterior + irrealis + nonpunctual is "an unrealized condition in the past, of a nonpunctual nature," e.g., *I would have been looking for something else.*

C. *Focussing.* For all early-creolized creoles, focussing is uniquely realized by left-dislocating the focussed NP. Everywhere except in Hawaii, where there is no equative copula, this copula precedes the focussed NP:

(11) *li ap achté chat-la,* "He is buying the cat."
(12) *sé chat li ap achté a,* "It's the cat that he's buying."

Outside Hawaii, the focussed NP leaves no pronoun copy; in Hawaii, a pronoun copy may be left if the object is focussed, and must be left if the subject is focussed (otherwise focussed and nonfocussed sentences could not be distinguished):

(13) *jan laik go*, "John wants to go."
(14) *jan i laik go*, "It's John who wants to go."
(15) *i bin hapai da wahini*, "He has taken the girl."
(16) *da wahini i bin hapai* (*am*), "It's the girl he's taken."

D. *Copulative constructions.* All early-creolized creoles make a distinction between attributive and locative-existential constructions. Attributive constructions (handled by copula plus adjective in English) are expressed by means of stative verbs, e.g., *li malad, i sik,* "he is ill." Locative and existential constructions contain a distinctive locative copula (*stei* in Hawaii, *yé* in Caribbean French creoles, *de* in Anglo-Creoles), which may be deleted (optionally in locative contexts for some Anglo-Creoles, obligatorily in locative contexts for French creoles unless it occurs clause-finally, but not in existential contexts, cf. Jourdain 1956, p. 141), but which cannot commute with the equative copula (*sé* in most Franco-Creoles, *a* or *da* in most Anglo-Creoles) that occurs between two coreferential N P. Hawaii is, apparently, alone in that it makes no distinction between attributive (*jan sik*) and equative (*jan mi brada*) contexts. However, it can hardly be accidental that, for all speakers who have it, the English copula *iz* occurs more frequently in N＿＿N environments than in any others.

E. *Negation.* In early-creolized creoles, so-called multiple negation is standard, i.e., all nondefinite N P, as well as the verb, must be individually negated (*nonbadi na go du nating,* literally 'Nobody won't do nothing').

These are some of the more obvious similarities; others, particularly in the formation of relative clauses and various embedding transformations, are less easy to document, owing to the paucity of descriptions of creole languages and the inadequacy (particularly with respect to more complex structures) of the descriptions that do exist. It should further be noted (although there is not space here to document this) that, with a single exception, pidgin and creole languages from those areas that have not undergone population displacement differ, with respect to the grammatical areas described, not only from the early-creolized creoles, but also from one another. That exception—West African Pidgin English—quite closely resembles the early-creolized model. However, there are two possible explanations for this apparent anomaly. West African Pidgin, in its modern form, may very well be a repidginization of Sierra Leone Krio, a creole language that was strongly influenced by, if indeed it did not originate directly from, Jamaican Creole (via the rebellious Maroons returned from Jamaica to Africa in 1800). Alternatively, an earlier pidgin may have creolized in Africa in the seventeenth or eighteenth century, in the mixed townships that grew up around the European forts, as suggested by Hancock (1972) and other writers, and the resultant creole may, again, have repidginized. While there is as yet insufficient evidence to decide between the two explanations, either would adequately account for the grammatical similarities between West African Pidgin and the early-creolized creoles.

It should be pointed out that a number of these similarities were first brought to light by Taylor nearly two decades ago (Taylor 1956, 1960). Prior to the early 1970s there were two possible explanations for them:

I. Substratal influence. Since it was believed that the substratal languages of Caribbean, Bight of Benim, and Indian Ocean Creoles could have been in large part, or in some cases perhaps exclusively, drawn from the West African area, in particular the Kwa group, it could be claimed that the early-creolized creoles reflected broad similarities in Kwa and related languages. However, the belief that West Africa could have provided any substantial input to the Indian Ocean area has been thoroughly discredited by Chaudenson (1974), while work by Daelmann (summarized in Daelmann 1971) has shown that at least one Caribbean creole, Saramaccan, was more strongly influenced in its lexicon by Kongo, a Bantu language, than by any member of the Kwa group. Moreover, as must be obvious to anyone who has carried out the most superficial examination of African languages, the differences between even related languages, in those grammatical areas presently under discussion, are quite considerable, and while partial resemblances have occasionally been pointed out between the characteristic creole tense-aspect system and the systems of various African languages, no case of anything approaching identity has as yet been uncovered. Indeed, in the highly unlikely event of some indigenous African language's being found that showed point-by-point identity with the creole model, 'substratomaniacs' would still be faced with the problem of explaining how that language (which must obviously be a minor and little-known one) could have won out against all competing models, sub- and superstrate, during the period of creole formation. Finally, the similarity of Hawaiian Creole to the general pattern of early-creolizing creoles constitutes perhaps the most powerful single argument against substratal influence, insofar as, in its formation, there can be no possibility of an African substratum of any kind.

II. Monogenesis. The monogenetic theory survives the objections, fatal to any theory of substratal influence, raised by the presence of overall creole similarities in the Indian and Pacific Oceans. However, the main positive argument in its favor was that, until recently, there was no other discernible explanation of these similarities. So far is it from being plausible in itself that I was asked by several linguists not previously familiar with the pidgin-creole field why I should have spent so much time in Bickerton 1974 attacking what must obviously have been a straw man of my own invention! We are asked to believe that an original contact language could be disseminated round the entire tropical zone, to peoples of widely differing language background, and still preserve a virtually complete identity in its grammatical structure wherever it took root, despite considerable changes in its phonology and virtually complete changes in its lexicon. We are not asked to believe that this colossal task was accomplished by a tiny minority of persons for whom the language in question was not even their native tongue, since to ask this would be to widen the credibility gap past all bridging; but a moment's thought will suffice to convince one that monogenesis entails precisely such a belief. There was very little easterly movement of population from the supposed birthplace of the language in West Africa: the population of the Indian Ocean islands was recruited mainly from India and Madagascar, while in Asia and the Pacific regions there were, until the late nineteenth century, no large-scale population movements that could have influenced the spread of such a language. Transmission must therefore have been predominantly via Portuguese seamen, merchants, and administrators in the early stages, and later on by their equivalents of other European nationalities. These must have been, in the main, first-generation pidgin speakers of the language they allegedly transmitted, and we saw earlier in this paper the kind of thing that first-generation pidgin speakers do to a language. Moreover, in any region where they travelled, the bulk of them were transients; those who settled or had any long or meaningful contact with the regions involved could have constituted only an insignificant minority of the population that learned and used the contact language.

Though neither paper specifically challenged either the substratal or monogenetic positions, the idea that universals might be somehow involved in the process of creolization was expressed, from somewhat differing viewpoints, by Traugott (1973) and Givón (1973). Unfortunately, neither paper distinguishes adequately between the very different processes involved in pidginization and early creolization (a defect Givón corrects in a postscript to his original paper dated 1975). The first process involves the gradual elimination of substratal influences that are heavily present in the initial stages; the second involves the acquisition of grammatical rules, the vast bulk of which are not present in either substrate or superstrate languages. The present writer was the first to propose a cogent alternative to previous explanations of creole similarities in Bickerton 1974, a paper that (a) showed striking similarities between the Hawaiian Creole and some Caribbean Creole tense-aspect systems, which could not be derived from any of the various languages in contact, and (b) indicated that these similarities could not have come about through diffusion of a pre-existing contact language, since it was precisely the features Hawaiian Creole had in common with other early-creolized creoles that were rarely or never found among surviving speakers of Hawaiian Pidgin.

The explanation hardly seems revolutionary in view of developments in general linguistic theory over the past two decades. Thanks to the work of Chomsky and his associates, it has come to be accepted by probably a majority of linguists that the possible forms human language can take are rather sharply circumscribed by innate characteristics of the human species—characteristics that, admittedly, we are still far from being able to define in any satisfactory way. These constraints are normally taken as being formal rather than substantive; in other words they limit the forms a language MAY take rather than determine those it MUST take. We know that, in the absence of any linguistic input, a child cannot acquire language. We know that, in the presence of an adequate linguistic input, a child will arrive at a grammar that will not differ significantly from those of its elders.

What we lack is a definition of 'adequate'. 'Any input that is not completely null' must clearly constitute an unsatisfactory definition. But, if that is the case, there must exist situations intermediate between that of the normal child in a normal community, with a total mastery over the ancestral language, and that of the feral or traumatized child in isolation, with a total lack of mastery over any language. One situation that stands between these poles is surely that of the child of speakers of an unstable pidgin in a displaced community where ancestral languages are of very limited utility. If the situation of the pidgin speaker is one of handicapped *second*-language learning, then that of the first-generation creole speaker is surely one of handicapped *first*-language learning. The pidgin he is presented as a model (and which he chooses, over its ancestral-language competitors, presumably because it enables him to communicate with a wider range of persons) is, in comparison with its competitors, too impoverished and unstable a medium to serve all the communicative needs of an individual. This matters not at all to the pidgin speaker, who will still usually have fellow-speakers of his own language to consort with. (Even if he does not, like Tsou's SWONALS, this will not, apparently, lead him to acquire any of the classic creole features described above.) But the child creole speaker will be driven to 'expand' the pidgin. Practically every account of the relationship between pidgins and creoles has suggested that some such 'expansion' must take place, but no account has previously suggested how this might be done. It is obvious that the process must consist of internalizing linguistic rules for which there is no evidence in terms of linguistic outputs. If such rules are not induced from primary data, they must be derived directly from the human *faculté de langage*, which must in consequence contain some kind of analog for the instructions, 'If your input language has no nonpunctual aspect marker, employ a locative expression preverbally'; 'if your input language has no system of determiners, distinguish formally between the three existential classes of NP'; etc.

Critics of the original statement of this theory (in Bickerton 1974) seem to have somewhat misunderstood it. Some seem to have been under the impression that the theory is invalidated if any of the claimed common features are found elsewhere than in creoles; yet obviously, if creoles reflect natural semantactic structures, one would expect these to surface from time to time elsewhere, especially in child speech and in nonstandard languages. Some seem to have been under the impression that the theory could be refuted simply by pointing out one or two creoles that did not possess one or another of the claimed features, or one or two creole rules that could plausibly be attributed to a substratum. Yet it is obvious that while the basic conditions of early-creolizing societies were similar, details must have differed widely; if one substratum feature comes through here, if one 'natural' feature is blocked there, this makes absolutely no difference to the central argument of natural semantax: that there can be rules of language that are not derived from any linguistic input.

The position of my critics may best be illustrated by the old story about the girl who was asked, "Would you sleep with me for five million bucks?" "Guess I might." "Fifty?" "Whaddaya think I am, a whore?" "We just settled that, now we're fixing the price." The critics can, of course, defend their virtue at any cost, but the cost in this case is a high one: it involves their claiming that *every rule in every creole language can be shown to have been derived directly from some rule in the antecedent pidgin or one of the contributory* (i.e., substrate or superstrate) *languages.* If they take this position, they are at least honest. If they do not, then the matter is settled, and we are just fixing the price—the price being, in this case, just exactly how many, and which, of the linguistic structures involved were derived directly, without any evidence in the form of outputs from older speakers.[9] For those of us who are seriously interested in discovering the language capacities of our species, and through them, the way in which the human mind works, the empirical charting of this area surely constitutes one of the readiest and most promising avenues of advance.

NOTES

1. For example, the account in Naro 1971, which is almost word for word Bloomfield, does not mention Bloomfield's name. But this is only poetic justice, since Bloomfield does not cite Schuchardt's (1914) very similar account.

2. I am indebted to Bill Wilson, one of my graduate students, for first drawing my attention to literary attestations of pidginized Hawaiian. Subsequent research in the community has produced more direct and indirect evidence of the existence of this previously unknown variety of language, of which it is still hoped to find a few surviving speakers.

3. For example, as late as the early 1900s, pidginized Hawaiian was used as the language of command by foremen on the Parker Ranch in Waimea (admittedly, one that still contained a good percentage of Hawaiians in its work force, but it is worth noting that this was still, apparently, a more convenient medium than *hapa-haole* or any kind of English). Persons who

remember this pidgin recall that it had SVO word order and contained numerous expressions that seemed absurd to native speakers of Hawaiian, such as *pi'i makai*, intended to mean "go towards the sea," but meaning literally something like "ascend seawards"!

4. A full account of this development is given in Bickerton and Odo 1976 and Bickerton 1977.

5. Coded references to informants give sex ([M]ale or [F]emale) followed by ethnicity ([J]apanese, [F]ilipino, etc.), followed by age and island of residence ([K]auai, [H]awaii, etc.).

6. A point as yet by no means clear is whether this kind of relexification can apply to substrate structures that are the product of transformations or only to the output of the phrase-structure component. This point is of some general theoretical interest, since it has an obvious bearing on the point at which lexical insertion takes place in a grammar. A strong claim would be that products of substrate transformations cannot be relexified. This claim will be empirically tested in future work on Hawaiian Pidgin.

7. One exception that should be made to this generalization is in the area of negation. Howell (1975) has pointed out that in the contact language of Japanese bargirls and American servicemen, negation follows neither the Japanese nor the English pattern, but consists of an invariant *no* inserted immediately before the negated predicate (as seems to be the case in most pidgins and creoles). But one swallow doesn't make a summer; what universals are accessible to adults remains an empirical question, with the probability that they are relatively few.

8. In Bickerton 1974 it was claimed that tense-aspect characteristics (ix) and (x) existed in Hawaii. This assertion is now doubtful in view of the fact that the only informant who produced, in natural speech, examples of the relevant structures that appeared to have the meanings predicted denies that those meanings were what he intended. This ought to close the matter, and for those who believe in the *ex cathedra* infallibility of informants, it will doubtless do so. However, some very funny things go on in pidgin and creole continua, of which those who do not know them at first hand (and even a good many who do) seem to be unaware. For instance, in his corpus, drawn entirely from residents of Oahu, Perlman (1973) found only five occurrences of preverbal *stay*, from which it was impossible to determine the meaning of this structure; his attempts to elicit sentences from informants produced only a greater confusion, causing him to doubt whether the construction really existed. In fact, in recordings made on the outer islands, we have over two hundred occurrences of *stay* plus verb, from which it is clearly apparent that the structure corresponds to tense-aspect characteristic (iv) described above. Our research, more extensive than that which Perlman's limited resources permitted, also found a very small number of *stay+V* users on Oahu. Obviously, *stay+V* once existed throughout the islands but has now largely

disappeared from Oahu due to decreolization. There is therefore the possibility that *bin+go+V* (with the meaning given) did previously exist on the outer islands (where decreolization, though slower than in Oahu, is also in progress) but has now changed its meaning, for some speakers, or ceased to exist, for others. There certainly exists the form *bin+laik+go+V*, with very similar meaning, which was found in spontaneous speech subsequent to the writing of Bickerton 1974.

9. Recent research on sign language at the University of Pennsylvania by Heidi Feldman and Susan Meadow (under the supervision of Leila Gleitman) indicates that among deaf children of hearing parents, "the child seems to be capable of organizing a linguistic system *without an environmental model*" (my emphasis) and follows "rules of order for semantic relations," whereas "the mother shows no such rules in her multi-gestural phrases," according to a report in *Signs for Our Times* (Linguistics Research Laboratory, Gallaudet College, Washington, D. C., No. 33, April-May 1975, p. 3). Not only does this report suggest that linguistic rules can be 'acquired' without any linguistic input to base them on; the analogy that it suggests between, on the one hand, hearing parents and deaf children, and on the other, pidgin-speaking parents and creole-speaking children, provides strong and quite independent evidence for the central argument of the present paper.

REFERENCES

Alleyne, Mervyn C. 1971. Acculturation and the cultural matrix of creolization. In *The Pidginization and Creolization of Languages*, D. Hymes, ed., pp. 169-86.

Bickerton, Derek. 1974. Creolization, linguistic universals, natural semantax and the brain. *Working Papers in Linguistics*, (University of Hawaii) 6. 3:124-41.

———. 1975a. *Dynamics of a Creole System*. Cambridge: Cambridge University Press.

———. 1975b. Reference in natural semantax. *Pragmatics Microfiche* 1:D1-G8.

———. 1977. *Change and Variation in Hawaiian English, Vol. II: Creole Syntax* (Final Report on NSF Project No. GS-39748).

Bickerton, Derek, and Odo, Carol. 1976. *Change and Variation in Hawaiian English, Vol. I: General Phonology and Pidgin Syntax* (Final Report on NSF Project No. GS-39748).

Bloomfield, Leonard. 1933. *Language*. New York: Holt, Rinehart & Winston.

Chaudenson, Robert. 1974. *Le lexique du parler créole de la Réunion.* Paris: Champion.

Daelmann, Jan. 1971. Kongo words in Saramacca Tongo. In Hymes, ed., pp. 281-83.

Ferguson, Charles A. 1971. Absence of copula and the notion of simplicity. In Hymes, ed., pp. 141-50.

Gilbert, Glenn, and Orlovic, Maria. 1975. Pidgin German spoken by foreign workers in West Germany. Mimeo.

Givón, Talmy. 1973. Prolegomena to any creology. Mimeo.

Hall, Robert. 1966. *Pidgin and Creole Languages.* Ithaca: Cornell University Press.

Hancock, Ian F. 1972. A domestic origin for the English-derived Atlantic Creoles. *Florida FL Reporter* X:1/2.

Howell, Richard W. 1975. Bamboo English revisited. Mimeo.

Hymes, Dell, ed. 1971. *The Pidginization and Creolization of Languages.* Cambridge: Cambridge University Press.

Jourdain, Elodie. 1956. *Du Français Aux Parlers Créoles.* Paris: Libraire Klincksieck.

Kay, Paul, and Sankoff, Gillian. 1974. A language-universals approach to pidgins and creoles. In *Pidgins and Creoles: Current Trends and Prospects*, D. DeCamp and I. A. Hancock, eds. Washington, D. C.: Georgetown University Press, pp. 61-72.

Koefoed, Geert. 1975. A note on pidgins, creoles and Greenberg's universals. Mimeo.

Labov, William. 1971. On the adequacy of natural language. Mimeo.

Nagara, Susumu. 1972. *Japanese Pidgin English in Hawaii.* Honolulu: University of Hawaii Press.

Naro, Anthony. 1971. Review of Carvalho, *Estudios Linguisticos. Foundations of Language* 7:148-55.

_____. 1975. The origins of Pidgin Portuguese. Mimeo.

Perlman, Alan. 1973. Grammatical structure and style-shift in Hawaiian Pidgin and Creole. Unpublished Ph.D. diss. University of Chicago.

Robson, Barbara. 1975. On the differences between creoles and other natural languages. Mimeo.

Schuchardt, H. E. M. 1914. *Die Sprache der Saramakkaneger in Surinam.* Amsterdam: Muller.

Silverstein, Michael. 1972. Chinook jargon: Language contact and the problem of multilevel generative systems. *Language* 48:376-406, 596-625.

Stewart, William A. 1962. Creole languages in the Caribbean. In *A Study of the Role of Second Languages in Asia, Africa and Latin America*, F. A. Rice, ed. Washington, D. C.: Center for Applied Linguistics, pp. 34-53.

Taylor, Douglas. 1956. Language contacts in the West Indies. *Word* 12:399-414.

––––––. 1960. Language shift or changing relationship? *International Journal of American Linguistics* 26:144-61.

Thompson, W. A. 1961. A note on some possible affinities between the creole dialects of the Old World and those of the New. In *Creole Language Studies* II, R. B. Le Page, ed. London: Macmillan, pp. 107-13.

Todd, Loreto. 1974. *Pidgins and Creoles*. London: Routledge and Kegan Paul.

Traugott, Elizabeth C. 1973. Some thoughts on natural syntactic processes. In *New Ways of Analyzing Variation in English*, C. -J. Bailey and R. Shuy, eds. Washington, D. C.: Georgetown University Press, pp. 313-22.

T'sou, Benjamin. 1975. The language of SWONALS (speakers without a native language). Mimeo.

Whinnom, Keith. 1965. The origin of the European-based creoles and pidgins. *Orbis* 14:509-27.

––––––. 1971. Linguistic hybridization and the special case of pidgins and creoles. In Hymes, ed., pp. 91-116.

Pidginization, Creolization, and Language Change

Elizabeth Closs Traugott

Pidgins and creoles were for a long time considered 'marginal' or 'special' languages. To call them this was to label them and the processes by which they developed as marginal to linguistic theory—and conveniently so, because what evidence we have of pidginization and creolization barely fits the traditional concept of comparative linguistics and historical reconstruction, particularly as it was developed in America during this century. Recent interest in language acquisition and in language variation and its social correlates have encouraged new perspectives on the subject of language change. From being the special and the marginal case, pidginization and creolization have become, for some linguists, the test case for any theory of change. The issues are many and complex. Disagreements among historical linguists on the theoretical and methodological issues remain great after well over a hundred years of extensive study. Disagreements among creolists are even greater, as is hardly surprising, considering the newness of the field. For the most part such disagreements have been productive and have provided the basis for further advances. Despite new theories, new methodologies, and new data, the basic questions remain: what is the nature of human language, why does it change, and how does it do so? It is the purpose of this paper to discuss some of the implications of pidginization and creolization for three theories of change, specifically the 'family tree', the generative 'acquisitional', and the dynamic 'wave' theories. In the first case, incorporation of pidginization and creolization necessitated modification of the theory, in the second, processes of pidginization and creolization came to be used as evaluation metrics for alternative claims about the role of language acquisition in a theory of language change, and in the third, these processes came to be salient to the theory itself. Length limitations prevent detailed discussion of the issues, and have necessitated omission of many relevant topics. Focus is here on broad conceptual issues. Other chapters in the volume will provide much of the necessary empirical evidence, and will reopen many of the issues.

THE GENETIC MODEL

Ever since William Jones's discovery in the latter part of the eighteenth century that patterned phonetic-semantic correspondences ('cognates') existed between languages like English, Latin, Greek, and Sanskrit, the idea of language 'kinship' has played a major role in conceptualizing language change. We speak of families of languages (e.g., the Indo-European language family, including English, German, Dutch, French, Spanish, Portuguese, Gaelic, Italian, Greek, Russian, Persian, Hindi, and Bengali; or the Finno-Ugric language family, including Finnish, Hungarian, Estonian, Lappish; or the Niger-Congo language family, including the Kwa languages Twi, Efik, Ewe, etc., and the Bantu languages). We also speak of parent and daughter languages (e.g., French is the 'daughter' of Vulgar Latin), of degrees of relationship (e.g., German and English are more closely related to each other than to French), and of Proto-languages—original, unattested 'parents' from which the divergent languages developed because of migration. The idea of a genealogical family tree was formalized by Schleicher in 1871, and is widely known as the 'Stammbaum theory'. Heavily influenced by Darwinian ideas on the origin and development of the species, Schleicher thought of his Indo-European family trees as representing the development of an organism. This organic view of language has largely been rejected— the tiny time span for which languages have been known to exist (some seven thousand years at the most), allows no such biological view; more importantly, plant and animal organisms reproduce. Languages are not organisms, and do not reproduce. Nevertheless, the genetic model has value as a metaphor, and analogs to biological concepts such as evolution of the species have helped focus on variation through time, selection given certain specifiable conditions, and such issues as rate of change.[1] The methods of natural science have been successfully used in linguistic studies to group languages into families according to their similarities and differences, and to infer successive stages of evolution from coexistent systems.

Particularly after the advent of structuralism and De Saussure's postulation (1916) of a dichotomy between synchrony and diachrony (that is, between atemporal language systems and what he conceived to be individual, nonsystematic historical changes), the main focus in historical linguistics was on comparison of known language states and reconstructions of previous synchronic states, with concentration on the establishment of proto-languages.[2] The reconstructed proto-languages and proto-forms came for many to be essentially homogeneous, mathematical formulae from which attested variants could most easily be derived.[3]

No reconstruction is of course possible without some postulation of change (evolution from Stage A to Stage B, and so forth). Any evolutionary theory must take into consideration such factors as mutation and decay. On the basis of the Indo-European languages, it was assumed that mutations (radical restructurings of languages) were relatively few and far between. The method of glottochronology developed by Swadesh (e.g., 1951) provided a mechanism for 'decay-dating'. One of its fundamental assumptions was that 'basic vocabulary' items (i.e., names of body parts, lower numerals, personal pronouns, basic actions and objects, immediate members of the family, and so forth) would be preserved longer, that is, be less subject to decay than non-basic vocabulary, and that about 80% of a two-hundred-word core vocabulary would be preserved over about one thousand years. Time-depth for splits in family relations could therefore be plotted, it was argued, in part according to degree of deviation in core vocabulary. Although severely challenged from the beginning, glottochronology nevertheless seemed valuable as an approximation.

The genetic theory of language change was originally developed for Indo-European languages—languages that were fairly well attested in written documents. These written documents were of course essential in the development of the method, since they provided the empirical data for reconstruction. However, they posed a fundamental problem for the study of language change—written documents tend to be relatively homogeneous and relatively standardized. They usually represent one style of language only. Before the age of printing, when the materials used were hard to write on, like stone or clay, or expensive, like parchment, and each copy of a text had to be handwritten separately, only something that was thought to be of vital importance to the community or the future was written down. The bulk of everyday language remained unrepresented. When the genetic approach was applied to unwritten languages, for example, the American Indian languages (cf. Bloomfield 1946, Haas 1969), linguists were applying methods developed for written languages to unwritten ones, and continued reconstructing relatively homogeneous and probably formal styles.

Pidginization and creolization present a formidable challenge to the genetic view of historical linguistics. First and foremost, pidginization and creolization, however defined, involve the development of new languages out of convergent contact situations—the characterization of pidgins and creoles as having the lexicon of one language and the grammar of another, although highly oversimplified, nevertheless captures an important generalization. Furthermore, except in advanced stages of pidginization and creolization, these languages are unwritten par excellence, developed in limited contexts, such as trade, slavery on a plantation, and so forth. Could a proto-form of a language with not one but at least two and often many more parents be reconstructed? Could a language with functions as limited as those of a pidgin be the worthy object of such study? Equally problematic was the fact that pidgins are known to develop rapidly. They may have long histories, like Sabir or West African Pidgin English, or short ones like Hawaiian Pidgin. Creoles may or may not develop after a relatively long period of pidginization (e.g., Tok Pisin after approximately one hundred years), or after a short one (e.g, Hawaiian Creole). In any event, time spans of five hundred to one thousand years have no significance for pidginization and creolization. As for the lexicon, basic vocabulary seems to change quite rapidly as part of the pidginization process. There is accumulating evidence that at least some sort of relexification (renewed borrowing of large segments of vocabulary from some different, more prestigious language) occurs, presumably as the result of repidginization of a pidgin. This suggests that basic vocabulary can be altered and realtered within a very short period of time.[4]

What solution can be proposed other than ignoring the processes of pidginization and creolization (and therewith, processes discernible in nearly all of the Third World, as well as elsewhere)? One of the first to incorporate pidginization and creolization into genetic linguistics was Hall (see especially 1966). He pointed out that if the splits and divergencies in change of the family tree of, say, Indo-European are explicated on the grounds of migration, migration probably also brought with it contact and hence some convergence with other systems. It may well be that Proto-Germanic and Proto-Romance were in fact hybridized languages of some sort, he argued.[5] If so, pidginization and creolization can be regarded not as different in kind from other processes of language change, but as extreme cases of the hybridization that goes on in language all the time. He proposed that if one allowed for highly variable decay dating, one can include pidginization and creolization in genetic theory, retaining the concepts of parent language, regular change, and so forth. For Hall, retention of the genetic model implied not a mixed marriage of two different languages, but rather a mingling of a superstrate, prestigious, usually Indo-European language with elements of a substrate, non-prestigious one (e.g., a West African language, or Chinese). For example, he says:

> We . . . must not think of a pidgin as representing a simply bilateral function: it is rather, a development of a single language (usually a European language in modern times) with strong influences from one or more others, sometimes a great many, and usually non-European (1966, p. 25).

In fact, linguists often resort to the substrate only when explanation on the grounds of the superstrate cannot be made; where this strategy fails, some reference to general properties of communication may be made. In this view, West African Pidgin English, Haitian Creole, and so forth are, as the names suggest, simplified forms of English, French, etc., accountable by the formula:

$$\frac{\text{Superstrate A}}{\text{Substrate B}} \longrightarrow \text{modified A}$$

From a lexical point of view, this formula may appear attractive, since the basic vocabulary is often in the main from the superstrate language. But it largely ignores the importance of the grammatical relations and promotes (although it does not necessitate) the idea that pidgins develop primarily in the mouths of European speakers simplifying their speech for foreigners.

Probably the larger number of creolists in the seventies reject the assumption that a language like West African Pidgin English is simplified English, and its corollary that African forms are 'borrowed'. Instead, they insist that the two or more languages that functioned as input to the pidginization process were equal partners linguistically (but not socially), or would go so far as to suggest that the superstrate language, being socially at a considerable distance, did not function as real input to the pidginization process, only some hypothesis as to its nature. This latter proposal is an appealing one for at least some situations in which pidgins arise, and has been modeled by Whinnom (1971, p. 106) as:

$$\frac{\text{Target languages}}{\text{Substrate languages A X B (X C ...)}} \longrightarrow \begin{array}{l}\text{Target-}\\\text{language-}\\\text{based pidgin}\end{array}$$

It calls into question the possibility of using any genetic model at all because of the indirect nature of the relationship between the source languages and the resulting pidgin.

Nevertheless, many who espouse a theory of pidginization of this sort turn to genetic theory, or at least to a version of it modified by variation theory (cf. the last part of this paper), when attempting to account for the fact that a large number of maritime pidgins and creoles, whatever their main source of vocabulary, share lexical and grammatical properties traceable to Portuguese and West African languages, especially the Akan languages.[6] For example, Portuguese-related *pikinini* 'child' and *savvy* 'to know, to be able to, to do habitually' are found in many maritime pidgins and creoles, whether of the Atlantic, the Indian Ocean, or the Pacific. So are grammatical structures typical of Akan languages, such as the formation of questions, and some verbal structures indicating tense, mood, and aspect (cf. especially Thompson 1961, Stewart 1962, Taylor 1963, Whinnom 1965, Voorhoeve 1973). Unlike Hall, who prefers the view that pidgins develop independently in each new contact situation, Stewart, Thompson, Whinnom, and others argue more or less strongly for a proto-pidgin that was a mixture of Portuguese and African languages (*not* simplified Portuguese), perhaps itself a relexified, repidginized form of Sabir, a lingua franca of the Mediterranean recorded from the twelfth to the twentieth century. The lack of continuity in the history of this Portuguese-African pidgin is explained by multiple stages of contact with different languages as a result of slave trade, colonial expansion, and so forth, and relexification is

postulated at each point. It is important to notice that, in contrast
to Hall's view of pidginized European languages, we are here
talking about Europeanized pidgins.

A family tree of pidgins and creoles based on this
monogenetic theory has been proposed by Todd (1974, p. 40),
with two major subfamilies reflecting eastward and westward
trading routes: Atlantic Portuguese Pidgin and Indo-Pacific Portuguese Pidgin (Fig. 1). Others, like Hancock (1970), prefer not to
find a Proto-Portuguese pidgin as the basis of most Caribbean and
maritime creoles, but nevertheless establish smaller families, for
example, Guinea Coast Pidgin English (with Krio, Gullah, and
others as its descendents).

As Todd says, any genetic approach begs many questions,
the most important of which is what the proto-language might
have been like. Another major problem is that the family tree (at
least in the above form, without the benefit of wave theory) fails
to suggest the wave after wave of contact already mentioned.
Therefore it cannot model what the monogenetic theory rests
on—the claim that the proto-pidgin spread and was relexified,
sometimes many times over. Another problem is that, while the
monogenetic theory accounts for the presence of Portuguese
forms in all the languages in this family, it does not account for
other kinds of similarities with pidgins and creoles in other
'families'. These similarities are not lexical, but typological and
probably universal. They need to be accounted for, not in terms of
kinship and descent, but of constraints on the nature of human
language in given types of context (cf. Bickerton 1975a, Traugott
1974b).

Interest in typologies and in universals of change goes back
to the beginning of interest in language families. It is basic to any
claim about the naturalness of the changes postulated (cf.
Jakobson 1958). Nevertheless, studies of typologies and of
universals tended, until recently, to be regarded primarily as the
domain of synchronic studies, presumably because the family tree
model demanded inspection of individual languages and language
families.[7] Current concern with universals of change stems largely
from two sources: Greenberg's work on typologies of languages
and their relation to language universals (e.g., 1969, 1974) and
Chomsky's interest in distinguishing what has to be learned in the
acquisition of language from what is universal and therefore
perhaps innate (e.g., 1965, 1967, 1975). Greenberg's work has
largely been concerned with defining tendencies to be found
among languages, and classifying languages according to such

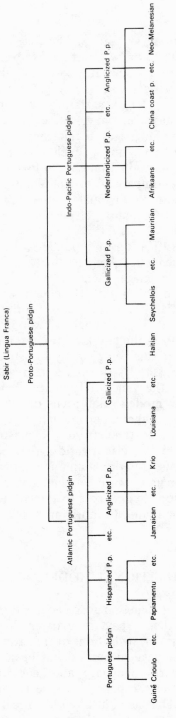

Fig. 1

tendencies, e.g., tonal vs. atonal, languages with or without nasalized vowels, with or without verbs overtly distinguishing 'being in a place' from 'being of a certain quality', and so forth. Such typological classification crosscuts genetic groupings entirely, since within any one language family it is possible for some languages to have nasalized vowels (e.g., French) or not (e.g., English), or for some languages to change with respect to nasality. This does not mean that typology excludes genetic theory; rather, it is a higher level of study that can be used to evaluate genetic analysis. Indeed, no comparison of changes can be made without study of cognates within individual languages or language families. Typology provides a different perspective, but not an exclusive one.

Detailed classification of typologies, largely through statistical methods, has led Greenberg to the study of generalizations concerning human language. Generative linguists, on the other hand, have come to the study of tendencies among linguistic structures from initial hypotheses about universal properties of language (cf. Chen 1973). Although it has not always been clear how a marriage between the two kinds of approaches to universals could be effected, the one being largely statistical, the other being largely logical, the possibility of such a marriage seems closer and closer, especially in the field of language change. Here we will consider two recent models that focus on universals of change from the perspective of what a possible language can be and how it can be acquired, rather than from the perspective of genetic comparison or typological classification—the acquisitional model developed in the transformational and generative semantic framework, and the dynamic wave model developed by linguists working with variation theory. It is in the latter that the marriage between Greenbergian and Chomskyan universals comes most nearly to fruition.

THE ACQUISITIONAL MODEL OF CHANGE

While acknowledging language acquisition as a likely cause for change, genetic theory paid it relatively little explicit attention. One of the major contributions of transformational grammar to the theory of language in general has been Chomsky's claim that our ability to learn a language, and hence the constraints on what a possible language can be, must be accounted for in any theory of language. This claim inspired historical linguists working in the transformational generative framework to turn their attention to the long-postulated relation between language learning and language change.

A basic tenet of transformational historical linguistics is that it is not merely people's performance that changes, but rather their 'grammar', that is, the underlying set of rules that represent the language user's knowledge of the language (Kiparsky 1965, 1968; King 1969). This was in direct contrast to the earlier claim that sound change was imperceptible and gradual (e.g., Hockett 1965). Gradualness, transformationalists claim, is a function of performance, as originally suggested, that is, of implementation of rules in the actual speech situation, but insofar as the language user's system or competence is concerned, a rule either is or is not present. For example, in the change from Proto IE voiceless stops to Germanic voiceless fricatives, individual performance may have varied considerably, but the change itself was abrupt. A speaker either did or did not have an [f] in the internalized representation of the word for 'father'; at the transitional period, some speakers may not have had [f] at all, others may have had both [f] and [p], others only [f]; this situation would naturally give the impression of a gradual change occurring, but for each speaker the change was abrupt. Empirical evidence that gradualness of articulatory shifts cannot account for everything in sound change is provided by such changes as [x] → [f], as in Old English [hlæxter] → [læftər] 'laughter'. How an articulatory shift from the velar to the labial without intervening [s], [θ] and other unlikely and unattested pronunciations could have occurred is unclear. Furthermore, abruptness of change is characteristic only of changes in the non-phonological structure of languages. There is no way to conceive of the gradual addition of a word like *sputnik* to one's grammar; either one uses it or one does not; however, frequency of use, that is, implementation of this word, may be gradual. Similarly, one either says *I him saw* or *I saw him*, or both; there is no way to conceive of a gradual shift from the one order to the other except where potential for use is concerned.

The claim that grammar changes was in direct opposition to the usual assumptions of genetic linguistics, at least as far as phonology was concerned. However, certain assumptions of earlier historical linguistics remained. In particular, the assumption that historical linguistics was to be based on comparison of largely homogeneous synchronic states persisted, at least in the earliest years, and significantly controlled thinking on the relations between language acquisition and language change.

The tenet that grammar, not merely performance, changes was directly linked to the hypothesis that language change comes about primarily because each generation has to learn the language anew. Children construct hypotheses about how the language works and may not develop the same hypotheses as those around them. If not, they have a different grammar. It had been felt for many centuries that children could have a deeper impact on the language than adults because of the very nature of the task of acquiring language. Transformational grammarians sought to explain this by postulating that radical changes (mutations or restructurings) could be brought about by children, not only between generations, but also in the acquisition of their own language. Adults, however, were considered capable of changing neither the language nor their own system radically (Halle 1962). Recent studies have tended to confirm that after puberty speakers have increasing difficulties in learning the exact contextual probabilities of a non-native language variety; for example, they are not likely to learn all the appropriate stylistic modifications of the new system. Nevertheless, teenagers do modify their grammars, and indeed may provide the main impetus to spread of language change in certain circumstances, for example, urban communities (Labov 1972). Whether teenagers' modifications are always merely innovations and never radical restructurings remains to be seen. Certainly, many adults can learn the syntax of a second language in such a way for it to be reasonable to speak of the adults' having acquired and internalized the grammar of the language; here again, however, a full range of variation may never be learned, but the grammar of one style, typically the written formal style, may be fully internalized.

A highly fruitful attempt was made to yoke together conceptually the claim 'grammars change' (and the assumption that children can mutate, but adults can only innovate) with the time-honored principle 'languages simplify over time'. As many have pointed out, if languages did nothing but simplify, our linguistic repertoire might just be *Ah,* or nothing at all. Certain principles must allow for a continual balance to occur between simplification and elaboration. It was the generative transformational claim that simplification was the result of children's generalization processes at all levels of grammar, whether phonological, lexical, or syntactic,[8] hence of their ability to mutate, while elaboration was the result of the adults' ability to add (or innovate) without modifying their system.

The comparative model emerging from these reformulations of the theory of language change is in skeletal form:

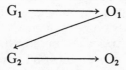

$$G_1 \longrightarrow O_1$$
$$G_2 \longrightarrow O_2$$

(cf. Kiparsky 1965, King 1969). In this model, G_1 represents the relatively homogeneous adult 'grammar' of the first generation. O_1 is the output of that grammar, what is actually said in performance; it is also the input to the second generation. G_2 represents the grammatical system developed by the second generation, roughly at the point of puberty. O_2 is the output of this generation's grammar and is itself the input to the third generation, and so forth. It is important to note that in this model the left-right arrows indicate production; the right-left arrow relating O_1 and G_2 is a perceptual one, implying children's use of universals in constructing G_2 on the basis of their input.

The Kiparsky-King model was felt to capture the generalization that languages simplify, since it was considered axiomatic that children develop 'optimal', that is, maximally efficient and simple grammars (Halle 1962). Therefore G_2 would by definition be no more complex and probably considerably simpler than G_1. For those concentrating on relating language acquisition to language change, however, a paradox soon presented itself. The result of acquisition (G_2) was supposedly as simple as or simpler than G_1. Yet what children actually do in learning a language is acquire progressively more complex structures, that is, they restructure their own grammars in ways that lead to overall elaboration. Furthermore, it was by no means clear that a young child's grammar was in any useful sense 'optimal'. As studies of language acquisition came to be more numerous (cf. especially Bloom 1970, Bowerman 1973, Brown 1973), and as investigation of the relation of language acquisition to language change began to be taken seriously, particularly the ways in which acquisition recapitulates known linguistic change (cf. Baron 1972), it became clear that the phenomenon to study was not so much comparison of static moments in the history of languages with static moments in children's language just preceding puberty, but rather comparison of dynamic processes of change in children's acquisition and in the development of languages (Traugott 1973).

In the latter part of the sixties attention was turned to the possibility that language acquisition and language change should both be explored in terms of (1) universals of language, i.e., constraints on what a possible language might be; (2) perceptual strategies, i.e., constraints on how language is perceived, that is, on learnability; and (3) strategies of production, called 'natural processes' by some, i.e., constraints on expressibility (cf. Kiparsky 1971; Andersen 1973; Traugott 1973, 1974b; and, with a focus on acquisition, Slobin 1975).

The argument, most clearly articulated by Stampe, was that children are born with certain innate processes that would eventually lead them to simplify their phonology to "verbal pabulum" if unhindered. A child's task in acquiring the adult system is "to revise all aspects of the system which separate his pronunciation from the standard," and revision involves "suppression, limitation, and ordering" (1969, p. 44). What is suppression, limitation, and ordering but the opposite of generalization? It is the development of constraints, the result of which is what linguists call elaboration. Phonetic change, Stampe points out, happens when children fail to suppress, order, and limit, and such failure often results in comparative simplification; the failure in itself, however, is not a simplification, nor for that matter an elaboration. Ontogenetically nothing has happened. Similarly, in syntax, natural processes involve constraints on expressibility. Innate cognitive structures must be organized in an ordered, time-limited sequence at the level of expression. The sequence is limited not only by the constraints of utterance production, but also by a principle of accessibility, which requires that material be laid out in ways readily decodable by the listener. One expects fundamental semantic-syntactic ('semantactic') constructs, without which language cannot be language, such as negativity, counterfactuality, relationships of real and unreal time, and so forth[9] to be expressed phrasally, to allow for maximum clarity of expression. If this is the case, one would expect a relatively analytic system, that is, one with few inflections. Since phonological processes tend to reduce distinctions, the child has to learn how to suppress, limit, and order the syntactic principles (these act to lay out the semantactic categories analytically) in relation to the phonological principles (these compress linguistic materials, and typically reduce adverbs, participles, and so forth to inflections). The constant adjustment that goes on accounts for balances between syntax and phonology and for changes that affect both at the same time.

Acquisition, in sum, is determined in part by the interplay between the principles underlying constraints on possible languages, on perception, and on production. None of these principles would result in acquisition in the absence of input. The structure of the input is proving more and more to be a crucial factor in acquisition—not in the sense originally understood, of any linguistic utterance at all heard by the child, but rather in the sense of utterances directed specifically to the child (Snow forthcoming). It seems that the nature of the input may be a prime reason for the mismatches between acquisition and language change.

Of particular importance, too, is the question whether the kinds of rule changes that are possible in early language acquisition are different from those possible at later periods of life. Since early language acquisition involves the development of surface expressions for very broad underlying categories, it would appear that more sweeping, fundamental rule changes would occur early, more specific ones later, but that there is an absolute difference between early and late acquisition seems unlikely. The language user who learns a second or third language has already made a hypothesis about at least one language (the native tongue) and therefore necessarily has a somewhat different input to non-native language learning than a child. That is, his or her own output is different; so, too, is that of adults who address the second language learner, since they use styles appropriate for addressing adults rather than children. Of primary importance is the fact that first language acquisition involves learning language as well as learning a language, and that it proceeds "concurrently with enculturation" (that is, with being socialized), while second language learning primarily involves learning a language and acculturation, that is, "modifications in the way in which language is used to meet social needs" (Valdman and Phillips 1975). Nevertheless, there is evidence that second language learning parallels first language learning in striking ways, at least on the syntactic level. Children already in near-adult command of native language A, that is, with a well-developed grammar, will treat a second language B like a first, making hypotheses about it that lead to development of output closely resembling that of the first language learners of Language B (cf. Ervin-Tripp 1970). The main difference between first and second language learning seems to be the speed at which developmental stages are reached—second language learning is considerably faster, but we find the same reliance on word-order to mark possessive, subject-verb-object, etc., the same lack of functors, and the same sorts of over-generalizations.

Why might this be? There seems to be a tendency to reactivate basic expressive strategies, that is, natural processes, and to redevelop constraints on them in terms of the new language, a tendency that supports in some measure the hypothesis that there are universals of language acquisition. It is also possible, indeed likely, that certain perceptual strategies that relate to phonological discrimination, awareness of morphological contrast, and processing of syntactic strings (cf. especially Bever 1970, Slobin 1973) will operate in second language acquisition, for example, Slobin's operating principle, "underlying semantic relations should be marked overtly and clearly" (the principle that accounts for why children *'ceteris paribus'* mark semantic notions earlier if their morphological realizations are perceptually more salient).

Which of the two approaches seems more explanatory for a theory of language change—the one that concentrates on comparison of static states, or the more dynamic one that concentrates on comparing processes of acquisition and change? One criterion of evaluation can be, and has been, whether both can account equally well for pidgins and creoles.

The process by which interlingual improvisation develops between two languages and results in a 'jargon' or 'trade language' (Whinnom 1971) seems to support the proposal that adults merely innovate but do not restructure. Indeed, Silverstein (1972) has explicitly claimed that Chinook jargon demonstrates only surface modifications of Chinook and English, but no restructuring of the underlying system of the donor languages. In contrast to the development of trade jargon, pidginization is often conceived as involving the creation of new rules. The issue is a controversial one, and sharp polarization has grown up between creolists like Bickerton, who regards trade jargons and pidgins as earlier and later stages of the same kinds of processes of intense relexification, and others like Sankoff, who focusses on the emergence of new rules in the development of pidgins. If the emergence of new rules that radically modify the system is indeed an essential aspect of pidginization, then it offers a direct challenge to the claim that all that adults can do is innovate. For one, the new rules involve the development of grammars in overall ways simpler than those of the donor languages, but elaborations of the language users' own systems of sound-meaning relationships. By contrast, creolization involves the development and internalization by children of rules comparatively far more complex than those of the donor pidgin.[10]

If this sketch is true, then pidgins and creoles present a counter-example to the basic concerns of the original transformational generative view, which focuses on comparison of synchronic states and relates simplification to child language acquisition, elaboration to adult innovation. On the other hand, the second view, concentrating on processes of change and acquisition incorporates pidginization and creolization naturally, since it does not tie simplification or elaboration directly to either adults or children and, furthermore, suggests that adults can return in learning second languages to earlier processes. It can therefore be said to be a more highly valued theory. This is particularly true if the generative theory espoused is one that allows not only for competence for the rational function of language (Chomsky 1965), but also for competence for use (cf. R. Lakoff 1972, Fillmore 1973, G. Lakoff 1974), since many of the characteristics of pidginization and creolization ultimately refer to processes of acquisition given certain functions (uses) and principles of communication.

If we reconsider what was said about first and second language acquisition, a problem may seem to arise in equating pidginization with second language acquisition, although none arises with equating creolization with first language acquisition. If we espouse the view that pidgins are simplified English, French, Portuguese, or whatever, then the problem is minimal, because we conceive of a superstrate language already in existence being learned, but we still have to face the fact that the result is a new language. If we accept right from the start Whinnom's view about substrate speakers making hypotheses about superstrate languages, we cannot fool ourselves into trying to find parallels between native language acquisition of, say, English, and the development, by second language learners, of a pidginized English. Yet, the fact that pidgins share remarkable similarities around the world must logically be tied to second language acquisition in some way. Tendencies have long been noted toward restricted vocabulary, few transformations, little embedding (particularly of relative clauses), comparative lack of morphological inflections but presence of overt, usually analytic markers of negation, tense, aspect, and sequencing (see, for example, Hall 1966; Hymes 1971, pp. 65-90 and Part III; Smith 1972). Such tendencies can be accounted for in terms of the acquisitional scheme that requires consideration of universals of language, perception and production and influence of input, provided we focus not so much on the processes and order of acquisition, but on the principles that make it possible. Pidginization, in other words, can be explained in part by a return to basic communicative principles, principles that are clearly prerequisites to language learning—one must know or develop the knowledge of what a language is for in order to acquire it (Halliday 1975).

Differing proposals about the nature of communicative principles have concentrated on different aspects of pidginization resulting from reduced function. Cassidy (1971), for example, hypothesizes that at the core of 'universals of communication' are (1) establishment of group identity (*I* vs. *you*; ingroups vs. outgroups); (2) differentiation between statements, questions, commands, and requests (differences between the latter two depend largely on role identification within the group); (3) naming trade objects and basic concepts like time and body parts. As the pidgin elaborates, Cassidy hypothesizes, modifications referring to quality, condition, manner, etc., develop; so do terms expressing aspect (completion, iteration, ongoing activity, habitual activity), modalities (possibilities, contingencies), and so forth. Ferguson (1975; cf. also Ferguson and DeBose in this volume) focusses not so much on these basics of communication, but on the fact that in the enculturation process we all learn certain ways to simplify language in functionally restricted situations, and these are brought to play in the creation of a pidgin.

The question remains how much such 'simplified registers' depend on universal principles such as Cassidy discusses, how much on language-specific, learned strategies. Whatever the principle or principles that bring about pidginization, they must refer at some point to the universals of what a language can be and how it can be expressed. In the situations that give rise to pidgins, we would expect to find little embedding (complementation, relativization, *if-then, before-after*) and similar types of hierarchization; certainly minimal subtlety of expression, for subtlety of discourse is largely contingent upon the presuppositional complexities associated with the use of specific linguistic structures in specific contexts, and with the inferences invited by the speech act. The restricted function of pidgins readily explains why there tends to be relatively little difference between underlying (semantic) and surface (syntactic) structure in pidgins (Kay and Sankoff 1972). One of the correlates of the relative closeness of underlying and surface structure is the tendency of pidgins to be analytic—the natural semantactic processes of maximum differentiation predominate, giving individual expression to individual concepts.

Creolization processes inevitably involve the same communicative principles as pidginization. However, since first language acquisition involves learning language as well as learning a language, and also enculturation, not just acculturation, creolization necessarily involves far more than pidginization—specifically, elaborating the language to make it a viable communicative system in a relatively large number of contexts. Bickerton has suggested that pidgins are "impossible languages to learn" (1975a) as native languages since they are so deficient in the possible distinctions that can be made in a language (e.g., between assertion and presupposition, or between action and state), and that this is why children must make recourse to their innate knowledge of what a language is and how it is to be expressed. Nobody develops a language in a vacuum, so to this knowledge we must add children's reference to perceptual strategies that analyze the input provided both by the pidgin, however inadequate, and the native languages heard, though not necessarily well understood, by the child. In any event we need to speak not so much of a return to basic principles of communication, at least where creolization is the result of first-language learning strategies, but of use of these principles as the groundwork on which to build more complex systems of communication through elaboration and restructuring.

Greater variety of function allows for greater variety of combinations; it is not surprising then that embeddings of various sorts develop in creoles (e.g., Sankoff and Brown 1976).[11] Creoles tend to develop not only more complex embeddings and word order patterns than pidgins, but also considerably more complex morphological structures. In particular, adverbs and particles become cliticized or even inflectional (e.g., Sankoff and Laberge 1973, Labov 1971). This seems to be attributable at least in part to the force of the natural phonological processes that lead to maximum cohesion and non-differentiation. Since pidgins tend to be spoken slowly and somewhat unrhythmically, the force of the phonological processes cannot be expected to be very great in pidgins. In creoles, however, they can have considerably greater importance since, like other native languages, creoles are spoken with speed and fluency. They develop in situations where there is relatively little identification by adults with the pidgin, because it is not their native language. Therefore, first generation creole speakers are presumably subject to relatively little suppressive judgment by older speakers. Unusually many experiments with language may thus survive, since there is minimal need to create 'cover-up' rules to accommodate oneself to the speech patterns of one's own class—though systematic variation certainly does develop, given the needs of communicating with members of other classes. That the structural elaborations developing in the creolization process do not generalize very fast, at least in some creole situations, and do not proceed in steps as predictable as those of first language acquisition, would seem to be explained by the absence of a native language model, and the social distance from the superstrate language or languages. Study of the constraints on transfer of new forms from individuals to larger social groups in newly emergent creoles should prove to be of vital importance to the theory of language variation.

THE DYNAMIC WAVE THEORY

This brings us to the most recent and most comprehensive, but as yet least formalized, approach to language change, the dynamic wave theory. A dynamic approach to language is far from new. It controlled nineteenth-century thought. Even after De Saussure's establishment of a sharp dichotomy between the study of synchrony and diachrony, the dynamic view never died completely. It was called for repeatedly during the fifties and sixties by a variety of linguists including, most notably, Greenberg (e.g., 1966) and Labov (e.g., 1965), but was not formulated in detail until Weinreich, Labov, and Herzog (1968) and subsequently, in a rather different way, Bailey (1973). Its present form, or rather variety of forms, is heavily dependent on work done within the framework of the acquisitional approach to language change, but differs substantially from it in its concentration on language variability,[12] on the evidence for language change that can be found in the current linguistic scene of any linguistic community (Labov, Yaeger, Steiner 1972), and in its reliance on what is known about pidginization and creolization of language as a partial basis for formulation of the theory (Bailey 1972). Emphasis on social correlates of change results in focus not so much on acquisition, which is seen only as a precondition for change, but on spread of changes ("the language has changed only when a *group* of speakers use a different pattern to communicate with each other" [Labov 1972, pp. 277]), therefore on what makes spread possible and what its results are. Most important of all, the dynamic theory explicitly rejects the claim still made, at least by proponents of comparing static stages in language development and language acquisition, that there is an opposition between diachrony and synchrony.[13] It demands that the framework in which linguistics as a whole should operate is a dynamic one that "includes time as a fundamental dimension of all analysis" (Bailey 1973, p. 21) (*all* is the key word here).

In beginning to formalize this theory, Bailey has modified the old rival to genetic theory, the wave theory of Schmidt (1872), which was developed to account for heterogeneity in language.[14] Basically, the claim is that in a situation without contact, or where contact has little linguistic significance, changes will follow unidirectional wavelike patterns of generalization (comparative simplification, resulting from children's failure to learn all the constraints on the innovated form). Given a relative time 0 at some focal point in social or geographical space, a feature *a* may enter variably at time (i) and spread to a larger social space; at time (ii) a more general version *b* of rule *a* will enter variably at the same focal point and spread, but usually not as far as *a*; at time (iii) a new, even more general form of a rule will enter at the focal point, and so forth. This account of change not only characterizes 'simplification', but also the tendency of peripheral changes to be archaic, as the following simplified model demonstrates:

Time (0) 0 Time (i) $\textcircled{a}$ 0 Time (ii) $\textcircled{\textcircled{b}a}$ 0 Time (iii) $\textcircled{\textcircled{\textcircled{c}b}a}$ 0

Such a wave shows an implicational scale, whereby *c* implies the presence of *b* and *b* implies the presence of *a*. This implicational scale is meant to be valid both temporally and spatially: "The wave model is essentially a temporal model that defines and generates static patterns out of dynamic process, the present being understood to be a cumulation of the past" (Bailey forthcoming).

The theory, as developed by Bailey, sets out to explain the dynamic variable properties of language. It establishes as its aim an explanation of the differences between situations with little contact, such as those modelled above, and various kinds of language mix, whether resulting in pidginization and essentially a new system or, at the other extreme, resulting in levelling and obliteration of distinctions, and ultimately giving rise to a koine (cf. eighteenth-century American colonial English, Attic Greek, and so forth).[15] Radical changes are seen as the result not of children's acquisition (this is supposed to lead to unidirectional shifts within a system), but of contact; contact involves borrowing, mixes, changes in the system, and out of it can emerge a new system.[16] Here we find the old idea of divergence, but explicitly stated as the result of convergence. Wave theory does not exclude

Stammbaum theory. It acts as a corrective on the over-algebraic formalism and the search for homogeneous systems. Naturally, it has been highly productive as a frame of reference for the study of pidgins and creoles. It allows both for a modified concept of monogenesis, since it could allow for certain elements to persist despite mix (why just those elements and not some others is a puzzle still not adequately answered),[17] and also for at least some degree of polygenesis, since each time language mix occurs, there is potential for independent development of a pidgin, given basic principles of communication in restricted contexts. Furthermore, it specifically allows for continua, and does not demand that artificial decisions be made about where one language or language type begins and another ends.

Particularly promising for pidgin and creole studies is the fact that, in keeping with some of the most recent work in linguistics, dynamic wave theory is based on a theory of language that insists that the structures of language can themselves not be forced into totally discrete categories. Just as no absolute boundaries exist between a trade jargon and a pidgin, none exist between semantics, syntax, phonology, and lexicon. The lexicon is seen as intimately connected with all aspects of language.[18] We can no longer hide behind easy definitions such as 'pidgins and creoles have the lexicon of one language and the grammar of another' and investigate the history of the lexicon one month and the history of the grammar another (usually to the detriment of the grammar), but are required to focus on the processes that make these particular lexical items the realizations of these semantic-syntactic relationships in this contact situation at this particular time.

CONCLUSION

Pidginization and creolization processes, then, are no longer seen merely as types of change that can be used to evaluate a theory; they have come to be of fundamental importance to the theory's very conception. Insofar as pidginization represents an extreme case of language mix, whatever processes are involved can be seen as setting limits on the theory of mix. Insofar as creolization represents relatively unhindered experiment with the creation of a new system, the processes involved can be seen to represent the maximum limit on what is possible in language elaboration. Insofar as both pidgins and especially creoles undergo modification toward the standard language, the processes of decreolization, which have been shown to progress not always by a direct but at least sometimes by an indirect path toward the standard (Bickerton 1975b), again represent the maximum limit on 'hypercorrection' in Labov's sense of generalization and overgeneralization of certain prestigious forms in the language.

As is inevitable when a new subject is incorporated into a discipline and demands the development of a new frame of reference, that new subject may seem to dominate the scene for a while at the expense of better-known subjects. The evidence pidginization and creolization give us for principles of communication, acquisition, possible language variation, and possible language change should not blind us to the fact that much is still not understood about such linguistic phenomena, and that while pidginization and creolization are certainly among the processes to which we must turn in developing theories of language, they are not the only (and possibly not even the best) sources of information. What is language-specific and what is universal are problems that have been central to all studies of language that permit of universal claims; they remain so now that pidginization and creolization have become central to linguistic theory. Recent studies of input in acquisition have emphasized the importance of not over-universalizing (cf. Snow forthcoming). Some creolists, too, have stressed input rather than universals. Alleyne (1971), for example, focusses on the differences between cultural matrices as keys to differences between pidgins and creoles, and Le Page (1974) insists that "different generations of speakers have different models, different goals." The acquisitional model of change, and especially the dynamic wave theory, have ushered in what can be expected to be a long period in which it will be possible to study language as a social instrument. The most fruitful results will come from addressing first and foremost the problem of the relation between general, universal processes of change and individual differences in the development of individual linguistic systems.

NOTES

I am grateful to Derek Bickerton for comments on an earlier draft of this paper. I am, as usual, solely responsible for errors of fact or judgment. Permission to reprint the genetic model of pidgins and creoles (Todd 1974, p.

40) is gratefully acknowledged to Loreto Todd and to Routledge and Kegan Paul.

1. For excellent discussion, see Anttila 1972, Chap. XX. Analogs to biological hybridization are also central to Whinnom's views on language mix (1971).

2. Detailed accounts of the comparative method in historical reconstruction can be found in Meillet 1934, Hoenigswald 1960, Anttila 1972. A good example of detailed application of the method in Indo-European studies is Lehmann 1955.

3. Not all comparativists agree that it is possible to reconstruct a uniform proto-language. Dyen (1969), for example, insists that only a uniform proto-idiolect can be assumed (or, even more weakly, "reconcilable reconstructions have proto-idiolectal identity"); however, Dyen still does not allow for language variation at the 'idiolectal' level.

4. Alternatively, in some situations, there is evidence of extensive 're-syntactification' (Gumperz and Wilson 1971).

5. Contemporary examples of pidgins and creoles in the 'Old World' are rare, presumably because of the relative length of contact. However, Indo-European migrations in pre-Christian times and after doubtless resulted in the development of at least some pidgins and creoles. Certainly, large numbers of different types of contact situations still persist and present problems for genetic theory, whether or not pidgins and creoles are involved. For a pioneering study, see Weinreich (1953).

6. For discussion of the possibility of using genetic theory with reference to pidgins and creoles see especially DeCamp 1971a, Hymes 1959, Taylor 1963. The last gives an excellent account of the controversies involved.

7. Undoubtedly, De Saussure's synchrony-diachrony dichotomy contributed significantly as well. Although the Saussurean dichotomy has been undermined consistently ever since it was proposed, it is only recently that full attention has been paid to systematicity in change—since typologies and universals deal with systems par excellence, their incorporation into historical theory naturally came somewhat late.

8. This view of generalization, developed by Kiparsky (1965, 1968), is in direct denial of the obviously inadequate claim of the neogrammarians that sound change occurred without exception and that apparent exceptions were the result of relatively random analogical processes at the morphological level. Kiparsky suggested that all rule-generalization, at whatever level of the grammar, involved simplification.

9. For an explicit hypothesis concerning the nature and range of such universals, see Bickerton 1975a.

10. That some creoles may develop as the result of second language

learning by adults is suggested by Gumperz and Wilson (1971). In these cases, principles of second language acquisition apply, at least in the early stages.

11. Sankoff and Brown actually show that embedding of relative clauses was initiated by pidgin-speaking adults; children, however, generalized the structure and use it far more extensively. The Halle-Kiparsky-King hypothesis of language acquisition can therefore adequately account for this situation. With Tok Pisin we have a case of an extensively elaborated pidgin; whether adult innovation of this sort would occur in situations of rapid creolization after a short period of pidginization remains to be tested.

12. DeCamp 1971b is, however, an important attempt to incorporate variability into the transformational-generative frame of reference.

13. Although generative phonological theory has been evaluated in part on dynamic grounds since Chomsky-Halle (1968), historical generative linguists have tended to treat synchrony as in some way 'basic'. For example, Kiparsky presupposes two different types of grammar when he says that "much progress in historical linguistics depends on sharpening synchronic theory so that it will provide the right basis for diachronic explanation" (1971, p. 578).

14. For a useful summary of differences and similarities between traditional concepts of family tree, wave model, and dialectology, see Pulgram (1953).

15. The differences between the development of a koine and a pidgin are well outlined in Samarin (1971).

16. The claim is further made that acquisition brings about 'natural' change; 'borrowing' does not. Insofar as all children can be said to borrow language-specific aspects of their language from the input provided them, this distinction seems strained. The distinction should not be one of borrowing versus non-borrowing, but of whether the systems from which borrowing takes place are the same or not. Clearly differences do need to be made between acquisition of a given system (where, by definition, 'system' is understood to involve consistent variation among related lects) and acquisition of several systems, or of aspects of several systems.

17. Bickerton suggests that we should not think of persistence at all, but rather of reappearance because such elements are 'natural'.

18. For a seminal account of a grammar in which lexical items are surface realizations of complex predications (e.g., *kill* = cause to become not alive), see McCawley 1968.

REFERENCES

Alleyne, Mervyn C. 1971. Acculturation and the cultural matrix of creolization. In *Pidginization and Creolization of Languages*, Dell Hymes, ed., pp. 169-86.

Andersen, Henning. 1973. Abductive and deductive change. *Language* 49: 765-93.

Anttila, Raimo. 1972. *An Introduction to Historical and Comparative Linguistics.* New York: Macmillan.

Bailey, Charles-James N. 1972. The integration of linguistic theory: internal reconstruction and the comparative method in descriptive analysis. In *Linguistic Change and Generative Theory*, Robert P. Stockwell and Ronald K. S. Macaulay, eds. Bloomington: Indiana University Press, pp. 22-31.

————. 1973. *Variation in Linguistic Theory.* Arlington, Va.: Center for Applied Linguistics.

————. (Forthcoming.) Old and new views on language relationships and language history. *Journal of East European Social History*, special ed. by Eric P. Hamp.

Baron, Naomi. 1972. The evolution of English periphrastic causatives: contributions to a general theory of linguistic variation and change. Ph.D. diss., Stanford University.

Bever, Thomas G. 1970. The cognitive basis for linguistic structures. In *Cognition and Development of Language*, John R. Hayes, ed. New York: Wiley, pp. 279-362.

Bickerton, Derek. 1975a. Creolization, linguistic universals, natural semantax and the brain. International Conference on Pidgins and Creoles, University of Hawaii, January 1975.

————. 1975b. *Dynamics of a Creole System.* New York: Columbia University Press.

Bloom, Lois. 1970. *Language Development: Form and Function in Emerging Grammars.* Cambridge, Mass.: MIT Press.

Bloomfield, Leonard. 1946. Algonquian. In *Linguistic Structures of Native America.* Viking Publications in Anthropology, 6. New York: Viking Press.

Bowerman, Melissa. 1973. *Early Syntactic Development: A Cross-Linguistic Study with Special Reference to Finnish.* New York: Cambridge University Press.

Brown, Roger. 1973. *A First Language: The Early Stages.* Cambridge, Mass.: Harvard University Press.

Cassidy, Frederic G. 1971. Tracing the pidgin element in Jamaican creole (with notes on method and the nature of pidgin vocabularies). In *Pidginization and Creolization of Languages*, Dell Hymes, ed. London: Cambridge University Press, pp. 203-22.

Chen, Matthew. 1973. Predictive power in phonological description. *Lingua* 32:173-91.

Chomsky, Noam. 1965. *Aspects of the Theory of Syntax.* Cambridge, Mass.: MIT Press.

————. 1967. The formal nature of language. Appendix to Eric Lenneberg, *Biological Foundation of Language.* New York: Wiley.
————. 1975. *Reflections on Language.* New York: Pantheon.
————, and Halle, Morris. 1968. *The Sound Pattern of English.* New York: Harper and Row.
DeCamp, David. 1971a. The study of pidgin and creole languages. In Hymes, ed., pp. 13-39.
————. 1971b. Toward a generative analysis of a post-creole speech continuum. In Hymes, ed., pp. 349-70.
Dyen, Isidore. 1969. Reconstruction, the comparative method and the proto-language uniformity assumption. *Language* 45:499-518.
Ervin-Tripp, Susan M. 1970. Structure and process in language acquistion. *Georgetown University Monograph Series on Languages and Linguistics* 23:313-53.
Ferguson, Charles A. 1975. Toward a characterization of English foreigner talk. *Anthropological Linguistics* 17:1-14.
Fillmore, Charles J. 1973. A grammarian looks to sociolinguistics. *Georgetown University Monographs on Languages and Linguistics* 25:273-87.
Greenberg, Joseph H. 1966. Synchronic and diachronic universals in phonology. *Language* 42:508-17.
————. 1969. Some methods of dynamic comparison in linguistics. In *Substance and Structure of Language,* Jaan Puhvel, ed., pp. 147-203. Berkeley and Los Angeles: University of California Press.
————. 1974. *Language Typology: A Historical and Analytic Overview.* The Hague: Mouton.
Gumperz, John J., and Wilson, Robert. 1971. Convergence and creolization: a case from the Indo-Aryan/Dravidian border. In Hymes, ed., pp. 151-68.
Haas, Mary R. 1969. *The Prehistory of Languages.* The Hague: Mouton.
Hall, Robert A., Jr. 1966. *Pidgin and Creole Languages.* Ithaca: Cornell University Press.
Halle, Morris. 1962. Phonology in generative grammar. *Word* 18:54-72.
Halliday, M. A. K. 1975. Learning how to mean. In *Explorations in the Development of Language.* London: Arnold.
Hancock, Ian F. 1970. A provisional comparison of the English-based Atlantic Creoles. *African Language Review* 8:7-72.
Hockett, Charles. 1965. Sound change. *Language* 41:185-204.
Hoenigswald, Henry. 1960. *Language Change and Linguistic Reconstruction.* Chicago: University of Chicago Press.
Hymes, Dell. 1959. Genetic classification: retrospect and prospect. *Anthropological Linguistics* 1:50-66.
————. ed. 1971. *Pidginization and Creolization of Languages.* London:

Cambridge University Press.

Jakobson, Roman. 1958. Typological studies and their contributions to historical comparative linguistics. Proceedings of the VIIIth International Congress of Linguistics, Oslo, 1958, pp. 17-25.

Kay, Paul, and Sankoff, Gillian. 1972. A language-universals approach to pidgins and creoles. In *Pidgins and Creoles: Current Trends and Prospects*, David DeCamp and Ian F. Hancock, eds. Washington, D. C.: Georgetown University Press, pp. 61-72.

King, Robert D. 1969. *Historical Linguistics and Generative Grammar*. Englewood Cliffs, N. J.: Prentice-Hall.

Kiparsky, Paul. 1965. Phonological change. Ph.D. diss., MIT.

_____. 1968. Linguistic universals and linguistic change. In *Universals in Linguistic Theory*, Emmon Bach and Robert T. Harms, eds. New York: Holt, Rinehart and Winston, pp. 170-202.

_____. 1971. Historical linguistics. In *A Survey of Linguistic Science*, Linguistics Program, University of Maryland, ed., pp. 576-649.

Labov, William. 1965. On the mechanism of linguistic change. *Georgetown University Monographs on Languages and Linguistics* 18:91-114.

_____. 1971. On the adequacy of natural language. Ms.

_____. 1972. *Sociolinguistic Patterns.* Philadelphia: University of Pennsylvania Press.

_____; Yaeger, Malcah; and Steiner, Richard. 1972. A quantitative study of sound change in progress. Report to NSF, Contract NSF-GS-3,287. University of Pennsylvania.

Lakoff, George. 1974. Interview with Herman Parret (to appear in Herman Parret, *Discussing Language.* The Hague: Mouton). Berkeley Studies in Syntax and Semantics I.

Lakoff, Robin. 1972. Language in context. *Language* 48:907-27.

Lehmann, Winfred. 1955. *Proto-Indo-European Phonology*. Austin: University of Texas Press.

Le Page, Robert B. 1974. Processes of pidginization and creolization. *York Papers on Linguistics* 4:41-69.

McCawley, James D. 1968. Lexical insertion in a transformational grammar without deep structure. Papers from the Fourth Regional Meeting of the Chicago Linguistic Society, pp. 71-80.

Meillet, Antoine. 1934. *Introduction à l'étude comparative des langues indo-européennes.* 7th ed. Paris: Librairie Hachette.

Pulgram, Ernst. 1953. Family tree, wave theory, and dialectology. *Orbis* 2:67-72.

Samarin, William. 1971. Salient and substantive pidginization. In Hymes, ed., pp. 117-40.

Sankoff, Gillian, and Brown, Penelope. 1976. The origins of syntax in discourse: a case study of Tok Pisin relatives. *Language* 52:631-66.

————, and Laberge, Suzanne. 1973. On the acquisition of native speakers by a language. *Kivung* 6:32-47.

Saussure, Ferdinand de. 1916. *Cours de linguistique générale.* Geneva: Payot.

Schleicher, August. 1871. Introduction to *Compendium der vergleichenden Grammatik der Indo-germanischen Sprachen.* Weimar: Böhlan.

Schmidt, Johannes. 1872. *Die verwantschaftsverhältnisse der indogermanischen Sprachen.* Weimar: Herman Böhlan.

Silverstein, Michael. 1972. Chinook jargon: language contact and the problem of multi-level generative systems. *Language* 48:378-406, 596-625.

Slobin, Dan I. 1973. Cognitive prerequisites for the development of grammar. In *Studies of Language Development*, Charles A. Ferguson and Dan I. Slobin, eds. New York: Holt, Rinehart and Winston, pp. 175-276.

————. 1975. The more it changes . . . : on understanding language by watching it move through time. Papers and Reports on Child Language Development 10. Stanford University: Department of Linguistics.

Smith, David. 1972. Some implications for the social status of pidgin languages. In *Sociolinguistics in Crosscultural Perspective*, David M. Smith and Roger W. Shuy, eds. Washington D. C.: Georgetown University Press.

Snow, Catherine E. (Forthcoming.) Mother's speech research: an overview. Proceedings of the Conference on Language Input and Acquisition, Boston, 1974.

Stampe, David. 1969. The acquisition of phonetic representation. Papers from the Fifth Regional Meeting of the Chicago Linguistic Society, pp. 443-54.

Stewart, William A. 1962. Creole languages in the Caribbean: a study of the role of second languages in Asia, Africa, and Latin America, ed. by F. A. Rice. Washington D. C.: Center for Applied Linguistics, pp. 34-53.

Swadesh, Morris. 1951. Diffusional cumulation and archaic residue as historic explanations. *Southwestern Journal of Anthropology* 7:1-21.

Taylor, Douglas. 1963. The origin of West Indian Creole languages: evidence from grammatical categories. *American Anthropologist* 65:800-14.

Thompson, R. W. 1961. A note on some possible affinities between the creole dialects of the Old World and those of the New. *Creole Language Studies 2.* Robert Le Page, ed. New York: St. Martin's Press, pp. 107-13.

Todd, Loreto. 1974. *Pidgins and Creoles.* London: Routledge and Kegan Paul.

Traugott, Elizabeth C. 1973. Le changement linguistique et sa relation à l'acquistion de la langue maternelle. *Langages* 32:39-52.

————. 1974a. On the notion "restructuring" in historical syntax.

Proceedings of the IXth International Congress of Linguists, 1972. Luigi Heilmann, ed. Bologna: Mulino, pp. 921-28.

————. 1974b. Explorations in linguistic elaboration: language change, language acquisition and the genesis of spatio-temporal terms. In *Historical Linguistics,* John M. Anderson and Charles Jones, eds. New York: American Elsevier, Vol. 1, pp. 263-314.

Valdman, Albert, and Phillips, John S. 1975. Pidginization, creolization and the elaboration of learner systems. *Colloque Theoretical Models in Applied Linguistics IV.* University of Neuchatel, May 1975.

Voorhoeve, Jan. 1973. Historical and linguistic evidence in favor of the relexification theory in the formation of creoles. *Language in Society* 2:133-45.

Weinreich, Uriel. 1953. *Languages in Contact.* New York: Publications of the Linguistic Society of America.

————; Labov, William; and Herzog, Marvin I. 1968. Empirical foundations for a theory of language change. In *Directions for Historical Linguistics,* Winfred P. Lehmann and Yakov Malkiel, eds. Austin: University of Texas Press, pp. 95-195.

Whinnom, Keith. 1965. The origin of the European-based creoles and pidgins. *Orbis* 14:509-27.

————. 1971. Linguistic hybridization and the 'special' case of pidgins and creoles. In *Pidginization and Creolization of Languages,* D. Hymes, ed. New York: Cambridge University Press, pp. 91-115.

Simplified Registers, Broken Language, and Pidginization

Charles A. Ferguson and Charles E. DeBose

O. INTRODUCTION

0.1. Linguists have generally been concerned primarily with full, natural languages even though the data available for study may in some instances be very limited or marginal, as in an epigraphic corpus of an extinct language or in the poorly remembered folktales of the last living informant of a language. Yet arguments can be made for the systematic study of special and restricted varieties of language for the value they may have in showing the limits of human language. Even a very specialized study of the conventionalized animal calls of a particular speech community may be rich in implications for the phonological, grammatical, and functional properties of human language in general (cf. Schultheiss 1912, Chandola 1963, Bynon 1975). In the last few years one kind of partial and restricted language, so-called pidgin, has received a great deal of attention, partly because of questions about the social conditions of appearance and maintenance of pidgins, partly also for their relevance to fundamental questions about language change and the nature of human language (cf. Hymes 1971).

The present paper[1] deals with three types of language that are not the full, natural languages that constitute the traditional object of the linguist's study. All three are in some sense reduced in comparison to full languages, and they are not natural in that they do not serve as the normal mother tongue of a speech community. The first type are 'simplified registers', which are more-or-less conventionalized varieties of language used by members of a speech community to address people whose knowledge of the language of the community is felt to be less than normal (cf. Ferguson 1975a). The second type is 'broken language', the imperfect approximations of a language by speakers of another language who are in the process of learning it (cf. Ferguson 1963). The third type is the pidgin itself, which the authors of the paper regard as typically resulting from the use of both simplified register and broken language in the same communication situations.

Simplified registers are reductions of a source language; broken language is a reduction of a target language; and a pidgin is both, i.e., it is a reduction of a so-called base language that is at the same time the source language for its native speakers and the target language for the non-native speakers involved.

1. SIMPLIFIED REGISTERS

1.1. *Variation*

In any speech community observed over a period of time suitable for analysis, the forms and meanings of the language(s) in use exhibit variation, i.e., elements and relations among them that are held in some sense to be 'the same' appear sometimes in one way sometimes in another. This variation is to be analyzed along four different dimensions or conditions of occurrence: grammatical (i.e., narrowly synchronic linguistic conditions), dialectal, registral, and diachronic. Grammatical variation is the kind that is conditioned by the linguistic environment of the form and meanings in question and is the focus of the 'allo' statements, derivational statements, and so on of phonology, morphosyntax, and semantics that constitute the bulk of a synchronic grammar. Dialectal variation within the community reflects discontinuities in communication, intergroup attitudes, and other social dimensions, and thus tends to be analyzed in terms of the regional provenience, socioeconomic status, age, sex, and similar basic social/demographic characteristics of groups of speakers. Although the language of an individual, as a result of his or her life history, may exhibit dialectal variation, this is in a sense accidental to the notion of dialect variation. Registral variation, on the other hand, reflects the occasion, topic, and respective roles of the language users, and hence every individual has a repertoire of registral variation corresponding to a range of different occasions and users of language. Registral variation is conventionalized and shared by the community, much like grammatical variation, although it is less frequently the object of linguistic analysis, while dialectal variation represents differences in conventionalization and hence potential or actual differences in the boundaries of speech communities themselves. Finally, variation may be part of ongoing language change, i.e., change over time in the conventions of language behavior in the community. Variation along all four dimensions may occur in phonology, morphosyntax, semantics, lexicon, or discourse structure, and there may be complex interrelations among the four dimensions, but a pair of morphological examples will serve to illustrate, in an uncomplicated way, the dimensions of variation.

The variation in stem form of *speak* ~ *spoke* and *eat* ~ *ate* is grammatical. The variation between /eyt/ and /et/ as the past of *eat* is dialectal, the former being standard American, the latter standard British or uneducated American. The variation between *spoke* and *spake* is registral in that the latter is used principally on occasions of public worship by people who use *spoke* on other occasions. Both /eyt/ ~ /et/ and *spoke* ~ *spake* also happen to be diachronic variation: /eyt/ and *spoke* are the dominant newer forms replacing /et/ and *spake,* which persist in dialectal and registral variants.

Sometimes a number of features of dialectal variation ('isoglosses') cluster together consistently enough in correlation with the regional/social conditions of occurrence to call the varieties exhibiting them a 'dialect' (e.g., coastal New England dialect, working-class dialect). The term 'dialect', although essentially arbitrary and requiring definition whenever it is used in linguistic description, is of significance at least in diachronic terms as designating a demarcatable variety that is potentially a new language, given appropriate conditions of communication and attitude (Ferguson and Gumperz 1960).

Similarly, a number of features of registral variation may cluster together consistently enough in correlation with the conditions of use to call the variety so characterized a 'register' (e.g., allegro register, classroom teaching register). Although the notion of register is essentially as arbitrary as that of dialect, it is a valuable concept in analyzing the linguistic repertoires of individuals and communities, both synchronically and diachronically (Ellis and Ure 1969).

1.2. Simplified registers

The kind of simplified register that has been most intensively studied is 'baby talk' (BT), the variety of language that is regarded by a speech community as primarily appropriate for addressing young children. Two main streams of research have contributed to our knowledge of this register. The anthropological linguistic stream has consisted chiefly of data elicited from adults in different societies on how they address children, and a limited amount of naturalistic observation in those societies. Substantial studies of this kind go back as far as the 1940s (with more limited studies even earlier); the first general, comparative treatment was Ferguson 1964. This stream has tended to focus on phonological and lexical features of BT and on displaced and extended uses of BT (e.g., reporting children's speech, to pets, between lovers). The other stream is psycholinguistic experimentation, which has consisted chiefly of the recording and analysis of adult speech to children under controlled conditions and the comparison of such speech with adult-adult speech under similar conditions. Although studies touching on these issues appeared in the 1960s, the first published account of a full-scale study of this kind was Snow 1972. The psycholinguistic stream has tended to focus on syntactic and intonational features of BT and on the relation between modified input to children and the children's language development. The bulk of this psycholinguistic research has been on speakers of American English, although there are good studies on Dutch and several other languages. A small but growing kind of research is studying BT within a larger context of language socialization in different cultures and is providing a useful perspective for the two mainstreams (cf. Blount 1972). A set of papers reviewing and adding to these streams of BT research appears in Snow and Ferguson 1977.

Widespread characteristics of BT registers include the following: slow, exaggerated enunciation; higher overall pitch; exaggerated intonation contours; full vowels for reduced vowels and some vowels lengthened; short sentences; little or no embedding; frequent use of devices for attention and feedback of words, phrases, and sentences; use of kinterms and names (with third person constructions) instead of personal pronouns; use of first plural pronoun for second singular; avoidance of inflections and use of lexemes in multiple word class functions; preference for CV and CVC syllables and reduplications; simplification of consonant clusters; avoidance or substitution of highly marked sounds; interchange among *l r w y*; use of labialization and palatalization; use of diminutive and hypocoristic formations; and a special lexicon for body parts and functions, close kin, food, clothing, small animals, toys and games, and a few predicates (e.g., nice, hot, enough, 'all gone').

This impressive list of widespread features suggests universal tendencies at work, but the extensive differences in detail among different speech communities also show that BT registers are conventionalized and language-specific. The conventionalized nature of BT is most evident in certain phonological and lexical characteristics, and its universal aspects are most evident in certain prosodic and syntactic characteristics. It seems reasonable to assume that BT, like language in general, is completely conventionalized but operates within universal constraints and reflects the interaction of universal tendencies of change. Thus if one language's BT uses [tʃ] in place of adult [s] and another's uses [ts] in place of adult [tʃ], this shows both the conventionalized, arbitrary nature of BT and the universal BT tendency to replace a sound in the adult speech by one that the speech community treats as easier to perceive or produce.

One other fact about BT registers must be noted. In any speech community there can be variation in the degree of 'babyishness' of the register, i.e., the incidence of BT features may vary from very slight to very full. To take two simple examples, the pitch level may vary from almost natural adult usage to a pervasive, very high fundamental, or the use of diminutives may vary from a sparing use to the diminutivizing of every word. Much of this variation corresponds to the adult's (usually unconscious) assessment of the child's linguistic competence and thus depends on the child's age or stage of language development.

Another simplified register that has been studied, and is more directly relevant to the concerns of this paper, is that of 'foreigner talk' (FT), the variety of language that is regarded by a speech community as primarily appropriate for addressing foreigners. Although the term was probably first used in Ferguson 1971, the concept goes back at least as far as Schuchardt (cf. Schuchardt 1909, Meijer & Muysken this volume). There has been less research on FT than on BT and it would be premature to attempt the kind of generalizations possible for BT, but at least some comments can be made. Many speech communities have one or more FT registers, and the small amount of research done has usually focussed on the kind of FT used in 'talking down' to speakers of other languages who are felt to be socially inferior in some important respects (e.g., less civilized, of 'inferior' religion, low social status). The FT modifications made in speaking to people regarded as socially equal or superior have been mentioned (e.g., Heidelberger Projekt 1975), but the only systematic study known to us is Henzl 1974, which investigates the variety of Czech used by native speakers of the language in addressing American college students of Czech. Three methods have been used in FT research: (a) elicitation from informants who report on how they or others in the speech community speak to foreigners, e.g., Ferguson 1975a; (b) experimental investigation in which investigators play the role of foreigners in selected communication situations, e.g., Hatch et al. 1975; and (c) recording of native-foreign interaction in a natural communication setting, e.g., Heidelberger Projekt 1975, pp. 85-98.

FT features that are probably widespread although not yet sufficiently documented to make such a claim with assurance include the following: slow, exaggerated enunciation; greater overall loudness; use of full forms instead of contractions; short sentences; parataxis (pure or with adverbial connectives such as *maybe, bye-and-bye*); repetition of words; analytic paraphrases of lexical items and certain constructions; reduction of inflections (often by the selection of one or two all-purpose forms, e.g., *me* for *I, my, mine, me* in English, infinitive for all non-past verb forms in Italian, *die* for all forms of the definite article in German); lack of function words (e.g., articles, prepositions, auxiliaries); use of feedback devices such as invariable tag questions; avoidance of strongly dialect or slang forms in favor of more standard forms; limited number of phonological simplifications (e.g, occasional addition of vowel to final consonants in English, *b* for *p* in Italian); special lexicon of quantifiers, intensifiers, and modal particles used in constructions not matching 'normal' language; use of foreign or foreign-sounding words (e.g., English *savvy*).

As with BT, features of FT suggest universal processes but in detail turn out to be highly conventionalized. A number of features are common to BT and FT and some are distinctive of one or the other, and it is sometimes possible to discern the special 'functions' or 'purposes' served by particular features by studying the way they occur in other registers. To take an obvious example, the loudness of FT is probably at least partly for increased audibility, since it is also used in addressing the hard of hearing. The higher pitch and use of *we* for *you* of BT apparently express the notion of caretaking and the incapacity of the addressee, since they are used in the kind of partial BT addressed to hospital patients (Brown 1973, p. 397). Also, as BT registers may vary in 'babyishness', so FT registers may vary in degree of 'foreignness', i.e., the incidence of FT features may vary from slight to very full depending chiefly on the speaker's assessment of the addressee's status and level of competence in the language. More typical of FT variation, however, is the 'vertical' dimension of 'talking up' versus 'talking down' mentioned above.

1.3. *Modifying processes*

If the usual conversational speech of a community is regarded as the norm and simplified registers as modifications of it, then the differences between the two may be described in terms of modifying processes of various kinds. Some are 'simplifying processes' that may be seen as reducing or simplifying the normal speech in some way and so justify the term 'simplified registers', but some are not. Three types of non-simplifying processes will be identified here: clarifying, upgrading, and expressive (cf. also Ferguson 1975b).

The notion of simplicity in language is difficult to define with precision, and we make no attempt here to offer an adequate definition, but modifications that seem intended in a fairly obvious way to make utterances easier to perceive, understand, or produce may be regarded as simplifying processes if they omit material, reduce irregularity, or make sound-meaning correspondences more transparent. Such modifications occur in phonology, morphosyntax and lexicon. Let us take modifications at the morphological level as an example, using the German definite article. In standard German there are six phonetically different forms of the article (manifesting declensional categories of two numbers, four cases, and three genders), stressed and unstressed variants of these, and contracted forms of the oblique cases of the article in combination with prepositions. Simplifying processes modifying the article could include: omission of the article under some or all of the conditions of its occurrence; reduction of the category system by generalizing one or more forms to manifest them; generalizing of one form for stressed and unstressed, contracted and uncontracted. In fact, examples of all these modifications can be found in BT and FT registers of German (Heidelberger Projekt 1975).

Some modifications that seem intended to make the language easier are not simplifying in the sense just described, but are 'clarifying', i.e., they add redundancy to the message by such means as increasing the substance, supplying material that is normally omitted, or separating elements normally fused in some way. Such modifications as repetition of words, reduplication within words, adding a subject *you* to imperatives, pronouncing carefully syllable by syllable, saying *day after today* for *tomorrow*, or using full forms for contractions are examples of clarifying processes that occur in English BT and FT (Ferguson 1975a). Often simplifying and clarifying processes intersect, as in the German definite article examples already mentioned.

One kind of modification that appears in simplified registers seems intended to make the language more 'correct' or 'standard' than the normal usage of adult-adult informal conversation. Modifications of this kind that represent 'upgrading' processes are more common in language teacher registers and 'talking-up' kinds of FT than in BT or 'talking-down' FT (Henzl 1974), but examples can be found in almost any kind of simplified register. A clear example in talking-down FT is documented in Heidelberger Projekt 1975: A German speaker who uses the infinitive of the verb in place of the inflected forms when addressing a foreign worker uses the standard German infinitive ending *-en* instead of the local dialect ending *-e*, which he uses when addressing a German-speaking employee.

Finally, some of the registral modifications found in simplified registers are not simplifying, clarifying, or upgrading, but simply seem to signal attitudes or affect appropriate to the communication situation. Thus, the proliferation of diminutive and hypocoristic formations in BT does not seem intended to make the language easier to process, but rather to express the speaker's attitude toward young children. The presence of such 'expressive' processes is doubtless a factor in the extension of registers to affectively comparable situations (e.g., BT to pets). In FT registers expressive processes tend to mark the status and role relationships between the speakers, as in the German FT use of familiar *du* instead of polite *Sie,* 'you', which seems to signal a superior-to-inferior relationship.

Not all features of simplified registers can be neatly classified in these four types of processes, but once a particular feature becomes conventionalized it can serve the purpose of signalling the use of the register, and features that do not exemplify the other processes at least can fill this identification function, so that such features have been assigned to a miscellaneous set of 'identifying' processes (Ferguson 1975b).

2. BROKEN LANGUAGE

2.1. *Learners' grammars*

Whenever the speaker of one language learns to speak another language the acquisition takes place gradually, not all at once, and is characterized by successive changes in the person's knowledge of the second language and his or her ability to use it. The development proceeds from zero mastery of the new language (except insofar as universal human language capabilities and mastery of the first language constitute knowledge of the new language) toward full mastery, although en route there may be detours and retracing of steps and full mastery may not be achieved. It is reasonable to assume that at any point in the development the speaker has a 'grammar', a linguistic system that is an incomplete and in part incorrect version of the grammar of the target language, and his 'errors' in comprehension and production of the target language may be used, along with his 'correct' behavior, as evidence for the current stage of his learner's grammar. Ferguson 1963 pointed to the value of studying such partial grammars for the construction of general linguistic theory. Corder 1967 initiated discussion of the systematic study of these learners' grammars, to which Nemser 1971 gave the name of 'approximative systems' and which Selinker and his colleagues have called 'interlanguage' (Selinker 1972). In consonance with this line of research the field of 'error analysis' is beginning to broaden its purely pedagogical goals to include a concern with basic questions of the nature of human language and the nature of language acquisition (Richards 1971).

Thus a number of studies have been undertaken recently that provide data on learners' grammars, put into a theoretical context of linguistics or psycholinguistics. Much of the literature presents the data in support of arguments on which is *the* primary source of error (e.g., interference, developmental processes) and on whether first and second language acquisition are essentially the same process or different processes (among many such studies see, e.g., Dulay and Burt 1972, Ervin-Tripp 1974, Felix 1975). Extreme views on these questions are not likely to be tenable in the long run, since even the most cursory investigation of learners' grammars shows that there are multiple sources of error and that there are both similarities and differences between first and second language acquisition. In particular, the accumulation of data on second language acquisition in childhood under 'natural' conditions (i.e., without formal instruction) is proceeding apace and will soon be comparable in quantity and degree of sophistication with the first language acquisition data already available (for a review of the 'natural' acquisition research see Cazden et al. 1975, pp. 3-8).

Unfortunately for our purposes there are few studies of adult 'natural' second language acquisition, but the need for such is now recognized (cf. the reference to *ungesteuert* language acquisition, Heidelberger Projekt 1975).

2.2. *Broken language*

In spite of the dearth of reliable data and the tendency to argue over equally untenable extreme positions, certain comments can be made about the characteristics of 'broken language' (BL), i.e., learners' productions of a target language.

First, many of the features of BL represent simplification or reductions of the target language and as such are similar in kind to the simplifications found in first language acquisition, simplified registers, language loss, and elsewhere in language variation and language change. Such 'errors' typically include omission of inflections or confusion among them, overgeneralization of morphological and syntactic patterns, preference for general and undifferentiated lexical items.

Second, many features represent transfers of structure from the first language, and as such are similar in kind to the borrowings and accommodations between languages in contact. Such 'errors' typically include substitutions of sounds and assimilation patterns from the first language and mismatches of grammatical categories and ranges of meaning of lexical items.

Third, many features of BL reflect individual histories of exposure to the target language, idiosyncratic details of the linguistic system of the learner's preceding stage of 'grammar', favorite strategies of the learner, and other factors that are neither developmental in nature nor due to interference. Examples include the use of 'prefabricated routines' (i.e., chunks of language picked up before their internal structure is differentiated) and the invention of categories not found in either source or target language.

It must also be noted that the sources of particular errors are often difficult or impossible to ascertain (e.g., the 'ambiguous goofs' of Dulay and Burt 1972) and that some errors may even turn out not to be systematic in any linguistically relevant sense at all.

Finally, the characteristics of BL differ depending on the social context of the use of the language, and this dimension of variation is particularly important for the purposes of the present study. For example, 'classroom' errors, or errors in a learning situation with sharp social barriers, may differ systematically from 'natural' errors—those in a situation without such barriers (cf. Richards 1972 for a discussion that is particularly relevant for the pidginization process).

With the present state of knowledge, it is difficult to offer with confidence any generalization about the incidence of simplification, transfer, and other types of error in BL. It seems likely, for example, that there is much more transfer in formal instruction than in 'natural' acquisition, but considerable simplification is attested under certain conditions of language use after classroom instruction (e.g., Powell 1975). Or, it seems likely that there is much more simplification in syntax than in phonology or lexicon, but transfer is attested for certain kinds of syntactic patterns (e.g., Schachter 1974). One of the principal tasks of language acquisition research is to discover general principles that will account for the differential incidence of various error types.

2.3. *Interaction*

The modifications of normal interadult speech that constitute simplified registers addressed to special categories of people, and the approximations to a target language that constitute the broken language of learners, are similar in many respects, and it is typically not possible, for example, to distinguish between texts of FT and BL without additional diachronic or variational information about the reference language(s). The FT register of a particular language may differ extensively in detail from the BL of a particular learner of the language at some stage in his/her development, but the large component of simplifying or 'developmental' phenomena in both makes for great similarity, and the users of the base language (matrix of FT, target of BL) may think of these as the same thing. For the same reason, linguistically sophisticated investigators may analyze cases of pidginization in terms of a single simplification process, missing the dual aspects of more-or-less conventionalized FT and the BL of learners (cf., e.g., Schumann 1974).

In analyzing reduced speech varieties that have resulted from the use of FT and BL in the same communication situations, it is often difficult to determine the origin of particular features, but in some cases the evidence may be fully adequate for the determination. For example, if a pidgin resulting from interaction of languages A and B is largely a reduced form of A, then simplified features of it cannot readily be identified as FT or BL in origin, but a grammatical feature in it that exists in B and not in A (e.g., inclusive-exclusive distinction in the first person plural pronoun) can be unequivocally assigned to origin in a transfer 'error' of BL.

The interaction of FT and BL can be seen as a kind of summation of elements of both, in which those features that occur in both are reinforced, i.e., are more likely to appear in the final product than are features that occur in only one. In this sense the model is like that of areal diffusion of linguistic features, by which trends in one language are reinforced by similar trends in another so that the languages move closer together typologically (e.g., the post-posed article in Balkan languages or the definite-object marker in South Asian languages). The notion of simple summation is not adequate, however, to account for the interaction of FT and BL, which are much more labile than full-language mother tongues. The speaker of A who is using his FT in talking to a speaker of B may adjust his FT to the latter's BL to an extent not found in other uses of simplified registers (e.g., BT to child). Similarly the FT that the speaker of B hears may be the source of features in his BL that he would not have heard from normal A. Until we have actual texts of interaction of this kind, the origin of a pidgin cannot be followed in detail, and we hope that the texts now becoming available in the study of Gastarbeiterdeutsch promise further research in varied circumstances of pidginization.

3. PIDGINIZATION

3.1. *Informal definition of pidginization*

As we attempt to lay the groundwork for a precise definition of pidginization, we may tentatively define it as the rapid structural modification of a language in certain contact situations in which it serves both as the target of broken language and the source of foreigner talk. Whenever speakers of one language acquire another, they produce broken language, and every speech community has simplified registers in its repertoire. Also, a language in the normal processes of diachronic change may be modified in ways similar to pidginization. The term pidginization, however, seems best limited to those situations in which the structural change is relatively rapid and results from the communicative interaction of native and non-native speakers of the common source/target language. To the extent that commonly occurring pidginized forms are perceived by the users as a structural whole, with some semblance of stability, they may be referred to as a *pidgin*. Pidgins are commonly referred to as languages (cf. the title of Hall 1966, *Pidgin and Creole Languages*) although this usage tends to attribute to them a greater degree of autonomy and stability than many observed instances of pidginization actually show.

The expression 'a language' is multiply ambiguous, and many criteria may be used to answer the question of what properties X must have in order for us to say 'X is a language'. At least three criteria are relevant here: autonomy, stability, and fullness. In one sense of 'a language', X is said to be a language if it is distinct to some specified degree from all other languages, i.e., X and Y are two languages if they differ beyond a certain criterion (e.g., of structural similarity, shared historical change, mutual intelligibility, or speakers' attitudes); otherwise they are varieties of one language. In another sense of 'a language', X is said to be a language if it has some minimal degree of stability. Although all languages in active use are in a state of flux, when the flux apparent in a given set of data X is greater than a certain degree, then X is regarded as transient, incipient, or approximative to a language, rather than being itself a language. In the third sense, X is said to be a language if it is a code with several levels of structure corresponding to phonological, morphosyntactic, lexical, and discourse regularities shared by a community of speakers, and if it is used in a wide range of communicative functions. In this sense a variety without such levels and uses may be called a special language, restricted language, or register, and may be regarded as part of, supplementary to, or parasitic on a full language.

One of the issues examined in this paper is when to consider that a set of pidginized forms constitutes a language, and we are suggesting that when a pidgin meets accepted criteria of autonomy, stability, and fullness it no longer meets the criteria of a pidgin in the restricted sense we are using. To be recognized as a language a pidginized variety must be sufficiently different from the source languages to be mutually unintelligible without special exposure and acquisition, and it must be felt by its users to be a separate entity. It must also be sufficiently homogeneous and stable to be described by a single grammar with variation rather than a combination of grammars. And, perhaps most critical, it must be sufficiently elaborated ("depidginized") to be used in a wide enough range of communicative contexts. These criteria, especially the third one, are often associated with the existence of a mother tongue community, but there is no necessary connection between them. On the one hand "the babies do not wait" for the criteria to be met (Bickerton 1974), and on the other hand a pidginized variety may come to serve a wide range of functions in lingua franca use.

Typical examples of pidgins as defined here are Tây Boi, the pidgin French spoken in Viet Nam, and the Chinook Jargon used in the American Northwest Coast area. Reinecke 1971 described Tây Bồi as consisting chiefly of French words pronounced with French sounds by native speakers of French and with Vietnamese sounds by the Vietnamese and combined in accordance with a reduced and highly variable inventory of French and Vietnamese patterns. Silverstein 1972 describes Chinook Jargon as having a largely Chinook vocabulary pronounced with the phonologies of the various mother tongues and in reduced and variable patterns derived from the respective grammars. Such pidgins are not only reduced in structure and restricted in use but also highly variable and generally intelligible to native speakers of the base language (in the sample cases, French and Chinook respectively).

Certain languages that have traditionally been considered pidgins are similar to creoles in their autonomy, stability, and fullness. Such languages as West African Pidgin, Tok Pisin, and Sango[2] have evolved to the point that they meet the criteria of full languages. For the purpose of brevity in the following discussion, whatever we have to say about creoles may be understood as equally applicable to pidgins that have undergone sufficient elaboration and stabilization to meet the criteria of full languages, although they may not meet the traditional criterion of having a community of mother tongue speakers. What we have to say about pidgins should be understood as limited to pidgins like Tây Bồi and Chinook Jargon. Whatever we choose to call the other type of 'pidgins', it should be clear that they represent a different stage of development than the reduced, hybridized forms of language identified as broken language and foreigner talk.

Generalizations that apply to pidgins in the more restricted sense cannot be extended to all varieties of language traditionally included within the pidgin category, and even the more restricted category we have adopted must ultimately be seen as an idealization. The various forms of language known as pidginized, jargonized, creolized, decreolized, etc., lie at different points along a continuum of linguistic development, of which the initial stage is represented by pidginization. The process that converts pidginized varieties of language into full languages is a different process, even if the end result is sometimes called a pidgin (cf. Whinnom 1971). While we have attempted to restrict the present discussion to the initial process (i.e., pidginization), careful scrutiny of the two sample cases, Tây Bồi and Chinook Jargon, suggests that the latter may lie slightly further along the continuum toward a full language than the former. While Tây Bồi was restricted mainly to communication between native speakers of French and native speakers of Vietnamese, Chinook Jargon often functioned as a lingua franca in situations that excluded native speakers of Chinook and included speakers of several different substrate languages. The relative functional elaboration of Chinook Jargon in comparison with Tây Bồi is matched by such structural elaborations as the appearance of auxiliary verbs in the former (4.3.). Chinook Jargon may be seen as slightly more creolized than Tây Bồi but sufficiently less stable and less elaborated than creoles to be included within a study of pidginization. This last observation should make it clear that the pidgin/creole dichotomy represents an idealization that may be useful as a preliminary means of organizing our research objectives, but it must ultimately give way to a realization that no definite point of transition from a pidgin to a creole can be identified. In the following paragraphs we illustrate some of the distinctive characteristics of pidgins, as opposed to full languages, by pointing out certain inadequacies of traditional grammatical models when applied to pidginization and the need for a dynamic model of verbal interaction to represent adequately its essential characteristics.

3.2. *Pidgin grammars*

The conventional idealized model of a language as a static, homogeneous, synchronic system fails to capture important aspects of any kind of languages, but for 'normal' languages it may still serve as a useful model in many respects. For pidgins, however, it is completely unsatisfactory. The closest we can come to describing a pidgin in static, synchronic terms may be to assume an idealized speaker of some primary language P, who has acquired a minimal degree of proficiency in some second language S, and attempt to characterize his or her linguistic reduction and hybridization of pidgins by specifying the reduced set of morpheme classes, lexical items, and grammatical patterns that tend to be found in broken and foreigner talk varieties of S, filtered through the phonological, lexical, and, to a lesser extent, morphosyntactic system of P.

An idealized grammar of a pidgin English, for example, might be restricted to such major morpheme classes as nouns, pronouns, verbs, adjectives, and adverbs, excluding such minor categories as articles, prepositions, copula, auxiliary *do*, and inflectional affixes. The lexicon might contain only a subset of the basic vocabulary of English, characterized by the elimination of such allomorphic variation as *I ~ me, he ~ him*, etc., and the elimination of near synonyms as *put ~ place, got ~ have*, etc. The grammar might include devices to map S (English) vocabulary items onto components of the P system. Thus the grammar might replace each lexeme of the basic P vocabulary with its closest S equivalent but replace the phonemes of the S lexeme with corresponding P phonemes. The idealized pidgin grammar would probably have to specify very few morphosyntactic patterns derived from P, since most differences of patterning on this level would tend to be cancelled out in the process of reduction, leaving little basis for interference (see Reinecke 1971, however, for examples of morphosyntactic interference in Tây Bồi). The kinds of morphosyntactic interference most likely to occur in a pidgin would be those in which features of reduced S resemble normal P features. The English copula, for example, frequently absent in pidginized English is normally absent in Russian. Negation by means of a single negative particle before the verb phrase is found frequently in pidginized English, but is a normal feature, for example, in Spanish. The grammar would not need a device to map such P features onto the pidgin structure since they are already accounted for by reduction. Instances of substrate interference on the morphosyntactic level are more frequent in creoles than pidgins (e.g., the often observed similarity of Caribbean creoles to West African languages), but even in creoles many instances of possible substrate interference may be just as adequately accounted for on the basis of universal processes of grammatical reduction or elaboration.[3] Possible sentences of the pidgin grammar, therefore, might include any combination of vocabulary items that conforms to the basic word order of S or P. Because of the absence of minor morpheme classes and near synonyms, some of these sentences might be vague or highly ambiguous, but some model of grammar writing could be used to specify the relationship of surface structures to their intended meaning (see Liem 1975 for the use of Fillmore case grammar in this way). The 'ideal pidgin' grammar in effect reduces or 'simplifies' S (presumably by some universal criteria of simplicity) and then maps it onto (or through) P.

3.3. Variation model

While highly idealized and abstract, the 'ideal pidgin' approach has some appeal because it seems to capture two of the main features of pidgins: that they are reduced and hybridized versions of a source language. One shortcoming of the model, however, is its failure to capture the characteristic instability of pidgins in comparison to normal languages. For example, the categorical absence of minor morpheme classes does not correspond to the concrete fact that they are often present to a variable extent in empirical samples of broken language, foreigner talk, and pidgins. Normal English utterances almost always include those features that are variably present in reduced varieties, and thus the description of them in conventional grammars of English as categorically present conforms to observed empirical data to a high degree. The categorical exclusion of such forms, however, from the 'ideal pidgin' is at odds with the high degree of variability in observed data.

Another aspect of the instability of pidgins is seen in the possibility of ranking speakers of broken language along a continuum representing various stages of the language acquisition process, with the implication that speakers closest to the zero point (incipient bilinguals) most closely resemble the ideal pidgin speaker and those nearest the other extreme (full bilinguals) approximate most closely the ideal speaker of normal language.[4]

To reflect adequately the instability of pidgins, our grammatical description would have to depart from the time-honored separation of diachrony from synchrony and of langue from parole and treat the various levels of the continuum according to a variation model of grammar such as an implicational scale (DeCamp 1971, Bailey 1973, Bickerton 1973) or a system of variable rules (Labov 1972, Cedergren and Sankoff 1974). Using the continuum as a frame of reference we could consider given examples of pidgin text as unpidginized or depidginized to the extent that the variable features are present.

3.4. *Interaction model*

Another aspect of pidginization that a static model fails to capture is the distinctiveness of the foreigner talk and broken language components from one another and their influence on one another. Even the specification of two or more discrete 'dialects' of the pidgin, one for native speakers of each source language and one for native S speakers, generated by the respective grammars and universal simplification processes (Silverstein 1972) would give no indication of the interaction effects discussed above in 2.3.

It is clear that foreigner talk represents in part the native speaker's attempt to approximate some notion of broken language, although little is known of the nature and extent of direct borrowing from broken language into foreigner talk.[5] It is reasonable to assume that broken language is also influenced by the foreigner talk component (Schuchardt 1909, Bloomfield 1933, Hall 1966, Ferguson 1971) but here again, the detailed facts of how this influence operates remain to be established through empirical studies.

Interaction models of language behavior are not well developed, although important beginnings have been made. The work of the ethnomethodologists and others who engage in conversational analysis is explicitly interactional (e.g., Goffman 1969, Sudnow 1972) but it pays little attention to developmental change or acquisition. Giles and his colleagues are studying general characteristics of linguistic accommodation between interlocutors (Giles, Taylor, and Bourhis 1973), but their work is far removed from the specifics of pidginization. Probably the most encouraging line of research is in the interactional study of first language acquisition (e.g., Keenan 1974). There are many places in the world today where the interaction between broken language and foreigner talk may be observed firsthand, and carefully planned empirical studies of these language situations could lead to fruitful hypotheses about how incipient speakers of a language interact verbally with mature speakers under a variety of conditions.

Such hypotheses would be expected to fit into a more inclusive framework of communicative competence. Part of communicative competence, we believe, is the ability of incipient speakers of a language to make themselves understood in a language of which they know mainly a reduced set of basic vocabulary items. So too is the ability of mature speakers to reduce and modify the structure of their linguistic output to a level and form deemed appropriate to the lower level of proficiency of their foreign interlocutors. Finally, the ability of speakers of various mother tongues to interpret the variously simplified versions of a lingua franca and to adjust their own productions in accordance with the input is a component of communicative competence. The scientific study of verbal interaction and communicative competence is still in its infancy, and the success of studies within this perspective will depend a great deal on the creativity and resourcefulness of the investigators.

4. CONCLUSIONS

We see pidginization as *a process that accepts normal language as input and produces a reduced, hybridized, and unstable variety of language as output, identified as broken language when used by non-native speakers and foreigner talk when used by native speakers, and identified as a pidgin when viewed as the linguistic output of verbal interaction between native speakers and foreigners in some particular contact situation.* We leave open to empirical research the yet unanswered questions: What sets the pidginization process into motion? Under what conditions does it result in a 'full-blown' pidgin? If the difference between pidgins and creoles is a matter of autonomy, stability, and fullness, what are the criteria, e.g., how stable is stable? In the following paragraphs we shall attempt to answer these questions in a tentative way based on our limited experience and some generally known facts.

4.1. Situations conducive to pidginization

Whenever a language spreads to new speakers it undergoes a certain amount of reduction and instability, even in the case of children learning their mother tongue. It is only in cases of second language acquisition, however, that the characteristic hybridization of pidginized language is found.

A contact situation involving two or more different languages appears to be the most fundamental precondition for pidginization to occur. It is well known, however, that most contact situations do not result in the degree of reduction and stability characteristic of pidgins like Tây Bôi or Chinook Jargon. If the source languages are closely related (e.g., Spanish and Italian in Argentinian *cocoliche*) the output of the contact will be more akin to dialect levelling. The closely related morphosyntactic patterns of the two languages will tend to be substituted for one another rather than simplified as in massive pidginization. Even in the case of unrelated languages, however, if the contact situation is characterized by a relatively high ratio of native target-language speakers to non-native speakers, and by interaction in a wide range of communication situations, any pidginization that occurs will tend to be brief and transient as reduced idiolects rapidly and regularly develop into normal, foreign-accented varieties of the target language.

When a language is learned through formal pedagogic means there seems to be a tendency for speakers to monitor consciously their linguistic performance, correcting observed deviations from the norms of consciously learned 'school' grammar (Krashen 1975, unpublished). Many of the deviations from normal patterns observed at the early stage of naturally-acquired second languages might tend to be eliminated by the self-monitoring of formally taught speakers.

Even if there are a large number of non-native speakers in proportion to native speakers it is less than certain that a full-blown pidgin like Tây Bôi will result. If the languages in contact spread at a symmetrical rate into their respective communities of native speakers, another possible outcome is stable bilingualism, with the component languages assigned to complementary functions (e.g., Spanish and Guaraní in Paraguay). Chances for full development of a pidgin are lessened, as incipient bilinguals of either language will have a better chance of encountering members of the other group who speak their primary language well and fewer reasons to attempt communication in their reduced second language.

The foregoing observations suggest that small scale, transient pidginization merging into foreign-accented normal language is widespread and common, but that the emergence of pidgins like Tây Bồi and Chinook Jargon is relatively uncommon.

4.2. *Preconditions for pidgins*

Chances for the emergence of a pidgin appear to be optimal when the rate of spread of the source language is asymmetrical, with a high incidence of incipient bilingualism among one group that is subordinate in status to another group that places little value on knowledge of the subordinate group's language. Under such conditions, which Bloomfield (1933) discusses under the heading of *intimate borrowing*, speakers of the 'lower' language have no choice but to make themselves understood as best they can in whatever degree of proficiency in the 'dominant' language they may command. He further speculates that speakers of the dominant language assume that the normal variety of their language is too complicated for their subordinates and respond to them in a stereotyped imitation of their broken language (i.e., foreigner talk). Bloomfield's notion of an intimate contact situation summarizes rather well what we consider the preconditions for the development of pidgin. These preconditions may be summarized as follows:

(a) *Asymmetrical spread* of a dominant language among speakers of one or more subordinate languages without reciprocal spread of the subordinate language(s) among dominant language speakers.

(b) A relatively *closed network* of verbal interaction, limited as to speakers and uses, conducive to some degree of stabilization.

(c) An *attitude* on the part of a significant number of users that recognizes the pidginized speech as a separate entity. This may be a condescending attitude on the part of speakers of the dominant language who see the others as unable or unworthy to acquire their language. It may also be the recognition of lingua franca function by speakers of different nondominant languages.

A pidgin emerges if the contact situation in which the pidginization occurs meets these preconditions. As noted above, creole lingua francas like Chinese Pidgin English are not pidgins according to our definition. This point is worth repeating here since Bloomfield lists such languages among his examples of "conventional jargons" and implies that they are representative, in their stability, of the linguistic output of pidginization. Whinnom (1971) proposes to call Chinese Pidgin a pidgin for virtually the same reasons we prefer to call it a creole. The differences are mainly terminological. Whinnom would probably agree that Tây Bôi and Chinese Pidgin are different kinds of entities but chooses to label instances of the former type pidginization and the latter type pidgins. The terminology itself is not as important as understanding the relevant differences, but we see some value in restricting the use of 'pidgin' and classifying together as creoles the varieties that seem to belong with full, normal languages.

4.3. *Pidgin to creole*

When we consider the range of regional, social, stylistic, and individual variation characteristic of normal language it seems clear that the greater stability of normal language in contrast to pidgins is a matter of degree, and that the instability of pidgins represents a component of the total instability of the normal languages of which they are extensions. The question of how stable a pidgin must become before it turns into a creole properly belongs to the study of creolization, and we must limit our comments here to the problem of identifying the terminal stage of pidginization. We have proposed that the initial stage corresponds to the contact situation in which a second language is spreading among speakers of one or more different primary languages, and that given certain preconditions of spread, network, and attitude, the pidginized forms may become a pidgin. Under appropriate conditions the pidgin may begin to stabilize further and develop features that have no counterpart in the source language. A nice example is the appearance of the auxiliary verbs 'make', 'come', and 'go' in Chinook Jargon (of Nootkan etymology, cf. Silverstein 1972, pp. 614-17). The alternation between normal and reduced forms may give way to invariable use of reduced forms: invariable use of English *me* as a first person singular marker, or invariable absence of the English copula, which was variably present in pidginized forms. The competing phonological systems from different source languages merge toward a single system combining elements from various languages and new elements derived through internal processes of change. Pidgin speakers may evolve new aspect markers, subordination devices, and so on to express grammatical relations that cannot readily be inferred from linguistic context and extra-linguistic cues. At the point that processes of stabilization and structural elaboration such as those just mentioned begin to appear, we would consider the pidgin to have embarked upon the stage of incipient creolization, and given the proper conditions, it might continue along the path toward a full creole.

This paper has focussed on the interaction of foreigner talk and broken language in the formation of pidgins. The pidgin/ creole dichotomy adopted for the purpose of delimiting the scope of the study is an admitted idealization of what would be more accurately described in terms of a continuum. Discrete stages of the continuum could be represented within a typology of language situations that would correlate forms of language representing varying degrees of pidginization, creolization, and decreolization with several types of interaction networks characterized by different combinations of variables. A number of these variables have been mentioned in the paper, but others equally important have not been. We need a taxonomy that distinguishes, for example, number and similarity of source languages (Tây Bồi has two unrelated, Chinook Jargon at least four, related and unrelated); degree of dominance of source languages (Sango has one dominant language, Russenorsk had two); shifts in dominance including 'relexification' (the dominance in Chinook Jargon moved from Chinook toward English during its history); presence of a model source language (Krio is 'covered' by Standard English, Sranan is not). Many other variables could be listed, all with effects on the varieties of language in question, and it is our conviction that generalizations about pidginization and creolization are premature and likely to be wrong until a more inclusive taxonomy is available. In the meantime our paper calls attention to one important aspect of the total picture.

NOTES

1. This joint paper grew out of Ferguson's interest in simplified registers and language acquisition and DeBose's interest in creoles and his work on Papiamentu. The paper benefitted from Ferguson's participation in the Conference on German in Contact with Other Languages, held at the University of Essen, December 1975.

2. The difficulty of drawing this line is shown by the fact that there are apparently small populations of mother tongue speakers of these three, especially Tok Pisin (Sankoff and Laberge 1973).

3. Note that this analytic strategy of identifying a phenomenon as interference only when it cannot be accounted for by more general processes is followed also by some investigations in error analysis (cf. Felix 1975).

4. The notion of a unidimensional continuum is used here as a convenient simplification of the situation. We assume that in reality such continua are multidimensional, reflecting the complexity of social groupings and language functions.

5. One of the authors casually observed a native Spanish speaker in Puerto Rico substitute the retroflex *r* of American English for the Spanish trilled *r* in foreigner talk addressed to a native speaker of English. This is an isolated but convincing example of phonological interference from the performance of non-native speakers upon the foreigner talk of native speakers.

REFERENCES

Bailey, Charles-James N. 1973. *Variation and Linguistic Theory.* Arlington, Va.: Center for Applied Linguistics.
Bickerton, Derek. 1973. The nature of a creole continuum. *Language* 49:640-69.
————. 1974. Creolization, linguistic universals, natural semantax and the brain. *Working Papers in Linguistics* 6:125-41. University of Hawaii.
Bloomfield, Leonard. 1933. *Language.* New York: Holt, Rinehart & Winston.
Blount, Ben G. 1972. Aspects of Luo socialization. *Language in Society* 1:235-48.
Brown, Roger. 1973. *A First Language: The Early Stages.* Cambridge, Mass.: Harvard University Press.
Bynon, James. 1975. Domestic animal calling in a Berber tribe. In W. McCormack and S. Wurm, eds., *Language and Man.*
Cazden, Courtney B.; Cancino, Herlinda; Rosanky, Ellen J.; and Schumann, John H. 1975. *Second Language Acquisition Sequences in Children, Adolescents and Adults.* Final Report, Project No. 730744. U. S. Dept. of Health, Education and Welfare, NIE.
Cedergren, Henrietta, and Sankoff, David. 1974. Variable rules: performance as a statistical reflection of competence. *Language* 50:333-53.

Chandola, A. C. 1963. Animal commands of Garwali and their linguistic implication. *Word* 19:203-207.

Clyne, Michael G. 1974. German and English working pidgins. *Linguistic Communications* 13:1-20.

Corder, S. P. 1967. The significance of learners' errors. *International Review of Applied Linguistics in Language Learning* 5:161-70.

DeCamp, David. 1971. Toward a generative analysis of a post-creole speech continuum. In *Pidginization and Creolization of Languages,* D. Hymes, ed., pp. 349-70.

Dulay, Heidi C., and Burt, Marina K. 1972. Goofing: an indication of children's second language learning strategies. *Language Learning* 22:235-52.

Ellis, J., and Ure, J. 1969. Language variety: register. In *Encyclopedia of Linguistics, Information and Control.* London: Pergamon Press.

Ervin-Tripp, Susan M. 1974. Is second language learning like the first? *TESOL Quarterly* 8:111-27.

Felix, Sascha W. 1975. Interference, interlanguage, and related issues. Paper read at the conference on German in Contact with other Languages. Essen.

Ferguson, Charles A. 1963. Linguistic theory and language learning. *Monograph Series on Languages and Linguistics* 16:115-24. (Washington, D. C.: Georgetown University Press.)

————. 1964. Baby talk in six languages. *American Anthropologist* 66.6 Pt. II:103-14.

————. 1971. Absence of copula and the notion of simplicity: a study of normal speech, baby talk, foreigner talk and pidgins. In *Pidginization and Creolization of Languages*, D. Hymes, ed., pp. 141-50.

————. 1975a. Toward a characterization of English foreigner talk. *Anthropological Linguistics* 17:1-14.

————. 1975b. Baby talk as a simplified register. *Papers and Reports on Child Language Development* 9:1-27. In C. E. Snow & C. A. Ferguson, eds., *Talking to Children.* London: Cambridge University Press.

————, and Gumperz, John J. 1960. Introduction. *Linguistic Diversity in South Asia IJAL* 26:3, Part II: 1-18.

Giles, Howard; Taylor, D. M.; and Bourhis, R. 1973. Towards a theory of inter-personal accommodation through language: Some Canadian data. *Language in Society* 2:177-223.

Goffman, Erving. 1969. *Strategic Interaction.* Philadelphia, Pa.: University of Pennsylvania Press.

Hall, Robert A. 1966. *Pidgin and Creole Languages.* Ithaca: Cornell University Press.

Hatch, E.; Shapira, R.; and Gough, J. 1975. "Foreigner-Talk" discourse.

Working Paper in English as a Second Language, U.C.L.A.

Heidelberger Forschungsprojekt "Pidgin Deutsch." 1975. *Sprache und Kommunikation ausländischer Arbeiter.* Kronberg/Ts.: Scriptor Verlag.

Henzl, Věra M. 1974. Linguistic register of foreign language instruction. *Language Learning* 23:207-22.

Hymes, Dell, ed. 1971. *Pidginization and Creolization of Languages.* London: Cambridge University Press.

Keenan, Elinor O. 1974. Conversational competence in children. *Journal of Child Language* 1:163-83.

Krashen, Stephen. 1975. A model of adult second language performance. Paper read at Linguistic Society of America meeting, San Francisco.

Labov, William. 1972. *Sociolinguistic Patterns.* Philadelphia, Pa.: University of Pennsylvania Press.

Liem, Nguyan Dau. 1975. Case in Tai Boy verbs. Paper presented at the International Congress on Pidgins and Creoles, Honolulu.

Meijer, Guus, and Muysken, Pieter. 1977. Chapter 2, this volume.

Nemser, William. 1971. Approximative systems of foreign language learners. *International Review of Applied Linguistics in Language Learning* 9:115-23.

Powell, Patricia B. 1975. Moi Tarzan, vous Jane? A study of communicative competence. *Foreign Language Annals* 8:38-42.

Reinecke, John E. 1971. Tây Bồi notes on the Pidgin French spoken in Vietnam. In *Pidginization and Creolization of Languages,* D. Hymes, ed., pp. 47-56.

Richards, Jack C. 1971. Error analysis and second language strategies. *Language Sciences* 17:12-22. Reprinted in Oller, John, W., Jr., and Richards, Jack C., eds., *Focus on the Learner.* Rowley, Mass.: Newbury House Publishers, pp. 137-52.

————. 1972. Social factors, interlanguage, and language learning. *Language Learning* 22:159-88.

Sankoff, Gillian, and Laberge, Suzanne. 1973. On the acquisition of native speakers by a language. In *Pidgins and Creoles: Current Trends and Prospects,* David DeCamp and Ian F. Hancock, eds. Washington, D. C.: Georgetown University Press, pp. 73-84.

Schachter, Jacqueline. 1974. Contrastive analysis and error analysis.

Schuchardt, Hugo. 1909. Die Lingua Franca. *Zeitschrift für Romanische Philologie* 33:441-61.

Schultheiss, F. 1912. Zurufe an Tiere im Arabischen. *Abhandlungen der kön. Preussischen Akademie der Wissenschaften* (Phil.-hist. Klasse) 1-92.

Schumann, John H. 1974. The implication of interlanguage, pidginization and creolization for the study of adult second language acquisition. *TESOL Quarterly* 8:145-52. Also in Schumann, John H., and

Stenson, Nancy, eds., *New Frontiers in Second Language Learning*. Rowley, Mass.: Newbury House Publishers, pp. 137-52.

Selinker, L. 1972. Interlanguage. *International Review of Applied Linguistics in Language Learning* 10:209-32.

Silverstein, Michael. 1972. Chinook Jargon: language contact and the problem of multi-generative systems. *Language* 48:378-406, 596-625.

Snow, Catherine E. 1972. Mothers' speech to children learning language. *Child Development* 43:549-65.

———, and Ferguson, Charles A., eds. 1977. *Talking to Children: Language Input and Acquisition*. Cambridge: Cambridge University Press.

Sudnow, David, ed. 1972. *Studies in Social Interaction*. New York: The Free Press.

Whinnom, Keith. 1971. Linguistic hybridization. In *Pidginization and Creolization of Languages*, D. Hymes, ed., pp. 91-115.

iii.

The Life-Cycle: Pidginization, Creolization, and Decreolization

Processes of Pidginization in African Languages

Gabriel Manessy

1. INTRODUCTION

1.1. "*Pidginization* is that complex process of sociolinguistic change comprising reduction in inner form, with convergence, in the context of restriction in use.... Pidginization is usually associated with simplification in outer form." This well-known definition given by Hymes (1971, p. 84) describes rather well the topic of my paper, except that "convergence," that is, the totality of the interference phenomena that usually result from language contact, does not appear to me, in Africa at least, to be necessarily related to the process of pidginization nor entailed by it. The Kenya-Pidgin-Swahili of Nairobi described by Heine (1973, pp. 70-118) is certainly much less marked by the influence of the substrate language than is the Katangese Swahili Creole of Lubumbashi (Polomé 1968), which is strongly influenced by Luba. Conversely, ethnic languages such as the varieties of Senufo found in Mali exhibit numerous features ascribable to the dominant language (in this case Bambara) without, so far as we can tell, showing any trace of pidginization. It is not certain, on the other hand, that restriction in use leads in every case to what is ordinarily considered a pidgin or a pidginized variety; one of the results may be the formation of koines, as defined by Samarin (1971, p. 133): "what characterizes them linguistically is the incorporation of features from several regional varieties of a single language." Such regional koines are used in Dyula-speaking regions (Casamance, southern Senegal) where mutual comprehension is often difficult or even impossible between speakers of neighboring villages; these koines are based on the dominant dialects, Fogny in the north, Kasa in the south. It would be interesting to examine from this standpoint the urban varieties of languages such as Wolof in Senegal or Bambara in Mali, which, spoken in the center of the areas where these languages are dominant, serve as a means of communication both for Wolofs or Bambaras speaking different dialects and for foreign speakers of various linguistic backgrounds. Town Bemba, described by Richardson (1961, 1963), is also considered by Samarin (1971, p. 135) as a "kind of koinè with pidgin features."

1.2.   It is important, moreover, to take into consideration, in defining the field of research, the variety of sociolinguistic situations observable in sub-Saharan Africa. There are quantitative and qualitative differences in the restriction of use shown by second languages and in the resulting effects. Nida and Fehderau (1970) make a useful though limited distinction between what they label koines (to which they assign a definition markedly different from Samarin's)—namely, vehicular varieties of a "standard" language recognized as such—and pidgins, defined as autonomous language varieties considered independently of any normative reference to a vernacular (ethnic) language. Thus we may assign to the second group languages such as Lingala in Zaïre, whose origin is a matter of debate, Pidgin English spoken on the coast of the Gulf of Guinea, from Ghana to Cameroon (Mafeni 1971), and even Sango in the Central African Republic, given the very limited influence that vernacular Sango seems to exert on the common language. That vehicular varieties constitute an altogether different case is illustrated by Lacroix's (1959, p. 57) description of the linguistic situation in Ngaoundéré, an urban center in central Cameroon: "learned" Fula speakers know the "correct" language, *fulfulde laam~de*, a literary variety based on the conservative usage of certain rural groups; but the common language is "standard Fula," a variety considered less pure and that shares certain features and tendencies with Fula as spoken by non-native speakers; the latter are either former serfs who have adopted their masters' language or people who have kept their own language but use Fula as a language of wider communication. There results from this situation an extreme variability in the usage of speakers, depending on their degree of sensitivity to the prestige of the correct language or their relative tolerance toward vernacular speech. An analogous difficulty has led Heine (1973, pp. 71, 76) to establish, in his description on what he holds to be a pidginized variety of Swahili, a distinction between maximal and minimal structure at the phonological as well as the morpho-syntactic level in order to account for the pressure that Standard Swahili, broadcast by radio stations, exercises on speaker usage.

1.3.   The interpretation of linguistic variations is further com-plicated by the fact that the dominant norm is not always, and in any case not for all speakers, the vernacular norm. For a long time those among the Bakongos who are the most closely attached to their traditions have been chagrined by the fact that young people hardly use any other variety than Kituba, a corrupted form of the language according to traditionalists and a bona fide pidgin according to Nida and Fehderau (1970, p. 148), but which in the eyes of the present generation represents the modern form of the ancestral language. The sociolinguistic study G. Partmann (1973) devoted to Ivory Coast vehicular Dyula demonstrates conclusively that for the Dyula schoolchildren that composed her control sample, the target norm is no longer represented by their elders' speech, the medium of transmission of the ethnic group's inner values, but by "trade" Dyula, the symbol of modernism. Reputed to speak Dyula well are those engaged in a modern profession: cocoa or coffee growers, businessmen, radio announcers. The same phenomenon is observed in communities where the language still assumes the function of ethnic identifica-tion: it is rare for young people, at least those who have been educated (by means of French), not to distinguish between "old people's speech" and their own usage. But the latter very often shows characteristics that, if they were noted in a speech variety recognized as a contact vernacular, would be interpreted as features of pidginization; for instance "learned" Dagaras[1] effect the following replacements: (1) such synthetic forms as *nɔ̄rá* "rooster" or *pélē* "lamb" by analytic compounds: *nɔ̄-dāā* "male of the hen," respectively *pēr=bīlē* "young of sheep"; (2) variant forms of the object pronoun attested after certain monosyllabic verbs (*ὼ sò-ṁ à* "he washed me," *ὼ sò-b́ à* "he washed you") by the full forms of that pronoun and of the post-posed particle *ὼ sò mé nà, ὼ sò fὼ nà;* (3) the interrogative marker consisting of the lengthening of the final vowel of the utterance by an explicit marker (adapted, moreover, from French *est-ce que*): *ísíké fὼ nà wá nā* "will you come?" instead of *fὼ nà wá nāā*. This usage is in no way viewed as slipshod; on the contrary, it is expressly proposed as a norm whenever the standardization of the language (for example, for pedagogical objectives) is considered.

1.4.   Thus it seems that the pidginization process is not necessarily linked to speech varieties having the status of lingua franca. It is likely to occur whenever there is a break in linguistic tradition, whatever the causes for that break may be. If one takes into account the political and socioeconomical upheavals to which Africa has been subjected, he can readily perceive the magnitude of this phenomenon and the importance of its analysis for the interpretation of linguistic facts. My aim is to attempt this analysis, within the limits set by available documentation, without taking into account a sociolinguistic typology whose relevance does not appear evident to me. It is clear that the effects of the break in the linguistic tradition should be particularly noticeable in speech varieties liberated from all inherited norms, that is to say, in "pidgins" as defined by Nida; but actual processes of pidginization are likely to appear with greater clarity to the extent that one can compare speech varieties where they apply to those that result from the "normal," continuous evolution of the language under consideration. My study below will therefore focus on these privileged cases, and pidgins will simply furnish complementary illustration.[2]

2. MORPHOPHONOLOGICAL ASPECTS OF PIDGINIZATION

2.1. *Phonetic replacements*

Generalizations are certainly most hazardous at the level of phonological structure. It appears that the number and the diversity of distinctive features found in non-native varieties of African languages are more reduced than in corresponding vernacular languages: this fact has been reported for the A 70 pidgin (vehicular Bulu) of southern Cameroon (Alexandre 1963, p. 579); for the Fula "koine" of Ngaoundéré (Lacroix 1959); for the non-native Hausa used by an Ibo informant, at least insofar as consonants are concerned (Hodge 1958), for Nigerian Pidgin English (Mafeni 1971), for Nairobi vehicular Swahili (Heine 1973, 1975); this reduction also characterizes Fanagalo in South Africa, as shown by the comparison of the phonemic inventory established by Heine (1973) with that proposed by Doke for the Nguni languages (1954, p. 92). The phonological distinctions that are most often eliminated involve adjustment of the glottis (voicing in vehicular Swahili, injectives in Fula and Nguni, glottal stops in Fula, ejectives in Hausa) or of the tongue musculature (affricates in Hausa and Swahili, tongue height level for mid vowels in Fula and Bulu).

The interpretation of these facts is unclear. The explanation that comes first to mind is that of a dual economy, reduction of articulatory effort and ease of the perception of the auditory signal. It does not, however, account for the preservation of pre-nasalized stops of Fula as spoken by non-native speakers or of a distinction as subtle as that which exists in Fanagalo between alveolar laterals: non-fricative *l*, voiceless fricative *ɬ* and voiced fricative *lʒ*. Two factors seem to come into play: on the one hand, interference from the users' native language, and on the other hand, the functional load of oppositions. It is certainly not by chance that Kituba, spoken in the Kikongo domain (and indeed far beyond), exhibits a phonological system identical to that of Kikongo (Fehderau 1966, p. 58); similarly, Samarin (1970b, p. 668) accounts for the maintenance in Sango of the three punctual tones of Ngbandi-Sango-Yakoma by the single fact that vehicular Sango is utilized by speakers of tone languages, which confirms the magnitude of the variability observed in this area (Samarin 1970a, p. 13). It is, moreover, remarkable that distinctions normally eliminated are preserved, by exception to the general tendency, precisely in situations where they are of some utility: thus, in Lubumbashi Swahili, initial *h* is rarely heard and alternates with ϕ, except in negative verb forms, where it serves precisely to indicate the negative marker *ha-* and where it is never lost (Annicq 1967). Nothing allows one to suppose that the pidginization process implies on the paradigmatic axis a restructuring of the system of the source language; on the contrary, one has the impression that the users of the pidginized variety exploit their own phonological system by adapting it and suppressing its most salient particularities[3] and by observing some lexical conventions, such as the pre-aspiration of the vowel marking negation in the above-mentioned case from Swahili. To support this hypothesis, one may point to the extreme variability of phonetic realizations, which casts a doubt on the validity of the system that the linguist is forced to posit in order to devise a coherent transcription: as for example when Heine (1973, p. 72) opposes a phoneme /ch/ realized as [ɟ, ç, c, ʃ] to /j/ which appears as [ɟ, dʒ, ndʒ, c, y], to /sh/ ([s] or [ʃ]), to /s/ ([ç] or [s]), to /z/ ([s] or [z]); this means that each of these various phones may be interpreted as the realization of at least two phonemes: [ʃ] is the realization of /ch/ or /sh/, [ç] of /s/ or /ch/, [s] of /sh/, /s/ or /z/, etc.

2.2. *Syllable structure*

On the other hand one must impute to pidginization the widely attested tendency toward optimal syllabification, in which vocalic and consonantal segments alternate regularly. The manifestations of this tendency are multiple and diverse. In Nairobi vehicular Swahili, and to a lesser degree in that of Lubumbashi, there appear supporting vowels in initial consonant clusters of the type NC: *i* before *n* and *u* before *m* (*inchi* "country," *umbwa* "dog," as opposed to Standard Swahili *nchi* and *mbwa*, respectively; Heine 1973, p. 47). In Kituba, contiguous vowels are excluded (Fehderau 1966, p. 47); they are also partially excluded in Zaïre Swahili, where an epenthetic -*l*- is frequently inserted between hetero-syllabic vowels: *kilatu* "shoes," instead of St. Sw. *kiatu; kufula*, instead of *kufua* (Polomé 1968, p. 18). The same concern for syntagmatic regularity might perhaps justify in part the care with which speakers of vehicular Dyula pronounce the intervocalic velar stop, often not very audible in the pronunciation of real Dyulas (Partmann 1973, p. 60). In Pidgin English, consonant clusters are reduced, either by the elimination of one of the consonants or by the insertion of a vowel; this fact is reported for Nigerian Pidgin English (Mafeni 1971, p. 108) and for Cameroon Pidgin English (De Féral 1975, p. 54). The latter author lists *pun* "spoon," *tanop* "stand up," *milik* "milk," *simok* "smoke"; it appears furthermore that in CVC syllables, -C constitutes the weak position where neutralizations are numerous and deletions frequent "not only in rapid speech, but also in isolated words" (De Féral 1975, p. 55). In Sango final vowels are elided in utterances after an immediately preceding or before an immediately following word-initial vowel: *lo* (ɛ)*kɛ* (*a*)*pɛ* "he isn't here," *mbi bá*(*a*) (*a*)*pɛ* "I don't see" (Samarin 1970a, p. 16). In all these cases, the result is the organization of utterances into a succession of open syllables.

2.3. *Optimum perceptibility of formatives*

Such an organization allows for as clear a realization of significant contrasts as possible and it no doubt facilitates the identification of distinctive units. An analogous explanation might account for the tendency to model formatives on dominant patterns: in Nairobi vehicular Swahili monosyllabic verbal bases are systematically extended by the use of a prefix *ku-*, which is used moreover to form infinitives; i.e., on the basis of St. Sw. *-ja* (infinitive *kuja* "to come") is formed Veh. Sw. *kuja* and its corresponding infinitive *kukuja* (Heine 1973, p. 108). According to Heine (1973, p. 144; 1975, point 9), in the vehicular varieties of Bantu languages the number of syllables per word is supposed to aim toward an optimal figure of two, a number smaller than that which is in fact attested in corresponding vernacular varieties. Heine (1973, p. 145) points out moreover that in Chinese and Melanesian Pidgin English this number tends, on the contrary, to be higher than the average observed in English, namely 1.26 syllables per word; from this he concludes that the disyllabic structure of the word is a substantive feature of pidginization. If this generalization is confirmed by other studies it would account for particularities such as that reported by Partmann (1973, p. 70) for vehicular Dyula: in that speech variety the French word *craie* "chalk" has been borrowed with its definite article, *lakre*, although the syllable type CCV (where -C- is *r* or *l*) conforms to ethnic Dyula syllable structure and the word *crayon* "pencil" has been adopted without any other modification except the deletion of the glide, *kreõ*.

2.4. *Invariability of formatives*

A tendency that manifests itself even more clearly is that which tends to endow formatives with a form at the same time full and stable. In Nairobi, vowel initial disyllabic verbal bases such as *-enda* "to go," *-isha* "to have finished" are regularized, as are monosyllabic CV bases, by the adjunction of *ku-*, realized in that case as kw- (*-kwenda, -kwisha*); this has the effect of maintaining for the prefix, when it functions as infinitival morpheme, its full form *ku-* (*ku-kwenda, ku-kwisha*, instead of St. Sw. *kw-enda, kw-isha*; Heine 1973, p. 108). In the same speech variety, the morphophonemic alternation *i/e* that appears regularly in verb derivational suffixes in Lubumbashi as well as in vernacular Swahili (*i* after the pre-suffixal vowels *a, i, u; e* after *e* and *o: -pok.e.a.* "to receive," *-tum.i.a.* "to have sent") is eliminated and speakers may choose between the two vowels (Heine 1973, p. 100). In the Fula "koine" of Ngaoundéré and also in urban varieties of the language, especially among young speakers, the complex consonantal alternation of the "correct" variety is suppressed, which, at the beginning of verb forms, opposes the three persons of the singular to corresponding persons of the plural (compare *ʔo haari*, "he ate his fill" vs. *ɓe kaari* "they ate their fill," *ʔo wari* "he came" vs. *ɓe ~gari* "they came," with koine *gorko wari* "a man came" vs. *worbe wari* "some men came") (Lacroix 1959, p. 61). Dyula, where utterance constituents are usually composed of invariable lexemes, scarcely offers a fruitful ground for morphophonemic simplification.[4] The latter process nonetheless manifests itself in the vehicular variety by the elimination of a frequently appearing morphological mechanism, reduplication; instead of *a ka sogo tige tige* "he cut (*tige*) the meat (*sogo*) in small pieces," Partmann's informants produced *a ka sogo tige fitini fitini*, thus transferring from the verb to an explicit modifier (*fitini* "small") the process of emphasis. Another alternative, whose result is also to preserve the invariability of the verb, consists in repeating the entire verbal phrase: instead of *a ka a sē ko ko* "he ceaselessly washed (*ko*) his foot (*sē*)," speakers use *a ka a sē ko ka a sē ko* (Partmann 1973, p. 78).

3. THE EXPRESSION OF GRAMMATICAL CATEGORIES AND SYNTACTIC RELATIONSHIPS

The morphophonemic modifications that languages undergo because of their specialization in referential function facilitate the identification of formatives in the speech chain continuum. An analogous explanatory principle seems to account for the particular features pidginized speech varieties show in the expression of grammatical categories and syntactic relationships.

3.1. *Paradigmatic univocity*

3.1.1. By "paradigmatic univocity" I mean, following the definition proposed by Hjelmslev (1938, p. 285; 1939, p. 373), the stable relationship that obtains between a content level unit (a "morpheme" in Hjelmslev's terminology) and an expression level unit (or "formative"). The latter tends to be explicitly expressed: for instance, in the equational construction Sango systematically makes use of the copula ɛkɛ (*í ɛkɛ ázo* "we are people"), which does not appear at the surface level in Ngbandi (*é ázi* "we are people"; Samarin 1971, p. 125); instead of the tonal derivational process used in the latter language to derive nouns from verbal bases, Sango substitutes an affixal derivation in *-ngó* (Samarin 1970b, p. 668; 1970a, p. 70). In vehicular varieties of Swahili (Le Breton 1936, p. 16; Heine 1973, p. 81), prefixes and infixes, which, in Standard Swahili, express within verb forms subject and object pronoun (*ninakupiga* "I hit you," *alimpiga* "he hit me") are replaced by full and invariable pronominal forms (*mimi napiga wewe, yeye alipiga mimi*). Moreover, the morpheme must be, as much as possible, distinct from any other: vernacular Dyula contains a suffix *-ya* which makes it possible to derive from an adjectival base (for example, *jugu* "bad, evil") a verbal (*a jugu-ya-ra* "he became bad") as well as a nominal (*jugu-ya lo* "that's badness"). In vehicular Dyula, the verbal derivative has become rare, but it is attested; on the other hand, the nominal has practically disappeared, and it is being eventually replaced by an analytic expression such as *a ka jugu* "he is bad" (Partmann 1973, pp. 79, 81). One may ascribe to the same concern for the removal of ambiguity the distinction effected in Lubumbashi Swahili between the Class 7 prefix and singular marker *ki-* (*kilima,* pl. *vilima* "hill, mountain") and *ka-*, a diminutive prefix borrowed perhaps from Chiluba (*chupa<*ki-upa* "bottle," *kachupa* "small bottle"; Polomé 1968, p. 20). Vernacular Swahili assigns the two functions to *ki-: kisu* "a knife," *visu* "knives" but *kibuzi* "a small goat (*mbuzi*)," *kilima* "a small mountain (*mlima*), a hill" (Ashton 1944, p. 295). Nairobi Swahili no longer has *ki-* as a number marker, but it has preserved *ka-* as a diminutive (Heine 1973, p. 84).

3.1.2.   A third characteristic of univocity consists in the singleness of the "formative." It manifests itself by the elimination of agreement mechanisms that require the expression of the same "morpheme" in several points of an utterance. The Bantu languages exhibit, with respect to their noun class system, a process of that type whose complexity elicited the admiration of C. Meinhof and the first Bantuists: it involves the totality of noun determiners and substitutes as well as verb forms, and may be governed by an adverbial form with a pronominal base (Swahili *hapa pamekufa simba* "here died a lion") as well as by a noun (Swahili *wanafunzi wasoma vitabu vingi* "the pupils read numerous books"). This process, which is well attested in vernacular varieties of Swahili, has completely disappeared from vehicular varieties of the language, where adjectives and numerals are invariable (Nairobi Swahili *watu kidogo* "a small number of men," *pesa kidogo* "little money"; Lubumbashi Swahili *kitanda muzuri* "a good bed," *batu*

tatu "three men") and where the pronominal system is no longer
related to the noun class system (Polomé 1968, p. 20; Heine 1973,
pp. 77-80). Similarly, in Lingala adjectives and numerals are
invariable (Guthrie 1939, pp. 42, 46). In vehicular Bulu, noun
modifiers are sometimes inflected for plural, but they usually
remain invariable (Alexandre 1963, p. 581). Expressed only once
in a clause, a grammatical morpheme appears in principle under a
single form. This may be illustrated by observing the manifestation
of the negative copula in various forms of Swahili. In vernacular
forms, it is *si* (*si kijiko* "it isn't a spoon," *sisi si wevi* "we aren't
thieves"), whereas the affirmative copula is *ni.* In vehicular
Swahili, this copula is generally *iko*; for negation, the Lubumbashi
variety has available two forms, the presentative *haina* (*haina bey
nguvu* "it isn't a high price") and the equational *hana* (*dada yangu
hana ya tumbo moya* "my sister is not from the same belly [as I
am]"). In "Congo" Swahili material collected in Astrida by B.
Lecoste (1960), the negative copula is formed by the adjunction
of the prefix *ha-*—normally appearing initially in verbal forms—to
the copula (*pombe haiko kitu mubaya* "beer is not a bad thing");
in Nairobi, use is made of the negative adverb *hapana* (*matunda
mingi hapana iko* "there isn't much fruit," *Bwana Kamau hapana
iko mwalimu* "Mr. Kamau isn't a professor" (Heine 1973, pp.
95-96.) In the latter two cases the negative marker that obligatorily accompanies the verb has been extended to the copula with a
resulting unification in the expression of the negative. In the same
way, Sango has retained only one of the connective particles *té*
and *tí* that characterize in Ngbandi the determination relation
(Samarin 1970, p. 128). Commercial Dyula utilizes only one of
three attributive particles of Bambara: *ku* (actual holding), *bolo*
(possession), *fè* (property). It is remarkable that this particle is not
the one that in the source language is the least marked
semantically, but *fè*, whose distribution is the widest, for it
indicates temporal and spatial localization as well as attribution
(Partmann 1973, p. 96).

3.1.3.   The most striking example of simplification in the mode
of expression of grammatical categories is furnished by vehicular
varieties of languages with class systems. "Correct" Fula distrib-
utes singular noun forms in nineteen classes and corresponding
plural forms in five, all of them characterized by a suffix, by the
presence or the absence of consonant alternations at the beginning
of the noun root, and by a particular anaphoric element. There
exists in addition in all Fula dialects an irregular plural formation

process consisting of the adjunction to the singular form (containing its suffix) of a suffix *-ji* or *-je* (belonging respectively to the plural classes with pronouns *ɗi* and *ɗe*) or, for nouns referring to human beings, of the morpheme *-ʔen*. It is this process that is being generalized in the koine variety, where only the frequently used correct forms, i.e., those that are strongly lexicalized, are preserved. And even the latter tend to be regularized: one hears *dõngalji* "loads" instead of *donle* (sg. *dõngal*), *faãndeeji* "stewpans" instead of *payande* (sg. *faãnde*), *gorkoen* "men" instead of *worɓe* (sg. *gorko*), *laamidoen* "chiefs" instead of *laamiiɓe* (sg. *laamido*). The same phenomenon is noted in the normal usage of urbanized Fulani (Lacroix 1959, pp. 62-66). A quite analogous phenomenon is developing in Kituba. The latter language has preserved six "genders," that is to say six pairs of singular and plural classes remaining from the dozen that are found in Kikongo (plus the locative classes). But in the Brazzaville region and, to a certain extent, in the other regions, one notices a tendency to make the prefix *ba-* the unique plural marker, whether it be substituted for the other prefixes (*bwala* "village," pl. *babwala* instead of *mabwala*), added to them (*diboko* "arm," pl. *bamaboko* instead of *maboko*), or pre-posed to the singular form (*kinzu* "pot," pl. *bakinzu* instead of *binzu*) (Fehderau 1966, p. 114). It is clear that in such a usage, morphophonemic variation in the noun form is no longer interpreted as the expression of number but as a phenomenon of suppletion undergoing regularization. This is the conclusion reached by Heine (1973, pp. 84-85) when he interprets the contrast sg. *mtu* vs. pl. *watu* "man" of vehicular Swahili as the contrast ϕ vs. *wa-*, *-mtu* and *-tu* constituting two variant forms of the same root, the first one being moreover compatible with the expression of plurality: *mtu kumi* "ten men." Nairobi Swahili has only three "genders," based on the contrast of a single singular form ϕ to three plural markers: *wa-* (*mlevi*, pl. *walevi* "drunkard"), assigned to alternating roots;[5] *ma-* (*shamba*, pl. *mashamba* "field," *rafiki*, pl. *marafiki* "friend"); ϕ (*miti*, pl. *miti* "tree," *kisu*, pl. *kisu* "knife"). The noun class system of vehicular Bulu does not appear to have reached such a degree of reduction, but rather, it seems to be characterized, at least on the basis of the summary indications provided by Alexandre (1963, p. 580), by the confusion of "genders" and the predominance of the plural prefix *be-* (*oceŋ* pl. *beceŋ*, or *beoceŋ* "knife," instead of *oceŋ*, pl. *aceŋ*). In Fanagalo, of the fifteen classes and eight genders of Zulu there remains but one contrast consisting of sg. ϕ vs. pl. *ma-* or *zi-*, except for a few forms that preserve the prefix *um-* in the singular and, in the plural, the prefix *ba-* in the case of nouns referring to human beings, and *mi-* in the contrary case (Cole 1953, p. 5; Heine 1973, pp. 125-28).

3.2. Syntagmatic univocity

3.2.1.   A remarkable feature of the pidginized varieties of African languages is the decomposition of complex forms, or in other words, the frequent substitution of an analytic construction for a synthetic one. In the preceding section examples were provided in the course of the discussion of the use of pronominal forms and of the negative copula in vehicular Swahili. With regard to the latter feature, it is necessary to point out that *hapana* is the regular negative marker in the Lubumbashi as well as the Nairobi variety, being pre-posed to the infinitive form in the former variety (*mi hapana kulala kesho* "I won't sleep tomorrow") and to the verb root in the latter (*mimi hapana piga wewe* "I don't [didn't, won't] hit you") (Annicq 1967, passim; Polomé 1968, p. 22; Heine 1973, p. 93). There remain only lexicalized and no doubt opaque synthetic forms: *sijui* "I don't know," *sitaki* "I don't want." Similarly Fanagalo has replaced the complex system of positive and negative conjugations of southern Bantu languages[6] by a single negative element, *aikhona*, preceding a verb form (Heine 1973, p. 133). In Swahili, what Polomé terms "complex structures"[7] (1967, p. 131) have more or less disappeared from vehicular varieties; in Lubumbashi, the locative suffix *-ni*, in speech varieties where it is preserved, has fused with the noun root (*mukini* "village"), place being indicated by means of a preposition (*katika*) or by a periphrastic construction (*ndani ya nyumba* "inside the house") (Polomé 1968, p. 20).

3.2.2.   The latter example illustrates the importance assumed in pidginized varieties by semantically full lexemes (*ndani* is a noun) at the expense of grammatical markers. In vernacular Hausa, the formation of the plural of nouns is a very complex process involving a dozen suffixes and diverse modifications of the noun stem: partial or total reduplication, vowel alternations; furthermore, several plural forms may correspond to the same singular form (Brauner 1965, p. 117). In the vehicular variety the plural is obtained by the adjunction of *deyawa* "much" to the singular form (Hodge 1958, p. 59). In Pidgin English, it is the third person plural pronoun that assumes this function: *à nó sí dì tíchà-dem* "I didn't see the teachers" (Mafeni 1971, p. 110). Vernacular Dyula, like Bambara, and other Mandé languages, disposes of an abundant set of derivational affixes on the basis of which, starting with nominal or verbal stems, are formed diminutives, augmentatives, agentives, nouns of state, quality, tribal groups, etc., and, starting with verb stems, transitives and inchoatives. Partmann's study has revealed a distinct abandonment of this process on the part of non-native Dyula speakers as well as on the part of those for whom it is the first language. Both groups of speakers prefer to the use of the diminutive prefix *-ni* and the augmentative suffix *-ba* that of the modifiers *fitini* "small," *deni* "child," and *gbele* "big"; to the suffixes of agent (*-la*), of state (*-mã*), of origin (*-ka*), they prefer periphrases such as "people (*mɔgɔ*) of the smithy" or clauses such as "he comes from . . .," "he lives in . . . ." It is as if the speaker would free himself from the constraining framework of the grammatical category to confer greater precision on the referential content of the utterance: the choice of *fitini* or *deni* rather than *-li* enables him or her to differentiate a person of small stature from a young one. Likewise, the "correct" expression *a juguyara* "he became bad" decomposes itself into two statements, one underscoring the factual state (*a ka jugu* "he is bad") and the other the contingent or recent nature of the phenomenon by the substitution of the adverb *sisã* "now" for the suffix *-ya* (Partmann 1973, pp. 73-83). If my interpretation is correct, this is a manifestation of the same concern for explicitation which, in my opinion also manifests itself at the morphophonemic level (cf. 2.3. and 2.4.). More simply, the utilization of lexical resources may avoid the risk of confusion: in vehicular Bulu, tonal contrasts are preserved but nevertheless "it seems . . . that homophonous minimal pairs distinguished by tone are avoided, either by the disuse of one of the words of a pair or by its incorporation into a complex expression. Thus it is that the minimal pair *m̀bàŋ: m̀bǎŋ* 'elephant tusk: palm nut' is replaced by the paired expressions *mbaŋ-alen: mbaŋə-zok* 'mbang of a palm tree: *mbang* of an elephant' where tone no longer plays a differentiative role" (Alexandre 1963, p. 579).

3.3. *The linear organization of utterances*

3.3.1.   This type of organization is in itself a direct consequence of the principle of syntagmatic univocity, which excludes the fact that several content level units be represented by the same expression level unit. What is important in this regard is that, in all the cases studied, the position of the expression level units relative to each other becomes the index of the relationship between

them.[8] This may be illustrated by the comparison of two
synonymous utterances ("the old man said to the policeman") in
standard and in vehicular Hausa: *tsoofo m mùtum yaagayà wàd'-
ansàndaa* versus *sofo mutum geya dansanda* (Hodge 1958, p. 60).
The latter version exhibits the elimination of (in addition to the
redundant 3 sg. prefixed pronoun *yaa-*) the particle *n* (here
realized as *m*) post-posed to the head element of the determinative
construction and a signal of this syntactic relationship[9] and the
functive *wà*, the marker of the "dative"; the syntactic structure of
the utterance is then indicated only by the relative position of its
constituents: subject before predicate, head element before
modifier, complement following verb. The same generalization
may be made about vehicular Swahili. In the standard variety, the
relations among the various clauses are signalled by conjunctions,
by the selection of mode and "tense" (what Ashton [1944, p.
395] labels "conjunctions expressed in verb forms") and by
relatives.[10] Nairobi Swahili preserves most of the conjunctions of
standard Swahili, except for the use of *kama, ya kuwa,* and
kwamba to introduce object clauses, and substitutes for the other
processes two rules that operate conjointly: on the one hand,
when an element is shared by several clauses constituting the same
sentence, it is normally deleted after having been expressed the
first time (Heine 1973, p. 118); on the other hand, to embedded
clauses, that is, clauses functioning as sentence constituents, are
applied the same ordering rules that apply to the latter: the object
follows the verb (*baba nasema mtoto bado iko kidogo sana* "the
father says that the child [*mtoto*] is still too small"); the modifier
follows the head constituent (*mtu ile mimi naona φ jana kwisha
kufa* "the man [that] I saw yesterday [*jana*] is dead") where φ
marks the place of the deleted object pronoun (*mimi naona yeye
jana* "I saw him yesterday"). Finally vehicular Swahili, like the
standard variety, employs embedded clauses to express adverbial
complements, but instead of marking these clauses by means of
complex morphemes (*-po-, -mo-, -ko-, -vyo-*) that refer to the
general functioning of a noun classification system, it makes
explicit the adverbial relation by representing it by means of a
substantive (*saa* "hour," *siku* "day," *pahali* "place," *namna*
"manner") (cf. Heine 1973, p. 117), the latter, occupying in the
utterance the position assigned to adverbial complements: *saa ile
mimi nakuja hapa mimi naona mtu ya biashara* "as soon as I came
here, I saw the tradesman (lit. the man of trade)"; *dereva kwisha
sahau pahali ile gari yake iko* "the driver forgot the place (where)
his car (*gari*) is"; *yeye bado eleza mimi namna ile pesa napotea* "he

hasn't yet explained to me the way (by which) the money disappeared." The structure of the sentence is essentially the same in vehicular and in standard Swahili, but the means of expression are fundamentally different.

3.3.2. A significant consequence of the importance accorded to the position of the word in an utterance, as an indicator of its function, is the high degree of word class shift often observed in vehicular varieties. Hodge (1958, p. 62) points out that, whereas standard Hausa uses nouns functioning as predicates only if they are "actualized" by *nàà* "to be in" or, in the case of a completed action, by *yi* "to do" (*naayi màganà* "I have spoken [lit. I have made speech]"), vehicular Hausa readily treats the noun as a verb: *naamagana,* lit. "me speech." Similarly in Krio (Jones 1971, p. 79), the same term is indifferently noun, verb, or adjective, depending on the place it occupies in an utterance: *a de sing* "I am singing," *a lɛk dis sing* "I like this song," *dis sing biznes ya dɔn mɔna mi o* "I've had too much of this singing business." It is no doubt by virtue of the same principle that vehicular Dyula has eliminated the distinction between cardinal and ordinal numerals in favor of the former (Partmann 1973, p. 81).

4. MODIFICATION OF INNER FORM

It is difficult to evaluate the modification undergone by what Hjelmslev (1968, p. 13) calls "content form." It is easy enough to confuse the content system with its expression. From the rarity of "coordinators" (relative prefixes, prepositions, tense markers, etc.) Scotton concludes in favor of the existence in vehicular Swahili of "an abbreviated syntax, consisting mainly of content words, with the listener left to make the connections" (1969, p. 101). I believe, together with Polomé (1968, p. 23), that there are no profound divergences between vernacular Swahili and its vehicular varieties in the domain of syntax, and that "abbreviation" is a superficial phenomenon (cf. above 3.3.1.). Moreover, it is probably not justified to view as a mark of reduction of inner form the suppression of grammatical constraints linked to certain formal characteristics of utterance constituents. The elimination in vehicular Hausa of the gender opposition masculine versus feminine indicated in the standard variety by the form of personal pronouns and, in the singular, by that of the presentative, of the determiner suffixed to the substantive, and of the adjective

(Hodge 1958, p. 59) implies nothing more than the disappearance of a traditional distinction, however empty semantically, between two classes of substantives. The simplification of systems of nominal classes functioning as means for the representation of number represents the same order of phenomena (Martinet 1967, p. 19).

In a few cases, however, analogies noted between vehicular varieties of languages very distant one from another from a typological, genetic, and geographical point of view suggest that certain shared innovations, consisting of reductions or restructuring, may stem from the pidginization process itself.

4.1. *Reduction*

4.1.1.   An example of reduction is provided by the elimination, when it is attested in vernacular varieties, of the distinction between immediate determination (also termed necessary, natural, or inalienable) and mediate determination (contingent, contractual, or alienable). Vernacular Dyula juxtaposes immediately the determining to the determined noun (in that order) only if the second element is a noun referring to a part of the body or to certain kinship relationships; in all the other cases, a particle (*ka, ta,* or *la*) is inserted between the two terms (Long and Diomandé 1970, p. 36). In vehicular Dyula the content difference implied by the presence or the absence of the particle is no longer perceived; *ka* has become the marker of the determination relation and ϕ is simply one of its variant realizations. As is generally the case, it is the explicit variant that has been generalized (Partmann 1973, p. 90). An identical phenomenon has occurred in Sango (Samarin 1971, p. 128). Contrary to what happens in Ngbandi, where necessary determination is marked by the contiguous juxtaposition of the two constituents of the syntagma and contingent determination by the insertion of *tí* or *té*, Sango employs in all cases *tí* or *nà* "for" (with very diverse semantic values, cf. Samarin 1970a, p. 58), and, more rarely, ϕ in lexicalized phrases that Samarin considers to result from the deletion of *tí* (1970a, p. 70).

4.1.2.   Such a restructuring indicates a reorganization of the semantic system evidenced also by the high degree of polysemy observed in the vocabulary of the pidginized speech varieties. Thus vehicular Dyula tends to use only a single word *yiri* where the vernacular variety establishes a distinction between *yiri* "tree or wood," *logo* "firewood," *-sū* "plant" (*kafesū* "coffee plant," *tigasū* "peanut plant"); similarly, when native speakers of Dyula make use of *fitini* or *deni* instead of the diminutive suffix *-ni* (cf. 3.2.2. above), they do so deliberately and designate a young person (as opposed to an adult) by *deni* and an individual of small stature by *fitini*; non-native speakers are indifferent to this distinction and, as a general rule, employ the most frequent term, namely *fitini* (Partmann 1973, pp. 46, 80). For Sango, Bouquiaux (1969, p. 64) estimates at about a thousand the common vocabulary and Roulon at a little more than two hundred "the average basic vocabulary necessary for someone to correctly handle the language" (1972, p. 157); *nyàmà* refers to any animal and any type of meat, *mànyēer* or *màyérè* is translated by Bouquiaux as "manner, way, skill, hability, ruse, pride, haughtiness, artifice, science." This polysemy is compensated for, in communication, by the use of periphrases of which a certain number are widely employed (*mólèngē tí kɔlī* "male child, boy," *mólèngē tí wálī* "girl"), but most of which are *Augenblicksbildungen* (nonce forms), for example, for "roof" the use of *ndō tí dà, lì tí dà* "top of a hut, head of a hut" (Roulon 1972, p. 157).

4.2. Restructuring

4.2.1. As Samarin points out (1971, p. 125), pidginization does not necessarily entail the impoverishment of a vernacular language. If certain semantic distinctions are eliminated, others may appear or develop. Such a case seems to be evidenced by vehicular varieties of classifying languages where the formal process of the classification of substantives tends to give way to meaningful contrasts on the content level. Thus, in vehicular Bulu speakers sometimes still observe the agreement rule between the subject substantive and the verb prefix, but they take into consideration the meaning of the former: they use *a-* for the singular and *be-* for the plural in the case of an animate, and *e-* for the singular and *mi-, me-,* or *bi-* for the plural in the opposite case (Alexandre 1963, p. 580). In the Fula koine of Ngaoundéré, the adjective-noun agreement is based on an analogous principle: the class *o* and *be* suffixes are utilized if the noun designates one or more human beings but *-jum* (sg.) and *-ji* (pl.) if the referent is non-human. In Lubumbashi and Nairobi, in the most "correct" varieties of local vehicular Swahili, a distinction is effected between the demonstratives designating persons and the others. At most four forms are used in Lubumbashi Swahili: *huyu* (proximity) and *ule* (distance) for persons; *hiyi* (proximity) and *ile* (distance) for things, without any distinction of number. The variety described by Polomé (1968, p. 21) opposes persons and things for the proximate demonstrative, *huyu* and *hiyi*, but preserves this distinction for the distant demonstrative only when it is post-posed to the noun (*ile kintu* "this thing there," *ile muntu* "this man there," *mtoto ule* "this child there"). In Nairobi two sets of demonstratives, proximate and distant, are attested for certain speakers, but the one applying to persons incorporates a distinction of number (sg. *huyu*, pl. *hawa*; sg. [*y*]*ule*, pl. *wale*) that is absent from the other (sg./pl. *hii, ile*); most speakers only know *hii* and *ile* (Heine 1973, p. 80).

4.2.2. The correlation observed between the presence or the absence of the feature [Human] (or perhaps [Animate]) and the expression of number is probably not fortuitous. Even in Nairobi, where nouns are distributed formally in three genders (ϕ/*wa-*, ϕ/*ma-*, ϕ/ϕ, cf. 3.1.3. above), Heine notes among certain speakers a tendency to reserve the second gender for nouns referring to human beings (other than those that remain classified under ϕ/*wa-*); moreover, *ma-* may be pre-posed to forms of the third gender when it is necessary to indicate plurality. The outcome of this tendency would be a system where the number contrast marked by *ma-* (*wa-* in a few substantives) was obligatorily expressed for humans and optional in all the other cases. The Lubumbashi variety has preserved a much more complex nominal system, but an analogous rule applies to the pronominal prefixes of verbs: these are sg. *a-* and pl. *ba-* (or *wa-*), if the subject is animate, but *i-* sg./pl. in the opposite case: *bintu inaisha kukauka* "the things have finished drying" (Annicq 1967, p. 8). Lingala possesses a rule quite analogous for prefixed personal pronouns (persons sg. *a-* vs. pl. *ba-*; things sg./pl. *e-*) as well as for absolute pronouns (persons sg. *ye* vs. pl. *bango*; things sg./pl. *yango*), proximate demonstratives (persons sg. *óyo* vs. pl. *baóyo*; things sg./pl. *óyo*), and distant demonstratives (persons sg. *yangó* vs. pl. *bangó*; things sg./pl. *yangó*) (Guthrie 1939, pp. 21, 24, 48). In Kituba, for the third person, number is marked for animates (sg. *yándi* vs. pl. *báwu*) but not for inanimates (sg./pl. *yáwu*) (Fehderau 1966, p. 50). In vehicular Fula, the emphatic demonstrative forms, which are as numerous as noun classes in the vernacular variety, are reduced to three for most speakers: for animates, sg. *kãŋko* vs. pl. *kãmbe*; for inanimates, sg./pl. *kanjum* (Lacroix 1959, p. 68).

4.2.3.   More striking because of its greater generality is the restructuring of the verbal system starting from two oppositions, one belonging to chronology and opposing an unmarked term to two others marked for past and future, respectively, and the other to aspect. The clearest picture of this model appears in Cameroon Pidgin English; for instance, the following forms occur for the first person singular of *tok* "to talk" (De Féral 1975, p. 82):

	Unmarked	Completive	Non-Completive
Unmarked	a tok	a don tok	a di tok
Past	a bin tok	a bin don tok	a bin di tok
Future	a go tok	a go don tok	a go di tok

The verbal systems of pidginized varieties considered here appear as approximate realizations of the model under discussion. Nairobi Swahili is quite close to it in opposing to a form *na-/ana-* (prefixed to the verb root) with aorist value a future in *ta-/ata-* and a past form obtained by the pre-position of *kwisha* to the verb root; the corresponding negative forms contain, respectively, in front of the verb root *hapana, hawezi* or *hapana weza* and *bado*. Moreover non-completive process is expressed by *-kuwa* "to be" followed by the verb stem; *-kuwa* receives the marks of the aorist, of the past (*-li-*, in all other cases replaced by *kwisha*) and of the future (Heine 1973, pp. 90-94). In Lubumbashi the expression of tense seems to be dissociated from that of aspect: the former involves infixed markers (present *-na-*, *-φ-* [negative]; past *-li-*, *-ku-* [negative]; future *-ta-* [affirmative and negative]) and the latter auxiliaries (*kwisha* for the completive, *iko* for the non-completive) (Annicq 1967, pp. 5, 49; Polomé 1968, pp. 22, 23). In vehicular Hausa, as in Sango, a progressive form containing the verb "to be" (*na* in Hausa, *ɛkɛ* in Sango) but no explicit indication of tense contrasts with aorist, future and past forms. The morphological processes utilized differ markedly, however: an amalgam of the tense marker and the prefixed pronoun in Hausa (Hodge 1958, pp. 59-60), and in Sango, pre-position of *fadé* "soon" for the future, the post-position for *awɛ* "it is finished" for the past, and the absence of any marker for the aorist (Bouquiaux 1969, p. 63; Samarin 1970a, pp. 89-95; 1971, p. 128). The case of vehicular Bulu (Alexandre 1963, p. 581) is not very clear; there appear to exist an aorist marked by *φ*, a past in *-nga-*, and a periphrastic future composed of the auxiliaries *ye* "to wish" or *ke* "to go" (these markers are identical to those of the vernacular languages of the A

70 group); the completive is indicated by means of the auxiliaries *man* or *fini* "finished." In Fanagalo, only the temporal marker remains: an aorist marked by ϕ, a future formed by the pre-position to the verb form of *zo* or of the auxiliary *yazi* "to be able to," and a past marked by the suffixation of *-ile* (Heine 1973, p. 131). The same scheme is attested in the most "corrupted" version of Upland Country Swahili described by Le Breton (1936, p. 22), where the verb form with prefixed *na-* indicates at the same time the present and the future and, when preceded by *nakwisha*, the past. On the contrary, koine Fula marks only aspect: completive (suffixation of *-i*), non-completive (suffixation of *-a*), but it also comprises a progressive obtained by the pre-position of the particle *don* to the non-completive form. The verb system of Kituba (Fehderau 1966, pp. 53-54) constitutes a special case. One finds in that language a distinction between an unmarked aorist, a present, a future, and a past signalled, respectively, by the pre-posed "auxiliaries" *ké, ta,* and *mé*; but this distinction is combined with an opposition between actual (ϕ) and non-actual (the suffix *-aka* adjoined to the verb stem).

Certain of the analogies that I have just proposed might seem far-fetched, even forced. They would be more convincing if I could provide here an analysis of the verb systems of the vernacular languages to which are connected the various vehicular varieties just examined. There is practically nothing in common, from a typological point of view, among the verb system of Hausa, which aligns six paradigmatic sets corresponding to five aspects (Gouffé 1977, 3.11; Brauner 1965, p. 25), that of Fula, which combines three voices and three aspects comprising several tenses (Lacroix 1959, p. 68; Arnott 1970, pp. 179-82), and the system of the Bantu languages, whose simplest expression, that of Swahili, comprises four moods, ten tense-aspect modalities, and numerous compound tenses (Polomé 1967, pp. 110-26). The same thing could be said of the other African languages cited, as well as for English, which one must consider the base language of Cameroon Pidgin English.

5. CONCLUSION

The preceding presentation is above all descriptive; the facts provided are too fragmentary and incomplete to allow useful generalizations. It seems possible nonetheless to draw from it some indications on the significance of the facts observed. It appears probable that the explicitation of contrasts in the speech chain, the stabilization of the form of formatives, paradigmatic and syntagmatic univocity, the grammaticalization of word order, the elimination of arbitrary constraints, and the simplification of content form compensated by recourse to discursive expressions where lexicon plays a predominant role[11] contribute to facilitate the encoding and the decoding of the message (Hymes 1971, p. 73). These processes thus make mutual comprehension easier and confer on a vehicular variety "a form that corresponds to the communicative needs imposed by the context of situation" (Houis 1971, p. 159). More important to me seems to be the fact that these processes apparently do not operate on an intangible structure that would remain identical to itself through all its fluctuations in the vernacular or the vehicular varieties but on a restructured on. To judge from the verb systems examined in 4.2.3. the principle of this reconstruction is independent of the genetic origin or the typological characteristics of the speech variety in which it manifests itself. In 1924 Father Jaffré, a missionary, explained the formation of Kituba in the following way:

> By means of an inexorable correlation, as we deliver to our wards a disfigured language, these, giving us back our formula, present theirs to us in a deformed form. Thus, to give an example, instead of "il est allé le chercher", one utters "lui y en a allé pour chercher ça", and Blacks, to conform themselves to the mold of our thought, calque their translation: *yandi kele kouenda mou bonga iaou*; they ignore the real form which exists, as adequate as the French form, short, clear, and as easy as it: *ouele* (il est allé) *ia* (le) *bonga* (prendre).[12]

The hypothesis of a translation, from Kituba to Petit-Nègre[13] or from Petit-Nègre to Kituba, is hardly likely; the latter existed long before French and Belgian colonization (Fehderau 1966, pp. 98-101) and Petit-Nègre has been employed far beyond the Kongo-speaking area. It all happens, however, as if the "mold" in which the two interlocutors model their message were shared by them. If that were the case, the practical efficiency of pidginized varieties might be the result of three correlative properties: their simplicity, or more exactly, their narrow adaptation to the referential function; their neutrality, that is to say, the fact that their use does not habitually evoke any categorization or any value judgment;[14] and finally, their conformity to what might turn out to be the elementary structures of human language.

Translated by Albert Valdman

NOTES

1. Dagara is a Gur language spoken by a rural population in the southwest of the Upper Volta.

2. Among the languages examined here, five belong to the Bantu group: Swahili (G.42 in Guthrie's classification [1948]) comprises numerous dialects in Tanzania, Kenya, Somaliland, Mozambique, and the Comore islands, and vehicular varieties found nearly everywhere in East Africa, notably in the interior of Kenya, Uganda, and eastern Zaïre; Lingala (C.26d) and Kituba (or Monokutuba), the vehicular form of Kikongo (H.16), both of which are national languages of Zaïre, the first spoken in the Congo valley from Kisangani to Kinshasa, to the north of the valley and in most of the large cities, and the second in the southwest region of Zaïre and in the southern portion of the Democratic Republic of the Congo; Bulu (A.70; Guthrie 1953) in southern Cameroon, whose vehicular variety is also labelled Pidgin A.70; Fanagalo of the mines of South Africa, whose base language is Zulu (S.32). The other languages are Sango (Adamawa Group, I.A. 6 in Greenberg's classification), whose domain covers the Central African Republic and neighboring regions; Hausa, a Tchadic language (Afro-Asiatic, III E, according to Greenberg) that enjoys a very broad distribution in Nigeria, Niger and far beyond the borders of these states; Dyula (I.A. 2a), a Mande language close to Bambara and Malinke, a vernacular language of the north of the Ivory Coast and an important vehicular language in West Africa; Pidgin English, widespread in coastal areas, from Ghana to Cameroon, and Krio, an English-based creole of Sierra Leone, probably related to Pidgin English. The inventory of African trade languages has been established by Heine in German (1968) and in English (1970); these works contain all information of historical, geographical, sociological, and demographic nature available at the date of publication. The extensive bibliography provided in Heine (1973) should also be consulted.

3. It is possible that the mechanism analyzed by Samarin (1966), which consists in characterizing the second language by contrast with the native tongue, operates at this level.

4. If not, perhaps, insofar as tone patterns are concerned whose variation characterizes, in Bambara, compounds (in contrast to discursive syntagma) and serves to express the nominal modality of definiteness. This question has not been investigated by Partmann.

5. It is remarkable that the morphophonemic oddities of vernacular Swahili have been preserved in this gender. Thus, note the composition of "woman" *mwanamke*, pl. *wanawake*, made up of *-ana* "son, daughter," and of *-ke* "feminine, female" (with class agreement: sg. *mw-* . . . *m*, pl. *w-* . . .

wa-), or that of "Arab" *mwarabu*, pl. *waarabu* with the non-reduction of *wa-* to *w-* (normal before a vowel) specific to borrowed nouns. Here, obviously, a group of fossilized forms are involved.

6. Doke 1954, p. 70: "There is no general method of deriving negative from positive forms."

7. "Various morphemic complexes ... which cannot be readily included in the regular inflectional patterns, though they show inflectional affixes."

8. This represents the third feature of creole languages according to Hjelmslev (1939, p. 373): "paradigmatic univocity" (the absence of different "declinations" and "conjugations"); "syntagmatic univocity" (every morpheme has its unique expression); "word order having grammatical value."

9. This particle is *n* after determined masculine singular, *r* after feminine singular, and *n* after plural: *mùtum*, pl. *mutàànee* means "man"; the expression should be interpreted literally as "an old sort of man."

10. Cf. Polomé 1967, pp. 140-66, the use of the subjunctive mood (suffix *-e*; the only verb modality admitted: consecutive *-ka-*) in the subordinate clause is sufficient to indicate finality: *nenda ukanunue ndizi* "go (*nenda*) buy bananas (*ndizi*)," *tunamzuru Hussein atuambie habari yake* "we (*tu-*) are paying a visit to Hussein in order that he tell us his news (*habari yake*)." The interplay of "tenses," that is to say, of verb modalities, manifests itself in such utterances as *tuliwasikia wakiimba* "we heard them singing" (*-ki-* in the second verb form, the non-completive marker, indicates that the song was being performed at the time it was heard, and *-li-* denotes the past), or *angalitoka bara asingalisema kikae* "if he had come from the mainland, he wouldn't have spoken kikae" (in the two verb forms *-ngali-* indicates the past irrealis). With regard to the use of relative forms, it constitutes a frequent embedding process. These are complex verb forms containing the referential particle *o*, whose presence indicates that the form is not a primary sentence constituent, and of a "concord" element linking it to the antecedent substantive: *vitabu wasivyovisoma watoto* "the books (*vitabu*) that the children (*watoto*) did not read"; the concord element *-vi-* appears twice in the verb form: as a "relative" in *-vyo-* and as an infixed object before the verb stem *-soma*. If this concord element belongs to one of the locative classes (*-ku-, -pa-, -mu-*) or to the class *vi-* (whose prefix serves to form manner adverbs on adjectival stems: *-zuri* "good," *vizuri* "well"), the relative form has the value of a circumstantial adverb: *tuliposikia vile tukaogopa* "when (*-po-*) we heard (*-li-* past) how matters were (*vile*), then (*-ka-*) we became frightened"; *nisipokuja hataweza kufanya kazi hii* "if I don't come, he won't be able (*-weza*) to do this work (*kazi hii*)"; *tuonavyo sisi hawakusikia maneno haya* "as we think (*-ona*; the position of the relative varies depending on whether the verb modalities are or are not expressed), they haven't understood (*-sikia-; -ku-* marks the completive) these words." In addition to

its adnominal use, the relative form makes possible the expression of a large number of circumstantial relations.

11. For Partmann's informants, to speak Dyula well entails, above all, to know a lot of vocabulary (1973, pp. 117, 127).

12. Cited by F. Lumwamu (n.d.); the Kituba and Kikongo utterances should be read as, respectively, *yandi kéle kwénda mu bonga yawu* and *welé ya bonga.*

13. Petit-Nègre is a pidginized variety of French, probably highly stereotypic in nature, formerly employed widely in French-influenced West Africa. It is highly doubtful that it ever constituted a stable pidgin.

14. All the speakers interviewed by Partmann admitted being quite satisfied with the type of Dyula they spoke, recognizing willingly at the same time that it was not the purest (Partmann 1973, pp. 118-19, 127, 130).

REFERENCES

Alexandre, Pierre. 1963. Aperçu sommaire sur le Pidgin A 70 du Cameroun. *Cahiers d'Etudes Africaines* 3:577-82.

Annicq, Camille. 1967. *Le swahili véhiculaire.* Lubumbashi: Editions IMBELCO.

Arnott, D. W. 1970. *The Nominal and Verbal Systems of Fula.* Oxford: Clarendon Press.

Ashton, E. O. 1944. *Swahili Grammar (Including Intonation).* London: Longmans, Green.

Bouquiaux, Luc. 1969. La créolisation du français par le sango véhiculaire, phénomène réciproque. *Le français en France et hors de France. I. Créoles et contacts africains.* Paris: Les Belles Lettres.

Brauner, Sigmund, und Ashiwaju, M. 1965. *Lehrbuch der Hausa-Sprache.* Leipzig: VEB Verlag Enzyklopädie.

Cole, Desmond. 1953. Fanagalo and the Bantu languages in South Africa. *African Studies* 12:1-9.

De Féral, Carole. 1975. Le Pidgin-English au Cameroun: quelques aspects linguistiques. Unpublished maîtrise thesis, University of Paris X.

Doke, C. M. 1954. *The Southern Bantu Languages.* London: Oxford University Press.

Fehderau, H. 1966. The Origin and Development of Kituba (Lingua Franca Kikongo). Unpublished Ph.D. diss., Cornell University.

Gouffé, Claude. 1977. La langue haoussa. *Description linguistique du Monde.* Paris: Centre National de la Recherche Scientifique (in press).

Greenberg, Joseph. 1963. *The Languages of Africa.* The Hague: Mouton.

Guthrie, Malcolm. 1939. *Grammaire et dictionnaire de lingala.* Cambridge: W. Heffer.

———. 1948. *The Classification of the Bantu Languages.* London: Dawsons of Pall Mall.

———. 1953. *The Bantu Languages of Western Equatorial Africa.* London: Oxford University Press.

Heine, Bernd. 1968. *Afrikanische Verkehrssprachen.* Köln, Infratest, Schriftenreihe zur empirischen Sozialforschung, Band 4.

———. 1970. *Status and Use of African Lingua Francas.* München: IFO - Institut für Wirtschaftsforschung, Afrika-Studien 49.

———. 1973. *Pidgin-Sprachen im Bantu-Bereich.* Berlin: Dietrich Reimer Verlag.

———. 1975. Some generalizations of African-based pidgins. (Paper presented at the International Conference on Pidgins and Creoles, Honolulu, January 1975.)

Hjelmslev, Louis. 1938. Relations de parenté dans les langues créoles. *Revue des Etudes Indo-Européennes* (Bucarest) 1:271-86.

———. 1939. Caractères grammaticaux des langues créoles. *Congrès International des Sciences Anthropologiques et Ethnologiques. Compte-rendu de la 2e session,* 373. Copenhague.

———. 1968. *Prolégomènes à une théorie du langage.* Paris: Editions de Minuit.

Hodge, Carleton. 1958. Non-Native Hausa. *Monograph Series on Language and Linguistics* 11:57-69.

Houis, Maurice. 1971. *Anthropologie linguistique de l'Afrique Noire.* Paris: P.U.F.

Hymes, Dell, ed. 1971. *Pidginization and Creolization of Languages.* London: Cambridge University Press.

Jaffré, C. 1924. *Méthode pratique de Lari-Français.* Paris-Brazzaville.

Jones, Eldred. 1971. Krio: An English-based Language of Sierra-Leone. In *The English Language in West Africa,* J. Spencer, ed. London: Longman, pp. 66-94.

Lacroix, Pierre-Francis. 1959. Observations sur la "koinè" peule de Ngaoundéré. *Travaux de l'Institut de Linguistique* 4:57-71.

Le Breton, F. H. 1936. *Up-Country Swahili, for the soldier, settler, miner, merchant and their wives, and for all who deal with Up-Country natives without interpreters.* Richmond: R. W. Simpson.

Lecoste, B. 1960. A grammatical study of two recordings of Belgian-Congo Swahili. *Swahili* 31:219-26.

Long, R. W., and Diomandé, R. S. 1970. *Basic Dyula.* Bloomington, Ind.: Indiana University. Intensive Language Training Center.

Lumwamu, François. n.d. Recherches sur la koinè Kongo. Unpublished doctoral diss., University of Paris-III (in preparation).

Mafeni, Bernard. 1971. Nigerian Pidgin. In *The English Language in West Africa*, J. Spencer, ed. London: Longman, pp. 95-112.

Martinet, André. 1967. Que faut-il entendre par "fonction des affixes de classe"? In *La classification nominale dans les langues négro-africaines*, G. Manessy, ed. Paris: Centre National de la Recherche Scientifique.

Nida, Eugene, and Fehderau, H. W. 1970. Indigenous pidgins and koinés. *International Journal of American Linguistics* 36:146-55.

Partmann, Gayle. 1973. Le dioula véhiculaire en Côte d'Ivoire. Etude comparative des jeunes locuteurs primaires et secondaires du dioula. Unpublished Ph.D. diss., Stanford University.

Polomé, Edgar. 1967. *Swahili Language Handbook*. Washington, D. C.: Center for Applied Linguistics.

_____. 1968. Lubumbashi Swahili. *Journal of African Languages* 7:14-25.

Richardson, Irvine. 1961. Some observations on the status of Town Bemba in Northern Rhodesia. *African Language Studies* 2:25-36.

_____. 1963. Examples of deviation and innovation in Bemba. *African Language Studies* IV:128-45.

Roulon, Paulette. 1972. Etude du français et du sango parlés par les Ngbaka-Ma'bo (République Centrafricaine). *Ethnies* (IDERIC, Nice) 2:133-65.

Samarin, William. 1970a. *Sango, langue de l'Afrique centrale*. Leiden: E. J. Brill.

_____. 1970b. Lingua francas in the world. *Readings in the Sociology of Languages*, J. A. Fishman, ed. Paris, the Hague: Mouton, pp. 660-72.

_____. 1971. Salient and substantive pidginization. In D. Hymes, ed., pp. 117-40.

Scotton, C. M. M. 1969. A look at the Swahili of two groups of Up-Country speakers. *Swahili* 39:101-10.

Creolization: Elaboration in the Development of Creole French Dialects

Albert Valdman

0. INTRODUCTION

0.1. *Complexification in creolization*

According to the classical life-cycle theory (Hall 1966), a creole derives from the nativization of a pidgin, i.e., its acquisition as a first language by a new generation of speakers.

The expansion of linguistic functions served by a creole is accompanied by a set of processes subsumed under the term *creolization:* (1) relative stabilization of variation; (2) expansion of inner form; (3) complexification of outer form (Hymes 1971). While the corresponding mirror-image process, *pidginization*, has received detailed attention (Alexandre 1963; Bouquiaux 1969; Cole 1953; Hymes 1971; Partmann 1973; Polomé 1968; Samarin 1970, 1971, to mention just a few studies), creolization has remained by and large ill described.

The link between reduction of inner form and simplification of outer form and, conversely, expansion of inner form and complexification of outer form, has been noted by several authors. For instance, Manessy (1975) cites the levelling of the semantic distinctions of alienable versus inalienable possession in Dyula and Sango—two widely used vehicular languages of West Africa—as the result of the generalization of a relational particle. But only in

Bickerton's account of the decreolization gradatum of Guianese English (1975, p. 114) does one find a detailed account of the interaction of modification of surface structure, principally by means of lexical borrowing, and extensive restructuring of semantactic structure:

> The process that we have observed in the developmental phase between the basilect and mid-mesolect consisted to a large extent in introducing formatives modelled on English ones, using them (at least initially) in a quite un-English way, and only slowly and gradually shifting the underlying system in the direction of English.

Whereas pidginization may be viewed as facilitating the decoding of messages on the part of the hearer by the mapping of semantic formatives onto invariant forms and the establishment of isomorphism between form and grammatical function (Hymes 1971, p. 73), creolization on the contrary effects the compression of linearly ordered simplex formatives into complex units (Traugott, this volume).

How is one to account for this apparently paradoxical aspect of creolization—paradoxical in that it scrambles semantic information and increases the knowledge the hearer must possess of the grammatical system? The answer lies in our assessment of the relative importance of the cognitive, expressive, and integrative functions of language and of the nature of grammar. Pidgins are inadequate languages, not only in that they lack explicitly expressed semantic distinctions, but also because of their slow rhythm (Bickerton 1975, Labov 1971). The latter points out that in comparison to Buang, a Melanesian language spoken in the same area, New Guinea Tok Pisin (Melanesian Pidgin English) has more heavy stresses, shorter phonological phrases, and fewer close junctures. He proceeds to demonstrate that one of the constants of the creolization of English-based pidgins is the replacement of optional time adverbials placed outside the predicate by obligatory tense particles occurring within it. This restructuring does not primarily serve the need for more delicate semantic differentiations since no profound deep-level reorganization is involved and since, according to Labov, grammar is not directly related to cognitive structures:

> On the whole, grammar is not a tool of logical analysis; grammar is busy with emphasis, focus, down-shifting and up-grading; it is a way of organizing information and of taking alternative points of view (1971, p. 72).

Tense markers replace time adverbs because they provide speakers with a certain degree of stylistic flexibility; they can be contracted in allegro style or expanded in lento style. When combined to form an elaborated auxiliary, they provide a broader base for the application of morphophonemic rules that define a wider range of styles between formal and informal.

0.2. *Complexification and restructuring*

As mentioned by several authors in this book, the terms "simplification" and "complexification" are not altogether appropriate to refer to the various processes that lead to pidginization and the transformation of pidgins and pre-pidgin continua into creoles. As Robert Le Page suggests, the difference between pidginization and creolization rests on a shift between context-bound and context-free speech, between what is linguistically implicit and explicit, between dependence on non-linguistic semiotic channels and the use of an elaborate grammatical apparatus to transmit meaning. It is not readily apparent, for example, how the signalling of tense by means of particles instead of adverbs introduces greater complexity. Bickerton (1975) shows that the development of the verbal system of Guianese (English-based) Creole from basilect to mesolect and acrolect takes the form of successive restructuring, chiefly the replacement of an aspect-oriented system by a tense-oriented system, rather than the addition to a simple base of new categories and more elaborated means to express them.

In the study cited above, Bickerton draws an analogy between decreolization and natural second-language learning; the Guianese Creole-English gradatum stems, as it were, from the postponed acquisition of Standard English by speakers of the creole basilect. In this regard, that author's view of second-language learning is of some importance, and it is noteworthy that it shares several key features with those currently being emitted by some applied linguists, e.g., Corder (1975). A considerable body of research (e.g., Dulay and Burt 1972, 1974a, 1974b) has revealed striking similarities between the development of the linguistic competence of children acquiring their first language and the learning of a second language on the part of children and adults. In this volume, Ferguson and DeBose argue that adults possess the capability of reducing fully formed language to produce various types of "simplified" registers employed in certain socially determined circumstances. Corder rejects the notion of simplification, which he views as reflecting a comparative, evaluative stance toward the language of children, reduced registers, pidgins and creoles, and second-language learners' approximative systems. He suggests instead that these varieties of language are basic and that normal, fully formed adult speech represents the complexification of a universal base that these less elaborated varieties reflect. In fact, the existence of reduced registers constitutes for Corder evidence that speakers are endowed with the capability of reverting to an ontologically earlier, more basic stage of linguistic development. These, together with pidgins, creoles, and second-language learners' approximative systems, represent fossilized intermediate stages in the process of elaboration. Corder suggests further that the heuristic device available to the second-language learner consists not of a set of strategies for simplification but of the universal linguistic base reflected in less elaborated varieties of language. The form of this heuristic device varies with the individual inasmuch as it depends on his or her previous language acquisition and learning experience: first-language acquisition, the use of special registers, previously acquired second languages, etc. Interestingly enough, Bickerton suggests that a determining factor in the development of European-based pidgins and creoles was the substrate language speakers' multilingual background. Their experience in the acquisition of several second languages equipped them with more generalized hypotheses for second-language learning than monolingual speakers, hypotheses based not on the grammar of their native language so much as on those they had found to be shared by all the languages they knew (1975, p. 174).

A final point made by Corder that deserves mention is that linguistic elaboration is determined by communicative demands and the function of the discourse: "a speaker adopts just that point on the simple-complex continuum which is complex enough for successful communication and . . . he 'shifts' up and down the scale as circumstances require (1975, p. 6)." In light of Labov's proposal, it is necessary to add that, at least for normal, elaborated varieties of language, success in communication transcends the efficient transmission of messages and requires demonstration of considerable stylistic maneuver on the part of the speaker.

0.3. *Elaboration and decreolization*

The above considerations lead me to adopt the term *elaboration* to refer to the various processes generally subsumed under expansion of inner form and complexification of outer form. Its similarity to second-language learning renders the process of decreolization less than optimal for the study of the actual operation of elaboration in the development of creole languages. Without excluding the possibility of pidgins undergoing a certain degree of elaboration, it would seem that this process is linked centrally to the acquisition of pre-pidgin continua or pidgins by children. Since, despite their similarities, first-language acquisition and second-language learning show substantial differences, I will assume that the processes of elaboration undergone by a creole differ qualitatively from the successive restructuring characteristic of L_2 learners' approximative systems and decreolization.

English creolists frequently contrast the decreolization gradata that renders difficult the analysis of the object of their study with the clear line that demarcates French-based creoles from French. As I have shown elsewhere (Valdman 1973, 1975), this is an idealized view of the situation. Nonetheless, decreolization has not yet affected the morphosyntactic system of Creole French (Créole). Most of the reasons for the greater structural autonomy of Créole are historical: to mention just one, the largest Créole-speaking territory, Haiti, was isolated from its former colonial power for more than a century, and its abysmally low level of economic development has cut off the bulk of the population from effective contact with French. But a linguistic reason offered by Hugo Schuchardt (see Meijer and Muysken, this volume) also deserves serious consideration. Schuchardt accounted for the widespread diffusion of pidginized and creolized varieties of English by the fact that its structure already showed a certain creolized character. In particular, its rich system of auxiliaries and modals represents an intermediate step between the totally analytic verbal system of English-based pidgins and creoles and the inflectional system of the Romance languages. Créole lends itself particularly to the study of elaboration since in many areas it has evolved independently of its base language and is relatively free of decreolization.

0.4.   My paper has a double objective within the framework of this volume. First, it purports to illustrate the structure of a characteristic creole language, Créole.[1] Section 1 provides a sketch of the phonological structure of the Haitian variety of Créole; section 2 contains a comparative study of the system of noun determiners in the various Créole dialects; section 3 describes complex sandhi phenomena in Haitian Créole (HC); finally, section 4 presents some aspects of the verbal system of Créole. Second, this paper attempts to make certain claims about the nature of elaboration. In sections 1-3 I show that the system of noun determiners has attained its most elaborated form in HC and that, further, that elaboration has provided the basis for the development of a rich set of morphophonemic variants, which affords speakers of HC with a broad stylistic range. In section 4 I try to show that elaboration is a type of linguistic change and that it occurs only after a pre-creole continuum has attained a certain degree of crystallization.

1. SOME ASPECTS OF THE PHONOLOGY OF CREOLE

1.1. *Differences in phonological inventories*

Superficially, Créole differs little from its base language at the phonological level. A comparison of the phonemic inventories of the two languages reveals only minor differences: the lack of a front rounded series in Créole, a somewhat richer system of nasal vowels and fewer gaps in the consonantal system (see Table 1).

The similarity between the two languages reflected in Table 1 is illusory. First, the Créole data are based on Caribbean varieties and fail to indicate that, for instance, Indian Ocean dialects lack the set of palatal obstruents.[2] Second, in the area of vowel nasality the two languages differ more profoundly than by the presence or absence of one or two units: the high vowels /ĩ/ and /ũ/ have marginal differentiative function, the phonetic values of corresponding vowels diverge considerably, and more importantly, in the Caribbean varieties vowels are usually nasalized in the context of nasal consonants (for details, see Tinelli 1974, Valdman 1977), although there are attested such triads as /mõ/ "mountain" vs. /mõn/ "world" vs. /mɔn/ "mountain, hill"; /šã/ "field" vs. /šãm/ "room" vs. /šam/ "amulet, magical potion." Third, Créole /r/ differs from the corresponding French phoneme not only by its velar and (in the context of a labial segment) labialized pronunciation but by its more limited distribution: it is absent in post-vocalic position, cf. /frɛ/ and *frère* "brother," /pak/ and *parc* "park." The loss of post-vocalic /r/ results in an increased differentiative function for the distinction high-mid vs. low-mid, since high- and low-mid vowels, in near-complementary distribution in Standard French (Valdman 1976), are found in all positions in Créole: /mo/ "word" (*mot* /mo/) vs. /mɔ/ "dead person" (*mort*/mɔr/); /pe/ "hush" (*paix* /pe/ ~ /pɛ/) vs. /pɛ/ "priest" (*père* /pɛr/).

	Standard French				Créole		

Vowels

i	ÿ	u		i			u
e	φ	o		e			o
ϵ	œ	ɔ		ϵ			ɔ
	a	ɑ			a		
					(ï)		(ü)
	ē	ã			ē		ō
	oē	õ				ã	

Consonants

p	t		k		p	t	č	k
b	d		g		b	d	ǰ	g
f	s	š			f	s	š	h
v	z	ž			v	z	ž	
m	n	ñ			m	n	ñ	ŋ
	l	r				l		r
w	y				w	y		

Table 1

Phonemic inventories of Standard French and (Caribbean) Créole

1.2. *Morphophonemics*

The most striking differences between Créole and French reside at the level of morphophonemic structure (chiefly external sandhi) and syllable structure; these have remained little studied (see, however, Hall 1953, Tinelli 1975, and Valdman 1977). Haitian Créole (HC) exhibits optional elision of the vowel of pronouns that superficially resembles liaison and elision in French. It will be recalled that in the latter language liaison is a phenomenon, obligatory in certain phonosyntactic contexts and optional in others, statable in the form of a simple rule couched in phonological terms:

(1) $\begin{bmatrix} +\text{cons} \\ -\text{voc} \end{bmatrix} \longrightarrow \phi \ / \ - \ [+\text{cons}]$

This rule accounts for such contrasts as:

(2) peti*t* train, peti*t* ruisseau vs. petit‿hôtel, petit‿oiseau
and applies to any morpheme of the language ending with a
segment specified by the input to the rule and occurring in the
appropriate phonosyntactic environment.

In HC elision affects mainly the personal pronouns:

(3)	Singular	Plural
1st	mwẽ~m	nũ~n
2nd	u ~ w	
3rd	li ~ l	jo~j

These optionally lose their final vowel (or in the case of *u*,
alternate with the corresponding glide) when they occur as subject
before verbs:

(4) m ale ~ mwẽ ale   "I go, I went"
     m te di u~mwẽ te di u   "I had told you"

This type of external sandhi is accounted for by the following
optional rule (Tinelli 1975):

(5) Pronoun Elision

$$[-\text{cons}]_{1.2} \longrightarrow \phi \ / \ \left\{ \begin{array}{c} [+\text{cons}] \\ <[-\text{cons}]> \end{array} \right\} \underset{\text{PPn}}{-\,]\!]} + \underset{\text{VP}}{[\![\,-\,} <[+\text{syll}]$$

However, as stated in (5) Pronoun Elision is not sufficiently
constrained; for example, it fails to account for the obligatory
deletion of the vowel(s) of personal pronouns before the verb
markers *ape* "continuative, iterative" and *ava* "irrealis":

(6) m ap di u ~ *mwẽ ap di u "I'm telling you"

as well as the fact that, when post-posed, they are not subject to
optional deletion when they follow a [-voc] segment:

(7) kote papa li~kote papa l "Where is his, her father?"
     kote timun li   "Where is his, her child?"

In post-position elision is also subject to grammatical factors; thus,
it is excluded after the copula verb *se*, the negative adverb *pa* and
monosyllabic prepositions:

(8) se mwẽ   ~   *se m   "It's me"
     se pa li   ~   *se pa l   "It's not him"
     se nu   ~   *su n   "on us"

Comparison with previous stages of HC reflected by some scant written texts dating back to the end of the eighteenth century and comparison with other dialects indicate that elision developed after the formative period of Créole. That this phenomenon progressed further in HC than in the other dialects is not surprising since it is in Haiti that Créole fulfills the widest range of linguistic functions and thus needs to provide its speakers with the widest range of stylistic diversification. But elision is only one of several complex morphophonemic phenomena that testify to the extensive elaboration undergone by Créole since its emergence from pidginized varieties of French. Most of these phenomena take the form of external sandhi occurring between nouns and following determiners. Before examining these morphophonemic alternations, it is necessary to review the development of the system of noun determiners that provided a suitable base for the development of this variation.

2. RESTRUCTURING IN THE SYSTEM OF NOUN DETERMINERS

2.1. *Conservative system*

The only feature shared by the noun determiner systems of the various dialects of Créole consists of the use of post-posed *-la* (subject, as will be shown in 3., to considerable morphophonemic variation in Caribbean varieties), whose semantic value is intermediate between that of the French definite and demonstrative articles. No doubt this determiner has its source in the French locative adverb *là*, more specifically the latter's cliticized variant *-là*; compare: *Koté kabrit-la* (Où est cette chèvre-là?) "Where is the goat (previously mentioned)." Otherwise, Créole dialects show two systems, with some dialects—notably, Louisianan and Guyanan—exhibiting features from both systems. The most widely distributed system found in the Indian Ocean as well as, in part, in Louisiana, Guyana, and Lesser Antilles, is characterized by the pre-position of determiners. In the other system, whose most evolved form appears in HC, all determiners, except the indefinite, are post-posed.

In view of its wider distribution and the fact that it diverges least from French, I assume that the determiner system featuring pre-position (labelled hereafter the conservative system) reflects earlier stages of Créole.

The conservative system is best illustrated by the Mauritian paradigm for *lisjē* "dog":

		Sg		Pl
Indef		en lisjē	*Indef*	lisjē
$\left\{\begin{matrix}\text{Poss}\\\text{Dem}\end{matrix}\right\}$ (Pl)	+N + Def	lisjē-la	*Def*	ban lisjē-la
		mo lisjē	*Poss 1sg*	mo ban lisjē
		sa lisjē-la	*Dem*	sa ban lisjē-la

All determiners except the indefinite combine freely with plural; indefinite plural is expressed by zero.

The French source of the formatives is fairly clear. The plural marker derives from the weakened collective *bande* "bunch," the Def *la* from the locative adverb *là*, the Dem *sa* from the demonstrative pronoun *ça,* the Indef from *un/une.* The near identity of form would suggest that the Poss determiners are derived from corresponding French forms.[3]

Two features of the conservative determiner system require comment. First, all determiners have invariant phonological representation; available descriptions (Baker 1972, Chaudenson 1974, Papen 1975, respectively) do not mention any morphophonemic alternations. Second, restructuring with reference to the French pronominal system is relatively modest since three sets of pronominals are differentiated.

2.2. *Innovative system*

One of the first phases in the development of the innovative system appears to have been the post-position of a plural marker identical in form with the 3rd pl pronoun. The absence of this feature from Indian Ocean dialects little influenced by West African languages (see Chaudenson this volume) and, on the other hand, its presence in other European-based Caribbean and African pidgins and creoles (cf., e.g., Bailey 1966, Bickerton 1975) and in West African languages (Goodman 1964) points toward an origin in the latter. That it constituted an early innovation is suggested by the existence of that feature in the two conservative New World varieties, Louisianan and Guyanan. According to a wave model of linguistic change (Bailey 1974) an early change would progress faster and would be found at the points most distant from the focus of the innovation, most likely some place in the Caribbean. In the latter area the new post-posed plural marker's progress appears to have been blocked in the Lesser Antillean varieties. These exhibit the use of a pre-posed plural marker derived from the French plural demonstrative determiner *ces*, e.g., Martinican:

      (9)   se iš-la   "the, these children"

cf. Guyanan:

      (10) zozo-ja   "the, these birds"
            bitasõ-je-la   "the, these plantations"

Turiault (1874, p. 441) cites a sentence containing both the pre-posed and the post-posed plural markers:

      (11) se bɛ f-la-jo mɔ   "The cows are dead"

on the basis of which one could hypothesize that either post-posed *-jo* or pre-posed *se* was introduced for emphasis. Only the discovery in older texts or isolated Caribbean dialects of alternations between the two forms could provide data permitting a choice between the two hypotheses.

    Another early change in the conservative system was the shift of position of Dem, for it is post-posed in all New World varieties:

      (12) Louisianan : rekɔl-sa "this (particular) crop"
           Martinican : bug-ta-la   "this guy"
           Haitian :   liv-sa-a/liv-sila-a "this book"

The occurrence of the obligatory combination Dem + Def in the Indian Ocean dialects and in early texts (for instance, an early nineteenth-century Créole adaptation of the parable of the Prodigal Son contains such sequences as *pays là ci là là* "that country" and *robelà cilàlà* "that gown, these clothes") suggests that Dem represents an emphatic form of Def.[4]

    A clear case of elaboration at the semantic level involves the development in HC of a three-way distinction between Def, Dem, and what appears on the surface to be a reduplicated form of Def:

      (13) liv-la   "the (previously mentioned) book"
      (14) liv-sa-a   "this, that (here) book"

(15) liv-la-a   "the particular (previously
                                  mentioned) book"

(15) also contrasts with the sequence N + Det + locative adverb:

(16) liv-la la   "the (previously men-
                                  tioned) book is there"

The relationship of what I have termed the "deictic" determiner
(Valdman 1977) and Def is not very clear, and since its occurrence
in texts is relatively infrequent, one is forced to resort to sounding
informant intuitions—a notoriously unsatisfactory elicitation
procedure—to determine how it combines with the other determiners and the plural marker and the exact semantic differentiation it affords. The deictic determiner (or Def if one chooses to
analyze *la-a* as the reduplicated Def) also combines frequently
with Poss:

(17) Kote mãže-mwẽ?   "Where is my food"
      Koté mãže-mwẽ-ã?   "Where is the food that is
                                  mine"

and Douglas Taylor even notes a combination Dem + Poss + Def in
Dominican (1968, p. 1043); I cite the French translation he
provides together with my own English rendition:

(18) se kaj-sa-mwẽ-a   "these-here houses that are
                                  mine -
                                  ces maisons-là (qui sont à
                                  moi) -"

    The post-position of the personal pronouns to express
Poss must have constituted the most recent change in the
determiner system of Créole since it had not reached Louisiana or
Guyana. In fact it must have taken place in two phases. The first
involved the expression of Poss by means of a prepositional phrase
introduced by the preposition *à*; this step is reflected by forms
presently attested in Guadeloupean and Northern HC as well as in
texts from the end of the Saint-Domingue colonial period (late
eighteenth century):

(19) Northern HC : pitit-a-j   "his, her child"
      Guadeloupe : wɔb-a-mwẽ   "my dress"
      Colonial   : liberté à yo   "their freedom"
                    zamour à moué   "my love"
                    gié à moi   "my eyes"

The deletion of the linking *a* developed at an early date, and there must have been fluctuation between N + *à* Poss and N + Poss for an extensive period. This fluctuation is reflected by the absence of linking *a* in a proclamation issued in 1796:

(pl)

(20) liberté vous autes   "your freedom"

and in the Créole translation of the parable of the Prodigal Son:

(21) papa moi   "my father"
      cochons-li-io   "his pigs"

Today, the construction N + Poss occurs invariably in all the other Caribbean varieties.

The shift of position of Poss appears to have been one of the consequences of the morphological restructuring of the system of personal pronouns. I have stated above that the present Indian Ocean dialects reflect the differentiation of subject and object (unstressed vs. stressed or pre-posed vs. post-posed) sets of personal pronouns in the early stages of Créole. That distinction is consistently noted in all Colonial texts. However, the texts also show the first stages of the generalized elision of the vowel(s) of personal pronoun described in 1.2. One of the written versions of the best-known Colonial songs (*Lisette quitté laplaine*, Anon. 1811) contains the variants *mo/m* for the 1st sg pronoun;[5] the latter alternant occurs before the continuative-iterative verb marker *a* (presently *ap*):

(22) la jour quan ma coupé cane   "In the daytime
                                     when I am cutting
                                     sugar cane"
      dan dromi ma songé toi   "in my sleep I keep
                                     thinking of you"

and before the only verb beginning with a vowel occurring in the text:

      laut' jour m'alé à la ville   "the other day I
                                     went to town"

The parable of the Prodigal Son shows that elision had been extended to pre-consonantal position:

(23) m' pas mérité   "I don't deserve"
      m' té péché   "I have sinned"

The development of the pronominal system in HC is summarized by (24):

(24) *Colonial Period*   *Present-Day HC*

	Subject	Object/Poss	
1 sg	mo/mõ	mwa/mwe/mwẽ	m~mwẽ
2 sg	to	twa/twe	w~u
	vu/u		
3 sg	li		l~li/i; li/j~i
1 pl	nu		
2 pl	(vu)zɔt		n~nũ
3 pl	jo		j~jo

The slash lines indicate variation not accountable in terms of morphophonemic processes (regional, stylistic, etc. variation) whereas ~ denotes morphophonemic alternations characterizable in terms of an elision rule and serving a stylistic function. This thoroughgoing restructuring, involving as it does the loss of some semantic distinctions (merger of 1 pl and 2 pl and of 2 sg formal vs. informal), the levelling of case distinctions but, on the other hand, the generalization of sandhi alternants, cannot be characterized simply in terms of simplification or complexification.

The diagram below presents in schematic fashion the determiner system of HC characteristic of the innovative system:

(25)

		Singular		Plural
		jũ liv	*Indef*	liv
	⎧Def ⎫	liv-la	*Def*	liv-jo
Indef + N +	⎨ (Deictic)⎬ (Pl)	liv-sa-a	*Dem*	liv-sa- jo
	⎩Poss ⎭	liv-li	*Poss 3 sg*	liv-li-jo
	Dem + Def	liv-la-a	*Deictic*	liv-la-jo
		liv-li-a	*Poss+Deic*	liv-li-a-jo

3. SANDHI ALTERNATIONS IN THE HC DETERMINER

3.1. *The definite determiner*

One of the effects of Pronominal Elision (see 1.2.) is to eliminate V V sequences. But it is not a natural rule since the vowel of a personal pronoun is not obligatorily deleted before a vowel, i.e., it cannot be formulated as

$$(26)\ V \longrightarrow \phi \ / \ \text{——} \ V$$

It is in fact a complex optional vowel truncation rule, whose correct formulation requires a statement of the features of the segments preceding or following the truncated vowel as well as a delicate definition of the syntactic environment in which it variably takes effect. It will be noted that Pronominal Elision does not apply if the truncation of the vowel would result in sequences glide + consonant:

(27)	j arete l	"They stopped him"	jo arete l
	w ale	"You went"	u ale
	but		
	jo vini	"They came"	*j vini
	u vɔje	"You sent"	*w vɔje

In Créole only initial clusters of the type obstruent + liquid are permitted. That Pronominal Deletion operates in the pronouns *mwē, li,* and *nū* rests on the fact that the resonants become syllabic before another consonant:

(28)	m̩ te di u	"I told you"	mwē te di u
	l̩ marje	"He got married"	li marje
	n̩ tunē	"We returned"	nū tunē

In HC, vowels are optionally truncated in a variety of forms, including verb markers, conjunctions, and even verb stems:

(29)	mwē pa té la	"I was not there"	m̩ pa t la
	sa ki vini	"The one that came"	sa k vini
	mwē vini	"I came"	m̩ vin bule l
			"I came to burn it"

It cannot be claimed, however, that there is a deep-seated "conspiracy" that tends toward the reduction of sequences of consecutive vowels (V V or V V V) since that tendency is countered by other rules whose output is precisely V V. The first of these determines the phonic representation of Def in HC and, to a variable extent, in all Caribbean dialects.

The *l* of Def *la* is truncated when it occurs after a vowel:

(30) l-Truncation

pitit-la	"the child"	dlo-a	"the water"
madãm-lã	"the wife"	šē-ã	"the dog"

The examples in (30) also show the nasalization of the vowel of Def. In HC this rule extends to the *l*, which is assimilated variably to the preceding nasal consonant:

(31) madãm-lã   ~   madãm-nã
     lalin-lã   ~   lalin-nã   "the moon"
     lãŋ-lã   ~   lãŋ-nã   "the tongue"

and even extends across non-nasal segments. In (32), the vowel of Det is nasalized when it follows a word containing a high vowel preceded by a nasal consonant and followed by up to two non-nasal segments:

(32) žẽnu-ã   "the knee"
     mãgo mi-ã   "the ripe mango"
     klinik-lã   "the clinic"
     kãnif-lã   "the pen-knife"
     fãmij-u-ã   "your (particular) family"

Nasalization does not appear to be variable in the environments illustrated by (32), but it is after words ending in a nasal vowel followed by an obstruent:

(33) mõt-la   ~   mõt-lã   "the watch"
     bãk-la   ~   bãk-lã   "the bank"
     mãsõž-la   ~   mãsõž-lã   "the lie"

and after a high vowel preceded by a non-nasal consonant:

(34) vodu-a   ~   vodu-ã   "the vaudoun"

These three morphophonemic rules affecting Def serve, on the one hand, to differentiate geographical varieties of Créole, and, on the other hand (at least in HC), to provide speakers with stylistic maneuver: the environments to which nasalization has spread are less extensive in lento style.

3.2. *Sandhi alternations in Northern HC*

Because of differences in the underlying form of Poss determiners, NH provides a more suitable base for the operation of morphophonemic rules that are found also in the other two main geographical dialects of HC, Western (Port-au-Prince, WH), and Southern (SH). In NH possession is expressed by the post-posed personal pronoun introduced by the preposition *a*. This creates the possibility of V V V that are reduced in a variety of ways.

Except in very lento styles, any noun-final unrounded

vowel is truncated; the vowel of the preposition appears in its underlying form or it is nasalized when followed by a nasal consonant (with the 1 sg or 1 pl Poss):

(35) Final Vowel Truncation

sulje-a-papa	suljapapa	"father's shoes"
papa-a-jo	papajo	"their father"
papa-a-mwẽ	papãm	"my father"
diri-a-nũ	dirãnũ	"our rice"

In WH and SH, V V resulting from the post-position of the 2 sg pronoun *u* are reduced by the formation of the corresponding glide:

(36) Back glide formation

dlo-u	dlow	"your water"
pje-u	pjew	"your foot, feet"

In NH (as well as some varieties of WH and SH) the 3 sg pronoun is *li~i* rather than *li~l: li* occurs post-posed after a consonant and *i* as subject (pre-posed) or post-posed after a vowel. In the latter case, it is generally reduced to the glide *j*.

(37) Front glide formation

jo kupe i	jo kupej	"they cut it"
lapo-i	lapoj	"his skin"

Some of the early structural descriptions of HC, notably Hall (1953) and Stewart (1963), correctly observed the reduction of the final vowel of the word preceding the indefinite determiner whose usual phonic realization is *õ*:

(38) Final Vowel Truncation

se õ mun	sõ mun	"it's a person"
li gẽ õ šat	l gõ šat	"he, she has a cat"

The existence of that rule in NH, as shown by the examples in (35), suggests that this is not an idiosyncratic phenomenon limited to the indefinite determiner. Final Vowel Truncation is accompanied by a type of vowel harmony when the second of a V V is rounded or when a V is followed by the glide *w* (i.e., after Back Glide Formation has applied):

(39) Vowel Rounding

pje-u (pjew)	pjow	"your foot, feet"
avɛ u	avɔw	"with you"
papa-u	papɔw	"your father"
m ap ba u	m ap bɔw	"I'll give you"
tu sa u vle	tu sɔ vle	"all that you want"

The intermediate form in which only Black Glide Formation applies is rare. The only alternate pronunciations are in fact one in which both rules apply as in (42) or one, characteristic of lento styles, in which neither applies and in which case an intervocalic glide is inserted to reduce potential V V terminating with a rounded vowel:

(40) papa-u   papawu   "your father"
     papa o   papawo   "Oh, father!"

V V in which the first vowel is unrounded are unreduced:

(41) vɛ -a   "the glass"
     bɔkɔ -a   "the witch doctor,
                           vaudoun priest"

I illustrate the application of Back Glide Formation, Vowel Rounding, and Final Vowel Truncation in WH and NC:

(42)

	WH	NC	
Input	ake u	sulje a u	papa a u
Back Glide Formation	ake w	sulje a w	papa a w
Vowel Rounding	ako w	sulje ɔ w	papa ɔ w
Vowel Truncation	----	sulj ɔ w	pap ɔ w
Output	[akow]	[suljɔw]	[papɔw]

Vowel Truncation does not apply when the first vowel in V V or V V V is rounded; instead, the rounded vowel is replaced by the rounded back glide *w*:

(43) On-Glide Formation

do-a-mwẽ	dwãm	"my back"
põ-a-nũ	pwãnũ	"our bridge"
ku-a-i	kwaj	"son cou"

That avoidance of vowel hiatus underlies HC phonotactics is underscored by an interesting analogical development in NH. In that variety post-vocalic *r* is generally maintained, particularly in final position. Thus, pairs such as *pɛ* "peace" and *pɛr* "priest," which fall together in the WH, are kept distinct. As one would expect, the final *r* appears in the possessive construction: for instance, "my sister" is generally realized as /sɛrãm/. But an epenthetic *r* crops up unexpectedly in forms ending with a vowel in their isolated form:

(44) R-Insertion

sɛr	sɛr a m		sɛrãm	"my sister"
papa	papa a m	papãm	paparãm	"my father"
pitapitit	pitapitit a m	pitapitãm	pitapitarãm	"my grandchild"
karako	karako a m	karakwãm	karakorãm	"my nightshirt"

In NH there exist, then, two mechanisms for the reduction of V V : (1) Vowel Truncation or Glide Formation, depending on the nature of the vowels involved; (2) R-Insertion. In most cases, either of the two alternatives is available to speakers, although there are numerous lower-level constraints that restrict the choice. Presumably, the alternation between the two variants is not "free" but determined by various sociolinguistic factors that require further investigation.

The following derivations summarize the interplay of the various morphophonemic rules that reduce vowel sequences in NH:

(45)

	sɛr a m	papa-a-m	papa-a-m	papa-a-u	do-a-m
Input	sɛr a m	papa-a-m	papa-a-m	papa-a-u	do-a-m
R-Insertion	------	paparam	------	------	------
On-Glide formation	----	-------	-------	-------	dw a m
Back Glide formation	------	-------	-------	papa a w	-------
Vowel Harmony	------	-------	-------	papa ɔ w	-------
Vowel Truncation	------	-------	pap a m	pap ɔ w	-------
Nasalization	sɛrãm	paparãm	papãm	------	dwãm
Output	[sɛrãm]	[paparãm]	[papãm]	[papɔw]	[dwãm]

These fall short of indicating the total range of variants available to speakers of the dialect. In lento styles, they may employ the full (non-truncated) form of the personal pronouns; for instance instead of *ser-a-m*, they might start from *ser-a-mwẽ*, in which case none of the rules apply and the output is [seramwẽ]. Since WH constitutes the prestige dialect, speakers of NH will shift in that direction under certain circumstances (Orjala 1970). The two possible WH outputs, [sɛm] or [sɛmwẽ] are added to the repertoire of NH, thus making a total of four phonic realizations for that particular combination of formatives.

4. ELABORATION AND THE TERMINUS
A QUO OF CRÉOLE

4.1. *The gradualness of elaboration*

The shift from pre-posed to post-posed noun determiners does not appear to have involved rapid and massive restructuring; rather, it must have taken the form of a series of small, gradual changes spreading differentially across social groups and geographical boundaries. The scarcity of recorded samples of Créole in its formative period (approximately 1650 to 1750 in the New World and 1700 to 1800 in the Indian Ocean) makes it difficult to reconstruct steps in the evolution of the language and to confirm or invalidate the hypothesis I have set forth in 2., namely, that the New World varieties of Créole, particularly HC, display an innovative determiner system and that the system found in the Indian Ocean dialects reflects more closely that of a common pre-creole base. The reconstruction of the determiner system of a hypothetical proto-Créole and the charting of its differentiation into the various systems attested today must proceed mainly by the use of the comparative method.

If, following language variationists, one assumes that language change starts out as synchronic variation, evidence for the evolution of Créole must be sought primarily in linguistic variants observable today. Students of Créole are in a rather privileged position since its dialects are disseminated widely in two geographically distant parts of the world and since there exist today several relatively isolated Créole-speaking communities, for example, the Leeward British-influenced islands of Grenada, Saint-Vincent, and Carriacou, as well as Saint-Barts (Saint Barthélemy), a tiny dependency of Guadeloupe settled originally by whites. I have pointed out that an important step leading to the post-position of Poss was the replacement in the pronominal system of case variation by sandhi alternation (see examples (22) and (23) in 2.1.). Sandhi variation taking the form of vowel deletion is found widely in New World varieties of Créole from Louisiana to Trinidad. That the seeds of this type of variation were already present in the vernacular forms of French in use in seventeenth-century overseas colonies is suggested by such sandhi alternations as *m~mwē* '1 sg' found in White Reunionnese or Créole des Blancs des Hauts (Chaudenson 1974, Corne 1975):

(46) m i māz lavian   "I eat meat"
mwē lete i māz lavian "I ate meat"

The presence of post-posed determiners in many languages of West Africa was no doubt an important factor in the restructuring of the Créole system in the Caribbean. The shift to post-position of determiners should not, however, be viewed as the direct transfer of a feature from the substrate languages. The presence of post-positions in the languages spoken by the imported slaves played the role of catalyst, for a tendency toward post-position was already found in overseas varieties of French; such focussing constructions as *le fils à Paul, c'est son fils à lui* constitute a salient feature of present-day colloquial styles of French and could have served as models for the Créole Poss constructions.

An important question in pidgin and creole linguistics is the degree of elaboration undergone by the terminus a quo of existing creoles. The standard view of pidginization and creolization as mirror-image processes (Hall 1966) implies a two-step development of creoles. The first step involves rapid and drastic restructuring producing a language variety reduced and simplified with regard to the base language. The second step consists of the elaboration of the product of pidginization as its functions expand and as it becomes nativized. But relatively stable and elaborated systems may emerge from contact situations that give rise to pidginized varieties of a language. For example, the pidginized variety of French in use in the Ivory Coast (Français Populaire d'Abidjan) exhibits a determiner system composed of post-posed Def *-la* followed by a number marker (*-lui* for Sg and *-leur* for Pl) that contrasts sharply with the absence of obligatory determiners or the widely variant use of pre-posed reflexes of French determiners characteristic of early-stage pidgin French (Valdman and Phillips 1975, Phillips 1975). There is no indication that this stabilized and elaborated subsystem developed over a longer time span than the thirty- to fifty-year period Chaudenson posits for the emergence of such characteristic creoles as Créole or Sranan on the strength of external evidence. Thus, creoles may be formed by means of a one-step restructuring process, as suggested by Alleyne (1971) and several of the contributors to this volume, and the distinction between pre-pidgin and pre-creole continua is unwarranted.

One of the reasons for the adoption of the two-step model

for the genesis of creoles is the assumption that pidginization was effected on highly standardized and inflected forms of western European languages. The restructuring process evidenced by the comparison of the structure of a present-day creole and its base language appears therefore to be very extensive and can be explained only by resort to an intermediate pidginization stage comprising reduction and simplification. As suggested by Schuchardt, from a typological point of view, the structure of English does not differ strikingly from that of its creole derivates; in the following discussion I should like to show that this is also the case for the varieties of French from which Créole no doubt evolved.

4.2. *Elaboration in the verbal system of Créole*

The verbal system of Créole indeed is markedly different from that of Standard French: (1) it gives priority to aspectual rather than tense distinctions; (2) tense-aspect categories are expressed by free morphemes occurring pre-posed to invariable stems rather than by inflectional suffixes and stem alternations. The basic system of Créole is found in the Caribbean varieties: in addition to a zero form that may refer to the present or past depending on whether the stem is stative or non-stative and on various contextual factors, tense-aspect categories are signalled by three particles (see Table 2). Except for the Lesser Antillean varieties of Créole (LAC), where the non-punctual is realized by *ka* and the irrealis by *ke* or *kaj*, verb particles correspond phonologically to French auxiliaries or modals: the non-punctual (Progr) marker (*pe/ap/ape/apre*) is derived from the preposition *après*; the irrealis particle *ava/va/a* has its source in the present tense form of *aller*; the anterior particle *te* originates in the imperfect or past participle of *être*. In the absence of detailed descriptions of the verb system of any dialect of Créole at the semantactic level, it is difficult to assert that HC and the LAC and Guyanan varieties share the same set of deep-level verbal categories despite differences in the phonological shape of morphemes. In fact there is one significant difference in semantic range between the Progr particle of HC and that of LAC. In the latter *ka* may also express habitual and iterative, whereas these categories are realized in HC by the zero form rather than by *ap*. Nonetheless it is clear that Caribbean varieties reflect a verbal system that is conservative with respect to that found in the Indian Ocean dialects.

ASPECTS→↓	PUNCTUAL	NON-PUNCTUAL	TENSE↓
REALIS	ϕ : ϕ	ap : ka	NON-ANTERIOR
	te : te	t ap : te ka	ANTERIOR
IRREALIS	a : ke/kaj	av ap : ke ka	NON-ANTERIOR
	ta : te ke	t av ap : te ke ka	ANTERIOR
	HC : LAC	HC : LAC	

Table 2

Tense-Aspect Markers of Haitian (HC)
And Lesser Antillean-Guyanan Créole (LAC)

The verb system of IOC, found typically in Mauritian and Seychellois, shows considerable elaboration. Differences between Caribbean and Indian Ocean dialects appear at the semantactic rather than at the phonological level; in fact, from the latter standpoint, Mauritian and Seychellois verb markers correspond closely to those of HC (see Tables 2 and 3). Elaboration in the Indian Ocean dialects has proceeded by the grammaticalization of distinctions incipient in HC, particularly the shift of the modals *fini* and *fεk* 'immediate past' to verbal particles. While recent descriptions of Mauritian and Seychellois differ in many details (Baker 1972; Corne 1973, 1974; Moorghen 1972; Papen 1975), they all identify the verbal categories appearing in Table 3.

Whereas in the New World dialects the zero form implies completion, at least for non-stative verbs, in IOC that aspect is expressed overtly by *fin* (~*in*~*n*), a reduced form of *fini* "to finish":

(47) letã ki li *n* met so maj   "When he had (com-
dã magazẽ, lera vini,   pleted) putting his corn
mãz so maj   in the barn, Rat came and
                            ate his corn"

	Pres	Past	Future$_1$	Future$_2$
ONE MARKER				
	φ	ti	a(va)	pu
TWO-MARKER COMBINATIONS				
Past	---	---	ti a	ti pu
Progressive	(a)pe	ti ape	a pe	pu pe
Completive	(fi)n	ti n	x	x
Actual	fek	ti fek	?	pu fek
THREE-MARKER COMBINATIONS				
Compl + Act	x	ti n fek	a n fek	pu n fek
Fut$_1$ + Act	x	ti a fek	---	---
Fut$_2$ + Act	x	ti pu fek	---	---
Progr + Act	fek pe	ti fek pe	x	x
	pe fek	ti pe fek	x	x
FOUR-MARKER COMBINATIONS				
Fut$_1$ + Compl + Act	x	ti a n fek	x	x
Fut$_2$ + Compl + Act	x	ti pu n fek	x	x
Fut$_1$ + Act + Progr	x	x	? a fek pe	---
Fut$_2$ + Act + Progr	x	x	---	pu fek pe
Fut$_1$ + Compl + Progr	x	ti a n pe	? a n pe	x
Fut$_2$ + Compl + Progr	x	ti pu n pe	x	pu n pe

(x represents a non-permissible combination)

Table 3

Tense-Aspect Markers of Mauritian
and Seychellois Créole

The completive marker may occur with the verb *fini:*

> (48) i *n* fini mãz sõ banan   "He has finished eating
> (Seych)   his banana"

In HC the reduced form *fin* also occurs, but it functions as a modal rather than a verb marker since, unlike the IOC Compl it is never followed by another verb marker. Compare:

> (49) li *fin* sɔti (HC)   "He has just left"
> (50) i a *n* ape mãze (Seych) "He will have been eating"

In addition, in HC, *fin* is not subject to further reduction, whereas in Maur and Seych the truncated form *n* is the most frequently used variant.

In HC *fek* is a modal verb functioning like *fin*. In IOC it appears to occupy a position intermediate between that of a modal verb, as in HC, and the full verb marker status attained by Compl *fin*. In Seych it occurs always following *fin*:

(51) i *n fek* al labutik   "he has just gone to the shop"

but in Maur it may occur preceding or following it:

(52) Li *fek fin* al labutik

versus

(53) Zan *in fek* soti   "Jane has just left"

In both dialects the occurrence of *fek* is variable with respect to the Progr marker *ape*:

(54) nu ti ape *fek* koz u la   "We were just talking about
     (Seych)   you"

(55) nu ape *fek* koz u
     (Maur)

versus

(56) mo *fek* pe (ape) zwe   "I have just been playing"
     (Maur)

(57) lor ki zot *fek* pe koze? "Who have you just been
                                 talking about"

The variation in syntactic position exhibited by *fek* suggests that it is a modal undergoing grammaticalization, an evolution now completed for Compl *fin* in IOC and incipient in HC.

Of the two irrealis markers, *pu* indicates the speaker's intent to carry out the action or the certainty of the action or state. Compare:

(58) li pu gaɲ en baba   "She'll have a child (it's
                           certain since she is already
                           pregnant)"

(59) li a gaɲ en baba   "She'll have a child (if she
                           continues not taking the
                           pill)"

Corne (1975, p. 58) states that in Seych the distinction between *pu* and *a* is reversed, the latter indicating certainty, and that the two markers differ with regard to the relative distance of a future event, *a* referring to a less distant event. Considerable fluctuation is observed in the use of the two irrealis markers, which suggests that the distinction is a vestigial feature being lost more rapidly in Seych than in Maur. The origin of the differentiation is clear, however. In HC *pu* occurs as a sort of complementizer with exhortative or obligative meaning:

(60) se pu ou fe sa   "You have to do that"
(61) m pu kuri vit si   "I'll have to run fast so that the
      pu lapli pa muje mwẽ   rain won't get me wet"

One can readily envisage the grammaticalization of HC *pu* accompanied by a semantic shift from weakened obligation to definite futurity, with the irrealis marker *a* taking on more restricted meaning.[6]

4.3. *The source of the Créole verb system*

It is in its verbal system that specialists of Créole have seen a clear effect of African servile languages. Even Hall—who could hardly be called a substratophile, let alone a substratomaniac—declares (1966, p. 109): ". . . the entire inflectional system of the Haitian Creole verb with its loss of tense and person-and-number endings and its use of aspectual prefixes, is straight African."[7] Bentolila (1971) suggested that the basic verbal system of Créole originates in Fon, and he was able to show remarkable similarities between the two languages (see Table 4). Not only do Fon and HC each have three tense-aspect markers with comparable semantic range but, with the exception of the anterior and irrealis, the markers occur in the same position relative to each other.

ASPECT	PUNCTUAL		NON-PUNCTUAL		TENSE
REALIS	φ	*φ*	ap	*do*	NON-ANTERIOR
	te	*ko*	t ap	*ko do*	ANTERIOR
IRREALIS	a	*na*	av ap	*na do*	NON-ANTERIOR
	ta	*na ko*	t av ap	*na ko do*	ANTERIOR

Table 4

Comparison of Tense-Aspect Marker Systems of
Haitian Créole and Fon (Italics)

Similarities involving complete subsystems can hardly be invoked to argue for a close genetic link between two languages, for they could be just as well explained by appeal to linguistic universals; and in fact Bickerton accounts for the similarities between the verb systems of creoles derived from different base languages and spoken in widely distant parts of the world (Jamaican Creole, Sranan, HC, Papiamentu, and Hawaiian Creole) by claiming that it represents the simplest and most "natural" system children can construct when confronted with an inadequate linguistic input (1974 and his contribution to this volume). Claims for the direct transfer of features from African languages to Créole can only be supported by the comparison of very specific features, such as the use of the third person plural pronoun as plural marker (see 2.2.) or focussing constructions involving clefting and nominalization of verbs evidenced by Caribbean creoles derived from different base languages (Williams 1976, Valdman 1977).

The verbal system of Créole appears strikingly different when compared to that of Standard French. But an examination of overseas vernacular varieties reveals that analyticity in the expression of verbal categories and the absence of person-number inflection are not alien to certain types of French. Appeal need not be made to decreolization to account for the presence of these two features in Créole.

Immediately after declaring that it is impossible to account for the verbal system of HC in terms of a normal evolution from French, Comhaire-Sylvain (1935, p. 106) mentions a large number of periphrastic constructions with aspectual meaning found in vernacular varieties of French. In a detailed study Gougenheim (1971, pp. 55ff.) lists numerous periphrastic constructions with durative and several with prospective meaning: *être après, être après à, être en voie de, être en route de*, etc., and *être pour* and *être en devoir de*, etc., respectively. One periphrastic construction that is particularly noteworthy is the use of embedded clauses introduced by *qui* to express Progr. This construction is noted by Grégoire in the speech of children (1947:II, p. 197):

(62) Ti frère qui pleure.   "Little brother is crying"
Y a petit frère qui pleure.

and in colloquial varieties of French (*Français populaire*) by Séchehaye (1926, p. 122):

(63) Ma poupée qui est cassée. "My doll is broken"

(64) Madame, vot' broche qui   "Lady, your brooch is
se décroche.   coming undone"

Reflexes of this construction are found in the speech of leeward Saint-Bart whites and in a more conservative variety of that speech attested in the Carénage section of Saint-Thomas in the U.S. Virgin Islands. In Carénage French (Valdman 1973, Highfield 1976) a construction with embedded main verb introduced by *qui* and where the higher verb is a form of *être* expresses present and past progressive as well as future:

(65) al e ki vej   "She's watching"
(66) al ete ki dize   "She was saying"
(67) al e ki va la fer   "She's going to do it"

This construction occurs with the same meaning in Reunionnese (Chaudenson 1974):

(68) li lete ki asiz   "She was sitting down"

and appears to be the source of one of the variant expressions of past tense:[8]

(69) mwẽ lete (te) i mãz lavian   "I ate meat"

It is likely that the varieties of French surviving in New World isolates (Valdman 1974) reflect those that were in use in the plantation colonies of the seventeenth and eighteenth centuries. These varieties show vestigial person-number inflection (for example, in Carénage French only in the present tense of *être* and *avoir* are there variant forms *sy/e/sõ* and *a/e* respectively). However, these varieties of French differ from Créole by the presence of stem alternation. For instance, in Carénage French, verbs have from three to four stems, e.g., *vwer/vwe/voje/vwere* "to see"; *prã/prãde/prãdre* "to take." This system of stem alternants survives in Reunionnese, in which *être* is realized by three forms in addition to a zero: *sora~sra* 'future', *sore~sre* 'past future (conditional)'; *ete~et~lete~te; le* (the last two stems do not by themselves express any grammatical categories, but instead appear to be variable forms of the base). Reunionnese also shows alternations in which one of the variants contains the reflex of a French-inflected stem and the other has a more analytic structure (Corne 1975, pp. 74, 91):[9]

(70) mwe lore mãz lavian   "I should have eaten the meat"
(71) mwe te i sa mãz lavian
(72) m i mãzra pa lavian   "I won't eat the meat"
(73) ma a mãz lavian   "I'll eat the meat"

It is difficult to interpret the widely variable data from Reunionnese that may result from dialect mixture. The same situation obtains in Acadian Louisiana, where a post-creole continuum seems to have formed not between the creole and the standard version of the base language as in the case for many English-based creoles, but between the creole and vernacular, 'advanced' varieties of the base language.[10] In any case, a preliminary comparison of the verbal systems of Créole and overseas vernacular varieties of French reveals that a structural bridge exists between them. This suggests that Créole dialects arose by the pidginization of overseas vernacular varieties of French in the special type of language contact situation that characterized the plantation colonies of the seventeenth and eighteenth centuries (see Chaudenson's contribution this volume).

In the verbal system pidginization operated on a base in which tense-person inflection was only vestigial, and it took the form of the replacement of a set of differentiated stems in favor of a more analytic system involving the use of particles expressing tense-aspect categories pre-posed to an invariable stem.

NOTES

*The research reported in this article was supported in part by a research grant from the National Endowment for the Humanities, No. 10298-74-251.

1. Créole dialects form four major groups (the number of speakers is indicated in parentheses): (1) Haiti (approx. 5,000,000), divided into three regional varieties—West (Port-au-Prince), South, and North; (2) Lesser Antilles: Guadeloupe (325,000), Martinique (350,000), Dominica (55,000), Saint-Lucia (75,000), marginally in Grenada, Saint-Vincent, and Trinidad (except for the overseas departments [D.O.M.] of Guadeloupe and Martinique, the Lesser Antilles dialects of Créole coexist with English, in both its creole and standard varieties); (3) the D.O.M. of French Guyana (45,000) and, marginally, Louisiana, which constitute conservative areas; (4) Mauritius (850,000), Rodrigues (20,000), the Seychelles (50,000), and the D.O.M. of Reunion (450,000); the latter variety is distinguished sharply from the other three.

From a sociolinguistic point of view three major types of situations are found in Créole-speaking territories: (1) strict diglossia with marginal bilingualism: Haiti; (2a) diglossia with bilingualism, where the dominant language is French: the French D.O.M.; (2b) diglossia with bilingualism, where the dominant language is English and where vernacular status is shared with creolized varieties of English: the British-influenced Lesser Antilles; (3) diglossia with multilingualism, characteristic especially of Mauritius but also to some extent of the Seychelles and Rodrigues, where Créole shares vernacular status with several varieties of Chinese and Indo-European and Tamil languages of India, and where English occupies a position of dominance alongside French.

Varieties of Créole form a closely knit group of dialects, but mutual intelligibility is probably quite low between dialects belonging to different geographical groups. Créole dialects share basic vocabulary, but they are set off by major differences in morphosyntax and phonology.

2. There are in addition two major differences in the structure of the vowel systems of New World and Indian Ocean dialects (IOC). First, in the latter, high-mid and low-mid vowels do not contrast and occur, more or less, in complementary distribution: the high-mid member of each pair of mid vowels occurs in open syllables and the low-mid member in checked syllables. In the transcription of IOC data, I will use the symbols *e* and *o* to represent both high- and low-mid allophones. The second difference is found in nasal vowels. In IOC, vowels occurring before a nasal consonant are not as strongly nasalized as in Caribbean varieties.

3. Another possible source is the subject (pre-posed) form of the personal pronouns that, except for the 3 sg, coincide with the Poss determiners; there is no differentiation of form for the plural persons:

	Subject	*Possessive*		*Object*
	(*Pre-posed*)			(*Post-posed*)
1sg	mo			mwa
2sg	to			two
3sg	li	so		li
1 pl			nu	
2 pl/3 pl			zot	

Additional support for this etymology is provided by 2 sg forms noted in Martinican (Jourdain 1956, p. 102):

m a prā iš-to   "I am going to take your children"
ki krije to   "Who called you?"

4. The Créole version of the parable of the Prodigal Son was composed, no doubt by a plantation owner or public official returned from Saint-Domingue, for a dialect survey organized in France by the baron Charles-Etienne Coquebert de Montbret in the early years of the nineteenth

century. It was first published in the annals of the Société des Antiquaires de France (Vol. 6, 1824, pp. 532-45) and then reedited in *Mélanges sur les langues et les patois* (Paris: Delaunay, pp. 5-29; 532-56). I am indebted to Arnold Highfield, College of the Virgin Islands, for having brought this text to my attention.

5. The first version of this song appeared in Moreau de Saint-Méry, *Description topographique, physique, civile, politique et historique de la partie française de l'île de Saint-Domingue* (1793); the second in a linguistic appendix to S. J. Ducoeurjoly's *Manuel des habitants de Saint-Domingue* (1802); the third, in an anonymous collection, *Idylles et Chansons de Saint-Domingue ou essais de Poésie Créole*, published in Philadelphia in 1811.

6. It is likely that *pu* definite future marker of Mauritian and the obligative complementizer of HC both originate in a periphrastic construction of older-stage IOC (Bourbonnais) with obligative meaning: *sa k lave pur ale* "those who had to die." The HC and the Mauritian developments are then independent.

7. Other creolists claim a direct African origin for the phonological shape of verb particles. Comhaire-Sylvain (1936) derives the irrealis marker *a* (~*ava*~*va*) from a Bantu root *bia;* Goodman (1964:85) finds various African etyma for the LAC Progr *ka* that Hull (1975) prefers to derive from Guinea Gulf Portuguese Creole by the intermediary of relexification.

8. The form *lete* (occurring also in a truncated variant *te*) would seem to have its source in the invariant past stem of *être, ete*. The prosthetic *l* comes from the pre-vowel form of the 3 sg pronoun; see the Carénage examples (65)-(67). Corne (1975) derives the mysterious *i* of Reunionnese, functioning as a predicate marker in (69), from *ki*.

9. The form *sa* occurs, also with prospective and irrealis meaning, in Louisianan Créole: *mo sa la* "I'll be there" (Broussard 1942), but only in the copula; the more general irrealis marker is *a*. Thomas (1869, p. 57) lists for Trinidadian Créole *se* as 'conditional' marker (*mwē se va/se a māže* "I should have eaten"). The latter combination alternates with *te va/te a*.

10. It is difficult, for both Reunion and Acadian Louisiana, to determine whether a form reflecting stem alternation or person-number inflection is the result of decreolization in the direction of Standard French or Acadian French or the survival of an older stage of decreolization or depidginization. Broussard notes for Louisianan Créole an alternation *mo te travaj*~*mo travaje*, but states that the latter is found in the speech of "Negroes who have been raised in closer contact with Whites."

REFERENCES

Alexandre, Pierre. 1963. Aperçu sommaire sur le Pidgin A 170 du Cameroun. *Cahiers d'Etudes Africaines* 3:577-82.

Alleyne, Mervyn C. 1971. Acculturation and the cultural matrix of creolization. In *Pidginization and Creolization of Languages,* D. Hymes, ed., pp. 169-86.

Bailey, Beryl L. 1966. *Jamaican Creole Syntax.* Cambridge: Cambridge University Press.

Bailey, Charles-James N. 1974. *Variation and Linguistic Theory.* Arlington, Va.: Center for Applied Linguistics.

Baker, Philip. 1972. *Kreol.* London: Hurst.

Bentolila, Alain. 1971. Les systèmes verbaux créoles: Comparaisons avec les langues africaines. Thèse de 3e cycle de l'Université de Paris V-René Descartes.

Bickerton, Derek. 1974. Creolization, linguistic universals, natural semantax and the brain. *Working Papers in Linguistics* (University of Hawaii) 6:125-41.

_____. 1975. *Dynamics of a Creole System.* London: Cambridge University Press.

Bouquiaux, Luc. 1969. La créolisation du français par le sango véhiculaire, phénomène réciproque. In *Le français en France et Hors de France I: Créoles et Contacts Africains,* pp. 57-68. Paris: Belles Lettres.

Broussard, James F. 1942. *Louisiana Creole Dialect.* Port Washington, N.Y., and London: Kennikat Press.

Chaudenson, Robert. 1974. *Le lexique du parler créole de la Réunion.* Paris: Champion. 2 vols.

Cole, Desmond T. 1953. Fanagalo and the Bantu languages in South Africa. *African Studies* 12:1-9.

Comhaire-Sylvain, Suzanne. 1936. *Le créole haïtien: morphologie et syntaxe.* Port-au-Prince and Wetteren.

Corder, S. Pit. 1975. 'Simple codes' and the sources of the second language learner's initial heuristic hypothesis. *Theoretical Models in Applied Linguistics IV* (Fourth Neuchâtel Symposium), S. Pit Corder and Eddy Roulet, eds. Paris, Didier and Brussels: AIMAV (forthcoming).

Corne, Chris. 1973. The tense-aspect system of Mauritian Creole. *Te Reo* 16:45-60.

_____. 1975. Tense, aspect and the mysterious *i* in Seychelles and Reunion Creole. *Te Reo* (1974-75):53-93.

Dulay, Heidi C., and Burt, Marina K. 1972. Goofing: an indicator of children's second-language strategies. *Language Learning* 22:235-52.

————. 1974a. Natural sequences in child language acquisition. *Language Learning* 24:37-53.

————. 1974b. Error and strategies in child second-language acquisition. *TESOL Quarterly* 8:129-36.

Etienne, Gérard. 1974. Le créole du Nord d'Haïti: Etude des niveaux de structure. Unpublished doctoral diss., Université de Strasbourg.

Faine, Jules. 1936. *Philologie créole; études historiques et étymologiques sur la langue créole d'Haïti.* Port-au-Prince: Imprimerie de l'Etat.

Goodman, M. F. 1964. *A Comparative Study of Creole French Dialects.* The Hague: Mouton.

Gougenheim, Georges. 1971. *Etude sur les périphrases verbales de la langue française.* Paris: Nizet.

Grégoire, Antoine. 1947. *L'apprentissage du langage*, vol. II: *La troisième année et les années suivantes* (Fascicule CVI, Bibliothèque de la Faculté de Philosophie et Lettres de l'Université de Liège). Paris: Belles Lettres.

Hall, Robert A., Jr. 1953. *Haitian Creole: grammar—texts—vocabulary.* Memoirs of the American Folklore Society 43. Baltimore: Waverly Press.

————. 1966. *Pidgin and Creole Languages.* Ithaca: Cornell University Press.

Highfield, Arnold R. 1976. The French dialect of Saint-Thomas, U. S. Virgin Islands: A descriptive grammar with texts and glossary. Unpublished doctoral diss., Ohio State University.

Hymes, Dell, ed. 1971. *Pidginization and Creolization of Languages.* London: Cambridge University Press.

Hull, Alexander. 1974. Evidence for the original unity of North American French Dialects. *Louisiana Review* 3:59-70.

————. 1975. On the origin and chronology of the French-based creoles. Revised draft of paper presented at International Conference on Pidgins and Creoles, Honolulu 1975.

Jourdain, Elodie. 1956. *Du français aux parlers créoles.* Paris: Klincksieck.

Labov, William. 1971. On the adequacy of natural languages: I. The Development of Tense. Unpublished draft. University of Pennsylvania.

Manessy, Gabriel. 1975. Pidgin et créole; pidginisation et créolisation. *Bulletin du Centre d'Etudes des Plurilinguismes,* No. 2:3-14. Nice: IDERIC, Université de Nice.

Moorghen, Pierre-Marie J. 1972. Etude structurale du créole de l'île Maurice: la phrase minimale, les transformations facultatives. Thèse de 3e cycle, Université de Nice.

Orjala, Paul R. 1970. A dialect survey of Haitian Creole. Unpublished doctoral diss., Hartford Seminary Foundation.

Polomé, Edouard C. 1968. Lubumbashi Swahili. *Journal of African Languages* 7:14-25.

Papen, Robert A. 1975. *A Short Grammar of Seychellois Creole.* Unpublished draft.

Partmann, Gayle H. 1973. Etude comparative du dioula traditionnel et du dioula commercial dans le parler des jeunes et dans le parler d'une génération supérieure. Unpublished doctoral diss., Stanford University.

Phillips, John S. 1975. Vietnamese contact French: Variation in a contact situation. Unpublished doctoral diss., Indiana University.

Robert, Peter A. 1971. *The verb in Grenadian French Creole.* Unpublished master's thesis, University of the West Indies, Jamaica.

Saint-Jacques-Fauquenoy, Marguerite. 1972. *Analyse structurale du créole guyanais.* Paris: Klincksieck.

Samarin, William J. 1970. Lingua francas in the world. In *Readings in the Sociology of Language,* J. A. Fishman, ed. The Hague: Mouton, pp. 660-72.

————. 1971. Salient and substantive pidginization. In Hymes (ed.), pp. 117-40.

Sankoff, Gillian, and Laberge, S. 1974. On the acquisition of native speakers by a language. In *Pidgins and Creoles: Current Trends and Prospects,* David DeCamp and Ian F. Hancock, eds. Washington, D. C.: Georgetown University Press, pp. 73-84.

Schuchardt, Hugo. 1883-91. Kreolische Studien I-IX. Sitzungsberichte des k.k. Akademie der Wissenschaften zu Wien. (Philosophische-Historische Klasse) 116:227-34.

Séchehaye, C. Albert. 1926. *Essai sur la structure logique de la phrase.* Paris: Champion.

Stewart, William A. 1963. The functional distribution of Creole and French in Haiti. In *Linguistics and Language Study* (13th Georgetown Roundtable Meeting), E. D. Woodworth and R. J. Di Pietro, eds. Washington, D. C.: Georgetown University Press, pp. 149-62.

Taylor, Douglas R. 1968. Le créole de la Dominique. In *Le langage,* A. Martinet, ed. Paris: Gallimard, pp. 1022-49.

Thomas, John Jacob. 1869. *The Theory and Practice of Creole Grammar.* Port of Spain: Chronicle Publishing Office. (Reprinted 1969, London: New Beacon Books Ltd.)

Tinelli, Henri. 1974. Generative and creolization processes: nasality in Haitian Creole. *Lingua* 33:343-66.

————. 1975. Elision rules, syllabic consonants, and vowel harmony in Haitian Creole. *Orbis* 2:358-76.

Turiault, Jean. 1874-77. Etude sur le créole de la Martinique. (*Bulletin de la Société Académique de Brest.* 2e série, 1:401-516; 3:1-111). Brest.

Valdman, Albert. 1973. Some aspects of decreolization in Creole French. In *Current Trends in Linguistics*, Thomas A. Sebeok, ed. Vol. XI: *Diachronic, Areal and Typological Linguistics.* The Hague: Mouton, pp. 507-36.

_____. 1974. Le parler vernaculaire des isolats français en Amérique du Nord. *Louisiana Review* 3:43-58.

_____. 1975. Créole et français en Haïti. *French Review* 49:174-85.

_____. 1976. *Introduction to French Phonology and Morphology.* Rowley, Mass.: Newbury House.

_____. 1977. *La structure, le statut et l'origine du créole.* Paris: Klincksieck (forthcoming).

Valdman, Albert, and Phillips, John S. 1975. Pidginization and creolization and the elaboration of learner systems. *Theoretical Models in Applied Linguistics IV* (Fourth Neuchâtel Symposium).

Williams, Wayne R. 1976. *Linguistic Change in the Syntax and Semantics of Sierra Leone Krio.* Unpublished doctoral diss., Indiana University.

The Question of Prior Creolization
in Black English

John R. Rickford

I. THE BASIC ISSUE

Of the many controversies that have attended investigations of Black English in recent years, no single issue has attracted greater interest and argument than that of its "creole origin." However, debate on this question, whether in the published literature or elsewhere, is frequently hampered by the absence of any clear statement about what the central issues and opposing viewpoints are. Many statements of the issue contain several propositions in one, or are too polemically worded to be useful. Sometimes, preliminary definitions are dispensed with altogether, and people begin trading arguments from the outset about whether BE has a different deep structure or not, how many Africanisms it contains, how much it resembles seventeenth-century colonial English, and so on. When the dust has finally settled, we remain no closer to a resolution of the central issues, because we have come to no agreement on what they are, or of how these diverse arguments relate to them.

The basic issue can be simply stated in terms of a single proposition: was there prior creolization in the history of BE? The "creolists" say yes, and the "non-creolists" say no. Other issues—such as whether and how fast the first generations of Afro-Americans acquired the speech patterns of whites around them, how many Africanisms they retained—are certainly relevant. But they need to be subsumed under the basic proposition, and their relevance to it explicitly justified.

Before we can actually investigate the probability of prior creolization in BE, there are some preliminary questions that we will need to consider.[1] What is involved in the processes of pidginization and creolization? Were social and historical circumstances in the United States of the kind that would favor such processes? What criteria exist for determining prior creolization in a language that is not now a creole?

Questions like these have been attracting considerable attention within the field of "creole studies" as a whole, but the discussions have not been brought to bear on the creole origins of BE in any systematic or explicit way. In section II of this paper, I shall explore each of these questions in turn, concentrating, however, on the use of various criteria for prior creolization, which we shall then apply to synchronic evidence from BE in section III.

II. SOME PRELIMINARY QUESTIONS

1. *Pidginization, creolization, and decreolization*

Clear, unitary definitions of the terms "pidgin" and "creole," of the type that Hall (1966) tried to establish, no longer meet with universal agreement. Hall's definitions were extended and qualified at the 1968 Mona Conference (Hymes 1971), and the question of definitions was still very much in ferment at the 1975 pidgin/creole conference in Hawaii.

However, certain basic characteristics of pidginization and creolization as processes, and pidgins and creoles as results, seem to be accepted by many creolists. The following sketch obviously owes much to the discussion in Hymes (1971, p. 84) and the work of the other scholars on which it is based. However, I have modified Hymes's definitions somewhat so that they depend less on his preceding discussion, and have added a definition of decreolization, since it is very much of relevance here.

The process of *pidginization* is usually assumed to begin when a language is used only for very limited communication between groups who speak different native languages. Sharply restricted in domains of use, it undergoes varying degrees of "simplification" and "admixture." If a new stable variety of the language emerges from this process, it might be described as a *pidgin.*

Creolization is the process by which one or more pidginized variants of a language (emerging from an initial multilingual contact situation of the type just described), are extended in domains of use and in the range of communicative and expressive functions they must serve. Frequently, but not necessarily, this process is associated with native use by children born into the contact situation. The pidginized variants are usually assumed to undergo "complication" and "expansion" of linguistic resources in the process, and the term *creole* may be used for any new stable variety that results from this process.

In *decreolization* the creolized varieties lose their distinctive features and begin to level in the direction of the original target language. This change occurs in the multilingual contact situation as the social and economic pressures to use the target language in more and more domains become increasingly pronounced, and as opportunities to master the language improve. A *(post-)creole continuum* of dialect varieties exhibiting varying approximations to the standard form of the target language is one typical result.

The preceding definitions, though inadequate in several respects, should help provide the basic orientation necessary to approach the issue of the "creole origin" of BE. I have chosen to center the discussion in this paper around the term "creolization," partly because it is the central link in the chain of processes described above, and partly because it makes more provisions for the existence of variation in the contact situation (cf. Alleyne 1971) than the term "creole" as normally used. Once we have established that prior creolization might have occurred in the history of BE (a slightly stronger claim than pidginization by itself), we might want to ask further if the result was stable enough to be called a *creole*. But we need not complicate our task by requiring that the kind of evidence that might be needed for subsequent and stronger claims be considered concurrently.

2. *Sociohistorical factors*

Pidginization and creolization of languages typically occur under certain kinds of sociohistorical conditions, though these differ in some details from case to case. Even before we turn to linguistic evidence, we could begin to assess the *probability* that such processes occurred in the history of BE by considering whether sociohistorical conditions in the United States might have been favorable to them or not.

This requires extensive scrutiny, from the standpoint of prior creolization, of the vast collection of original documents and existing historical studies relating to slavery and plantation life in the United States. Herskovits (1941, pp. 110-42) comes closest to providing what is needed, but even his study must be considered incomplete, partly because his interest was in the general persistence of Africanisms, and not in prior creolization of language by itself. In the absence of and as a preliminary to the much more comprehensive study that is required, I shall restrict myself here to a few possibly relevant observations.

Mintz (1971), Grimshaw (1971), and Alleyne (1971) have sketched some of the important sociohistorical conditions in the Caribbean that accompanied the development of pidgins and creoles in this region. They provide a useful basis for comparison with conditions in the United States at an earlier stage. We know, for instance, that in the United States, as in the Caribbean, large groups of slaves, speaking a variety of native languages, were imported as a subordinate labor force into a plantation environment and economy run by various European populations. We also know that in both areas the subordinate African populations were unable to maintain their native languages for any length of time under the conditions of the contact situation, and had to acquire some competence in the dominant European languages of their new environment.

One open question, however, is whether the slaves had enough access to the European models to permit fairly competent language learning without the intervention of "pidginizing" or "creolizing" stages. In this regard, people have sometimes noted informally that "in general," plantations in the United States were smaller than those in the Caribbean. From this one might predict more opportunities for European/African contact and more efficient language learning in the face of better exposure to the standard European norm. But Phillips (1918), among others, has pointed out that there were wide differences in the proportions of whites to blacks throughout the United States, and marked differences in plantation size. We need to avoid easy generalizations and investigate the specifics of different areas in greater detail.

Questions of motivation and attitude must also be added to data on numbers and apparent opportunities for black/white contact.[2] For instance, extensive intragroup use of the new contact language among the slaves could have helped it develop into a markedly different "code" (perhaps affected more heavily by native African patterns) than the version used in communication with white masters. And even if opportunities for interracial contact allowed the slaves to become proficient in "higher lects" (i.e., closer to the language of their masters), there might have been sufficient motivation and opportunity for them to maintain their more "pidginized" code as a means of communicating among themselves without fear of detection or punishment (see Rickford and Rickford 1976 for some actual lexical examples). If their children in turn grew up hearing these more pidginized varieties spoken in the slave quarters, they would have had almost the same chance of growing up with a "creole" as children in other areas whose parents controlled *only* the pidginized varieties because of more restricted social and linguistic exposure.

This chain of possibilities becomes even more relevant if we can establish that there were significant groups of slaves who arrived in the United States already speaking a pidgin (Dillard 1972, pp. 97, 142; Stewart 1967, p. 359). We would then have to look not at conditions for the *creation* of a code, but at conditions for its *transmission* to children and other adults, and for its further development (something more along the lines suggested in the preceding paragraph).

If we are to resolve such possibilities, we will need to sift through a great deal of historical and ethnographic evidence and interpret it with great sensitivity. In any case, until we have the required documentation and analysis, there is little more we can say about the extent to which conditions favorable to creolization were present in the United States. Let us turn instead to the third preliminary question—what kinds of *linguistic* criteria might be used to assess the possibility of prior creolization in BE.

3. *Linguistic criteria for prior creolization*

There are no hard and fast criteria by which the possibility of prior creolization can be assessed using linguistic data from a later period. In this section I shall elaborate four criteria that tend to be used more or less informally when considerations of prior creolization come up. Each one has stated or unstated justifications and stated or unstated weaknesses. There are some obvious difficulties about how these criteria should be applied, and I am by no means suggesting that these are the "right" or absolutely the "only" criteria that can be applied. But they do represent the criteria that creolists usually apply, and taken together they provide both a convenient yardstick against which the possibilities of prior creolization can be measured in some systematic and replicable way, and a means of avoiding endless arguments.

The four criteria are: (1) simplification, (2) admixture (in our case, African influence), (3) divergence from other dialects, and (4) similarity to other creoles. We shall discuss each of these in turn.

3.1. *Simplification.* At first sight, it seems an embarrassment to propose this as a criterion for prior *creolization*. Surely, one might ask, it is *complication* and not *simplification* that should be relevant here. However, it is difficult to use synchronic evidence to determine whether a hypothetical creole has undergone "complication" from a preceding pidgin stage, because the pidgin itself is usually replaced in the process and is not available for comparison. However, if it is assumed that the hypothetical creole, while being more complicated than the preceding pidgin in some respects, nevertheless retained some of the pidgin's greater "simplicity" vis-à-vis the standard language, then the apparent anomaly of using "simplification" to assess prior *creolization* in a language might be excused.[3]

It is arguments like this that Southworth (1971) and Berdan (1975) bring into play when using simplification to determine prior creolization, Southworth in the case of Marathi, Berdan in the case of Black English. However, Berdan points out that the significance of such simplification is not always clear-cut. He does indeed find that processes like relative clause construction and multiple negation seem to be more "simply" organized in BE than in Standard English (SE). The simplification would be sufficiently explained by prior creolization, but it does not necessarily imply this.

To the difficulty of interpreting the significance of "simplification" must be added the difficulty of determining what counts as simplification and what does not.[4] Reduction in vocabulary size is easy enough, but other cases in syntax and semantics can be much more ambiguous, as we shall see. We also need to confess that in comparing the *present* form of the standard language with the *present* form of the hypothetical creole, we are implicitly assuming that no major changes have taken place in the relevant features being compared in both languages since the periods at which the original pidginization or creolization might have occurred. Where this assumption cannot be verified, our comparisons to determine simplification might well be meaningless.

Finally, the use of this criterion does not imply any commitment to particular hypotheses about *how* the simplification might have come about, whether by deliberate simplification (Bloomfield 1933, p. 472) or through shared linguistic/cognitive universals (Kay and Sankoff 1974).

3.2. *Admixture (African influence).* The significance of simplification might be increased if we join it to evidence of "admixture" and "intergroup use" as Hymes (1971, p. 70) suggests. Intergroup use would be established by the historical fact that the African slaves came from a variety of regions and spoke a number of different languages. This fact would also satisfy Whinnom's (1971) observation that pidgins seem to emerge only where more than two languages are involved in the contact situation.

Admixture has its difficulties, because the nature and amount that should be taken as significant is not always clear. How much "mixture" must occur for us to consider the result pidginization or creolization as distinct from the more usual kinds of "substratal influence"? And how much weight should be assigned to mixture of phonological elements versus syntactic or lexical ones?

The tendency in creole studies has been to distinguish between grammatical syncretism and syncretism of other kinds. Lexical borrowing, for instance, occurs in many kinds of ordinary language contact situations, but grammatical syncretism seems to be more widespread in the languages called pidgins and creoles. Hence the simplified but not entirely inaccurate portrayal of pidgins and creoles as "the grammar of one language and the vocabulary of another." (Taylor 1956, p. 413; Southworth 1971, p. 256). Usually, the lexicon is provided mainly by the "superstrate" language, while the grammar shows considerable influence from the "substrate" language. Thus, for instance, New Guinea Pidgin is largely English in vocabulary, but many of its best-known grammatical features, such as the use of a predicate marker *i* or a transitivizing suffix *im,* derive from the native languages of the area. Again, at least some of the serial verb constructions common in English creoles (e.g., "Run go tell she send something") reflect the influence of West African patterns (Hall 1966, p. 77; Huttar 1975).

It is here, with the criterion of admixture, that discussions about the extent of African influence on BE or its predecessors become relevant to the issue of prior creolization. In keeping with the preceding discussion, we would assign minimal weight to the persistence of African influence in lexical features, but maximum weight to African influence in grammar.

We might note that some scholars who are skeptical about the extent to which the Caribbean creoles display simplification are more confident about describing them as the result of syncretism between West African and European patterns (cf. Alleyne 1971). On the other hand African influence is often as hard to establish as simplification, partly because other plausible explanations for structural parallels and similarities between certain West African languages and European-based creoles often exist, and because the necessary African data is often difficult to obtain.

3.3. *Divergence from other dialects.* The question of prior creolization of BE has been frequently defined in terms of how different it now is from other English dialects and how different we can presume it to have been in the past (Labov 1972, p. 8, Stewart 1970, p. 241). Thus, creolists usually devote a great deal of their argument to establishing how different BE always has been from SE and other white dialects, and non-creolists argue that BE is and always was no different from Southern or colonial white dialects (Kurath 1949).

How is divergence from other dialects relevant to the issue of prior creolization? Pidgins and creoles are usually thought to differ from dialects of a language in certain respects. Dialects are usually described as having "linguistic continuity" with earlier stages or other varieties of the language (Burling 1970, p. 185), while pidgins involve "a sharp break in transmission and the creation of a new code" (Southworth 1971, p. 255). As a corollary to this, pidginized and creolized varieties of a language are frequently not intelligible to speakers of the standard language or its dialects.

Unintelligibility is a clear indication of difference or divergence, although objective tests of this are not easily found. There are other problems with applying a criterion of this sort, for instance, the problem of deciding whether it is the *number* or *nature* of differences which is more significant. Davis (1971, p. 94) seems more concerned with the small number of differences versus the huge areas of similarity, while Labov (1972, p. 37) concentrates on determining whether BE contains subsets of rules (particularly those involving central parts of the grammar, like the tense/aspect system) that are not easily integrated into other English grammars. No one can deny that BE shares almost all its

vocabulary and many of its phonological and grammatical rules
with other varieties of English. But this is also true of many
English creoles, although admittedly to a lesser extent. If
divergence is to have any usefulness as a criterion of prior
creolization, it is the *nature* of differences, and not merely their
number that must be considered.

Finally we must note Wolfram's (1971, p. 143) caveat
against linking the issue of difference so invariably to the issue of
origins. On the one hand, earlier similarities between BE and other
American dialects might have been weakened through continued
social and geographical segregation. On the other, earlier differences might have been obliterated by the effects of decreolization.
However, the former theory becomes less plausible in light of both
our earlier criteria and our final criterion—similarity to other
creoles.

3.4. *Similarity to other creoles.* The final criterion is whether BE
is similar to other creoles whose status is well established. This
kind of criterion has been given little explicit justification in the
annals of creolist theory. Note for instance, that it is included in
none of the standard definitions of pidgin or creole. And yet it
remains the most frequently used criterion for classifying a
language as pidgin or creole.

Examples of the use of this criterion can be found
everywhere (cf. Tsusaki 1971, p. 332; Todd 1975). No one, to my
knowledge, has ever established that Gullah derived from an earlier
pidgin, or displays simplification, complication, or any of the
better-established criteria (except perhaps admixture—cf. Turner
1949). And yet everyone seems to agree that Gullah is a creole.
The reason for this apparently lies in the fact that Gullah, in its
most basilectal forms, has all the "classical" features of other
English creoles: serial verbs, locative *de,* habitual/continuative *da,*
etc. It goes without saying that if BE consistently displayed all the
same features, the question of its creole status would hardly be in
doubt.

The justification for using this criterion would probably go
as follows: If a certain set of clear cases are agreed upon by
everyone to constitute pidgins and creoles in terms of the standard
theoretical parameters, and these cases display certain characteristic linguistic features, then other cases that also display these
characteristics can be assumed to belong to the same type or class,
unless evidence to the contrary is shown.

While the criterion of similarity to other creoles has

received the least justification in creolist theory, it is easier to apply in practice than other, more established criteria like simplification. Armed with some amount of familiarity with what creoles look like (Dillard 1971), one can start comparing and checking off features. However, it is not enough to compare BE with basilectal varieties of creole, and it is these, unfortunately, that usually receive the most attention. The most revealing comparisons will involve the study of mesolectal or decreolizing varieties, and these are usually the most neglected areas in the field of creole studies as a whole (Rickford 1974). Nevertheless, a few studies of decreolization in progress have begun to appear (Day 1973, Bickerton 1975), and we can supplement these with unpublished evidence where available.

Some of the most revealing synchronic BE data has simply not yet been brought to general awareness, and other well-known features have never been examined according to any systematic criteria for prior creolization. In the next section of this paper we will attempt to fill in some of the gaps by considering various kinds of synchronic BE data in terms of the four criteria we have established. It is also possible to apply these criteria to written records of black American speech in earlier times, numerous examples of which are provided in Stewart (1967, 1968) and Dillard (1972). Both kinds of application are useful, but the latter will not be attempted here.

III. SOME LINGUISTIC EVIDENCE

1. *Phonology*

1.1. *Consonant cluster simplification.* One of the most thoroughly examined features of BE phonology is consonant cluster simplification. The type we shall consider here involves the loss of *t* or *d* when it is the second member of a word-final cluster (e.g., "tes*t*," "min*d*," "lef*t*," "stabb*ed*"). On the face of it, this would seem to fit the requirements of our first criterion for prior creolization—simplification—admirably.

However, consonant cluster simplification in BE does not occur categorically, but varies according to several conditioning factors—whether the cluster exhibits homophonous voicing or not, whether it is followed by a consonant or a vowel, whether the final *t* or *d* represents the past morpheme or not. While consonant cluster simplification by itself might be considered "simpler" in some articulatory sense, it is difficult to see how a system in which its application is contingent on a host of subtle factors could be considered "simpler" than one in which simplification is either categorically present for all final clusters (the case in some West Indian creoles?) or categorically absent (more nearly the case in Standard English).

What of admixture (substratal African influence)? Although Le Page (1960, p. 18) sees consonant cluster simplification in Jamaican Creole as one example of "the process of translation [of English] by West African ears," he provides no concrete evidence in support of this. Cassidy (1961, p. 402) points out that Twi does not have /st, ld, rd and nd/ clusters (among others) in single syllables, and presumably the Twi-speaking slaves would have had difficulty with these. On the other hand, he also points out that the West African languages as a group have several other single-syllable clusters that English does not have (e.g., *kp, gb, jw*), so we cannot argue from these for the transference of any *general* principle of consonant cluster simplification. In any case, in view of the widespread occurrence of some form of consonant cluster simplification in other dialects of English (both in the United States and elsewhere), arguments for substratal influence in this case might seem very strained.

Is there nevertheless enough difference between the patterns of simplification in BE and in white American dialects to satisfy our third criterion? Labov (1972, pp. 44-46) finds that for some of the BE groups, in some styles, the *grammatical constraint* (whether the final *t* or *d* in the cluster represents the past tense morpheme) is not as strong as the *phonological constraint* (whether the cluster is followed by consonant or vowel). For the white groups he studied, the positions are reversed.

Whether this would constitute a large enough difference to satisfy criterion three will depend on how it is interpreted relative to other aspects of the BE system. From the evidence that BE speakers seem to show greater attention to the grammatical constraint in more careful styles, Labov (1972, pp. 26-29, 45-46) suggests that one can say neither that BE consonant cluster simplification lacks grammatical conditioning nor that it shows the effect of a grammar in which there is no underlying -*ed* suffix. On the basis of his evidence and interpretations, criterion three would not seem to be satisfied.

Another difference may be that for some BE speakers, certain monomorphemic words appear to have no cluster in their underlying forms, particularly where the first consonant in the cluster is *s*. Evidence for this comes from the fact that simplification of these words takes place even in the least favorable environments, before a vowel. Labov (1972, p. 22) cites *des(k)*, *ghos(t)*, and *toas(t)* for New York City speakers, and Wolfram (1971, pp. 152-54) gives *tes(t)* as an example of a larger class of words for which there is "no underlying cluster" among some blacks in Lexington, Mississippi.

This is the case for virtually all final clusters of a similar type in the basilectal varieties of Caribbean creole. In these varieties, the basis for underlying full forms is so slight that one may even question the appropriateness of "consonant cluster simplification" as a descriptive label. However, beyond the one or two illustrative examples that are usually provided, we need to know how many and which words are similarly affected in BE. If the class is large enough, we will have grounds for more fully satisfying both criteria three and four.

In attempting to apply criterion four to consonant cluster simplification beyond the cases just discussed, we are hampered by the absence of any detailed quantitative evidence for the creoles comparable to what is available for BE. However, general statements for Jamaican Creole (Cassidy 1961, p. 38) and West African Pidgin (Schneider 1966) at least provide a rough basis for comparison. Both of these languages appear to carry out the simplification of word-final clusters more categorically than does BE. They also appear to have greater simplification of *word-initial* clusters (JC *plit* for "split"; *queeze* for "squeeze") and a more frequent use of *vowel-insertion* as a means of simplifying clusters (JC *sumúud* for "smooth"; WAP *sitík* for "stick"). Some of these features appear more frequently in earlier attestations of Black English (cf. *peech* for "speech" in Dillard 1972, p. 92) than they do today.

The JC patterns compared here with synchronic BE usage are presumably the most basilectal. Whether the patterns of consonant cluster simplification in more decreolized varieties of JC or other creoles will be more obviously similar to present-day BE patterns is an important question, which only further data will resolve.

1.2. *r-deletion*. The case of r-deletion is singularly instructive of some of the problems that we face in using phonological data to establish prior creolization. We can begin by considering Table 1 (from Labov 1972, p. 42), which shows the patterns of r-lessness (what Labov here calls R-vocalization) in two white and two BE dialects in New York.

Table 1. Application of R-vocalization rule to four vernaculars.

Vernacular	(VrV)	(r##V)	(r)
BEV	low	high	obligatory
BE Middle class	low	moderate	high
WNS	no	low	obligatory
White Middle Class	no	low	moderate

The BE groups are differentiated from the white groups in two respects: (1) they can have some r-lessness in (VrV) environments like *Ca(r)ol*, where the white groups have none; (2) they can have moderate to high frequency of r-lessness in (r##V) environments like *fou(r) o'clock*, where the white groups have considerably less.

Right away we are tempted to begin applying our criteria for prior creolization. With this amount of difference between the white and black patterns established, we might want to go on to argue that the BE patterns are simpler and suggest an even more general rule for r-lessness in the past.

Before we do all this, however, consider an important point. In Los Angeles, as Pfaff (1975, p. 17) points out, "the varieties of Black English . . . are overwhelmingly r-ful." This evidence is corroborated in Legum et al. (1971, p. 42). The complete divergence of this feature of the New York and Los Angeles varieties of BE clearly indicates that they are here responding to the dominant dialect patterns of their respective areas (New York's basic r-lessness, L.A.'s basic r-fulness), rather than reflecting the effects of some earlier and common creole origin.

Differences with respect to r-lessness are also found among the Caribbean English creoles. Trinidadian English is virtually stereotyped for its general r-lessness, but *r* before ##V is not as frequently lost in Guyana and Jamaica (Cassidy 1961, p. 39). In Barbados, according to Haynes (1973, p. 5), *r* tends toward strong retroflexion.

The Caribbean English creoles also differ on other phonological features. Each territory has some distinctive patterns (both segmental and suprasegmental) that make it possible to recognize which island a person is from by what is popularly called an "accent." For instance, Barbados speech is notorious for its glottal stops, Jamaican Creole for its substitution of *bw* for initial *b* (*bwai* for "boy") and replacement of dentals by velars before *l*, as in *likl* for "little" or *niigl* for "needle" (cf. Cassidy 1961, p. 40; Wells 1973, p. 31). In vocabulary, there are similar regional differences: Guyanese *golden-apple,* Jamaican *Jew-plum,* and Trinidadian *pomme-citerre,* all referring to the same fruit. These features perhaps owe their origin in part to differences in the backgrounds of the white groups that settled in each territory.

In the United States there are other phonological differences among varieties of BE that show the effect of different regional patterns. As Labov (1972, p. 9) points out, "a speaker from the South is plainly marked in the northern Black communities," by his or her "Southern" pronunciation (the presence of a back upglide in *ball* and *hawk,* for instance). The use of individual lexical items like *tote* for "carry" might also help brand him or her as a Southerner.

It is clear from the preceding discussion that some phonological patterns are subject to wide regional variation and the same kind of easy borrowing and replacement that is characteristic of simple lexical items. If we focus on phonological and lexical items of this type, it is easy to conclude that there are no significant differences between black and white speech in the United States (as many dialectologists agree—cf. Wolfram 1971, p. 155), and that the Caribbean English creoles share no typological similarities as a group.

However, we need to balance these kinds of examples with others that are more consistently present in different regional varieties of BE and Caribbean creole, and more consistently absent from regional white dialects. Such examples appear most strikingly with grammatical variables (see below). But there are at least two examples in phonology to which we will now turn.

1.3. *Loss of initial voiced stops in auxiliaries.* BE allows the morphophonemic condensation of certain auxiliaries in ways quite unparalleled in SE or white nonstandard dialects. "Don't," for instance, can be reduced to a single nasal vowel—$\tilde{\text{o}}$ or $\tilde{\omega}$ or $\tilde{o}$—and "didn't" can be reduced to $\tilde{e}nt,$ $\tilde{e}nt$ or $\tilde{m}.$ It is as a result of this latter process that BE speakers can use *ain't* for "didn't"—a feature that observers have frequently commented upon (Fasold and Wolfram 1970, p. 69; Labov et al. 1968, pp. 255-57). Other American dialects typically employ *ain't* only for the negative forms of "am," "is," "are," "have," and "has."

As an example of a similar phenomenon, consider the possible reductions of "I am going to." All dialects share the possibility of reducing this to *mgənə*. Beyond this point, however, the similarities disappear. SE and white nonstandard dialects always retain some trace of the initial *g* in "going," if only in the form of a velar nasal, as in ŋnə. But BE allows the assimilation of the *g* to the preceding nasal, and further reduction can apply to yield simply *mənə, mnə,* or *m*. Labov et al. (1968, pp. 251-52), from whom the above discussion is taken, point out that the BE reduction route is "unusual in English."

At first these divergent BE reductions of auxiliary *don't, didn't,* and *going to* seem like isolated phenomena. Notice, however, that as a group they share the "unusual" loss of an initial voiced stop. When we turn to other English creoles, we find a whole range of comparable examples. There is alternation between *ben* and *en* in Jamaican Creole, *da* and *a* in Gullah, *go* and *o* in Sranan, *gʋn* and *ʋn, bi* and *i, dʋn* and *ʋn* in Guyana Creole, *dəz* and *əz* in Gullah as well as in the creoles of Guyana, Trinidad, Barbados, and the Bay Islands. It should be noted that these are all auxiliaries or preverbal markers. As in BE, only this subset of the class of all words beginning with voiced stops is eligible to undergo the "deletion" process. Further discussion is provided in Rickford 1975a.

The kind of complex reduction rule that these cases would require cannot in any sense be considered a simplification of the more general English patterns (criterion one). Nor do I know if there are any parallels in West African languages (criterion two). On the other hand, it is difficult to see how BE could share such a subtle rule with the Caribbean creoles here (criterion four), and how they could both be so different from other English dialects on this feature (criterion three), without positing some shared typological or genetic relationship such as prior creolization.

1.4. *Intonation.* Although many people have remarked informally that there seem to be some consistent differences between black and white speakers in their use of suprasegmental features, and several people are supposed to be investigating these, no published studies have yet appeared. Because so little is known about an area that appears so promising, I should like to include here the results of a preliminary study that I carried out in 1972 (Rickford, in Ms.).[5]

The object of the study was to determine the extent to which black and white Americans could be identified on the basis of their social speech patterns. Twenty listeners (ten white and ten black) were asked to listen to a number of sentences of very short duration (each less than two seconds long), and to identify the race of the speaker. The sentences, prerecorded on tape, were produced by two white and two black speakers. The frequency of correct ethnic identification was 85.7%.

When asked what factors helped them in their identification, thirteen of the sixteen listeners who responded referred to suprasegmental rather than segmental features. Narrow phonetic transcription and spectrographic records of one of the sentences ("Hey, what's happening?") revealed that suprasegmental features in fact provided the most consistent phonetic difference. Both black speakers used higher pitch levels and more varied intonation than the white speakers. This is revealed in the following approximate representations of the fourth harmonic, taken from spectrograms of the same sentence as produced by the two male speakers:[6]

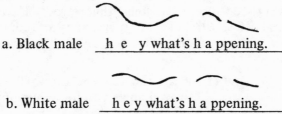

a. Black male   h e y what's h a ppening.

b. White male   h e y what's h a ppening.

The very tentative nature of these results must be emphasized. They require replication with many other subjects, and even more exact measurement. However, if the same kinds of differences receive more decisive confirmation, we would have another set of phonological evidence for prior creolization. Many Caribbean creoles are loosely described as having more varied and accidented intonation patterns than those of SE. And there has already been some discussion of whether these derive from the tonal patterns of West African languages (Cassidy 1961, pp. 26-32). Admittedly, the amount of solid empirical work in this area needs to go a long way and suffers from many of the limitations that beset the study of prosodic phenomena in linguistics as a whole. But what little has been done remains very suggestive, and cannot be ignored.

2. *Syntax/semantics*

In this section we shall concentrate on some of the central

syntactic/semantic features that distinguish the BE verb-phrase, although there are other phenomena (existential constructions, double negatives, means of expressing possession) that are equally deserving of careful scrutiny. The papers by Berdan and Pfaff cited above represent the most recent discussions of these other phenomena from the viewpoint of prior creolization.

2.1. *Stressed BÍN.* BE has a strongly stressed form, BÍN, which places the inception of the "process" referred to in the predicate at some point in the distant past. The form has been variously referred to as a "Completive Perfect" (Stewart 1965), "Remote Past" (Fasold and Wolfram 1970), and "Remote Perfective" (Dillard 1972). However, the impression these labels give of "total completion of event" is true only of *non-stative* predicates.

(1) She BÍN tell me that. (Black female, 32)

The meaning of this sentence is that the "telling," a completed event, occurred "a long time ago." However, with *stative* predicates, BÍN has no suggestions of completedness. On the contrary, it implies that the distantly initiated state is still in force:

(2) I BÍN know you you know. (Black male, 59)
    "I have known you for a long time, and still do."

SE cannot express such propositions with a single auxiliary, but depends on the use of adverbial phrases like "a long time ago" and "for a long time," coupled with preterit or perfect forms. In sharp contrast, there is an absolute restriction against the use of such phrases with stressed BÍN in BE:

(3) *I BÍN know you for a long time.

BÍN is much more frequent and productive in the grammar of BE than was previously supposed, and there is evidence that whites neither use it nor interpret its meaning correctly (Rickford 1975b, Labov 1972). Even those black Americans who speak more standard varieties of English and do not seem to use BÍN themselves are sensitive to the "remote" meaning of the form and the implications of the stative/non-stative predicates with which it is used. But whites typically see the form as meaning "simple past," and where it is used with a stative predicate, as in (2) above, usually see it as completed rather than still in force.

With respect to both interpretation and use, then, stressed BÍN satisfies our third criterion perfectly, perhaps better than any other feature, because the difference between BE and other dialects is well documented from native-speaker reactions. Again, it is difficult to consider BÍN a simplification of the SE system, and knowledge of African influence is completely lacking. However, the important question that still remains is whether it has any parallels in other creoles (criterion four).

On the face of it, the answer would seem to be no, since there is (to my knowledge) no comparable use of stressed BÍN in any English creole. There may be more indirect links, however. The crucial nature of the stative/non-stative distinction in determining the completedness of the action or state is characteristic of the verbal system in Guyana Creole and many other creoles (Agheyisi 1971, p. 133; Bickerton 1975, p. 28). And unstressed *bin* sometimes indicates a "past-before-the-past" or "remote past," when the predicate in Guyana Creole and West African pidgin English is non-stative (Agheyisi 1971:134, Bickerton 1975:45-59).

There are no simple equivalents of BE BÍN with any single creole form, however. Bickerton (1975, pp. 41-42) makes a comparison of the following two GC (Guyana Creole) sentences that is very relevant here:

(4) mi *bin* gat wan dag. "I had a dog"
(5) mi *don* gat wan dag. "I have a dog"

(4) implies that one got a dog some time ago, but may not still have it. It thus lacks the "incompleted" meaning of BÍN with statives. (5) provides this meaning (one still *has* the dog), but how long ago one got it (the "remote meaning" of BÍN) is left unspecified.[7]

My own suspicion is that BE BÍN is indeed a unique form, but may represent the very general decreolization phenomenon by which new forms are found or developed to carry the meanings of others that are disappearing (cf. Bickerton 1975, p. 69; Rickford 1974; Solomon 1972). It may represent a combination of the meanings that unstressed *bin, don,* and the verb stem by itself express quite separately in basilectal varieties of creole, selecting from and innovating upon these words in the process of decreolization. I have no definitive evidence to offer on this point now, but my hunch arises from a preliminary search of "decreolizing" data from the South Carolina Sea Islands. Unstressed *bin, don,* and the use of the verb stem by itself to signal past are all declining in frequency, as they are in inner-city varieties of BE. But at the same time, BÍN, which was never before recorded in earlier descriptions of Gullah, is showing up with increasing frequency. So also is anterior *had,* the form that we shall now discuss.

2.2. *Auxiliary had.* While there has been considerable discussion of how firmly auxiliary *have* figures in the grammar of BE, several observers have noted that *had* is more frequent than either *have* or *has.* The explanation usually given for this is that the phonetic processes that operate upon *d* are weaker than those that operate upon *v* or *s* (Labov et al. 1968, pp. 223-25). However, this would provide no explanation for the further claim made by Fasold and Wolfram (1970, p. 61) that BE speakers use more *had* than SE speakers. Differences in the susceptibility of *d* and *v* to phonetic erosion cannot be brought in here, since we are dealing with the same form—*had*—in both cases.

If the claim that BE speakers use more *had* than others is true, then there is a much more plausible explanation for this difference in patterns of decreolization elsewhere. Bickerton (1975, pp. 127-32) points out that perfective *had* (as well as unstressed *did*) enters the decreolizing mesolect of GC as a [+anterior] replacement for basilectal *bin.* That is, it serves to mark the earlier of two actions simultaneously under discussion:

> (6) She *go* back to see what *had happen* to this seed she *did plant.* "She *went* back to see what *had happened* to this seed she *had planted.*"

There is evidence in my Sea Island data that both *had* and *did* are also functioning in the decreolization of Gullah as [+anterior] replacements for unstressed *bin.* In the following sentence, *had* marks the earliest event in the sequence:

> (7) He *had* carry some [bush-medicine] fuh Joo-Joo *bathe* he feet. And Joo-Joo *tell* um to *tell* me how he *use* it. (Black female, 73) "He *had carried* some for Joo-Joo *to bathe* his feet with. And Joo-Joo *told* him *to tell* me how he *used* it."

If we assume that *had* enters BE in the decreolization process in much the same way, then we can argue that it is because *had* so nicely fills an earlier creole syntactic/semantic slot that it is used so frequently by BE speakers.

Present perfect *have,* on the other hand, does not correspond as neatly to any creole syntactic/semantic slot. And its nearest equivalent—*don*—does not disappear from preverbal environments in either Gullah or BE as quickly as unstressed *bin.* This would explain why it is adopted less frequently by BE than by SE speakers, and would also help explain why it is less frequent than *had* within the grammar of BE itself.

Note again the persuasive parallels from decreolization in GC. While almost all the perfective *had* users in Bickerton's sample use it accurately, only five of the twelve speakers who use present perfect *have* do so correctly (Bickerton 1975, p. 128). Experience with creole *bin* provides much better preparation for using SE *had* than creole experience with *don* provides for SE *have*.

In this case, criteria three and four converge nicely—a measure of difference between BE and SE usage leading us to parallels between the BE use of *have/had* and the patterns in other "decreolizing" creoles.

2.3. *Invariant be.* The standard example of how BE differs from SE is its use of invariant *be* to express "distributive" or "habitual" meaning, as in:

> (8) This woman *be waiting* on the bus. (Black female, 32) "This woman *is usually waiting* on the bus."

In view of the extensive literature already existing on this subject (Stewart 1970, Dillard 1972, Labov 1972, Fasold 1972, among others), further discussion of the syntax or meaning of this form is unnecessary here. We can go on to apply our criteria for prior creolization.

BE uses the single form *be* to express concepts that in SE require further adverbial specification or awkward circumlocution. It is possible to see this as simplification, but insofar as *be* increases the lexical inventory and complicates the deep structure, it can also be seen as an expansion and complication of the SE system. Our third criterion is better satisfied. In addition to the extensive evidence that *be* was not found in white nonstandard vernaculars in the North, Wolfram (1974) also established that it was "typically NOT found among Southern White speech, while it is an integral part of all varieties of vernacular Black English which have been studied."

The possibility that *be* somehow reflects African influence has been suggested by Dalby (1972) and Stewart (1970, p. 246), who point out that many West African languages (e.g., Wolof) seem to have a similar grammatical category. The most intriguing parallels, however, come from decreolizing processes on the Sea Islands (Rickford 1974). Among the older speakers, we find the widespread creole habitual marker—*doz*, which replaces the earlier forms *blan* and *da.* This often occurs with *be,* as in:

(9) She *doz be* sick. "She is usually sick."

However, because of condensation processes that include the one described in section 1.3. above, the *doz* in these constructions is often reduced to a mere *z* or zero, and younger speakers reinterpret the remaining *be* as a habitual marker by itself.[8]

The detail in which these processes are attested in the Sea Island area helps us to satisfy criterion four, and to argue that BE *be* may well have emerged in the same way.

2.4. *Copula absence.* Absence of inflected forms of *be* in BE is variable, not categorical. This has been quite firmly established in a series of empirical studies (Labov 1969, Wolfram 1969, Legum et al. 1971). At first, this might seem to weaken the possibility of prior creolization for BE, since the SE copula is either categorical-ly absent or more nearly so in some basilectal varieties of creole (cf. Bailey 1966). However, documented patterns of decreoli-zation in the New World again offer resemblances and explana-tions for the variable *patterns* of copula-absence in BE.

In BE, inflected forms of *be* are absent most often before *V-ing* and *gonna,* somewhat less before *adjectives* and *locatives,* and least often before NP. Stewart (1968) attempted to relate this to patterns of decreolization in Gullah. He pointed out that these differences corresponded to differences in the order with which the Gullah copula *da* was replaced by *iz* in verbal and nominal environments. *Iz* was more firmly established in nominal environ-ments before it spread to verbal ones, and the assumption that a similar process had operated in the history of BE would account for the statistical differences in copula absence found today.

Since then, both Bickerton (1973) and Day (1973) have found similar patterns in other "decreolizing" communities. In both GC and the Hawaiian Creole continuum, it is apparently true that the English copula first replaces creole equivalents in NP environments, then in locative and adjectival, and only last in continuative verbal ones. The possibility is strong then that the variation in BE copula absence might reflect some universal process of decreolization. This is only slightly weakened if we assume (as Labov has suggested in informal discussion) that nominal environments are universally more "copula demanding" than verbal ones. For as Kay and Sankoff (1974) suggest, pidgins and creoles might reveal the operation of language universals more frequently and directly than other classes of human language.

The BE patterns might also partially be explained by an appeal to substratal African influence in the parent creole. For the existence of the different creole copulas that are replaced in different stages by SE ones seems to relate to West African patterns. The distinction between nominal, attributive, and verbal environments affects the choice of copula in some West African languages (Dennis and Scott 1975, Berdan 1975).

Finally we must note here that patterns of copula absence similar to those of BE have also been found among one group of Southern whites, albeit to a much more limited extent. This would seem to limit the strength of our third criterion unless we can establish what Wolfram (1974) suggests—that the Southern whites he studied assimilated the patterns from decreolizing black speech.

3. *Lexicon*

3.1. *Some simple lexical items.* Most of the BE lexicon is shared with SE and other American dialects of English. However, some words that originated in the black community, such as *hip* and *cat*, are examples of calques and convergences of West African and English forms (Dalby 1972). And some of these, like *cut-eye* and *suck-teeth* (Rickford and Rickford 1976), are so well known within the black community, and so totally unfamiliar among white Americans, that one is led to wonder if the two communities could really have shared the close patterns of intercommunication that some people assume.

However, the significance of African influence, insofar as it pertains to prior creolization, is most questionable at the level of such simple lexical items (cf. the discussion in section II.3.3. above). More potentially telling are those words that have "grammatical" instead of simple "lexical" meaning, that form an integral part of grammatical paradigms, or that function as syntactic markers. The persistence of such items seems more characteristic of pidgin/creole situations than of other types of language learning. We shall briefly consider a few such examples that lie on the border between lexicon and grammar.

3.2. *They as possessive pronoun.* Both Stewart (1967) and Dillard (1972) have suggested that BE is characterized by undifferentiated pronoun usage—i.e., that neither *case* nor *gender* receive overt morphological marking. This represents the very strongest case that could be made about BE pronoun usage, and it would be most consistent with prior creolization. It would at once represent maximal simplification of the SE system, a certain amount of substratal African influence, sharp divergence from other American dialects, and strong similarity to basilectal varieties of Caribbean creole.

However, evidence for this most general claim seems to come mainly from written records of black speech in the eighteenth and nineteenth centuries. There does not appear to be any quantitative "accountable" evidence that BE speakers of today consistently use such features as *he* for all genders of third person singular subject, or *me* as first person singular pronoun in both subject and object position.

A weaker claim seems to be more widely supported by empirical data, however. This is that in BE, the forms *they* and *you* frequently lack any possessive case marking. Labov's most recent position on such forms as *you book* and *they book* mentions the possibility of creole influence here, but still seems to favor the interpretation that they are produced by general r-deletion rules (Labov 1972, pp. 24, 38). However, Pfaff (1975) has argued that the high frequency of *they* possessives in her BE data from Los Angeles cannot be related to such phonological processes, since the dialect is "overwhelmingly r-ful." While she does not find absence of possessive marking to be *generally* characteristic of BE pronouns, she concludes that this is indeed an underlying characteristic of *they*.

The significance of *they* by itself should not be under-played. My ongoing research into pronominal variation in GC reveals that *they* is one of the last mesolectal forms to acquire possessive marking. Other possessive SE forms that are more different from their mesolectal creole equivalents (such as *my* vs. *me, her* vs. *she*) are usually acquired first. If BE is in fact in the very last stages of decreolization, *they* is one of the creole pronoun forms that we would expect it to retain the longest.

3.3. *Say as complementizer.* One of the best-established African-isms in the New World is the use of *say* as a complementizer, as in:

> (10) They told me *say* they couldn't get it. (Black male, 31) They told me *that* they couldn't get it.

This form, superficially identical to the SE verb *say*, occurs in Gullah and in many West African and Caribbean creoles with a much wider variety of verbs: *tell, believe, think, know*, etc., and is apparently derived from Akan *se* (Cassidy 1961, p. 63; Dillard 1972, p. 121).

Dillard (ibid.) points out that the form is also found in BE, although "almost entirely restricted to *He tell me say. . . .*" Dillard claims that it is used "mainly by old people," but he conducted his studies in Washington, and his generalization may not be true everywhere. Most of the examples I collected in Philadelphia were from adults 20-40 years old. Some speakers approximate SE norms even further by incorporating tense marking into *say* to produce, "He told me *said. . . .*" Even in this form, however, its function as a complementizer and its relation to creole and African *se* is obvious.

Insofar as it can function in most cases as a simple equivalent of SE *that, say* seems to represent neither simplification nor complication of the SE system. Its relationship to African and creole patterns has already been suggested. From the perspective of its significance for prior creolization, all that remains is to establish to what extent it is used in other American dialects, so that the criterion of *difference* can be adequately assessed.

4. *Language use*

No one has yet considered the expressive and functional use of language within the black community as a potential indicator of prior creolization. And yet if we apply our criteria to what is already known about BE speech events and "ways of speaking," there seems to be much of relevance here.

First of all, it appears that the general preoccupation of BE speakers with verbal play and performance is not so characteristic of speakers of other American English dialects. Certainly, many of the specific BE speech events—*signifying, sounding, rapping, marking, rifting*—do not appear to exist in the same form or to the same extent among white Americans (Abrahams 1972, Labov 1972). If we apply these facts to Hymes's (1972) definition of a speech community as one "sharing rules for the conduct and interpretation of speech, and rules for the interpretation of at least one linguistic variety," then we might have to conclude that black and white users of English often do *not* form part of the same speech community. Even if we ignored the "shared variety" part of the definition (and the evidence of the preceding sections should make us cautious about doing this), the requirement of shared "rules for the conduct and interpretation of speech" cannot be as easily dismissed. The striking differences between black and white Americans' "ways of speaking" are enough to make us wonder if their historical development could really have been the same.

To these differences within America must be added similarities between BE speakers and creole speakers throughout the Caribbean. Such similarities in the area of *language use* have largely gone unrecognized—Abrahams (1970a) has provided some of the only published evidence. Abrahams points out that BE *sounding* or *playing the dozens* has direct parallels in the West Indian verbal activity called *rhyming*. The broad category of verbal "badinage," which he calls *talking broad*, is also found in both communities. Abrahams observes that he has witnessed the impromptu contests of wits that are characteristic of *broad talking* both "on the steps or at the pool hall in the big-city atmosphere of South Philadelphia," and "at markets, rum-shops, and especially on buses and boats in the British West Indies."

There are many more shared "ways of speaking" in these two communities. Apart from the shared prevalence of *talking good* (Abrahams 1970a) or *fancy talk* (Dillard 1972), there are other striking resemblances: patterns of *calling off* women on the street or *rapping* to them (both *rapping* and *sooring* are used for the latter in Guyana), patterns of *louding* or *granning* (the second term is identical in Guyana and American black communities), patterns of allusive reference that find expression both in the American *blues* and the Caribbean *calypso*.

Quite apart from structured speech events like those mentioned above, a great deal of ordinary conversation among BE speakers is marked by the same continuous exploitation of ambiguities that Reisman (1970) found so characteristic of creole speech in Antigua. I have avoided extending the discussion of BE/Caribbean creole similarities in language use beyond the broad sketch that is presented here, because it is a topic that easily deserves a separate paper (at least!). But I think enough has been said to justify the impression that BE and the Caribbean creoles at least form a single *speech area* (Hymes 1972, p. 55) if not a speech community.

Simplification would appear to be quite irrelevant where language-use features of this type are concerned. Further research might be devoted to exploring possible African influence (Abrahams 1970b) and building up even more data than presently exist on black/white differences within America, and BE/Caribbean similarities beyond those noted above.

IV. CONCLUSION

In this paper I have tried to define the controversy about BE origins in terms of a single proposition and have considered some preliminary questions relevant to it before introducing evidence for and against prior creolization. Some of the preliminaries might seem to be "old-hat" to the seasoned creolist. But creole studies as a field is changing and expanding rapidly, and the experienced creolist can profit as much as the neophyte from the process of reexamining some of its central tenets and considering how they relate to the specific issue of BE origins.

One of the most open areas in creole studies is the question of what criteria might be used to establish prior creolization. This is a key issue, as the relevance of pidginization and creolization to general linguistics becomes increasingly apparent, and people begin to speculate on the extent to which these processes have operated in the history of all human language. The criteria used in this paper were based on current terminology, information, and practice. Some of them might need to be rejected or revised, and others can undoubtedly be devised.

What of the basic issue, however? My own feeling is that the linguistic evidence satisfies the criteria used in this paper often enough to make the prior creolization of BE very likely indeed. Others might disagree. But it is hoped that they will be able to pinpoint the source of their disagreement (nature or application of the criteria, nature or interpretation of the evidence, other criteria, other evidence), so that we can avoid the kinds of standoff and stalemate that have been so typical in the past.

There is really too much interesting and useful work to be done for us to continue arguing. We are still only beginning to come to terms with the facts of variation, and as some of the cases discussed in this paper reveal (cf. sections III.1.3., III.2.3., III.3.3., above), we might profit more by confronting such facts than by ignoring or concealing them. There are also several important kinds of data and several "hunches" relating to the issue of prior creolization that require our attention: the role of social and historical factors, for instance, or the precise origin of BE BÍN.

Beyond the issue of whether creolization occurred in BE is the issue of how widespread and variable the processes of pidginization, creolization, and decreolization were. Hancock (1973) is now suggesting that there may have been several kinds of pidgin/creole English both in Africa and in the United States, and he is reopening the question of how unique Gullah was from some previously unexplored perspectives (Hancock 1973). All these possibilities require new data and new kinds of argument.

NOTES

I wish to thank Angela Rickford for encouragement and assistance in completing this paper. Table from Labov 1972 reprinted by permission of University of Pennsylvania Press.

1. One question that will not be considered at any length in this paper is the definition of Black English. Arguments on this point are too often ringed with political or ideological considerations that have little to contribute to the linguistic issues with which we are concerned. And there is an obsession with finding invariance, either by "normalizing" data or by claiming that one group or another speaks the most nonstandard or consistent variety of Black English. I do not think we have enough empirical data on how the very diverse sets of people who make up the black community speak in their most natural contexts. Until we do, we should be cautious about restricting our definitions of BE to any particular subgroup. The most general thing we might say is that BE is a convenient cover-term for a "continuum" of varieties spoken by black Americans, just like the Guyanese folk-term "creolese." Some BE features, like possessive *they,* might be more widely distributed across this continuum than others, like BÍN. But this does not make them any less relevant.

2. Herskovits (1941, p. 115) points out that greater personal contact with the masters' way of life did not always inculcate either love or respect for it on the part of the slaves.

3. As an example, creolization might introduce a diverse set of obligatory tense-aspect markers into a pidgin that previously had none, but the number and semantic complexity of its pronouns or prepositions might remain the same.

4. Cf. Samarin (1971, pp. 124ff.) for further discussion.

5. I should like to thank Leigh Lisker and Malcah Yaeger for their assistance with this study, which was done as a term paper at the University of Pennsylvania. However, they should not be held responsible in any way for its limitations.

6. Up to 18 years of age, the white male grew up mainly in Maryland, while the black male spent the same period of his life in Kentucky. Since Maryland is only on the fringe of the Southern region, it would be interesting to repeat the study with speakers who are all from the "deep" South.

7. Dillard (1972, p. 106) has suggested that *don* may have served as a recent past (contrasting with *bin* as remote past) in at least some varieties of BE. We still need to know whether the *bin* in this system was stressed or not (Dillard doesn't say), but the relation of these two forms is certainly worth further investigation.

8. Discussion of some other relevant questions—such as why *be* itself has not (yet?) become established as a habitual marker in the Caribbean—is provided in Rickford 1975a.

REFERENCES

Abrahams, Roger. 1970a. Patterns of performance in the British West Indies. In *Afro-American Anthropology,* Whitten and Szwed, eds., pp. 163-79.

Abrahams, Roger. 1970b. Traditions of eloquence in Afro-American communities. *Journal of Inter-American Studies and World Affairs* 12:505-27.

Abrahams, Roger. 1972. A true and exact survey of talking Black. Paper presented at the Conference on the Ethnography of speaking, University of Texas, April 20-22, 1972.

Agheyisi, Rebecca N. 1971. West African Pidgin English: simplification and simplicity. Ph.D. diss., Stanford University.

Alleyne, Mervyn C. 1971. Acculturation and the cultural matrix of creolization. In *Pidginization and Creolization of Languages,* D. Hymes, ed., pp. 169-86.

Bailey, Beryl L. 1966. *Jamaican Creole Syntax.* London: Cambridge University Press.

Berdan, Robert. 1975. Sufficiency conditions for a prior creolization of Black English. Paper presented at the International Conference on Pidgins and Creoles, Hawaii, January 6-11, 1975.

Bickerton, Derek. 1975. The structure of polylectal grammars. In *Proceedings of the Twenty-Third Annual Round Table,* R. Shuy, ed. Washington, D. C.: Georgetown University Press, pp. 17-42.

Bickerton, Derek. 1975. *Dynamics of a Creole System.* London: Cambridge University Press.

Bloomfield, Leonard. 1933. *Language.* London: George Allen and Unwin.

Burling, Robbins. 1970. *Man's Many Voices.* New York: Holt, Rinehart and Winston.

Cassidy, Frederic G. 1961. *Jamaica Talk.* London: Macmillan.

Dalby, David. 1972. The African element in American English. In *Rappin' and Stylin' Out,* T. Kochman, ed. Urbana: University of Illinois Press, pp. 170-86.

Davis, Lawrence. 1971. Dialect research: mythology and reality. In *Black-White Speech Relationships,* Wolfram and Clarke, eds., pp. 90-98.

Day, Richard R. 1973. Patterns of variation in copula and tense in the Hawaiian post-creole continuum. *Working Papers in Linguistics,* vol. 5, no. 2, Honolulu: University of Hawaii.

DeCamp, David. 1971. Toward a generative analysis of a post-creole continuum. In Hymes, ed., pp. 349-70.

DeCamp, David, and Hancock, Ian F. 1974. *Pidgins and Creoles: Current Trends and Prospects.* Washington, D. C.: Georgetown University Press.

Dennis, Jamie, and Scott, Jerrie. 1975. Creole formation and reorganization. Paper presented at the International Conference on Pidgins and Creoles, Hawaii, January 6-11, 1975.

Dillard, J. 1972. *Black English.* New York: Random House.

Edwards, Jay. 1974. African influences on the English of San Andres Island, Colombia. In DeCamp and Hancock, eds., pp. 1-26.

Fasold, R. W. 1972. *Tense Marking in Black English.* Washington, D. C.: Center for Applied Linguistics.

Fasold, R. W., and Wolfram, Walter A. 1970. Some linguistic features of Negro dialect. In *Teaching Standard English in the Inner-City,* R. Fasold and R. Shuy, eds. Washington, D. C.: Center for Applied Linguistics, pp. 41-86.

Grimshaw, Allan. 1971. Some social forces and some social functions of pidgin and creole languages. In Hymes, ed., pp. 427-46.

Hall, Robert A. 1966. *Pidgin and Creole Languages.* Ithaca: Cornell University Press.

Hancock, Ian. 1973. The relation of Black Vernacular English to the Atlantic creoles. Paper presented at the Fourth Annual Conference on African Linguistics, C.U.N.Y., April 6-8, 1973.

Haynes, Lilith. 1973. Language in Barbados and Guyana: Attitudes, behaviours and comparisons. Ph.D. diss., Stanford University. Ann Arbor, Michigan: University Microfilms.

Herskovits, Melville J. 1941. *The Myth of the Negro Past.* Boston: Beacon Press.

Hoenigswald, Henry. 1971. Language-history and creole studies. In Hymes, ed., pp. 473-80.

Huttar, George L. 1975. Some Kwa-like features of Djuka syntax. Paper presented at the International Conference on Pidgins and Creoles, Hawaii, January 6-11, 1975.

Hymes, Dell. 1972. Models of the interaction of language and social life. In

Directions in Sociolinguistics, John J. Gumperz and Dell Hymes, eds. New York: Holt, Rinehart and Winston, pp. 35-71.

Hymes, Dell, ed. 1971. *Pidginization and Creolization of Languages.* London: Cambridge University Press.

Kay, P., and Sankoff, G. 1974. A language-universals approach to pidgins and creoles. In DeCamp and Hancock, eds., pp. 61-72.

Kurath, Hans. 1949. *A Word-Geography of the Eastern United States.* Ann Arbor: University of Michigan Press.

Labov, William. 1969. Contraction, deletion, and inherent variability of the English copula. *Language* 45:715-62.

Labov, William. 1972. *Language in the Inner City.* Philadelphia: University of Pennsylvania Press.

Labov, William; Cohen, Paul; Robbins, Clarence; and Lewis, John. 1968. *A Study of the Non-Standard English of Negro and Puerto-Rican Speakers in New York City,* volume I. Final report, U. S. Office of Education. Cooperative Research Project no. 3288. Mimeographed, Columbia University.

Le Page, Robert B. 1960. Conclusion to Historical Introduction. In *Jamaican Creole: Creole Language Studies I,* R. Le Page and D. DeCamp, eds. London: Macmillan, pp. 115-21.

Legum, Stanley; Pfaff, C.; Tinnie, G.; and Nicholas, M. 1971. *The Speech of Young Black Children in Los Angeles.* Technical report no. 33. Inglewood, Cal.: Southwest Regional Laboratory for Educational Research and Development.

McDavid, Raven, and McDavid, Virginia. 1951. The relationship of the speech of American Negroes to the speech of Whites. *American Speech* 26:3-17.

Mintz, Sidney. 1971. The socio-historical background to pidginization and creolization. In Hymes, ed., pp. 481-96.

Pfaff, Carolyn. 1975. The process of decreolization in Black English. Paper presented at the International Conference on Pidgins and Creoles, Hawaii, January 6-11, 1975.

Phillips, Ulrich B. 1918. *American Negro slavery: a survey of the supply, employment and control of Negro labor as determined by the plantation regime.* New York.

Reisman, Karl. 1970. Cultural and linguistic ambiguity in a West-Indian village. In Whitten and Szwed, eds., pp. 129-44.

Rickford, John R. 1974. The insights of the mesolect. In DeCamp and Hancock, eds., pp. 92-117.

Rickford, John R. 1975a. How does *doz* disappear? Paper presented at the International Conference on Pidgins and Creoles, Hawaii, January 6-11, 1975.

Rickford, John R. 1975b. Carrying the New Wave into syntax—the case of BE *BIN*. In *Analyzing Variation in Language*, R. Fasold and R. Shuy, eds. Washington, D. C.: Georgetown University Press, pp. 162-83.

Rickford, John R. (Ms.) Sounding Black and sounding White: a preliminary acoustic investigation of a folk-hypothesis. Unpublished term paper, University of Pennsylvania.

Rickford, John R., and Rickford, Angela E. 1976. Cut-eye and suck-teeth: African words and gestures in new world guise. *Journal of American Folklore*, July-September, vol. 89, no. 353, pp. 294-309.

Samarin, William. 1971. Salient and substantive pidginization. In Hymes, ed., pp. 117-40.

Schneider, G. D. 1966. *West African Pidgin English*. Athens, Ohio: University of Ohio Press.

Solomon, Dennis. 1972. Form, meaning, and the post-creole continuum. Paper presented at the Conference on Creole Languages and Educational Development, April 1972, U.W.I., St. Augustine.

Southworth, Franklin. 1971. Detecting prior creolization: an analysis of the historical origins of Marathi. In Hymes, ed., pp. 255-74.

Stewart, William. 1965. Urban Negro speech: sociolinguistic factors affecting English teaching. In *Social Dialects and Language Learning*, R. Shuy, ed. Champaign, Ill.: The National Council of Teachers of English, pp. 10-18.

Stewart, William. 1967. Sociolinguistic factors in the history of American Negro dialects. *Florida Foreign Language Reporter*, vol. 5, no. 2. Page number references are to reprinted version in Williams, ed., pp. 353-62.

Stewart, William. 1968. Continuity and change in American Negro dialects. *Florida Foreign Language Reporter*, vol. 6, no. 2. Page number references are to reprinted version in Williams, ed., pp. 362-79.

Stewart, William. 1970. Historical and structural bases for the recognition of Negro dialect. In *Monograph Series on Languages and Linguistics— Twentieth Annual Round Table Meeting*, J. Alatis, ed. Washington, D. C.: Georgetown University Press, pp. 239-48.

Taylor, Douglas. 1956. Language contacts in the West-Indies. *Word* 12:399-414.

Todd, Loreto. 1975. Pidgins and creoles: the case for the creoloid. Paper presented at the International Conference on Pidgins and Creoles, Hawaii, January 6-11, 1975.

Tsusaki, Stanley. 1971. Coexistent systems in language variation: the case of Hawaiian English. In Hymes, ed., pp. 327-40.

Turner, Lorenzo Dow. 1949. *Africanisms in the Gullah Dialect*. Chicago: University of Chicago Press.

Wells, J. C. 1973. *Jamaican Pronunciation in London*. Publications of the

Philological Society, xxv. Oxford: Basil Blackwell.

Whinnom, Keith. 1971. Linguistic hybridization and the "special" case of pidgins and creoles. In Hymes, ed., pp. 91-116.

Whitten, Norman E., Jr., and Szwed, John F., eds. 1970. *Afro-American Anthropology*. New York: The Free Press.

Williams, Frederick, ed. 1970. *Language and Poverty*. Chicago: Markham.

Wolfram, Walter. 1969. *A Sociolinguistic Description of Detroit Negro Speech*. Washington, D. C.: Center for Applied Linguistics.

Wolfram, Walter. 1971. Black-White speech differences revisited. In Wolfram and Clarke, eds., pp. 139-60.

Wolfram, Walter. 1974. The Relationship of White Southern speech to Vernacular Black English: copula deletion and invariant *be*. *Language* 50:498-527.

Wolfram, Walter and Clarke, Nona S., eds. 1971. *Black-White speech relationships*. Washington, D. C.: Center for Applied Linguistics.

Processes of Pidginization
and Creolization

Robert Le Page

0. INTRODUCTION

I review here in outline various insights into the processes involved in pidginization and creolization, within the framework of my own somewhat idiosyncratic and sociolinguistically oriented approach, as developed in Le Page 1960, 1967, 1968, 1969, 1972, 1973, 1975a, 1975b.

0.1. I am concerned with the interaction between the intrinsic properties of mediating systems and behavioral processes, through which social systems such as languages emerge; in particular, with psychological and social acts of identity by individuals and by communities. One of the intrinsic properties of mediating systems is that while their internal economy works toward logical targets they nevertheless remain open systems interacting with their environment. "Cartesian grammar" is therefore too simplistic a tool to handle process in natural language (cf. Hockett 1968; also Feibleman and Friend 1945). Moreover, I have tried, for reasons given in Le Page 1969, 1975b, to avoid the point of view which requires that every speech event must belong to a nameable language system. Rather, I regard it as a reflex of the total behavioral system of the person who utters it, interacting with the context in which it is uttered; each speech act is therefore the reflex of an 'instant pidgin', related to the linguistic *competence* of more than one person (unless one can envisage an utterly solipsist speaker-hearer). Various kinds of systematic abstraction are made—by individual speakers, by social process, by linguists or other observers—to which we attach the name 'language' and, in doing so, tend to treat them as if they were all the same abstraction. Moreover, as individuals, as societies, and as linguists, we tend to reify and totemize these abstractions. The sociolinguist must be aware of such psychological and social processes and emphasize them as a corrective to the tendency of theoretical linguists to regard their reified abstractions as the only proper object of study—an approach that denies them the possibility of ever handling the processes of pidginization and creolization (or indeed, any natural linguistic process) satisfactorily.

0.2.   Thus, I distinguish between a child's acquisition of language and his or her creation of specific language systems. I distinguish also four meanings of the word 'language' as applied to systems. The first, Language One, is a hypothetical base, most closely approached in the child's most relaxed informal behavior, but ultimately inaccessible to either intuition or observation. The second, Language Two, consists of the systems the child induces for the various model groups he or she observes, including in particular the 'rules' of the totemized 'language' of his community; the third, Language Three, is the linguist's or the psychologist's or sociologist's abstraction from behavioral events within the framework of a general theory; the fourth, Language Four, is again hypothetical and in its totality inaccessible—it is inherent like Saussure's *langue* in all the social behavior of a community. (These four meanings of 'language' are dealt with in Le Page 1975b.) Language Four has the same relationship to a community as has Language One to an individual. Intuition leads us to Language Two, observation to Language Three.

0.3.   In section 1 I deal with the processes of pidginization under the following (far from discrete) headings:

    1.1. Necessity and heightened attention
    1.2. Perception and reinterpretation
    1.3. The universal and the learned expectancies of how to behave in a contact situation
    1.4. Redundancy and 'simplification'
    1.5. Chance and coincidence
    1.6. Universals

In section 2 I deal with the creolization-post-creolization-recreolization continuum, concentrating on sociolinguistic factors within the 'acts of identity' hypothesis. Thus I am concerned with the individual's establishment of his or her own identity, and with the choice of social models, when growing up in a creole society; with the models that are available to the individual; with the processes of 'focussing' or 'diffusion' in linguistic systems (see Le Page 1975b); and with the concomitant social processes through which a sense of communal identity emerges or disintegrates or is merged into another.

SECTION 1

1.1. *Necessity and heightened attention*

My hypothesis is concerned with opportunity and motivation in the creation (i.e., more conventionally, the 'learning') of a language. In normal face-to-face situations between members of the same language community, the attention given to an utterance is very variable, but a high degree of redundancy in the code helps to overcome the effects of inattention. In a contact situation, should one participant wish to distance himself from the other for some reason—for example, through feelings of insecurity—he can make any incorrect use of his code by the other a pretext for not understanding, and this reaction can set up a counterreaction in the other person. In the pidgin situation, as we shall see, redundancy in the code is reduced, but the necessities of the situation ensure that the participants are in a state of heightened attention to each other and to contextual clues, and psychologically willing to meet each other more than halfway in order to communicate or to commune. Each wishes to identify himself as a player in the game of 'instant pidgin'. Such considerations apply both to the 'secret in-group language game' practiced, according to Elton Brash, among the new urban dwellers of Port Moresby in New Guinea (as also presumably once among slaves in slave factories or on slave plantations), and to the 'trading lingua franca game' played on the slave trade coasts of West Africa between European and African traders. Thus a lower level of redundancy can be accepted in the code. When we come to the creolization phase, however, this consideration ceases to hold good and codes must evolve so as to reach the level of redundancy normal for any native language (cf. section 2; also, Labov 1971).

1.2. *Perception and reinterpretation*

The processes referred to here are familiarly invoked to account for 'interference', 'substrate or superstrate influence', and linguistic change, but lack any generally acceptable behavioral theory of perception and interference on which the processes of pidginization can be based. (For some of the arguments see Weinreich 1963; Kelly 1969; Alatis 1968, 1970, passim). All behavioral learning in humans is an active process in which data are perceived and interpreted in relation to the cognitive systems that the individual has already constructed; these are then possibly modified to take account of the new data—in Piaget's terminology, there is *assimilation* and *accommodation* (Piaget and Inhelder 1969, p. 6). Accommodation is always less than total; interference in language behavior is a case in point. Today, however, the cognitive system invoked is the so-called competence of the individual, rather than the externally abstracted and fully formed systems of 'langue', in which Weinreich's well-known study of *Languages in Contact* and much work in 'contrastive linguistics' deal. Studies of pidgin and creole behavior in contact situations show clearly what an unsatisfactory frame of reference Weinreich provided, but we are not agreed yet on the nature of 'competence' in its place. It is claimed that each person's cognitive capacities include innate capacities to search for linguistic universals, yet no such universals have so far been satisfactorily identified; nor are there any psychological answers yet (see, e.g., Carroll 1968) to questions about interference or 'transfer effects' in foreign language learning. As far as non-innate mechanisms are involved, we can only extrapolate back from observable linguistic systems to account for what has happened in terms of earlier interference; thus, we can take (as in Le Page 1967) the supposed phonology of the seventeenth- and eighteenth-century Akan languages and the supposed data afforded to their speakers by seventeenth- and eighteenth-century speakers of regional British dialects to account for Jamaican Creole phonology as a reflex of the latter perceived in terms of the former. Even thus simplistically it is clear that compensatory features from other levels of analysis must be taken into account.

I suggest below certain general rules for behavior in the contact situation—for example, that forms will be held as constant as possible; yet we now have to ask: at what level? and within what degrees of ambiguity and redundancy? We know that Jamaican Creole does not preserve the distinction preserved in modern RP between the vowels in *card* and *cord, garden* and *Gordon*; we know also that the absence of this distinction fits in well with the postulated seventeenth-century English vowel-values being interpreted in terms of a postulated Twi phonemic system. However, we also know that resultant homophones are in these particular sets distinguished by the use of a palatalized initial consonant for the first of each set, /kyaad/ *card* and /gyaadn/ *garden,* contrasting with a velar consonant in the second case, /kaad/ and /gaadn/. We also know that some dialects of English had (and some still have) a low front vowel in *card* and *garden,* others a low back, whereas *cord* and *Gordon* have always had back vowels. Some dialects of English have palatalized k, g before front vowels; Twi, according to Christaller's description, had palatal as well as velar values of k, g. At what level of the system, then, has 'interference' taken place? Is the necessity to preserve a spoken distinction between words like *cord* and *card* to be deemed part of the *competence* of the seventeenth-century slave coast or slave plantation pidgin speaker? A linguistic systematization that gave primacy to a semantic or semiotic deep structure would have to deal with this question. Is the distinction something that has been acquired from a model code in the subsequent creolization phase? Was that model Twi, or English, or coincidentally both? Would the juxtaposition of distinctive features rather than phonemic systems be more helpful?

The reasons for interference may be subsumed under any one of the four riders to my general hypothesis (Le Page et al. 1974):

> Each individual creates the systems for his verbal behaviour so that they shall resemble those of the group or groups with which from time to time he may wish to be identified, to the extent that: (a) he can identify the groups (b) he has both opportunity and ability to observe and analyse their behavioural systems (c) his motivation is sufficiently strong to impel him to choose, and to adapt his behaviour accordingly (d) he is still able to adapt his behaviour.

It is commonplace in the case of precreole pidgins to speak of English or French morphemes and sentences being reinterpreted through the grids of, for example, West African linguistic systems. Such gross statements serve to summarize the social consequences of a succession of constructs by individuals, some of whom were highly motivated to adapt, some grudgingly undertaking what was necessary to survive, some unable to understand very much of what was being demanded of them. We must remember, first, that in a contact situation children would often be able to learn quickly the language of the other culture, without interference, were it not for social factors such as the attitudes of their parents or of neighboring prestige groups or peer-groups to whom they may have easier access than to speakers of a standard variety of the European language; second, the fact that one's perceptual and cognitive systems form a closely interwoven mesh—we cannot keep phonological, grammatical, lexical, semantic, and contextual aspects of perception separate; third, that perception and systematization of linguistic data are biased for both participants in a contact situation and not just for one.

With these provisos in mind we can return to Weinreich's account of the importance of the psychological and sociocultural setting of language contact and try to carry his exploratory work a good deal further. He distinguished 'linguistic' from 'extra-linguistic' factors. "Of course, the linguist is entitled to abstract language from considerations of a psychological or sociological nature. As a matter of fact, he SHOULD pose purely linguistic problems about bilingualism" (Weinreich 1963, p. 4). Having done so, he may find the cause of the susceptibility of a language to foreign influence in its structural weaknesses, or in some social factor. My argument here is that what the linguist, or the speaker, chooses to regard as 'the language' is itself the result of individual, social, and psychological choice. The objects of our study are our own internal constructs. It is, therefore, not possible to deal with 'purely linguistic' problems, except as rather gross social abstractions or in terms of subjective idealizations. Thus in the case of pidgins and contact vernaculars one finds, and must expect to find, a wide variety of results emerging from what appears to be linguistically 'the same' situation. In the creolization phase, as we shall see, the amount of variation in the behavior of individuals is very quickly reduced by 'focussing' through daily interaction within small isolated communities, so that social norms emerge that differ to some extent from one community to another, depending on unique mixes of such features as the demographic and economic structure of that community (see Le Page 1975b). During such a period the model offered by a culturally dominant group is of great importance. Within the pidgin period, similarly, the role of a culturally dominant group would be important in crystallizing the form of the pidgin. In all probability agents and ships' captains on the one side and African slave traders ashore on the other made up such a group. Such people were already habituated to pidginlike behavior because of the nature of their calling. It would not give, therefore, a true account of linguistic development if we simply juxtaposed, for example, a West African phonology and an English or French phonology and explained the creole phonology in terms of interference between these two, the reinterpretation of the latter in terms of the former having given rise to a pidgin phonology that then led on to that of the creole. *Rather, one must see the 'interference phonology' as an abstraction toward which the practice of individuals in the contact situation converges.*

We can now return to the multidimensional nature of the perceptual process. The reinterpretation of the phonology and phonotactics of seventeenth-century English by West Africans led to the loss of a great many lexical contrasts. The stress and intonation rules for West African languages had to carry the syntactic prosodies of a pidgin English from which the formal marking of the parts of speech had disappeared. The formal markers of the English tense system disappeared, and the system's primary distinction became aspectual (see Alleyne 1971). The semiotic universe of the West African languages was to some extent superimposed on that which lay behind a European lexical system. There were many other interrelated examples of 'interference', and the multiple explanations and indeed multiple etymologies that have to be invoked to account for particular features presumed to derive from the pidgin code are amply illustrated in the *Dictionary of Jamaican English* and its historical introduction.

Alleyne (1971) has argued that the English strong preterite system *was* used, and *not* assimilated to the weak verb system so as to restructure English more simply in the pidgin situation. I discuss 'simplification' below. But the forms /brok/, /lef/, /los/ that he cites from Jamaican Creole may derive from the direct adoption of *broken, left,* and *lost* as stative predicates; they form a deprivative class of predicates, which includes also perhaps /gaan/ *gone.* I argue elsewhere that the basic creole grammar, and hence presumably the basic pidgin grammar, distinguish between active and stative predication before distinguishing between verb and non-verb forms, and that this fact is underlined by the generally aspectual implications of creole predicate paradigms basically concerned with distinguishing continuing from no-longer-continuing or punctual states and actions rather than with tense as a feature of actions. If this is correct, the reinterpretation that took place in the pidgin phase could have been due either wholly to West African semiotic distinctions or to a grammatical universal (predication; stative: non-stative predication) onto which was grafted the West African aspectual system.[1]

1.3. *The universal and the learned expectancies of how to behave in a contact situation*

Robert A. Hall, Jr. (1966) and Charles Ferguson (1971, 1975) have both dealt with this topic. Ferguson (1971) speaks of speech communities having "registers of a special kind for use with people who are regarded for one reason or another as unable readily to understand the normal speech of the community (e.g., babies, foreigners, deaf people). These forms of speech are generally felt by their users to be simplified versions of the language. . . ." I deal with 'simplification' below, and am here concerned with whether there are behavioral universals, or learned traits, that come into operation when we try to speak with somebody from another speech community or who, for any other reason, we think may not understand what we say.

We tend to speak more slowly, more loudly, and to enunciate more clearly, even though these practices may be self-defeating since they tend to run counter to the prosodic exponents of our syntax and semantics. We avoid ellipsis. We try to make explicit the prosodic frames of our parts of speech and syntax—exaggerated pauses between clauses, exaggerated intonational distinctions between statements and questions, etc.; because of the difficulty of maintaining these distinctions in slow time we tend to reinforce them by tags. In a contact situation we try to keep as many features of our language as invariant as possible—word form, word order—and avoid shifts of register, nuance, etc. Cassidy (1971) has mentioned the probability that in the early stages of pidginization prosodic changes would suffice for major transformations. Gestural language is normally employed to complement verbal syntax in a contact situation, and behind the gestural language there may be some kind of generally recognized linear sequences, e.g., of subject-predicate, subject-predicate-complement. It may therefore be a *universal* of behavior in a contact situation that the syntax of signs exercises pressure on the syntax of the emergent pidgin. A number of the tendencies referred to above may be innate, and therefore universal; a number may be learned. Linguisters (as they are often called in the literature) employed as interpreters in the West African slave trade were often Africans who had already had some contact with the

Portuguese. In addition to being agents for the transmission of Creole Portuguese, they would, when confronted with a hitherto unknown language group, be agents for the transmission of a generalized technique of 'talking to foreigners'. Ferguson (1975 and this volume) has carried further his analysis of foreigner talk. The list of features that his informants have generally agreed belong to this register are all familiar to us from pidgins: omission of the verb *be*, of all inflections, of conjunctions, of redundant pronouns; the use of iteration and of multiple negation; the addition of tags; analytic paraphrase as in *which place* for *where*; the reduction of the pronominal case-form paradigms; and use of a special vocabulary.

1.4. *'Simplification' and the reduction of redundancy*

I use the term 'redundancy' in the general sense in which any analyzable linguistic function may be performed more than once in an utterance, and may also be repeated in subsequent utterances. The rules of redundancy are probably different for speech as compared with writing, different within oral literature as compared with written, and different for monologue as compared with dialogue.[2] Redundancy in phonology occurs when more than one distinctive feature is involved in a phonemic contrast. In the contact situation this may allow for *partial* recognition and identification by each party recognizing (a) one of the two or three distinctive features involved, (b) the phonotactic rules, and (c) the semantic probabilities. In the grammar of spoken English the parts of speech and the modality systems are specified partly by prosodies, partly by inflection, partly by word order, and partly by the semantic probabilities; thus *I am going*, setting its prosody aside for the moment, can be reduced to *am go* without loss of syntactic specification. However, paradigmatically, *I am going* is related to *you are going, he is going, I always go, I went,* etc., and knowledge of one's language involves knowledge of such paradigmatic relationships. It involves also knowledge of the semantic relationships between *going* and *walking,* and between these and stative words like *red.* The user may draw on all these relationships within the network that is his or her language for analogical and creative purposes. Thus, apparent redundancy affords two facilities without loss of communication: first, it allows for the creative exploration of new kinds of relationships within the system—therefore, it allows for change, the use of unusual or unexpected forms, at all levels; second, it allows for loss of part of the message.

In a contact situation the formally marked paradigmatic, syntactic, and semantic relationships of the speaker's language may not be meaningful to the hearer. Then the function of morphs and prosodies becomes deictic, that is, pointing and positioning, in relation to the nonverbal context (which restores the overall level of information, of redundancy), and it is the nonverbal context and certain linguistic universals that complete the immediate grammar and meaning. Such a 'grammar' is, therefore, context-bound, in the sense that it cannot operate outside its particular context of situation. The progress of the autonomy of linguistic systems is from the context-bound toward the context-free, from the transient toward the permanent, from the idiosyncratic toward the completely general, from the semantically or deictically based toward the syntactically based. The goals of context-free, permanent, and universal are, of course, never reached; they are simply present in each individual as goals, and underlie the nature of the abstractions which he makes and the uses to which he puts those abstractions, whether in a linguistic or in any other mediating system.

'Simplification' is very difficult to define, though each of us feels that he knows how to speak simply, and it may well be that most of Ferguson's 'foreigner talk' rules would be regarded by their users as 'simplification'. Even within one language community we have no overall measure of linguistic complexity, if for no other reason than that the choice of a different lexical item may simplify the lexicon but complicate the syntax (as in 'which place' for *where*). Certainly it is difficult to imagine any universal hierarchy of linguistic complexity; one community's embedding of low codability may well be another's highly codable lexeme (see Brown and Lenneberg 1954/1970). Passive constructions seem to be comparatively rare in pidgins and creoles, but we do not know whether this is because they are avoided as being syntactically more complex than are active constructions, or whether there is a greater degree of coincidence and/or universality between the syntax of active than of passive constructions from one language to another (see below, 1.5. and 1.7.). I am inclined to the view that active constructions tend to be more readily available colloquially, and also that there is likely to be greater coincidence of form with the hearer's grammar in their case.

Both Hall (1966) and Ferguson (1971) instance the lack of

copular constructions in the simplified grammar of baby talk and foreigner talk, but if we accept the view of Lyons (1968, pp. 322-23) that the function of the copula in English is as a dummy carrier for markers of tense, aspect, or mood, then the lack of a copula in a 'basic' creole grammar and hence, by supposition, in its pidgin forerunner may be due to the lack of coincidence between specific marking systems for tense, aspect, or mood, or between the underlying conceptual analyses. I have suggested that in contact situations we keep features of our language as invariant as possible; if true, this itself constitutes one kind of simplification leading, as both Samarin (1971) and Labov (1971) have pointed out, to a "reduction of options," a *stylistic* limitation.

The restructuring of the rules inherent in one generation's speech data (in which some processes of systematic change are coming to an end and others are just beginning) by the next generation is generally assumed to be in the direction of greater simplicity; in English, verbs become assimilated to the weak paradigm, nouns to the strong masculine paradigm, and so on. This kind of restructuring is certainly a major feature of contact situations, so that processes already inherent in the underlying synchronic imbalances of the data of any one generation have been greatly accelerated. Thus the development of the various pidgin pronominal paradigms may be postulated as being partly due to the 'simplification' of foreigner talk and partly to this latter kind of restructuring, in which the partial logic inherent in the speaker's system is focussed more sharply by the hearer and improved upon to the extent, e.g., that the ambiguity of English *you* is removed by the introduction of West Indian /unu/. It seems that logical restructuring is a universal feature of the 'instant pidgin game', and that where trade rather than national pride is at stake, the economy of such a process, and its resultant surface forms, will be reinforced by both parties, and each will be able to accept the concomitant loss of stylistic redundancy because of their heightened attention and because of the role played in the grammar of their discourse by nonverbal features. Taking these nonverbal features (pointing, contextual clues, etc.) into account as part of the grammar of pidgin discourse, that 'simplified' grammar is likely to be as complex and redundant as that of either of the codes it replaces. It will, however, be completely context-bound, valid for one performance only; each successive performance will entail greater abstraction and the transfer of more and more features to the agreed syntax of the emergent pidgin code.

We must now consider the role in all this of chance and coincidence.

1.5. *Chance and coincidence*

Contact situations are bound to involve a good deal of exploration by both speaker and hearer, which will inevitably result in some lucky and many fruitless sallies. The lucky ones are likely to be reinforced by participants, eager to snatch at communication; the unlucky ones are less likely to be repeated. Some similarity in form and meaning between items from two codes will mean high probability of survival in the emergent pidgin code. A lexical example would be English *dirty* and Twi *doti* (see *Dictionary of Jamaican English*). But there will be examples at every level, including prosodic features. It may be that some coincidences are due not to chance but to 'universals'; or they may be in part universally derived, as with words that have a fairly recent echoic origin or whose form is influenced by echoic considerations. It may be that some syntactic features come under this head, e.g., the high probability of S V O order and hence of its survival as a means of defining the parts of a sentence where definition by morphology is lacking; or iteration for emphasis; or some prosodic features such as loudness for emphasis. Between any two linguistic codes there will be a certain amount of coincidence of form and/or function.

1.6. *Universals*

In some of the foregoing sections I have referred to the possible 'universality' of some aspect under discussion. Before going further we must, I think, try to clarify the term *universal*. Some linguistic processes or features derive their necessary appearance in all languages from the fact that languages are mediating systems and therefore reflect universals of human experience; thus, the expression of moods of affirmation, command, doubt, desire for communion, or of any contingency in a linguistic category we can call 'mood' is only secondarily a linguistic universal. We must distinguish such universals [a] from those which may derive from some supposed innate, language-specific characteristics of man on the one hand [b], and those which derive from the physical nature of the medium on the other [c]. In this volume Derek Bickerton discusses as a class of [b] some fairly specific rules which he claims must derive from the nature of man as a language-learning animal. It would be more in accordance with my own view of language to point under [b] to such universals as derive from acts of personal identity and from the processes I have referred to as 'projection' and 'focussing' (Le Page 1974, 1975b); Cassidy (1971) has done something along these lines, though Bickerton's is the more usual approach. Under [c] one must be aware of the differential properties of *speech* and language in an oral tradition as compared with those of *writing* and language in a literate tradition; it is too readily assumed that the abstraction 'language' means the same in each case. We must also distinguish universality of process from universality of feature; the exploitation of redundancy in contact situations would belong to the former, the emergence of a pronominal system, as posited by Cassidy, to the latter. Finally, some apparent universals [d] seem to belong to the category 'properties of mediating systems' and therefore are innate only in the sense that man uniquely has the mental capacity for symbolization and for relating symbols systematically. Thus it is a property of mediating systems that they are open systems, whereas most idealizations of language by linguists reflect their desire to impose the logical properties of closed systems on their data (see 0.1. above). Closed systems are autonomous; there is a strong tendency among linguists to idealize toward autonomy in the linguistic systems they discern, and the very search for something we can call a pidgin 'language' or a creole 'language' among the data afforded by speakers in contact situations is a reflection of this tendency. When pidgin speakers conduct the same kind of search it is an act of social identity that feeds back to and focusses the linguistic system, and so helps to create that which they need.

Cassidy (1971) derives his universals from semiotic aspects of the contact situation. "A first necessity . . . is to establish identifications . . . names for the interlocutors . . . a pronominal system to designate a *thou-you* party and an *I-we* party. . . . These would probably precede the designation of a *he-they* party. . . ." (p. 213). He does not, however, take sufficient account of the fact that each party to the discourse already has a native language and a well-established semiotic universe. Most adults (other than those who find their native-language *persona* profoundly unsatisfying and wish to start again) take their native-language semiotic with them in new situations. Bickerton (1975) implies a knowledge by all language users of universal linguistic categories, since otherwise understanding or learning somebody else's language would be impossible; but we cannot assume that 'understanding', with all its half-lights and contextual props, implies a competence isomorphous with 'using', and interference phenomena imply a failure to shift adequately from one register or language to another and seem to depend on our mapping new data onto existing linguistic categories and constraints directly rather than via universals.

I would propose (as has Christian 1970) a wholly relational model for the definition of the semiotic universe of an individual or of a culture, one in which all linguistic reference is to a relational network. Thus there is no point in looking for precise semantic universals or reference points as the basis for all languages and hence as the basis for an emergent pidgin. The *word* used by, for example, the European in the classical pidgin situation has a fuzzily defined potential for meaning in the speaker's code, in relation to the speaker's universe; it is used with a meaning more sharply focussed by the context; it is perceived by, for example, the African hearer in context as having a range of probabilities as to meaning, and this range is due partly to the context and partly to the hearer's own universe. The word of the emergent pidgin code then acquires its potential for meaning from the abstractions made by the participants in successive encounters. It is the context of use of the pidgin code which gives its words their meaning; but for each of the participants the potential for this meaning is a reflex of the potential of the corresponding term in his or her own language (cf. Silverstein 1972).

The situation from which a pidgin develops resembles a child-parent situation in that there is little formal instruction in grammar (probably less in the pidgin situation than for the child); also, in that both parties are eager to communicate, each conditions the other, and an oscillatory or echo-response pattern is quickly established and reinforced in the exploration of serviceable common elements. It reflects, as does the child-parent situation, the universals of mood referred to above, and these may have something approaching universal parameters of prosodic and gestural expression. There are, however, important differences between the two kinds of situation. In the later stages of the child-parent situation the parents retreat from their child's advance toward their model by correcting its mistakes and giving up baby talk; whereas the later stages of pidgin development are likely to reinforce and build upon the earlier shared near-misses. The parents mediate between the child's own rules and the rules of their model language; in the pidgin situation there is no shared model other than that provided by the logic of the need to communicate.

Under [a] we must group echoisms, which furnish a limited number of language universals, but here again one must be cautious. The sounds of nature are interpreted through our culturally acquired perceptual system just as speech-sounds are, so that the German cock says *kikeriki,* the French *cocorico,* the English *cock-a-doodle-doo;* Chaucer's ducks said *quek,* modern ducks say *quack.* A large number of the many near-echoisms of West Indian creole English are identifiably related to Africanisms, as in the common [boʃomm] or [bodomm] < Twi *borom* for the noise of something falling hard, or Emmanuel Rowe's 'imitation' of Bobiabu's noise in flight, ['bu'bu'bu'bu'bu'bu'bu'bu'bu'bu'bu 'bu] < Mende *bubu, to fly* (see *Dictionary of Jamaican English*).

Universals of type [c] would include loudness or repetition for emphasis, or closer linear juxtaposition for close syntactic structure. As to universals of underlying syntactic structure in the Chomskyan sense, if Silverstein's analysis (1972) of Chinook Jargon is correct, a pidgin has no deep structure, and within the terms of my own very similar analysis (1973) the pidgin code would have an underlying semantic deep structure for each of the participants (of whom of course there may be any number). It may be a type [d] universal of linguistic structures that they can be represented as being at some point on a continuum: at one extreme, concrete and directly referential, context-bound, idiosyncratic, and with a personal semantic deep structure; at the other, abstract, context-free, common, and with a syntactic deep structure exhibiting logical properties. In that case, pidgins are at one extreme of this continuum; the idealized speaker-hearer with logical syntax at the other extreme; and most natural linguistic structures somewhere in between. There seem to be few other agreed candidates for linguistic universality, but the theory of markedness has supplied one: all languages have unmarked and marked categories and it is the unmarked, being both of more general application and more frequent occurrence, that are likely to survive in the pidgin situation. It now seems to me, however, that this is simply a restatement in a different form of my earlier thesis that any kind and degree of coincidence between the features of linguistic systems in a contact situation is likely to favor the retention of those features in the pidgin. At first sight, Greenberg's (1969) suggestions in regard to marked features in grammar and semantics seemed to offer a promising kind of explanation for the emergence of certain pidgin features. However, the more one explores these features, the more difficult it appears to define any grammatical or semantic (as distinct from phonological) categories as universally 'unmarked'. Greenberg instances the category of number in the noun; but grammatical singularity and plurality turn out each to be complex amalgams, differing from culture to culture, of such other categories as uniqueness, mass, collectivity, etc. In the Jamaican pronominal paradigm, it is by no means obvious that the creole use of *mi, yu, im* for all cases represents the survival of an unmarked category.

1.7. *Conclusion to section 1*

My suggestions as to the processes involved in the emergence of a pidgin run counter to any genetic simile. Even though in early European/West African contact situations (and these would certainly antedate any records we have of the slave trade) a West African trader may have felt "I am speaking Portuguese" when playing his part in the game, that part would nevertheless still have been influenced by all the considerations noted above, as well as by his recourse to his native language or to any other language that it might occur to him to try when stuck. Subsequent comers to the coast, the 'linguisters' they employed, and the slaves they shipped were more likely simply to claim "I know how to talk to these people." Formative influences on emergent pidgins are many; however much creole successors may owe to the formative part played by the grammar or lexicon or phonology of speakers of one or another European or West African language, they are likely to owe as much or more to the subsequent focussing influence of various models in the stabilizing years, and something also to the general tendency of linguistic codes toward the more highly focussed, abstract, and general.

SECTION 2

2.1. *Creolization and post-creolization—projection, focussing, and diffusion*

Linguists necessarily idealize, and those working with creoles, more especially the English-based, have found it useful for descriptive purposes to construct an idealized basilect more conservative and more homogeneous than vouchsafed by actual speech samples, and to show divergences from such constructs as variation in the direction of one or more models (see, e.g., Bailey 1966, Chapter 7). We have usually recognized that in doing so we were imposing stasis on flux.[3] We recognize that, in the colonial situation, the expatriate model has been constantly changing, while the idealized creole base is always in artificially sharp focus, partly because of a lack of data about the past or because of the selective memory of linguist or informant.[4]

Nevertheless there is a good deal of evidence for a short period of rapid focussing during which the various Caribbean creoles developed their distinctive characteristics, followed by a comparatively stable period during which these characteristics did not greatly change. I discuss these periods in 2.2., and the subsequent periods of 'decreolization' and 'recreolization' in 2.3. First, however, it is necessary to say something about *projection, focussing, and diffusion* (see Le Page 1975b).

We have to consider adults competent both in their native languages and in a pidgin, using the latter to some extent among themselves and generally with the children growing up around them. Linguistic and conceptual focussing therefore are not as sharp for most first-generation creole children as for children in a monolingual or stable diglossic situation. Projection, however, is as important for the first-generation creole child as for any other. In contrast with the parents the child needs to externalize his or her concepts through the medium of the creole created from pidgin discourse; to create a language that will fulfill all needs of self-identification, perceptual analysis, interior monologue, and communication. The child must also, through projection and focussing, make a contribution to the emergence of a communal identity within which he or she can have a social role. The conditions under which the creole child grows up vary widely: some stable, some rapidly changing; sometimes in a minority enclave of an otherwise polarized society, sometimes among many other 'mixed' children in, for example, a newly urbanized society (see, e.g., Tabouret-Keller 1971). But we must now examine the homogenizing and stabilizing influences necessary for a creole language to emerge.

2.2. *The social setting of creolization*

Social rules, including language rules, grow out of daily intercourse. A sense of social or cultural identity can be the concomitant of a variety of factors: family ties, common economic or political or defense interests, a shared location, religious beliefs, mutual linguistic intelligibility, a shared upbringing. Moreover, one must observe the same constraints about the ascription of social identity as apply to the isolation of 'a language': some communities exist primarily in the mind of the social anthropologist who describes them and because of the perceptual categories and preconceptions that color the investigator's observation (for further extensive discussion see Barth 1969, LeVine and Campbell 1972). We must concern ourselves with the interaction between the growth of a sense of communal identity and linguistic focussing in creole communities.

The more intra-active the community the more homogeneous, stable, and prescriptive will its behavioral rules become. Thus the creole community of Belize—small, compact, and tightly knit through being surrounded on three sides by the sea, its only external communications until quite recently being by water, where all social ranks interacted daily and were united by the common threats of a hostile environment and the hostility of the Spanish—achieved a strong sense of its own creole identity and a strongly normative sense of 'creole' English. Many Jamaican plantations in the seventeenth and eighteenth centuries were little worlds of their own; communications from sugar plain to sugar plain on a mountainous island were very difficult—each plantation took its sugar down to a *barcadero* at the nearest point on the coast for loading—and so each had its creole, to be subsumed in a common and distinctive 'Jamaican' with the growth of a colored urban mercantile and professional middle class in Spanish Town and Kingston. The story of St. Lucia is one of the emergence of a sense of a community of interests between 'French' and 'English' in the face of external and internal threats at the end of the eighteenth and the beginning of the nineteenth century, and of a division between urban Castries, with its flourishing entrepôt status, and rural St. Lucia, with its poverty and very primitive communications at the end of the nineteenth and in the early twentieth century. The plantation communities of Surinam and Guiana were similarly isolated on their narrow coastal strips.

Thus, while a pidgin is a product of interaction between cultures, a stable creole is the product of subsequent intra-action, leading to focussing. Diffusion is the opposite of focussing; it is a concomitant of the breakdown of family ties or religious beliefs, a redistribution of economic or political or defense interests, of the decay of mutual intelligibility, of physical dispersion, of disparate upbringing. A culture, or a language, may be focussed at one level of use and diffuse at another; at other periods it may be equally focussed or diffuse at all levels. Thus, today the speaker of a nascent creole is almost immediately exposed to a model language through education; this was not so in the seventeenth or eighteenth century. On the other hand, independence movements lead on very rapidly to nationalism, which sometimes adopts the creole as its cultural badge in opposition to the former model language; this process, leading to re-creolization or 'hypercreolization' (see, e.g., Berry 1961), although mirrored in some seventeenth- and eighteenth-century attitudes, was less overt in those days except perhaps in Maroon or Bush Negro settlements. We know that slaves who had been born in the West Indies identified with a creole society in opposition to 'salt water negroes' (q.v. in *Dictionary of Jamaican English*) and such scraps of evidence as we have do suggest that Jamaican Creole and the creoles of other West Indian and Indian Ocean settlements jelled fairly early in the colonial history of these settlements and in general remained fairly stable as long as the settlements remained stable, in spite of influxes of large numbers of fresh slaves.

A creole language only exists insofar as it is inherent in the behavior of a creole-speaking person or community or in a book written in creole. I will assume that in the very early days of creolization a child may have had a number of models to choose among outside the home because of the arrival of large numbers of new African slaves, because of the existence of Maroon settlements, because of the existence of household slaves in privileged circumstances (as compared with field slaves), because of the children of European/African concubinage alongside those of pure African descent, and so on. We can observe similar multilingual choices confronting the children we have been working with in Cayo District, Belize, today (see Le Page et al. 1974) and also in West Africa. I am assuming further that during such a formative period some linguistic features become marked as belonging to a particular group that the child may or may not wish to emulate. Thus in Jamaica there would be those slaves who had reached the island via one of the Dutch depots; those who had come direct from Africa; those born on the island. There would be those who had seafaring connections. Among the poor whites, the indentured servants, former soldiers and seamen and their children, there would be parallel variations. Each group's characteristic usage would to some extent be socially marked.

The social stereotype might be endowed with formal linguistic characteristics at any systematic level, and as the creole society developed homogeneity and common behavioral patterns, some systematic markers and lexical items would become general-ly stigmatized and others acquire general prestige. Thus, for example, CVCV phonotactic structure, evidenced by Saramaccan and Sranan and by Papiamentu, was likely to be stigmatized in Jamaica in contrast with the CVC or CCVC structure of English (Sranan *beredi* English *bread*). Cassidy notes (1971, p. 210), "An important part of the decreolization of JC has consisted in the loss of these final vowels when, as here, they are unsupported by St. E. Hence JC *glaas* and *tob*" (by comparison with Sranan *grâsi* and *tóbo*, English *glass* and *tub*).

In order for systematic markers and lexical items to be stigmatized or to carry prestige, however, they had to be identifiable. Some features that we regard as 'typical' of the creole today were perhaps not always so but were identified partly as lower-class English. For example, some features of the phonology of JC are undoubtedly reflexes of African phonology and others of conservative dialects of rural English. The loss of the inflectional system of English is due to the contact situation; the use of past markers derived from *been* (*en, wen, ben, min, mi,* etc.) is due to the syntactic influence of western and northwestern British dialects, but the use of these forms with the uninflected verb form for past contexts is thought of as peculiarly creole.

Pidginization or the development of a pidgin language is a one-generation process, even though subsequent generations may constantly repeat the process and be strongly influenced in the way they do so by the form of the earlier pidgin. Creolization is also a one-generation process to some extent, since, by definition, once a generation has grown up making its language out of pidgin forms, that language is a creole. But, of course, the pidgin only supplies them with the nucleus of a grammatical code and a lexicon and certain analogical generative resources for syntactic, lexical, and semantic development; beyond these the new generation will turn, as will any generation, to other resource languages and to inherent processes.

Although pidginization through contact is general and constantly going on, the conditions that subsequently lead to the emergence of well-defined creoles are particular, and the characteristics of the creole in each case depend upon the relative size and prestige of the groups involved in the isolated community, the nature of their daily communion, the degree of their isolation, and other focussing factors such as the extent of a community of interest and the nature of that interest, the demographic structure of the community (predominance of young people vs. predominance of the old, predominance of male or female sex, etc.), and the replacement mechanisms of the population (see Le Page 1975b). The characteristics of the creole will also depend upon such linguistic features as the nature of the model language, and whether it is the same language as that involved in the contact that produced the original pidgin, or a different language.

There are two further respects in which the creole situation may be *sui generis.* The first is that the creole plantation communities were slave communities; the second, that they were colonial communities. Each member of the community thus had three ostensible options: to identify with the metropolitan country of the slave owners; to identify with the local creole community; or to identify with the country of origin of the slaves. The first and the last each had their local representatives: the first, in the governor and the army; the last, in runaway slave communities frequently dominated by former slaves with claims to high social status in Africa. In times of internal stress the social pulls were centrifugal, whereas in times of external threat the creole society could close its ranks so that blacks, whites, and colored people all identified themselves as creoles. In the post-creolization years similar forces have continued to operate. Many members of such communities have responded to the creole situation—as they may to any contact situation—by polarizing their behavior to a greater or lesser extent, depending on the hypothesis and four riders set out above in 1.2.

2.3. *The effects of education*

Early generations of creole children grew up in a relatively unfocussed linguistic environment. If, as I suggest, the normal progression of a nascent language community in a part-literate community is from a context-bound oral and gestural code toward a context-free oral and written code, the latter much more highly focussed than the former, then 'competence' statements about children in the latter situation will have a much more normative appearance than can any adequate statement about the competence of children in the former situation (see Le Page 1975a). However, the creole child has just the same need for identification as any other, and is subject to the same constraints under my hypothesis and four riders. The seventeenth- or eighteenth-century creole child had no difficulty in identifying some groups—the group of slaves on his plantation, or the group of white overseers; he or she could identify the group of upper-class speakers much less easily, and had little access to them. The at first gradual and then latterly quite sudden onset of education has, however, increased creole children's chances under rider [b], opportunities for learning, and the possibility of economic improvement their drive under [c], their motivation, while perhaps decreasing their chances under [a] to identify the model groups.

The early generations of creole children were in no doubt that there were people who actually did speak African languages—they met them and heard them referred to as 'Africans' or 'Congomen' or 'Ibos'. They were in no doubt either that there were people who actually spoke very white varieties of English; but their contact with such people, unless they themselves were the children of one or the other, might be very limited, and they did not get any schooling or learn to read. The advent of education was roughly contemporaneous with the abolition of slavery and the growth of absenteeism; creole children then began to have the opportunity to learn the system of the standard language, but their opportunities to identify at first hand the group who spoke it decreased to some extent. Instead, the most conspicuous indigenous interpreters of the educated model were the rapidly growing colored urban mercantile and professional middle class—in Jamaica, the 'brown men'. We can represent this changing situation by a series of diagrams, Figs. 1-4.

The free creole child was taught, through the educational system, what slaves were not taught to any great extent, that the system of the model language was a 'correct' version of which his own vernacular usage was a 'wrong' version. As a result not only were certain linguistic features stigmatized, but when any overt description of a linguistic system was available to and exemplified for the creole speaker it was that of the model language. (This situation is not, of course, confined to creole children.) The result of stigmatization for the creole child, as for any broad dialect speaker, has been that the effectiveness of schooling has depended on the rejection of the home, thus setting up divided motivation, whose effect is felt under my rider [c]. Being told that the vernacular was a bad variety of the model language led the creole child, as it would any broad dialect speaker, on the one hand to try to map the vernacular onto the grammar supplied for the model language, and on the other to regard the study of 'grammar' as something very important but very artificial—a white man's trick that had to be mastered. The big difference between the creole child and the, say, West Riding of Yorkshire dialect-speaking child is that, whereas it is not too difficult to map a West

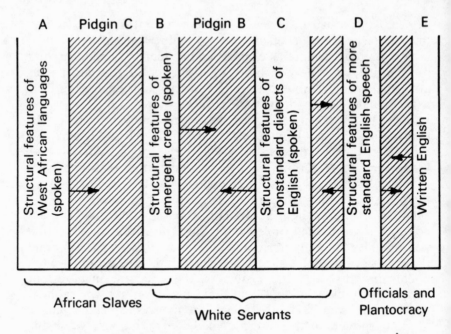

Fig. 1. Jamaican society in the late seventeenth century. Some individuals would have been monolingual in A; some bilingual in A and pidgin C; some bilingual in B and A; some in C and pidgin B; some in D and pidgin B; some monolingual in D.

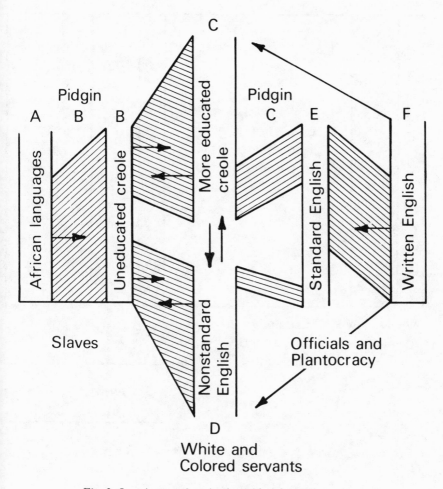

Fig. 2. Jamaican society in the mid-eighteenth century

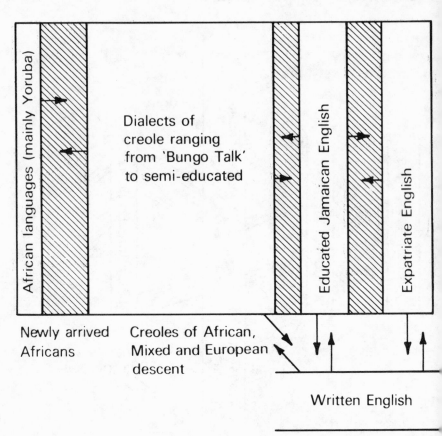

Fig. 3. Jamaican society in the mid-nineteenth century

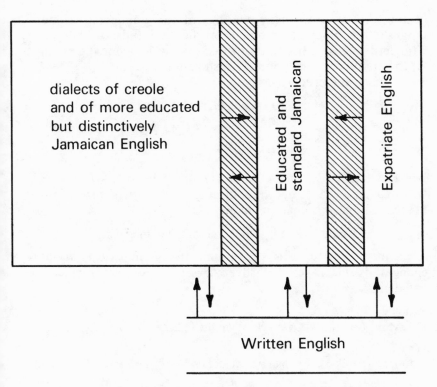

Fig. 4. Jamaican society in the first half of the twentieth century

Riding dialect onto many features of the grammar of standard
English, the inherent grammar of the two ends of the creole:
Standard English continuum just do not fit, let alone the grammar
of the creole with classroom English grammar.

Let us consider two cases:

Broad Jamaican Creole   Standard English

$$\text{im de} \qquad \left. \begin{array}{l} \text{He is} \\ \\ \text{was} \end{array} \right\} \text{there}$$

Beryl L. Bailey (*Jamaican Creole Syntax*, 1966) treats *de* as a verb.
It is easy to construct a continuum from that form to the
Standard English, something like:

ɩm de   i de   i dɛa   i ɩz deɐ   hi ɩz ðɛɐ

At some point in this continuum the grammatical structure
changes; is /dɛa/ verb or adverb? Let us consider further the
paradigms:

Standard English	I am sick	I was sick	I am the father	I am running	I ran
Jamaican Creole	mi sik	mi ben sik	mi di fada	mi a ron	mi ron
Belize	a sik	a mi sik	a di fada	a di ron	a ron

It seems that we have a broad creole grammar that does
not formally distinguish between verb predicates and non-verb
predicates, contrasting with a Standard English grammar that does.
In addition, within the Caribbean, we find reflexes of dialectal
varieties of English that mark aspect with the following forms:

Jamaican punctual completive	ben	< English *been*
continuative	a	< English *a-* as in *a-running*
Belize punctual completive	mi	< English *been* (bilab + V + Nasal)
continuative	di	< English *do*

Thus, whereas in the pidgin stage, Jamaican Creole

di biebi niem rabat

may have been related by the speaker to the grammar of his or her
native language and by the hearer to the grammar of his or hers,
with syntactically incompatible results but—at a superficial level—

no loss of communication (if one accepts Silverstein's argument), at the creole level the reflex of this sentence may be cognitively related to the grammar of the model language (with, non-cognitively, a syntactic deep structure) while in fact operating according to the (quite different) grammar (and semantic deep structure) of the creole speaker's vernacular. The implications of this for learning the model language are quite considerable.

Labov has discussed a similar problem in *Language in the Inner City* (1972b). "Is B[lack] E[nglish] V[ernacular] a separate system?" he asks. He concludes that the BEV speaker has at least a perceptual competence in various aspects of the grammar of Standard English, even if he cannot reproduce the SE forms: "This view of the relations of BEV and SE in the competence of black speakers shows that they do indeed form a single system. . . . The gears and axles of English grammatical machinery are available to speakers of all dialects, whether or not they use all of them in everyday speech." Much as I admire Labov's detailed and painstaking analysis, I fear that his results show nothing of the sort, any more than my own partial passive competence in 'French' shows 'French' and 'English' to be one system. This partial competence is part of *my* system, that is all (see Le Page 1973).

In 0.2., I have distinguished four senses in which the term 'language' is used. In homogeneous monolingual literate societies, a person's Language Two may be highly focussed and very close to his or her Language One, so that rules overtly stated for Two do not conflict too much with behavior triggered by One. In some recognized bilingual societies two distinct codes may be acknowledged—this is coming to be the case in some creole societies (e.g., Haiti) today. But in the past in creole societies it was felt (and frequently still is) that only the standard model has rules, and that the behavior of the individual in the vernacular is the result of failure to obey these.

In Belize, Young (1973) has analyzed the behavior of four groups of his fellow citizens: schoolteachers, second-generation civil servants, first-generation civil servants, and manual laborers. He has found the first two groups confidently bilingual in creole and educated Belize English, making a pronounced switch between two codes for different contexts and topics; the third group uneasily and partially bilingual with more of a continuum between their creole and their hypercorrect educated usage; and the fourth group monolingual in creole with some sporadic adjustments to a more elevated register closer to educated usage for certain topics.

R. Abrahams (1972) has shown that a creole can have its own
High varieties, distinct from the standard literary language of the
educated man. Here the rules are not those learned in school to
'correct' creole grammar, but those learned by observation of the
oral literature of creole rhetoric—of the preacher and the man of
words. But again, if the man of words were asked to formulate the
rules for talking sweet, he would be likely to respond, if at all,
with reference to the rules of the standard model language learned
in school.

2.4. *Lexical borrowing and supplementation; 'relexification'*

I wish to argue in this section that while lexical borrowing
and supplementation from a variety of sources are frequent in the
early years of a nascent creole, to speak of 'relexification',
especially if this means treating lexical development as if it
happened in isolation from 'the grammar' of 'a creole language', is
wrong. The most recent contribution to the discussion of
relexification is one of the most distinguished, not least because of
the author's very considerable knowledge of the unique case of
Surinam, in which a number of creole languages have developed
symbiotically. Voorhoeve (1973) argues that Sranan and Saramaccan speakers came to Surinam plantations with a basic knowledge
of Portuguese Creole. Sranan completely relexified in the direction
of English, Saramaccan only partly. The evidence suggests that
Djinka is not a product of relexification but developed from an
eighteenth-century English pidgin. "It is concluded that both
'normal' genetic developments and relexification may have similar
results and that comparative evidence alone is not a sufficient basis
for historical conclusions. . . ."

The records for Saramaccan and Sranan go back a good
deal further than those for most creole languages; the missionary
Christian Ludwig Schumann wrote a dictionary for each, in 1779
and 1783 respectively. I cannot dispute the verbal evidence
adduced by Voorhoeve and others for the use of similar lexical
items in various creole communities; but the evidence that is then
brought forward to 'explain' these similarities is essentially from
social history and not from historical linguistics. And in terms of
social history Voorhoeve and others may have given insufficient
weight to one possible factor in accounting for Portuguese words
in Sranan and Saramaccan, the existence of a large Dutch slave
depot in Curaçao in the seventeenth century from which the
plantations of many colonizing countries in the Caribbean were

supplied (see Le Page 1960, Chapter IV, especially pp. 58-59), and in which still today a Portuguese-influenced creole, Papiamentu, is spoken. Further, Voorhoeve refers to Schumann's Sranan dictionary annotation of certain words as 'Djutongo', which is taken to refer to Saramaccan, but which Schumann glosses as follows:

> Djutongo nennen die Neger hier die mit dem Portugiesischen vermengte Negersprache. [sic] Saramakka—Ningne habi Djutongo.

> (The Blacks here call Jew-Language that Negro language which is mixed with Portuguese. Saramaccans speak Jew-Language.)

To me (although not to Voorhoeve), the best interpretation of this is that the language under discussion was called Jew Language because it was used by Portuguese Jews and it was a lingua franca that had developed between them and the creole-English-speaking Negroes. Thus for two reasons it is not necessary, in order to suppose that slaves arrived in Surinam in the seventeenth century with some knowledge of a Portuguese-influenced creole, to suppose that they left West Africa with it.

The arguments for and against 'monogenesis' for creoles have gone on now for a number of years. I have tried to show elsewhere that genetic models for linguistic development are grossly misleading if pushed to this point, since 'languages' are abstractions that each of us makes for himself out of the behavioral data available to us; I would also maintain that large-scale lexical borrowing always has phonological and syntactic consequences, and that these aspects of one's linguistic system are interdependent.

2.5. *Conclusion to section 2*

Different generations of speakers have different models, different goals; they innovate, and children abstract from their parents' total behavior, including their innovation, systems that most economically handle, e.g., in the lexicon, rules that for their parents belonged to phonology or grammar and so on. The child so equipped then encounters his or her peers and teachers, and evolves with them the language of the community. Within a sociolinguistic and psycholinguistic framework such as I have tried to develop, it seems possible for a linguistic theory to emerge that can handle adequately the many-faceted phenomena of pidginization and creolization. I have sought to stress the psychological and social probabilities, trying always to work from inside the language

community. This does not mean that "purely linguistic" explanations of the kind so carefully and thoroughly explored by DeCamp
(1971), Labov (1972a and elsewhere), Sankoff (1974), and
Bickerton (1975) are no longer relevant; it does mean, however,
that the major revisions of linguistic theory being undertaken at
present in the light of the evidence from pidgins and creoles
should be in the direction of a fully integrated sociolinguistic
model for the processes of language.

NOTES

1. Since the first version of this paper was published (*York Papers in
Linguistics* 4, 1974, pp. 41-69) Derek Bickerton's *Dynamics of a Creole
System* has appeared; there he discusses at length (pp. 27-33) the parallel
situation in basilectal Guyanese creole. His discussion, however, starts from an
acceptance of the verb: non-verb distinction; he finds that, *within the verb
paradigm*, the distinction is that the stem's unmarked function with
non-statives signals past punctual, whereas with stative verbs it signals
non-past. The distinction between stative and non-stative must remain basic
to the grammar, however.
2. Samarin (1971) gives some specific stylistic examples from Tonga
which could be paralleled from most language communities.
3. There is a tendency for those working with French-based creoles
to deny the flux and to claim that French creoles are quite sharply distinct
from their models. My own experience in Mauritius, Grenada, and St. Lucia
does not wholly support this contention, which may to some extent at least
reflect the differential polarizing effect of the observer in two kinds of
community. The social value attached to the concept of "speaking correct
French to an educated man" is much more positive than that of "speaking
correct English." Behavior in private is another matter, as the observations of
Midgett (1970) in St. Lucia testify.
4. But see Bickerton 1975 for the most sustained attempt to date to
reconstruct the details of the historical past from those of today's continuum.

REFERENCES

Abrahams, R. 1972. The training of the man of words in talking sweet. *Language in Society* 1:15-30.

Alatis, J. E., ed. 1968. *Contrastive Linguistics and its Pedagogical Implications.* Washington, D.C.: Georgetown University monographs no. 21.

————, ed. 1970. *Bilingualism and Language Contact.* Georgetown University monographs no. 20.

Alleyne, M. C. 1971. Acculturation and the cultural matrix of creolization. In *Pidginization and Creolization of Languages,* Dell Hymes, ed., pp. 169-86.

Bailey, B. L. 1966. *Jamaican Creole Syntax.* London: Cambridge University Press.

Barth, F. 1969. *Ethnic Groups and Boundaries.* Boston: Little, Brown.

Berry, J. 1961. English loan words and adaptations in Sierra Leone Krio. In *Creole Language Studies II,* R. B. Le Page, ed., pp. 1-16. London: Macmillan.

Bickerton, D. 1973. The nature of a creole continuum. *Language* 49:640-69.

————. 1975. *The Dynamics of a Creole System.* London: Cambridge University Press.

Brash, E. 1976. Some stylistic responses to linguistic diversity in the English prose fiction of selected West African, Caribbean and Melanesian writers. Unpublished Ph.D. diss., University of Sussex.

Brown, R. 1973. *A First Language.* Cambridge, Mass.: Harvard University Press.

————, and Lenneberg, E. H. 1954/1970. A study in language and cognition. *Journal of Abnormal and Social Psychology* 49:454-62; reprinted 1970 in Brown, R., *Psycholinguistics.* New York: The Free Press, pp. 235-57.

Carroll, J. B. 1968. Contrastive linguistics and interference theory. In *Contrastive Linguistics and its Pedagogical Implications,* J. E. Alatis, ed., pp. 113-22.

Cassidy, F. G. 1971. Tracing the pidgin element in Jamaican Creole. In Hymes, pp. 203-21.

————, and Le Page, R. B. 1967. *Dictionary of Jamaican English.* London: Cambridge University Press.

Christian, C. C. 1970. The analysis of linguistic and cultural differences: a proposed model. In *Bilingualism and Language Contact,* J. E. Alatis, ed., pp. 149-62.

DeCamp, D. 1971. Towards a generative analysis of a post-creole speech continuum. In Hymes, pp. 349-70.

DJE. See Cassidy and Le Page, 1967.

Feibleman, James, and Friend, J. W. 1945. The structure and function of organisation. *Philosophical Review* 54:19-44.

Ferguson, C. A. 1971. Absence of copula and the notion of simplicity. In Hymes, pp. 141-50.

———. 1975. Towards a characterization of English foreigner talk. *Anthropological Linguistics* 17:1-14.

Greenberg, J. H. 1966. *Language Universals with Special Reference to Feature Hierarchies.* The Hague: Mouton.

———. 1969. Language universals: a research frontier. *Science* 166:473-78.

Gumperz, J. G., and Wilson, R. 1971. Convergence and creolization: a case from the Indo-Aryan/Dravidian border. In Hymes, pp. 151-67.

Hall, Robert A., Jr. 1966. *Pidgin and Creole Languages.* Ithaca: Cornell University Press.

Hockett, C. F. 1968. *The State of the Art.* The Hague: Mouton.

Kelly, L. C., ed. 1969. *The Description and Measurement of Bilingualism.* Toronto: University of Toronto Press.

Labov, W. 1971. On the adequacy of natural languages, I: the development of tense. Mimeo.

———. 1972a. Negative attraction and negative concord in English grammar. *Language* 48:773-818.

———. 1972b. *Language in the Inner City.* Philadelphia: University of Pennsylvania Press.

Le Page, R. B. 1960. *Jamaican Creole.* Creole Language Studies I. London: Macmillan.

———. 1967. Linguistic introduction: historical phonology. In Cassidy and Le Page, pp. xxxvi-lxiv.

———. 1968. Problems of description in multilingual communities. *Transactions of the Philological Society,* pp. 189-212.

———. 1969. How can we measure the effects which one language may have on the other in the speech of bilinguals? In *The Description and Measurement of Bilingualism,* L. G. Kelly, ed., pp. 142-47. Toronto: Toronto University Press.

———. 1972. Preliminary report on *The Sociolinguistic Survey of Multilingual Communities. Language in Society* 1:155-72.

———. 1973. The concept of competence in a creole/contact situation. *York Papers in Linguistics* 3:31-50.

———. 1975a. Sociolinguistics and the problem of competence. In *Language Teaching and Linguistics: Abstracts* 8, July 1975, pp. 136-56. London: Cambridge University Press.

———. 1975b. Projection, Focussing, Diffusion, or, steps towards a sociolinguistic theory of language as illustrated from the Sociolinguistic Survey of Multilingual Communities Stages I: Cayo District, Belize (formerly British Honduras). II: St. Lucia. In *Proceedings of* the International Conference on the Methodology of Sociolinguistic Surveys Montreal 1975. Washington, D.C.: Center for Applied Linguistics (to appear).

—————. Christie, P.; Jurdant, B.; Weekes, A. J.; and Tabouret-Keller, A. 1974. Sociolinguistic survey of multilingual communities, Stage I: British Honduras survey. The analysis of the sociolinguistic data. *Language in Society* 3:1-32.

LeVine, R. A., and Campbell, D. T. 1972. *Ethnocentrism.* New York: John Wiley.

Lyons, J. 1968. *Introduction to Theoretical Linguistics.* London: Cambridge University Press.

Midgett, D. 1970. Bilingualism and linguistic change in St. Lucia. *Anthropological Linguistics* 12:158-70.

Piaget, J., and Inhelder, B. 1969. *The Psychology of the Child* (trans. Helen Weaver). London: Routledge.

Samarin, W. 1971. Salient and substantive pidginization. In Hymes, pp. 117-40.

Sankoff, G. 1974. A quantitative paradigm for the study of communicative competence. In Bauman and Sherzer (eds.), *Explorations in the Ethnography of Speaking.* London: Cambridge University Press, pp. 18-49.

Silverstein, M. 1972. Chinook Jargon: language contact and the problem of multi-level generative systems. *Language* 48:378-406, 596-625.

Tabouret-Keller, A. 1971. Language use in relation to the growth of towns in West Africa: a survey. *International Migration Review* 5:180-203.

Voorhoeve, J. 1973. Historical and linguistic evidence in favour of the relexification theory in the formation of creoles. *Language in Society* 2:133-46.

Weinreich, U. 1963. *Languages in Contact* (2d printing). The Hague: Mouton.

Young, C. 1973. A sociolinguistic study of Belize Creole. Unpublished D.Phil diss., Language Department, University of York.

iv.

Problems of Genesis and Development:
The Historical and Social Matrix

Toward the Reconstruction of the
Social Matrix of Creole Language

Robert Chaudenson

The question of the genesis of creole languages has given rise to a large number of hypotheses that have often been as ardently defended as they were weakly argued.[1] This situation stems from two sets of causes. First, documents describing the early states of these languages are rare and, when available, are so fragmentary as to be relatively untrustworthy. Scholars are therefore tempted to adopt ingenious hypotheses without taking into account external facts that, though rare and difficult to obtain, might clarify certain aspects of the genesis of creoles and, in any event, would eliminate hypotheses that are clearly inconsistent with these facts. Second, many of the hypotheses that have been put forward are too often based on purely linguistic considerations and fail to take into account anthropological, historical, and sociological data. Without pretending to provide a comprehensive inventory of the possible sources of information or to illustrate all available methods of research, I will attempt to show how anthropological, historical, and sociological facts may be used to control hypotheses in regard to the origin of creoles.

1. THE MONOGENETIC HYPOTHESIS

Undoubtedly the monogenetic hypothesis is the most attractive of the hypotheses that fail to take into account all available external facts. In all its variant forms, the monogenetic hypothesis derives all creoles, or a group of creoles sharing the same European base language, from a single pidgin or "proto-creole." This common source may be a "nautical jargon" (Reinecke 1938; Faine 1939; Whinnom 1965), or an African or Afro-Portuguese pidgin[2] (Valkhoff 1960; Thompson 1961; Goodman 1964; Todd 1974).[3] The version of the monogenetic theory that assumes a proto-Afro-Portuguese pidgin is less objectionable than that which starts from a common African substratum.[4] The existence of Portuguese-based pidgins is firmly established, and these languages are reported on the coast of West Africa as well as that of India as early as the seventeenth century (de Saint-Lô 1637, pp. 60, 99, 143; Le Courbe 1688, p. 192; Hamilton 1727, p. XII). Nonetheless, in all cases, and even if we limit our consideration to the west coast of Africa, no proof is offered of the unity or the similarity of these pidgins, which these authors mention without providing any description or sample. Perhaps a comparative study of existing Portuguese-based creoles, such as that barely sketched out by R. W. Thompson (1961, p. 110), based on the more or less comprehensive descriptions of Schuchardt (1887), Dalgado, Lopes da Silva, Chataignier, etc., could shed some light on the relation between early Portuguese-based contact languages.

But even if it were proven that there existed on the coast of West Africa a relatively homogeneous Afro-Portuguese pidgin or creole, we could not infer from this fact a necessary genetic relationship between this pidgin and Dutch, English, and French creoles attested later in the same or neighboring regions. Indeed, even the successive presence of a pidgin and a creole derived from a common base language in the same geographical area does not necessarily prove a genetic relationship between the two. For example, Du Tertre (1654, p. 463) and, especially, Rochefort (1658, p. 523) mention the existence in the Caribbean of "baragoin," the lingua franca used by the Caribs in their dealings with Europeans, and provide some information about the circumstances of its use and list some lexical items. It does not seem, however, that, with the exception of some vocabulary elements, "baragoin" has left many traces in West Indian creoles, even on islands such as Dominica or Saint-Lucia, where the presence of a Carib population has been more lasting.

Regardless of the source it proposes for creoles, no monogenetic theory can fail to take into consideration the historical and sociological aspects of the problem: a language does not spread in time and space like a virus, and a few sporadic contacts between two linguistic groups are not sufficient to cause one group to adopt the language of the other. Thus the monogenetic theory that seeks to link all creoles to a Portuguese proto-creole completely evades the problem by arbitrarily assuming that the early texts (which often are not even studied) suggest the existence of a single Portuguese pidgin from West Africa to India. On the basis of similar evidence a linguist could in the year 2300 deduce the identity of Reunion and Martinican creoles!

Of course, sociohistorical data are superfluous for linguists concerned with strictly synchronic linguistic description. But in that case, they should rigorously abstain from taking any position with respect to problems of genesis; this has hardly always been the case.

2. THE SOCIOHISTORICAL APPROACH

Linguists have tended by and large to neglect or, in some cases, even totally disregard sociohistorical data. It is surprising, for example, how few references are made to Rens's admirable study of the historical and social background of Sranan (1953), based on a wide array of precise documents on early stages of the language. Some proposals for the possible contribution of historians, sociologists, and anthropologists to clarification of the genesis of pidgins and creoles have been put forward by Alleyne (1971), Hoenigswald (1971), and, particularly, Mintz (1971, pp. 473-96), but these proposals remain somewhat problematic and theoretical, as stressed by the preliminary remarks made by Hoenigswald and Mintz. In the case of Alleyne, he adheres to too narrow a linguistic description and, in his account of the development of creole languages in the West Indies, assigns too limited a role to the deculturation/acculturation process.

Within the framework of the sociohistorical approach, two points must be given special attention: (1) demographic patterns in the areas where the particular language under study appeared; (2) the socioeconomic structure.

2.1. *Settlement and demography*

For the linguist who is trying to determine the relative influence of servile languages on a given creole, the first step must be a detailed study of the settlement history of the area during the period in which the creole is assumed to have been formed. For example, it is hard to believe that Jourdain, in her classic work on the genesis of Creole French (1956), seriously considers the possible influence of the indigenous languages on Reunion French Creole when the island is known to have been uninhabited at the time of settlement. Before claiming the influence of such and such a language on the development of a pidgin or creole, it must first be proven that that language was indeed spoken in the area under study. This approach would permit one to eliminate certain gratuitous hypotheses such as the one, widely accepted, that postulates a common African origin for all French Creole dialects. Even a cursory survey of the settlement history of the plantation islands of the Caribbean and the Indian Ocean would reveal that, whereas slaves were imported to the Caribbean from the west coast of Africa, those shipped to the Indian Ocean came from the east coast of Africa. Moreover, slaves of East African origin ("Caffres") constituted a minority of the servile population and were imported after the formative period of the creole (Chaudenson 1974, pp. 1106-1109; 1976).

It is equally important to try to determine the span of time during which a creole was constituted. On that score, the study of Rens (1953) is exemplary: this author was able to show by the use of extensive and precise documents that Sranan was formed in Surinam within half a century (1953, pp. 53-54). For Indian Ocean Creole French dialects, examination of historical documents and comparative analysis lead me to the same conclusion (Chaudenson 1974, pp. 441-52). The delimitation of the formative period of creoles is important because it enables one to narrow down the study of the demographic patterns of the region concerned. That creoles emerge during a very short time span, as Rens and I have indicated, is an important factor in assessing the relative influence of the lexical base and servile languages on their structure. In the plantation colonies established in the seventeenth and eighteenth centuries, the population of European origin was no doubt much greater than is generally believed. In the case of the island of Bourbon (Reunion), contrary to all accepted opinions, it was only a half-century after the beginning of settlement that the servile population came to outnumber the whites (Chaudenson 1974, pp. 452-65). As we have seen, at that time the creole had already crystallized. Here again, errors are numerous and sometimes arise from prejudices and accepted opinions. In this light, Valkhoff's hypothesis of a determining African influence on Reunionnese is erroneous, hinging as it does on the disproportion between the white and black populations of Bourbon Island at the beginning of the eighteenth century (1960, p. 235). Valkhoff's hypothesis was based on population figures whose source he does not mention but which are obviously borrowed from Brunot (1967, VIII, p. 1050). In fact Brunot's figures are absolutely incorrect and are probably due to an unfortunate misprint that raises the black population from the probable 1,095 to 10,950 (1717 census figures show a population of 1,100).

In the French West Indies, where the whites presently constitute only an infinitesimal proportion of the population (0.7%; Benoist 1975, p. 18), one must bear in mind that this was not the case at the time of settlement. Thus, in Martinique census figures show that a quarter-century after the beginning of colonization, i.e., in 1664, there were 2,094 whites and 3,158 blacks (Funk 1953, p. 19); in 1740, whites still constituted 20% of the total population (Benoist 1975, p. 18).

The geographic origin of the various demographic groups is equally essential. For the islands of the Indian Ocean, whose settlement history is well known, the study of population origins quickly dispels the myth of the African origin of the French Creole dialects of that region. It is probable that these dialects derive directly from Bourbonnais, a creolized variety of French spoken on the island of Bourbon.[5] On the one hand, we know that this island was the first to be settled by the French, and on the other hand, we can refer to archival documents to determine the place of origin of the European settlers and the imported slaves and to follow the demographic development of the various ethnic groups (Chaudenson 1974, pp. 452-65). On the basis of documentary evidence, two important observations may be made: (1) a deliberate policy to prevent the formation of a homogeneous slave community resulted in a servile population that was highly varied from an ethnic point of view (for example, the 1709 census shows the following ethnic makeup: Malagasys 24%, Indians 24%, miscellaneous Africans [Caffres] 13%); (2) the "creole" slave group (slaves born in the colony) showed a rapid increase in size and attained 40% of the total in 1709.

Unfortunately, archival documents as accurate and complete as these are not available for all creoles. Nevertheless, careful examination of census figures, civil registries, slave inventories of estates, shipping documents, etc., would turn up important information, as would that of travelers' journals and other contemporary accounts. For example, in the West Indies, Father

Labat notes the multiplicity of languages spoken by blacks and makes some interesting observations:

> The most widespread of all these languages, at least so far as I have been able to learn from many people that have visited these countries and from my own experience, is the one spoken in the kingdom of Arda and Juda. We call blacks that come from that coast Aradas, and I have seen that all those from areas close to that country, sixty to eighty leagues to the east and to the west, understood or spoke Arada. That language is very easy. Verbs have only three tenses: present, past, and future. Nouns are not inflected; only the article changes. It contains many adverbs and, although it appears rudimentary, it still enables one to express oneself adequately (1724, pp. 11-45).

Systematic searches in local archives and the consultation of regional bibliographies, such as that of Comitas (1968) for the West Indies, and of works on the history of slavery would also shed light on population origins. Failing to do this, pidgin and creole linguistics will remain at the stage of speculations of the type proffered by Sylvain (1936), who draws unwarranted parallels between Haitian Creole and Ewe without offering documentary proof that the latter language was in fact spoken by slaves shipped to colonial Saint-Domingue.

2.2. *The socioeconomic structure*

The socioeconomic structure plays a key role in pidginization and creolization. In particular, two types of creoles corresponding to two different types of socioeconomic structures need to be distinguished:

(1) Endogenous creoles, arising from the contact of an indigenous population, servile or not, and an incoming European group whose activity was commercial rather than agricultural. These arose within the area where the vernacular language of an indigenous population was used or in the immediate vicinity. For example, "lanzado" communities seem to correspond to this type of situation. They appeared on the coast of West Africa and were formed at first by Portuguese, then by English settlers grouped in communities with native Africans: concubines, brokers, servants, etc. (Hancock 1972, Valdman 1977). The Portuguese creoles of Africa (Casamance, Guinea) would be examples of this type. These endogenous creoles, being in contact with the languages of the indigenous populations and no doubt structurally closer to them, would be particularly vulnerable to decreolization in the direction of these languages, as well as to repidginization.

(2) Exogenous creoles, often insular, arising in geographic areas from which, in general, none of the population groups in contact originate. These creoles correspond to plantocratic society communities, since these had from the beginning an agrarian orientation (food crops, coffee, spices, sugar cane, etc.).

Highly significant differences appear in the way in which these two types of creoles were formed. In the case of the endogenous creoles, the non-European population is relatively homogeneous, remains within its own territory or in adjacent areas, maintains, even under foreign domination, its ethnic identity, its traditions and, by and large, its language. A key feature of exogenous creoles is the ethnic diversity of the servile groups, speaking different languages, and often systematically separated from members of their African group and integrated into a new socioeconomic structure that aimed at their deculturation.

This analysis of exogenous creoles agrees in large measure with that proposed by Mintz (1971, p. 493).[6] In the Caribbean areas on which Mintz bases his analysis, the socioeconomic and sociocultural context in which the creoles emerged is very similar to the one that obtained for Reunion Creole (Chaudenson 1974): islands that were uninhabited (Mascarenes, Seychelles) or no longer occupied principally by their indigenous populations (West Indies); formation of multi-ethnic immigrant societies in which the group of European origin was socially and numerically dominant;[7] rapid acculturation of the servile groups, especially on the linguistic level (the relative rarity of the need for interpreters in court cases, as revealed by the study of legal archives, indicates that the slaves rapidly acquired the use of the creole; the rapid acquisition of the contact language by the slaves was due precisely to their linguistic diversity).

The numerous works on slavery are a rich source of information on the sociological structure of the plantation colonies. Detailed examination of these works largely confirms hypotheses formulated on the basis of study of early documentary evidence of the use of creoles and comparative analysis. On this point, Mintz's analysis of Caribbean plantation colonies can be made more comprehensive by the consideration of four sets of factors, which I have identified on the basis of close examination of descriptions of the establishment of the plantation colonies of Bourbon Island.

2.2.1. *Deculturation/acculturation.* This process is fundamental to an understanding of the colonial plantation societies of the seventeenth and eighteenth centuries. It was not a mere fortuitous phenomenon associated with the particular social structure of these colonies, but rather a concerted and systematic policy that constituted one of the colonies' main underpinnings.

For example, younger slaves were systematically sought out, since they were more easily assimilated into the plantocratic system.

> Children from ten to fifteen years make the best captives for sending to America. The Portuguese only take them at that age.... One has at least the advantage of raising them as one wishes; one trains them to adopt only those habits and behavior that are suitable to their masters; they more readily learn the language of the country and its customs, its Religion; they more readily forget their native country and the vices that abound there; they learn to like their masters and are less likely to escape (Labat 1731, II, p. 106-107).

The psychological and personality traits of the various ethnic groups were also taken into consideration. For instance, it was the indomitable character of the Caribs and their resistance to assimilation that led in large measure to their extermination (Du Tertre 1654, p. 473). On the other hand, certain African ethnic groups ("tribes") considered easily adaptable (slaves from Juda) were more favored on the market than others considered more prone to revolt, depression, and suicide (the Ibos for instance; cf. Randford 1971, p. 102).

2.2.2. *The role and function of "creole" slaves.* Born in the plantation colony, spared the deathly trials of the "middle passage," creole slaves enjoyed a higher social status than newly imported ("bozal") slaves and were often numerically preponderant. (In assessing the relative proportion of creole to bozal slaves, one must beware of slave immigration statistics and keep in mind the very high mortality rate for newly arrived slaves.) Creole slaves occupied a higher place on the occupational scale and constituted a social model for the newcomers. According to Rens (1953, p. 61):

> The creole slave became the ardent propagandist of the Caribbean ways and of his newly acquired tongue, teaching the newcomer the English names of the articles of ordinary use, initiating him into the languages of his new country, and thus leading him farther and farther away from Africa.

(Cf. also Wyndham 1935, p. 245; Randford 1971, p. 119; Chaudenson 1974, pp. 450-51.)

2.2.3. *The absence of a socio-cultural superstructure.* The population of European origin, often lower class and speaking substandard or dialectal forms of its native language, was insulated from the normative pressures and constraints exercised through the educational system and the direct influence of upper-class linguistic patterns. In the language contact situation of the plantation setting, the possibilities of very rapid evolution of the European languages increased, since in that setting inherent structural tendencies, generally inhibited by standardizing influences, were more likely to emerge freely (Chaudenson 1976b).

2.2.4. *The social structure of the plantation.* The colonial plantation was a veritable economic and social isolate, which lent itself perfectly to the process of deculturation/acculturation. The deliberate policy designed to prevent the formation of homogeneous slave communities manifested itself not only in the selection of imported slaves (for the islands of Bourbon and France [Mauritius], the letters and instructions of the Compagnie des Indes are very enlightening in this regard), but also in plantation organization. One important aspect of the integration of slaves into the plantocratic system was in the "seasoning" process described vividly in a chapter of Randford (1971) entitled "Hell in the Caribbean":

> The planters made a deliberate attempt to break the slaves' spirit and to loosen their links with Africa by judicious separation of tribes, by teaching them to speak only the master's language.... At the end of the seasoning the usual result was that the slaves' past had been annihilated and their tribal *mores* abrogated (1971, p. 104).

The process of deculturation was facilitated by the "vertical" structure of the plantation society (DeCamp 1961, p. 62) and the absence of horizontal communication between slaves on different plantations. This isolation made the maintenance of an ethnic consciousness among slaves from the same tribe or country of origin impossible. The creole that developed in the plantation colony thus represented not only the means of communication between the dominant group of European origin and the subordinate slave communities, but also between the various ethnic subgroups of each individual slave community. The physical atrocities of slavery have often overshadowed the effects of this policy of cultural alienation; this voluntary and systematic deculturation, though less spectacular, was extremely effective.

The documentary evidence on the basis of which a scholar can reconstruct the social setting of the plantation colonies and study the deculturation and acculturation of servile groups is extremely varied. It includes, in addition to the abundant literature on the history of slavery, correspondence and archives (immigration statistics, administrative and judicial records) as well as contemporary written accounts (travelers' narratives, diaries, memoirs, etc.).

3. THE COMPARATIVE APPROACH

The major difficulty in this approach lies, of course, in the almost total absence of written samples documenting early stages of creole languages, and rare are the cases such as Sranan, where one has access to reliable and extensive records (Rens 1953; Voorhoeve 1961, pp. 99-106). Nevertheless, this type of research is the most promising, especially in the area of lexicology. However, it must be oriented less toward the examination of published descriptions of pidgins and creoles, whose inventory in most cases is complete, than toward yet unexplored areas.

For the French creoles, for example, Goodman in his comparative study has been able to unearth some crucial data on the Caribbean area in particular (1964, pp. 104-107). More recently Valdman (1977), in a survey of orthographic practices, has undertaken an extensive inventory of early Creole French printed texts; for the Indian Ocean dialects, a similar collection is in preparation. It should be pointed out, however, that these early texts are not fully reliable documents about the structure of early stages of creoles, since they often exemplify European literary genres (fables, poems, etc.) and were composed by highly learned authors. It would be essential to compare these texts with more representative ones whenever the latter are available.

Notarial archives are useful for studies in lexicology. In particular, inventories of estates not only contain valuable information with respect to the cultural, economic, and social context (for example, the geographic provenience and ethnic origin of slaves), but in addition abound in the names of ordinary objects and indigenous plants. Judicial archives are more interesting in that they sometimes contain not only individual vocabulary items but complete utterances in creole languages. In general, recorders transcribed the responses of the defendant or of the witnesses in the official European language of the colony, but sometimes they noted original testimony given in the contact vernacular. For example, for Réunionnais, a very important piece of evidence for comparative study is a sentence in the contact vernacular of Bourbon Island that can be placed with certainty in the period 1714 to 1723; unfortunately, the original of this document has been lost, and only a copy has been preserved. This fragmentary evidence suggests that even at that time, that is, a half-century after the beginning of settlement, Réunionnais had already acquired the core of its structure (Chaudenson 1974, p. 444).

The comparative study of creoles should be developed on three different levels.

3.1. *Comparison of creoles from the same European base language in a single geographical area*

An example of this approach is my comparison of the four French Creole dialects of the Indian Ocean (Réunionnais, Mauritian, Seychellois, and Rodrigais), which traces these dialects to a common source, Bourbonnais, the creolized variety of French spoken on Bourbon before 1720 (Chaudenson 1974, pp. 1106-43).

3.2. *Comparison of creoles derived from the same European language in different geographical areas*

The principal study illustrating this approach is Goodman's comparison of Creole French dialects of the Caribbean and the Indian Ocean (1964), which is somewhat flawed by the relative paucity of information available to the author on the Indian Ocean dialects. Previous attempts at such a comparison had been undertaken by Adam (1883), Faine (1939), and Brunot (1967, VIII, p. 1132). Brunot's comparative study was undertaken with a view toward elucidating the problem of the origin of creoles, and while he did not grasp the problem in its entirety, he did nevertheless emphasize the importance of determining the place of origin of servile groups in constructing arguments for a genetic link between a given creole and the servile languages. The importance of this factor is particularly clear in comparative work on Creole French. The sociohistorical approach must necessarily precede comparative study since it alone enables one to determine which slave languages can be seriously taken into consideration.

In the case of the determination of the possible linguistic sources of a linguistic feature x present in one or more Creole French dialects, the following approach should be followed. Given:

C_1, a Creole French dialect of the New World

C_2, a Creole French dialect of the Indian Ocean

V_1, a language spoken by a large number of slaves imported to New World colonies

V_2, a language spoken by a large number of slaves imported to the Indian Ocean islands

F, standard, dialectal, or substandard French, or older stages of French.

If the feature x appears in both the New World and the Indian Ocean, then the following possibilities need be considered:

	C_1	V_1	C_2	V_2	F
1	+	+	+	+	+
2	+	-	+	-	-
3	+	+	+	-	-
4	+	-	+	+	-
5	+	+	+	-	+
6	+	-	+	+	+
7	+	-	+	-	+

In cases 1 and 2 the source of feature x is indeterminate since x is common to both groups of dialects and either appears in all possible source languages or is absent from them all.

Cases 3 and 4 are theoretically improbable, and the presence of the feature x in both groups of dialects must be attributed either to a chance coincidence or to the operation of some linguistic universal. Lexical items must be considered apart from phonological or semantactic features. Words are found in both groups of dialects for which a French origin is excluded absolutely. In fact, they can be traced to indigenous languages spoken in one or the other of the two geographical areas and abound in narrative accounts of French travelers and sailors. Probably these items, which I have labeled "vocabulaire des Isles" (Chaudenson 1974, pp. 590-632, 1090-93) and which refer to exotic flora and fauna, were transported from one area to the other—usually from West to East, along colonial trade and maritime communication routes.

In cases 5 and 6, the direct influence of an indigenous or servile language must also be excluded and a French source must be invoked. This is no doubt the case, for example, of *mũn* "person" (Chaudenson 1974, pp. 438-39), to which many creolists have assigned an African origin, and of the reflexive pronouns based on forms meaning "body" (e.g., *corps-moin, cadav'-moin*), for which some have argued an influence of parallel expressions appearing in Sudanese dialects (Jourdain 1956, p. 139). Given the absence of any direct link between West Africa and the Indian Ocean plantation islands, and the presence in many French dialectal varieties of these forms with the same generic meaning, a French origin is indubitable. The principal argument invoked against a French origin for these lexical items and constructions is their disappearance prior to the period of settlement of the West Indies (Jourdain 1956, p. 139; Goodman 1964, p. 57). In fact, today some dialects of western France still preserve the reflexive uses of *corps* and a generic meaning for *monde* (Chaudenson 1974, pp. 733-34).

3.3. *Dialect studies*

The comparative approach could be extended to regional and social dialects of the European base languages (Chaudenson 1973, pp. 342-72). In addition to shedding light on the genesis and development of creoles, this approach could lead to discoveries of interest to both general linguistics and the study of the structure and development of the particular European language.

3.4. *Universalist and innatist hypotheses*

The existence of structural analogies between genetically related languages, as is the case for the Romance languages on which most of the extant creoles are based, does not necessarily require recourse to a monogenetic hypothesis and the postulation of a proto-creole. Might it not be the case that primitive contact languages, given particular sociocultural circumstances (multilingualism in the communities, absence of normative institutions, lower-class or provincial origin of the European settlers, etc.), would show convergent evolutionary developments that would lead ultimately to similar structures? In the case of English creoles, parallels between certain structural features of American Black English and the English creoles and pidgins could be attributed to evolutionary tendencies of English, thus obviating the postulation of a previously existing rudimentary proto-pidgin (Bailey 1965, p. 172; Stewart 1967, p. 22; Wolfram 1969, pp. 11-14; Dillard 1971, pp. 393-408).

I have attempted to substantiate the existence of these convergent evolutionary patterns by comparing Indian Ocean Creole French varieties to substandard and dialect varieties of French and particularly to that substandard form of French labeled "français avancé" (Chaudenson 1974). Since then, I have continued in the same direction by examining some striking parallels between productive processes that appear in the course of first-language acquisition, and that determine successive child-language grammars, and those present in creole languages—for example, the prevalence of aspect over tense in verbal systems, the tendency toward the analytic expression of semantic categories—parallels that appear in Romance as well as Germanic base languages and their creole derivates (Chaudenson 1976a; Valdman and Phillips 1975). In this universalist and innatist orientation reappears the original hope of successfully accounting for the central aspects of pidginization and creolization within the framework of a general theory of language acquisition and language change, an endeavor with which are associated some of the most illustrious names in the history of linguistics (Schuchardt 1887, Jespersen 1921, Hjelmslev 1938, etc.). This hope is still very much with us today, and manifests itself particularly in Bickerton's insightful study of decreolization (1975; cf. especially pp. 4, 59, 173-74) as well as in several of the papers in this volume.

4. CONCLUSION

Long neglected or treated with some levity, set aside a priori by persistent synchronists, the problem of the genesis of creoles is of vital importance both for general linguistics and for an accurate account of the history and development of the various lexical-base and creole languages involved. The multidisciplinary approach, firmly grounded on external facts that I have outlined here, would enable us to refine the comparative method, which remains the principal tool of diachronic investigation. In this way we may avoid past reliance on flimsy and fanciful hypotheses, for sociohistorical facts allow one to identify those languages that have played a role in the genesis and development of a particular creole language, and to specify the precise nature and limits of this role.

Translated by Albert Valdman, Betsy Kerr-Barnes,
and Joseph W. Phillips

NOTES

1. The question of the dating of the first attestations of the word "creole" with the sense of 'language' must be reexamined; von Wartburg's *Französiches Etymologisches Wörterbuch* mentions: "Nf. créole: corrupted French spoken by the blacks of the colonies and by the creoles [locally born French] in their dealings with blacks (Larousse 1869)," II/2, p. 1296. Goodman points out a first attestation for Dutch creole: "Creol spreak. . . 1799," and for the French *langage créole,* Ducoeur-Joly 1802 (Goodman 1964, p. 11). Arveiller showed that the word had appeared more than a century earlier to designate the bastard Portuguese of Senegal: "These people [in Senegal] speak, in addition to the language of the country, a certain broken talk that bears little resemblance to Portuguese and which is called creole language, as in the Mediterranean Sea [one refers to the broken talk in use there] as lingua franca," Le Courbe, p. 192, text written circa 1688, quoted in Arveiller (1963, p. 208).

2. For French-based creoles, that common source has been characterized as an Afro-French proto-creole (Alleyne 1971), itself derived by relexification from a proto-Afro-Portuguese pidgin (Hull 1975).

3. We have only cited here the names of the authors of a few of the principal theories; for further details, cf. Hymes 1971, pp. 18-23; Todd 1974, pp. 28-49; Chaudenson 1974, pp. 400-420. Furthermore, the position of some of the quoted linguists has sometimes differed.

4. Todd herself, who goes so far as to set up a family tree specifying the derivation of existing creoles from Mediterranean lingua franca (Sabir) by the intermediary of a proto-Portuguese pidgin, acknowledges the fragility of the hypothesis (1974, p. 39).

5. Nevertheless the structural differences between these creoles are important and are due to various factors of evolution specific to each. Mauritian and Rodrigais creoles are more similar; Seychellois creole is characterized by features that are sometimes to be found in Réunionnais (Chaudenson 1974, pp. 113-19; Corne 1974-75 and 1976).

6. As my thesis was already completed in 1971, it is obvious that I

could not, at that time, have been acquainted with Mintz's article, but the analogy of our conclusions is all the more significant.

7. On this latter point, I take exception to Mintz, who describes the European group as "smaller and socially dominant." I have pointed out in 2.1. that one must not be deceived by subsequent demographic evolution; in any case, irrespective of their numerical importance, the whites constituted a much more homogeneous group from a linguistic and cultural point of view than the ethnically heterogeneous mass of slaves.

REFERENCES

Adam, Lucien. 1883. *Les idiomes négro-aryens. Essai d'hybridiologie linguistique.* Paris: Maisonneuve.

Alleyne, Mervyn C. 1971. The cultural matrix of creolization. In Hymes, pp. 169-88.

Arveiller, Raymond. 1963. *Contribution à l'étude des termes de voyage en français (1505-1722).* Paris: D'Artrey.

Bailey, Beryl L. 1965. Toward a new perspective in Negro English dialectology. *American Speech* 40:171-77.

Benoist, Jean. 1975. *Les sociétés antillaises.* Martinique: Centre de recherches caraïbes, 4th ed.

Bickerton, Derek. 1975. *Dynamics of a Creole System.* London: Cambridge University Press.

Brunot, Ferdinand. *Histoire de la langue française des origines à nos jours.* Paris: A. Colin (rev. ed., 1967), Vol. VIII, 5, Ch. II, III, pp. 1130-47.

Chataignier, André. 1963. Le créole portugais du Sénégal: observations et textes. *Journal of African Languages* 2:44-71.

Chaudenson, Robert. 1973. Pour une étude comparée des créoles et parlers français d'outre mer: survivance et innovation. *Revue de linguistique romane*, no. 147-48:342-71.

———. 1974. *Le lexique du parler créole de la Réunion.* Paris: Champion.

———. 1976. Créoles de l'océan indien et langues africaines. In *Readings in Creole Studies,* Goodman, Hancock, Heine, Polomé, eds. (in press).

———. 1976b. Créole et langage enfantin: phylogenèse et ontogenèse. (Ms.)

Comitas, Lambros. 1968. *Caribbeana: 1900-1965. A topical bibliography.* Seattle: University of Washington Press.

Corne, Chris. 1974-75. Tense, aspect and the mysterious *i* in Seychelles and Reunion Creole. *Te Reo* 17-18:53-93.

———. 1976. A note on "passives" in Indian Ocean creole dialects. *Journal of Creole Studies* I (in press).

Dalgado, S. R. 1900. *Dialecto Indo-Português de Ceylão*. Lisbon.

_____. 1900. *Dialecto Indo-Português de Damão: dialecto Indo-Português de Goa*. Lisbon.

DeCamp, David. 1961. Social and geographical factors in Jamaican dialects. *Proceedings of the Conference on Creole Studies* (Creole Language Studies II), R. B. Le Page, ed. London: Macmillan, pp. 61-84.

Dillard, Joseph L. 1971. The creolist and the study of Negro non-standard dialects in the continental United States. In Hymes, pp. 393-408.

Du Tertre, Jean Baptiste. 1654. *Histoire générale des Isles de S. Christophe, de la Guadeloupe, de la Martinique et autres de l'Amérique*. Paris.

Faine, Jules. 1939. *Le créole dans l'univers*. Port-au-Prince: Imprimerie de l'Etat.

Funk, Henry E. 1953. The French Creole Dialect of the Martinique. Unpublished Ph.D. diss., University of Virginia.

Goodman, Morris F. 1964. *A Comparative Study of Creole French Dialects*. The Hague: Mouton.

Hamilton, Alexander. 1727. *A New Account to the East Indies*. Edinburgh.

Hancock, Ian F. 1972. A domestic origin for the English-derived Atlantic creoles. *The Florida Foreign Language Reporter* 10:7-8, 52.

Hjelmslev, Louis. 1938. Relation de parenté des langues créoles. *Revue des Etudes Indo-Européennes* 2:271-86.

_____. 1939. Caractères grammaticaux des langues créoles. *Congrès International des Sciences Anthropologiques et Ethnologiques*, 373-74.

Hoenigswald, Henry M. 1971. Language history and creole studies. In Hymes, p. 473-80.

Hull, Alexander. 1975. On the origin and chronology of the French-based creoles. Revised draft of a paper presented to the International Conference on Pidgins and Creoles, Honolulu, Jan. 1975.

Hymes, Dell, ed. 1971. *Pidginization and Creolization of Languages*. London: Cambridge University Press.

Jespersen, Otto. 1921. *Language: Its Nature, Development and Origin*. New York: Holt.

Jourdain, Elodie. 1956. *Du français aux parlers créoles*. Paris: Klincksieck.

Labat, Jean Baptiste. 1724. *Nouveau voyage aux Isles de l'Amérique*. Paris.

_____. 1731. *Voyage du Chevalier des Marchais en Guinée*. Paris.

Larousse, Pierre, ed. 1869. *Grand Dictionnaire Universel du XIX Siècle*. Paris: Larousse.

Le Courbe. 1688. *Premier voyage*.

Lopes da Silva, Baltasar. 1957. *O dialecto crioulo de Cabo Verde*. Lisbon: Impresa Nacional.

Mintz, Sydney M. 1971. The socio-historical background to pidginization and creolization. In Hymes, pp. 481-98.

Randford, O. 1971. *The Slave Trade.* London: J. Murray.

Reinecke, John E. 1938. Trade jargons and Creole dialects as marginal languages. *Social Forces* 17:107-18. Reprinted in *Language in Culture and Society*, D. H. Hymes, ed., pp. 534-46. (New York: Harper and Row, 1964).

Rens, L. E. 1953. *The Historical and Social Background of Surinam's Negro English.* Amsterdam: North-Holland.

Rochefort, C. de. 1658. *Histoire naturelle et morale des Iles Antilles de l'Amérique.* Paris.

Saint-Lô, Alexis de. 1637. *Relation du voyage du Cap-Verd.* Paris.

Schuchardt, Hugo. 1887. Beiträge zur Kenntnis des creolischen Romanish. *Zeitschrift für Romanische Philologie* 12:242-54, 301-22.

————. 1889. Allgemeineres über das Indoportugiesische (Asioportugiesische). *Zeitschrift für Romanische Philologie* 13:476-516.

Stewart, William A. 1967. Sociolinguistic factors in the history of American Negro dialects. *The Florida Foreign Language Reporter* 5:11-29.

Thompson, R. W. 1961. A note on some possible affinities between the creole dialects of the Old World and those of the New. *Proceedings of the Conference on Creole Studies* (Creole Language Studies II), R. B. Le Page, ed. London: Macmillan, pp. 107-13.

Todd, Loreto. 1974. *Pidgins and Creoles.* London: Routledge and Kegan Paul.

Valdman, Albert. 1977. *Le créole: structure, statut et origine.* Paris: Klincksieck (in press).

Valdman, A. and Phillips, J. S. 1975. Pidginization, creolization and the elaboration of learner systems. *Theoretical Models in Applied Linguistics IV.* Brussels, Paris: AIMAV, Didier (in press).

Valkhoff, Marius. 1960. Some notes on creole French. *African Studies* 19:230-44.

Voorhoeve, Jan. 1961. A project for the study of creole language history in Surinam. *Proceedings of the Conference on Creole Language Studies* (Creole Language Studies II), R. B. Le Page, ed. London: Macmillan, pp. 99-106.

Wartburg, Walther von. 1922. *Französisches Etymologisches Wörterbuch.* Basel.

Whinnom, Keith. 1965. Origin of the European-based creoles and pidgins. *Orbis* 15:509-27.

Wolfram, Walt. 1969. *Detroit Negro Speech.* Washington, D.C.: Center for Applied Linguistics.

Wyndham, H. A. 1935. *The Atlantic and Slavery.* London: Oxford University Press.

Recovering Pidgin Genesis: Approaches and Problems

Ian F. Hancock

> "... both the Gothick and the Celtick, though blended with a different idiom, had the same origin with the Sanscrit." (From Sir William Jones's famous address to the Royal Asiatic Society [Bengal] in 1786)

For most of the pidgins and creoles currently being studied, the beginnings of European contact have meant the beginnings of the languages themselves.[1] Since from the earliest times ships have carried clerks whose job it was to document the various aspects of the situation, it might be assumed that samples of the nautical trade pidgins would be abundant; yet this is not so. Early records, if they mention them at all, speak of such languages as "bastard, broken" (Todd 1974, p. 35), "corrupted" (Hancock 1969, p. 13), etc., and the attitude has generally been that such forms of speech were unworthy of serious study.

In the few instances where the early forms of modern creoles have been recorded, it appears to have been by speakers of languages lexically unrelated to them; for example, J. D. Herlein, a speaker of Dutch, was among the first to record Surinam Creole English in 1718, although that creole was probably being spoken in Surinam for almost a century before that. Dutch speakers were also the first to record Java Creole Portuguese, long before the

277

Portuguese themselves acknowledged it in print. The earliest records of China Coast Pidgin English[2] and China Coast Creole Portuguese[3] were made by the Chinese, not the Europeans.

The reason is clear: foreigners would not always have known whether the Portuguese, English, etc., dialects that they were transcribing were "corrupt" or not; the name was usually the same whatever the variety.[4] Thus early records of the creoles are scant, and were nearly all made by non-native speakers, often speakers of lexically unconnected languages. This had at least one advantage: the creoles were represented in the orthography of the recorder's tongue. When speakers of the related *metropolitan* language have done this, there has been a consistent tendency to standardize the forms, even in modern times. Thus Alldridge (1910, p. 30), representing Krio speech, writes "de cotton tree deh walker" ("the Cotton Tree is walking") for what is actually pronounced [di kɔtin tri de waka]. A Creole Portuguese announcement written by a resident priest from Portugal has "Sinhor sa grandi serbiço" for [sinɔ sə grani sibrisu] ("the master's great works"). For Chinook Jargon there is "kloosh mesika kumtux" for [ɬoːʃ məsaygə kʌmdʌks] ("well you know"). This standardization sometimes leads to error: the Washington state place name Mount Kaleetan ("Mount Arrow") appears to have been taken from one of the numerous Chinook Jargon dictionaries in which the word is consistently spelt "Kalitan," rather than from actual speech, in which it is pronounced [kalaytən] (< Chinukan, *ditto*).

In historical-comparative linguistics, documentation is essential. For languages having a long literary tradition, such as Tamil, Arabic, or Icelandic, attestations of earlier forms are abundant and historical description has not been a difficult task. But, although many languages have been written for as long as there has been European contact,[5] for the majority there are no written documents much older than a century or two.

In creole language situations, for reasons already mentioned, early documentation is especially scant, and of course nonexistent from the precontact period. At best, documentation provides tantalizing but frequently inconclusive evidence for hypotheses that must still remain unproven. For example, early visitors to the Pacific Northwest, such as Meares in 1788, Jewitt in 1803, and Lewis and Clarke in 1803-1805, recorded words and phrases from Chinook Jargon, which was apparently already being spoken in the area. Jewitt observed that "it would seem that they [the Nootka] have two languages, one for their songs and one for common use" (1815, p. 166). The assumption that Chinook Jargon existed in the Northwest before the arrival of the Europeans was hinted at by Shaw (1909, p. ix) and plainly made by Thomas (1935, p. vii): "[Chinook] Jargon was in use among the natives of the region when the first explorers and maritime traders arrived." There is no reason why it should not have been, of course, although Thomas's speculation was vigorously refuted by Howay (1942). The arguments pro and con are discussed in Reid (1943), but so far evidence either way is lacking.

Similarly, while it has been suggested that "a pre-European Manding lingua franca" provided the substratum for the later European-related Atlantic creoles (Hancock 1978), there is as yet no substantiating documentation. A thorough examination of pre-fifteenth-century Arabic sources needs to be undertaken—with no guarantee of success. The known clues are all from the post-European, not the post-Arabic contact period. The earliest Arabic sources, including two Manding dialects from between A.D. 1100 and A.D. 1500, Malinke and Soninke (Dalby and Hair 1964, p. 174), have not been scrutinized with pidginization in mind.

The problem is well defined: pidgins have not usually been adequately recorded across their development, and as a result a comprehensive diachronic picture is often lacking (China Coast Pidgin is an exception). Thus the matter of determining what the earlier relationships were that are shared by the modern creoles is fraught with speculation. For these languages perhaps more than for others, the historical rather than the linguistic evidence must provide the principal leads. Reconstructions of individual historical situations have to be especially thorough, and the linguistic evidence compared to see whether both tally. The theoretical approach of the kind being undertaken by Sr. Canice Johnson (1974), using the techniques of external reconstruction, is a significant first step toward describing the Atlantic protocreole first suggested by Hall (1966, pp. 118-120),[6] and our increasing historical knowledge of the first African-European contacts seems not to contradict the historical picture that is also slowly emerging.

Some written sources have yielded no results to date. The (presumably) early twentieth-century New Testament translation into Krio has not been located despite a search in every church archive in Freetown and letters to all the biblical translation societies. And yet, according to Green, "Missionaries in Sierra Leone translated the whole of the New Testament into pidgin early this century. It was withdrawn from circulation soon afterwards, for

although the intentions were good, the results looked blasphemous"
(1954, p. 119). There are similar unsubstantiated reports of a New
Testament translation in Belizean or Jamaican Creole, current
among the inhabitants of Nicaragua.[7]

Equally vexing is the situation in which linguistic or
circumstantial evidence lacks the verification of any kind of
documentation. Reduced, restructured linguae francae, for example, appear to establish themselves most firmly in areas of the
greatest linguistic complexity: the Pacific Northwest; Papua New
Guinea, with not only post-European Tok Pisin but also at least
two pidginized indigenous languages, Motu and Siassi; Indochina;
the Guinea Coast, and so on. No pidgin has yet been reported
from another major linguistically diverse area, the Caucasus, but
one would expect investigation to reveal the existence of a lingua
franca there in light of the situation in other fragmentation areas.

Not all of the languages receiving attention are so poorly
documented, however. Hall has published examples of China Coast
Pidgin in various stages of its development from 1747-48 to the
present (Hall 1944, p. 109). The existence of such Portuguese-
derived items as *grande, querer, deus, pequeninho, comprador,
mandarim, mas que, mouro, padre, sabeir,* etc. suggests either
relexification from an earlier Portuguese-related creole, or
lexical adoptions from one coexistent with it. Bawden (1954)
provides the earliest documented samples of such a language,
transcribed from a Chinese-Creole phrase book written ca. 1751
and discussed further by Thompson (1959). In cases where the
early forms of the creoles or the pidgins are preserved, the extent
of phonological or syntactic reconstruction depends upon the
amount of the material available to us. It would not be difficult,
for instance, to write a fairly comprehensive basic description of
early Java Creole Portuguese from Meister's collection of words
and phrases (1692, pp. 215-22).

Other scholars must confine their research to the historical
aspects of the situation in their search for linguistic clues. Luiz F.
Thomaz, a scholar now with the Portuguese army in Timor, is
currently editing some two thousand documents from the Lisbon
archives relating to Malacca and the Portuguese occupation of that
city.[8] Half of these have not been examined since they were
written, but there is indication that they will shed light upon the
linguistic situation in sixteenth- and seventeenth-century Malacca.
Marshall Morris of the University of Puerto Rico is also searching
the Lisbon archives, as well as those in Oxford and London, for

documents indicating Creole Portuguese influences in Puerto Rican Spanish.

The recent research of Curtin (1969) has shown that the importance of the Dutch in the Caribbean slave trade has hitherto been underestimated. Newly assembled evidence indicates that the Surinam creoles, both English- and Portuguese-related, were introduced by the Dutch rather than (or in addition to) the English. Thus we may be able to extend the period of its transference from Africa to South America before and beyond their occupation of Surinam (1651-67). Even during this time, the English in Surinam were purchasing their slaves from the Dutch (Hancock 1978).

Others who have searched the early literature for linguistic evidence include Paul Teyssier (1959) and Freda Weber de Kurlat (1962), both of whom have examined the language of Gil Vicente's *Fragoa d'Amor* (1525) in an attempt to retrieve the earliest known West African Creole Portuguese features. The examination of a document he discovered, dated 1684, enabled C. Dyneley Prince (1912) to present a lexical analysis of the now-extinct Delaware River Pidgin Munsi. The orthoepist William Matthews (1935, 1937) began the description of a nautical dialect of English believed by some[9] to have been the variety initially used in the Euro-African contact situation, and as such to be of prime importance to the understanding of West African Creole origins.

More recent document-based work has been undertaken by Anthony Naro (1973), upon whose extensive survey of early Portuguese sources his reconnaissance language hypothesis is based; Ian Robertson (1974), who has collected many literary references to the continued use of a pidginized or creolized Dutch in the interior of Guyana, and who as a consequence visited the Canje and Berbice River areas, where he discovered many speakers still living, hitherto unknown to the world outside; Joe Dillard (1975), who is assembling documentation from which a reconstruction of early Afro-American English is emerging; and Donald Kloe (1974), who recently discovered and analyzed a poem dated ca. 1799, written in a western-hemisphere English-related creole showing features from Gullah, Jamaican, and Krio. William Samarin of the University of Toronto is studying a "Dutch-Bangala-Moganzoeloe" phrase book dated 1901 found in Tangerloo, Belgium, published by Catholic missionaries, for evidence that might shed light on the emergence of contact languages in the nineteenth-century Ubangi River basin (Sango, for example, has a high Bantu-derived lexical content).

For some languages, concrete historical evidence of their early existence is lacking, although linguistic clues in their contemporary forms allow creolists to hypothesize as to the time and circumstances of their origins and to posit their characteristics from those times. For other languages, we possess documentary references to their possible historical existence, but lack conclusive linguistic data to support them.

West African English-related Creole is an example of the first situation, viz., one lacking documented proof of the existence of such a language prior to 1734 (the date of the first known reference to a local West African variety of English), but that linguistically and circumstantially appears to have originated even earlier than 1600. Although Voorhoeve (1973, p. 137) cavils at this likelihood, we are nevertheless faced with the problems of how to explain lexical, phonological, and grammatical forms in the modern descendants of the language, which point clearly to a late sixteenth-/early seventeenth-century origin, and why modern Sranan and Krio share such a high percentage of these same features, although Surinam linguistic influence has only been *from*, not *upon*, West Africa, beginning over a century earlier than 1734.

To give just a few examples: lexically, modern Sierra Leone Krio contains such items as customance, "customer" (in Krio *kɔstamɛnt*, from a protoform *customant, a back-formation from a supposed plural *customants) last recorded in English in 1575 (OED); *poork poynt*, "porcupine"; *cheek*, "chin"; *lighten*, "lightning"; *even* "evening"; etc., obsolete in print by A.D. 1600 (OED), as well as many other archaisms (*skeat*, "skate fish"; *baluster*, "bannister"; *peradventure*, "perhaps"; etc.) that survived somewhat longer. Phonologically, many items reflect earlier, especially sixteenth- and seventeenth-century British pronunciations: *muskyat*, "muskrat"—itself from obsolete *musk rat* (last recorded use in fact from Sierra Leone, 1794 [OED] retains the high vowel /u/ rather than /ʌ/, a feature found in many Krio items ["cucumber," "shove," etc.], as well as a palatalized velar, also common [e.g., in *"galley," "gamble," "gate," "can," "cabin," "captain,"* etc.]). Other archaic phonological features include /ai/ for modern Standard English /oi/ (in *"groin," "boy," "poork poynt"*—in Krio *pɔk-pɛnt* with /ɛ/ as a normal reflexion of /ai/, cf. *"rice," "drive," "knife,"* etc.); close-o in *"poor," "report," "sport," "bore,"* etc.; final unstressed -ən as /in/ in *"bacon,"* *"button," "Johnson," "happen,"* etc. Stress patterns such as *"auntý," "charácter," "propertý," "penknífe,"* etc. might also be included here.

Grammatically, features such as the use of *do* (Krio *de*) as a marker of habitual or progressive action, or *done* to indicate the completed aspect of the verb, are also indicative of very early acquisition. The latter in particular has never been widespread in English, but did enjoy some use in the Anglo-Scottish dialects during the sixteenth century ("done discuss," "done invent"; OED, *do*, 31). Its widespread occurrence in other nautically derived English dialects (e.g., in St. Helena, Tristan da Cunha, Trinidad, etc.) probably results from syntactic convergence with the same functional morpheme in West African languages. This has passed into Southern U.S. white speech through Afro-American dialects. Negation with pre-verbal *not* (Scots *no, nae,* Krio *nɔ*) may also be an archaism.

Historically, the African rather than the English-derived items shared by the East Atlantic and West Atlantic creoles are the most significant as an indication of relationship; the Surinam creoles and Krio share a great many items not occurring in any other creole in the Atlantic area—the *be*-verb *na* is probably the most obvious. If the precise historical links between Upper Guinea and Surinam are determined and thorough examination of the Dutch involvement in the slave trade made (see Hancock 1978), the linguistic indications will probably be reinforced despite the absence of documented proof.

In the latter case, viz., the availability of documentary clues but few linguistic survivals, a good example is provided by Sabir, or the Lingua Franca, the origins of which are of some concern to creolists, since there are several scholars who believe all European-related pidgins to have developed from it.[10]

One opinion is that the Lingua Franca originated at the time of the Crusades (A.D. 1095ff.) on the Jerusalem battlefields, later spreading westward along the shores of the Mediterranean with the military and merchant vessels. Basing her hypothesis entirely upon a study of early documentary clues, Noeljeanne Adkins at the University of Texas at Austin believes that the beginnings of the Lingua Franca are to be sought perhaps as much as a thousand years earlier than the Crusades.

Since prehistoric times, Britain has been involved in commerce of one sort or another. From the time of Pythias, himself an enterprising merchant from the Greek colony at Marseilles, there have been two approaches from the Mediterranean to Britain: through the Straits of Gibraltar by sea, and overland to the coast of France and the Netherlands to the Channel. It was preferable for reasons of economy to use the sea route; however, when the Straits were held by a hostile power, trade had to resort to the alternate route, viz., from Gaul to Marseilles.

Strabo maintained that Caesar's war with the Veneti and his subsequent invasion of Britain were based on the desire to achieve maritime supremacy, and thus commercial advantage, from the Gallic merchants and British seafarers engaged in the lucrative cross-Channel trade. Caesar's scout, Volusenus, and the great general himself were greeted with battle by the Britons, who were extremely hostile to the invasion. Caesar withdrew, accomplishing little, and it remained to Claudius to try to collect Seneca's loans and to extend and protect the Gallo-Roman merchants, who had maintained and increased the commercial trade.

In the third century A.D., the Franks turned pirate, and Carausius was appointed by Maximian to cope with them. There is a question of Carausius's actual nationality; Aurelius Victor says *Menapiæ Civis,* leading scholars to believe that he may have been a Briton, while Eumenius states that he was *Bataviæ alumnus,* i.e., a Belgian. Whatever his nationality, he was so proficient at dealing with the Frankish pirates that he came to be suspected by some of collusion. Although Maximian grew to oppose him, Carausius was able to seize power and rule Britain from A.D. 286 to A.D. 293. Hiring a great number of Frankish mercenaries and building an impressive fleet that prevented Britain from being attacked from abroad for many years, he came to earn the epithet "The first sea-king of British history." Carausius's naval strategies are described by Eumenius.[11]

Given the prodigious amount of trade and the presence of a mixture of Gallo-Italian merchants speaking Vulgar Latin, the British seamen speaking either Celtic or a Latinized Celtic, and the Franks themselves speaking their Germanic tongue in whatever form it had at the time, plus the contact with the Greek mercantile system at Marseilles, there are grounds for assuming that some sort of trade contact or military contact language was in use. Note further that when Constantius put down these rebellions and established Britain more firmly within the Roman Empire, trade through the Straits with direct links to the Mediterranean became yet more frequently attested. At this time too, Christianity began drifting northward—significant because it provides the first clues as to the nature of the hypothesized contact language.

Evidence for such a contact language at this time (i.e., the third century A.D.) is scant. Most scholars would maintain that Vulgar Latin was the lingua franca of the time, particularly the variety they designate as Continental Vulgar Latin. Mackail (1895) makes an interesting reference to the fashionable, racy style of speech introduced in court circles during the reign of Nero (A.D. 54-A.D. 68) by his *arbiter elegantarium,* Petronius: "In the semi-Greek seaports of southern Italy it passes into what is almost a dialect of its own, the *lingua franca* of the Mediterranean under the [Roman] Empire, a dialect of mixed Latin and Greek." Kenneth Jackson (1953), in his discussion of "popular oral borrowings from colloquial Vulgar Latin" during the period between ca. A.D. 450 and the seventh century, questions the source of these adoptions: "Where they come from . . . is a very uncertain question." Of certain sound changes he says that they "might have been borrowed either from low-class urban dwellers in Britain or from the Gallo-Latin of the Continent," and adds, in support of the existence of a trade contact language, that "such words might have been introduced through trade with the Franks."

In the Lives of various saints, particularly the Cambro-British saints, some clues appear that are worth examining in detail. In the *Vita Sancti Cadoci*[12] we find the following passage:

Et ut verius fertur, attributa sunt ei a Domino illarum gentium idiomata, per quas eundo et redeundo transibat, loquebaturque variis linguis, ad instar primitive ecclesie in discipulorum.

(And, as it is most truly reported, a knowledge of the languages of those nations through which, in going and returning, he passed, was given to him by the Lord, and he spake in various tongues, like to the primitive church of the disciples in the time of Christ.)

Taking this passage less miraculously and in more practical terms, it is possible that Saint Cadoc was speaking the lingua franca of the time, or a trade contact language that enabled him to communicate with the peoples he encountered on his way to Jerusalem by way of Greece. A further curiosity is the likening of the *"variis linguis"* to the tongue used in the primitive Christian church by disciples at the time of Christ, i.e., Aramaic. The word *instar* here might more accurately be translated by "equivalent to." In other words, was the language(s) spoken by Cadoc the same language spoken by Christ and his followers, or is it more likely that the writer means that the language used was the lingua franca, or a descendant from it, in use at that time, i.e., Aramaic, or what Weinreich has labelled "Targumic" (see below)? Still one is left with the fact that the words to describe the means of communication are in the plural. Unless the author was trying to explain the phenomenon of pidginization, the more "miraculous" explanation must continue to be accepted.

There is another passage concerning Cadoc's disappearance from Britain to Beneventum (probably in France):

> ... *mirumque dictu, linguam illorum dono Sancti Spiritus, continuo integerrime novit, ipsique similiter suam.* ...
> (... and wonderful to be said, he constantly and perfectly knew their language by the gift of the Holy Spirit, and they likewise his. . .).[13]

If upon arriving in Beneventum Cadoc was able to converse immediately, perfectly, and continuously with the local people, it suggests either a prior knowledge of that language or the presence of a pidgin of some sort.

In the *Vita Sancti David*[14] a similar passage is encountered:

> *Cum autem trans mare Brittannicum vecti, Gallias adirent alienigenas diversarum gentium linguas audirent, linguarum gratia ceu apostolicus ille cetus ditatus est pater David, ut ne in extraneis degentes gentibus interprete egerent, et ut aliorum fidem veritatis verbo firmarent.*
> (When they had sailed over the British sea, and arrived in France, they heard strange languages of divers nations, and Father David was endowed with grace as the apostolic company, that when living in foreign nations, they might not want an interpreter, and that by their words they should confirm the faith of others.)

Here, some of the difficulties are cleared up. It is known that the company did go by sea, though probably across the Channel to northern France. However, the company was bound for Jerusalem, so they may possibly have gone through the Straits into the Mediterranean along the routes later to be followed by the Crusaders. However they reached it, they arrived in the Mediterranean, and the passage states that wherever they went they needed no interpreter, but were able to converse right away with the locals. This situation seems to suggest the use of a lingua franca, whether or not pidginized, although actual examples in the text itself are lacking.

Yet again, in the *Vita Sancti Paterni*,[15] one finds the passage:

> *Mox David as illos misit; illi nec mora venerunt; perrexerunt pariter trans barbaras gentes, gratiam linguarum accipientes; nam essent viri*

unius lingue, unumquemque hominem propria lingua in qua natus
fuerat, allo-quebantur.
(David sent presently to them, and they came without delay; they
passed together over barbarous nations, and received the grace of
languages; for although they were men of one language, yet they spoke
to every man in his own language, that of the country wherein he was
born.)

Again the company—David, Padarn, and another named Teilo—are
on their way to Jerusalem.

Documentation also suggests that the term *Franca* in the
Lingua Franca is older than the Crusades. It is commonly thought
that the term came into use at that time, employed by the locals
of Byzantium and environs to designate the language of the
crusading invaders whom they indiscriminately classified as
"Franks." However, the Franks were in the area long before the
Crusades. Reference has already been made to the Frankish
element in the Channel commerce during the third century, which
was presumably carried through the Straits into the Mediterranean. A question may arise as to the likelihood of the Franks' not
being known in the Mediterranean area but wholly confined to
northern Gaul, but there is some evidence that "Frank" may have
been a term similar to "Viking," used to cover one or any of the
Germanic (or Teutonic) tribal groups that moved into both
northern Europe and down through Macedonia and Thrace into
the regions of Ancyra (according to Fredegarius).[16] So the Franks
were certainly known in the Mediterranean, even the eastern
Mediterranean, before the Crusades. But were they called
"Franks"? In the west they were. In the *Vita Sancti Winfrede,*
there are several references to "Franks" where one would expect
to find Saxons or other "German" appellations. *Francis, Francus,*
Francorum are terms used, and more important, *Tempore quoque*
Francorum ("at the time of the Franks") seems to exhibit the use
of the term "Frank" for the Germanic tribes in general. There is
evidence for a Latin-Germanic contact language, so it is possible
that the further south it was spoken, the more it would be
influenced by the local indigenous languages.

Up to this point there is little evidence, but much
speculation, about the possibility of a pidginized lingua franca,
which actually may have been the forerunner of what was to
become the Mediterranean Lingua Franca or Sabir and (providing
that it wasn't the same thing), the "Genovese" or "Commercial"
Latin used by merchants in fifteenth- and sixteenth-century Spain

and Italy (Serrano y Sanz 1930, Pidal 1942). Such a trade vernacular would have exhibited a preponderance of Latin, both in
vocabulary and structure; some Greek words would have occurred,
since the titular head of the Roman Empire was maintained in
Byzantium after the fifth and sixth centuries (and cf. Mackail, op.
cit.). One would expect to find some Aramaic (Targumic) or
Hebrew words from the lexicon of Jewish traders and merchants
engaged in commerce in the area, and one would also look for
traces of other languages spoken in the major countries bordering
the Mediterranean: Turkish, Arabic, and so on. Assuming such an
eclectic lexicon for this theorized contact language, apart from
religious accounts what evidence is there to support its existence?
A document comes to hand that may contain some of the required
answers. Although the language in it is not called a pidgin or a
lingua franca, it seems to share some of the characteristics of the
phenomenon discussed here. It is called the *Lorica of Gildas the
Briton,*[17] probably written ca. A.D. 600.

What is a *Lorica*? Apparently a kind of charm to ward off
certain evils. Although originally (in Plautius's time) a kind of
leather coat, the term came to refer to the mail coats such as may
be seen on the Franks' Casket, and is described in *Beowulf*, where
it is called a *hringde byrnan*. In other words, it was a protection
against one's foes, whether real or supernatural (for example, the
garment saves Beowulf from Grendel's mother). Following the
idea that a virtuous life was a protection against fiends, certain
prayers came to be known as *loricae* and were considered
especially efficacious.

The earliest manuscript of the *Lorica* considered here can
be dated from the early ninth century. It seems to have been
extremely popular, since there are six extant manuscripts known,
three of which are glossed, allowing us to ascertain with some
certainty the interpretations of the words. However, it was clearly
composed at a much earlier date, approximately A.D. 600, as
mentioned above.

The most important aspect of the *Lorica* is the vocabulary
used in the composition of the work. Two other documents of
approximately the same time have vocabularies that resemble the
collection of obscure and exotic lexemes found in the *Lorica*, viz.,
the *Hisperica Famina,* a seventh-century document found in the
Vienna Library, and a hymn attributed to Saint Columbus (d.
A.D. 597), known from its opening words as *Altus prosator*, the
earliest manuscript of which dates from the eleventh century,
although, like the *Lorica of Gildas,* its actual data of composition

was much earlier. There is also another Celtic Lorica, the *Leyden Lorica,* that uses much of the same obscure vocabulary. Singer (op. cit.) says, "To the Anglo-Saxon clerics, who shared a knowledge of Latin with their Celtic colleagues, there was however an easy and natural means of communication, and of this interchange the Lorica of Gildas is a very early monument." Adkins agrees with Singer, but expands the area covered by the language, not limiting it solely to the British Isles, assuming that the vocabulary would have relexified from the various local languages as it moved eastward through the Straits of Gibraltar into the Mediterranean. Singer continues: "It is written in that very characteristic form of Latin known as 'Hisperic' or 'Hibernian', that was affected in south-west Britain and Ireland in the sixth and seventh centuries. . . . through the medium of these glosses and vocabularies the combined efforts of mediaevalists, and Greek, Semitic, Celtic and Anglo-Saxon scholars have now extracted the meaning and source of a great number of these obscure terms." A discussion of an Irish variety of Hisperic is given in MacAlister (1937).[18]

Recent research into the origins of Yiddish has brought to light some interesting similarities to the above situation. Weinreich (1954, pp. 73-101) has referred to Targumic, already mentioned, the Aramaic-like dialect(s) that came to be spoken by Palestinian Jews as Hebrew gradually fell from use as an everyday language. Jacobs (1975, p. 8) emphasizes the point that this was the source of the Jewish diaspora languages (see Gold 1974, pp. 47-53), one of which was Loez (La'az, Laazic), spoken during the first millennium A.D.:

> As the Jews were dispersed from Palestine after the destruction of the second temple (A.D. 70), they established Jewish communities in their new homelands. Naturally, the language they took with them out of Palestine was the language they had spoken among themselves in Palestine—Targumic. From the outset we can realize the necessity of a contact language for official purposes between certain members of the Jewish community and officials of the host culture. The base for such a contact language could be the host culture's language, or a pidginized form of it; or, a common lingua franca could have been employed, such as Latin in Europe.

The presence of Jewish trading communities in Sardinia, Sicily, North Africa, and elsewhere throughout the Mediterranean makes it not unlikely that the Jews might have used the early Romance-derived contact language themselves; it may further be speculated that Loez was a Jewish variety of the Lingua Franca; although it is assumed to be Old French and/or Old Italian (Jacobs op. cit., p. 9; Bunis 1975), Loez has nowhere ever been specifically identified. Jacobs further points out (op. cit., p. 10), that "The year A.D. 1,000 is commonly given as the time of the migration of the Loez-speaking Jews to the Rheinland, an area called Loter. This date is of course only a very rough estimation. But the point is that the migration of large numbers of Loez-speaking Jews set the stage for the birth of Yiddish."

Modern Yiddish contains several Romance-derived words, and earlier forms of the language contained even more (Samuel 1971, pp. 19-29), a fact put forward by Jacobs in support of the possibility of a Romance substratum for Yiddish. Although Marchand (1965, p. 249) maintains that "there are many things which militate against the assumption of a Romance base for Yiddish," an opinion he offers with little supporting argument, it is perhaps significant that Loez and Hisperic, if not the same thing, were both spoken at the same time in the same places: during the first millennium A.D., on the southwestern and northwestern coasts of France, traditional trading centers along the route from the Mediterranean to northern Europe.

To speculate yet further, it may also be possible that the pan-European underworld contact lexicon (called Cant, Rot-welsch, Bargoens, Hantyrka, Rodi, and a host of other names), with its high Latin- and Hebrew-derived content, may share in part the same origin. Words such as *pannam* (bread) or *mazuma* (money) are everywhere familiar among the European criminal element. Perhaps less probably linked is Russenorsk, which Fox (1973) has nevertheless shown to be derived in part from a northern European military pidgin ("soldiers' cant") spoken in garrisons throughout Scandinavia. Another element in the language, besides the speech of the fishermen themselves, was a Low German *Kaufmannsjargon;* Fox himself, in his discussion of Russenorsk agrees that "The present version of the relexification hypothesis is an extremely strong claim; it presupposes a continuous pidgin grammar roughly from the fifteenth century to modern times, and an unbroken line of transmission to many parts of the world" (op. cit., p. 24).

If current documentation-based research continues to yield such promising clues to the historical background of creole origins and development, we will one day be able to define the whole phenomenon more accurately. Already it may be necessary to adjust Fox's "fifteenth century" to read "second century," and if the Mediterranean is indeed the source of the relexification continuum, then Hall's suggested Ancient Egyptian soldiers' and traders' pidgin (op. cit., p. 3) may yet be unearthed.[19]

NOTES

1. It ought not be necessary to point out that creolization is not just a European process; nevertheless practically all of the creoles that have been studied to date are lexically related to European languages.

2. "A vocabulary of words in use among the red-haired people." See the *Pall Mall Gazette,* 1870.

3. Yin and Chan.

4. Cf. Papia Kristang, also called Portuguese by its speakers, or Krio, referred to as English by some Sierra Leoneans.

5. And for a great many others, *before* European contact.

6. Hall (op. cit., p. 120) referred to, but did not elaborate upon, a non-African nautical source for this protocreole, taking it back to London's dockland and other English seaports.

7. Thanks to Barbara Assadi for this information.

8. See *The Sunday Times*, November 29, 1970. Dr. Thomaz is planning to publish his findings with the Junta de Investigações Scientificas de Lisboa, and possibly the Malaysian National Archives.

9. See Hall (loc. cit., fn. 6), and Hancock (1972).

10. E.g., Thompson (1961), Whinnom (1965), Todd (1974).

11. Eumenius, *Panegyricus Constantio Cæsari,* c. 3.

12. Cott. Library, British Museum, Vesp. A., section 11 (manuscript).

13. Loc. cit., section 34.

14. Cott. Library, British Museum, Vesp. A (manuscript).

15. Ibid.

16. Fredegarius, *Chronicon Francorum.*

17. Reproduced in Singer (1928).

18. The section of this paper dealing with the origins of the Lingua Franca has been taken almost entirely, with permission and gratitude, from an unpublished term paper by Ms. Noeljeanne Adkins, who is continuing research along the same lines.

19. See Hodge (1971, 1975).

REFERENCES

Aldridge, T. J. 1910. *A Transformed Colony*. London: Seeley & Co. Ltd.

Bawden, C. R. 1954. An eighteenth century Chinese source for the Portuguese dialect of Macao. In the *Silver Jubilee Volume of the Zinbun Kagaku Kenkyusho,* Kyoto: Kyoto University Press, pp. 12-33.

Bunis, David M. 1975. A Guide to Reading and Writing Judezmo. Brooklyn: The Judezmo Society.

Curtin, P. D. 1969. *The Atlantic Slave Trade: a census.* Madison: University of Wisconsin Press.

Dalby, D., and Hair, P. E. H. 1964. "Le langaige de Guynee": a sixteenth century vocabulary from the Pepper Coast. *African Language Studies* V:174-91.

Dillard, Joe. 1975. *Perspectives on Black English*. Mouton.

Fox, James. 1973. Russenorsk: a study in language adaptivity. Unpublished term paper, University of Chicago.

Gold, David L. 1974. Review of *For Max Weinreich on his Seventieth Birthday: Studies in Jewish Languages, Literature and Society*, L. S. Dawidowicz et al., eds. *Language Sciences*, August 1974, pp. 47-53.

Green, L. G. 1954. *White Man's Grave*. London: S. Paul.

Hall, Robert A., Jr. 1944. Chinese Pidgin English: grammar and texts. *Journal of the American Oriental Society* LXIV:95-113.

————. 1966. *Pidgin and Creole Languages.* Ithaca: Cornell University Press.

Hancock, Ian F. 1969. A provisional comparison of the English-derived Atlantic creoles. *African Language Review* VIII:7-72.

————. 1972. A domestic origin for the English-derived Atlantic creoles. *The Florida Fl Reporter* X(1/2):7,8,52.

————. 1976. Gullah and Barbadian: origins and relationships. In *Proceedings of the 1975 International Conference on Pidgins and Creoles,* R. Day, ed. In press.

Hodge, Carleton, T. 1971. Egyptian and Mischsprachen. Lecture given at the Language and History in Africa Seminar, University of London. Also in *Festschrift for A. A. Hill*. Netherlands: De Ridder.

————. 1975. Lisramic II. *Anthropological Linguistics XVII:* 237-72.

Howay, F. W. 1942. Origin of the Chinook Jargon of the North West. *British Columbia Historical Quarterly* VI:225-50.

Jackson, Kenneth. 1953. *Language and History in Early Britain.* Edinburgh: Edinburgh University Press.

Jacobs, Neil. 1975. Yiddish origins and creolization. Unpublished paper, Dept. of Linguistics, University of Texas at Austin.

Jewitt, John R. 1815. *A Narrative of the Adventures and Sufferings of John R. Jewitt.* Middletown (written by Roland Alsop): Ye Galleon Press.

Johnson, Sister Mary Canice. 1974. Two morpheme structure rules in an English proto-creole. In *Pidgins and Creoles: Current Trends and Prospects,* David DeCamp and Ian F. Hancock, eds. Washington, D.C.: Georgetown University Press, pp. 113-29.

Kloe, Donald R. 1974. Buddy Quow: an anonymous poem in Gullah-Jamaican dialect written circa 1800. *Southern Folklore Quarterly* XXXVIII(2):81-90.

Macalister, R. A. S. 1937. *The Secret Languages of Ireland.* Cambridge: Cambridge University Press.

Mackail, John W. 1903. *Latin Literature.* New York: Scribner's.

Marchand, J. W. 1965. The origin of Yiddish. *Communications et rapports du Premier Congrès Internationale de Dialectologie Générale,* Part iii, pp. 248-52. Louvain: Louvain Catholic University Press.

Matthews, W. 1935. Sailors' pronunciation in the second half of the seventeenth century. *Anglia* LIX:192-251.

––––––. 1937. Sailors' pronunciation, 1770-1783. *Anglia* LXI:72-80.

Meister, George. 1692. *Der orientalisch-indianische Kunst- und Lustgärtner.* Dresden: C. Hekel Publishers.

Naro, Anthony. 1973. The origin of West African Pidgin. Paper presented at the Ninth Regional Meeting of the Chicago Linguistic Society.

Pidal, Ramón M. 1942. *La lengua de Cristóbal Colón.* Madrid: Espasa-Calpe S.A.

Prince, C. Dyneley. 1912. An ancient New Jersey Indian jargon. *American Anthropologist* n.s. XIV:508-24.

Reid, Robie L. 1943. The Chinook Jargon and British Columbia. *British Columbia Historical Quarterly* VI:1-11.

Robertson, Ian. 1974. Dutch Creole in Guyana: some missing links. *Society for Caribbean Linguistics Occasional Paper No. 2.* Georgetown: University of Guyana Press.

Samuel, Maurice. 1971. *In praise of Yiddish.* New York: Cowles Publishers.

Serrano y Sanz, M. 1930. *El archivo colombino de la cartuja de las cuevas.* Madrid: Bailly, Ballière & Hijos.

Shaw, George C. 1909. *The Chinook Jargon and How to Use It.* Seattle: Ranier Printing Co.

Singer, Charles. 1928. *From Magic to Science.* London: E. Benn, Ltd.

Teyssier, Paul. 1959. *La langue de Gil Vicente.* Paris: Klincksieck.

Thomas, Edward H. 1935. *Chinook, a History and Dictionary of the North West Coast Trade Jargon.* Portland: Binfords and Mort Publishers.

Thompson, R. W. 1959. Two synchronic cross-sections in the Portuguese dialect of Macao. *Orbis* VIII(1):29-53.

_____. 1961. A note on some possible affinities between the creole dialects of the Old World and those of the New. In *Proceedings of the Conference on Creole Language Studies,* R. B. Le Page, ed. London: Cambridge University Press, pp. 107-13.

Todd, Loreto. 1974. *Pidgins and Creoles.* London and Boston: Routledge and Kegan Paul.

Voorhoeve, Jan. 1973. Historical and linguistic evidence in favour of the relexification theory in the formation of the creoles. *Language in Society* 2:133-45.

Weber de Kurlat, Frida. 1962. El tipo cómico del negro en el teatro prelopesco. *Filología* VIII:139-68.

Weinreich, Max. 1954. Prehistory and early history of Yiddish: facts and conceptual framework. In *The Field of Yiddish: Studies in Yiddish Language, Folklore and Literature*, Uriel Weinreich, ed. The Hague: Mouton, pp. 73-101.

Whinnom, Keith. 1965. The origin of the European based creoles and pidgins. *Orbis* XIV:509-27.

Yin, K. J., and Chan, J. 1751. *Ao Men Chi Lüeh.* Macao: Government Printer.

Lingua Franca:
Historical Problems[1]

Keith Whinnom

With the possible exception of the Portuguese pidgins that achieved worldwide currency from the sixteenth century on, and that still survive in various creolized forms, Lingua Franca is probably the most important pidgin language about which we have information. Not only is it the earliest documented, and, by several centuries, the longest-lived of all pidgins, but it quite certainly provided the channel for a great deal of Mediterranean vocabulary-borrowing,[2] and it may well be the basis, whether by imitation or direct relexification, of many modern European-based pidgins and creoles.[3] The monogenetic theory of the origin of European-based pidgins is still a controversial issue, but one might note in passing the extraordinary fact that most students of Portuguese creole appear to be unaware that in the early days the Portuguese crown sold slave-trading concessions not to Portuguese but to Genoese Jews, who undoubtedly spoke Lingua Franca.[4]

All creolists are aware that there are serious obstacles in the way of the study of the early history of pidgins and creoles, and there is no need to spell them out in detail. First and most obvious is the paucity and unreliability of the written documents. Pidginists are forced to indulge in speculative reconstructions in a way unknown to students of the history of English, German, French, or even Arabic, Tamil or Tibetan; and for Lingua Franca our specimens are especially sparse and tantalizing, spread across

295

the centuries in (approximately or precisely) 1300, 1400, 1520, 1550, 1610, 1680, and, in greater abundance, later.[5] Furthermore, the earliest samples are hardly ever produced by writers thoroughly acquainted with the language: they are to be found in literary works, often in verse, and were almost invariably written with intent to amuse their Romance-speaking readers. In these texts, therefore, the language is visible only through the screen of the writer's ignorance and native linguistic habits, and such evidence can be hard to interpret. While we may feel entitled to discard aberrant forms (agreement of adjectives and the like) on the grounds that they could be due to the ignorance or carelessness of author or copyist, this may be dangerous: the strange Grion text, which exhibits various Italian inflections alongside genuine LF forms, may actually reflect a first stage in the formation of the pidgin. Conversely, the grammatical regularity of later texts may not accurately reflect the reality.

The second major difficulty lies in handling the ambiguous indirect historical evidence. It is true that many early references to pidgins and creoles describe them as "broken," "bastard," or "corrupt" varieties of the language from which the major part of their lexicon is derived, but just as frequently those qualifying adjectives are lacking. While it would be easy to multiply examples, one unequivocal case may suffice to illustrate this crucial point: the historians tell us repeatedly that the East India Company employed Portuguese as interpreters in the Far East. But closer scrutiny of the sources reveals that these "Portuguese" were Asiatic Christians with Portuguese names, and that the "Portuguese" language allegedly used throughout the Orient by Portuguese, Spaniards, Dutchmen, Danes, Englishmen, and Chinese, was actually a well-documented Portuguese pidgin.

In precisely the same way, the information one can glean about the language used in the Levant trade even as late as the eighteenth century can also be highly misleading. One discovers that the English Levant Company did have dragomen, or interpreters. But except in the very earliest days these were English students of the Turkish language, used exclusively for the company's dealings with Turkish ministers and local officials. They were few in number, normally only one per factory, and they were unusual men. In 1700 Sir Paul Rycaut wrote that the profession of dragoman required a man of learning, perfect in Turkish, Greek, and Arabic. But these superior and skilled interpreters, who could turn a request or a complaint into formal, flowery, and complimentary Turkish, had nothing to do with the day-to-day business of trading, for in the Ottoman Empire the merchants were not Turks. All business was dominated by Jews, and the English merchants traded mainly with these Jewish middlemen, though Greeks, Arabs, and Syrian Christians were also involved. On the other side, only the factors themselves were English, and their staffs were mostly Armenians or Greeks, with either an Italian or a Levantine occupying the important position of chief clerk, or *scrivan*—which, of course, looks very like a Lingua Franca word. The crucial question is what language was used in the basic commercial dealings of Jews, Maronites, Greeks, Arabs, Armenians, and Italians. We know that it was not Turkish, and we must be entitled to view with some suspicion assertions such as that "Italian was used as the lingua franca throughout the Levant."[6] It is at least as plausible that "Italian" here means Lingua Franca, and not L2 Italian; and it is now impossible to agree with those who have maintained that Lingua Franca was merely Italian, badly spoken.

There was an interesting correspondence in the *Athenaeum,* from April to June of 1877,[7] provoked by the publication of a book by J. Cresswell Clough.[8] The now largely forgotten polymath Hyde Clarke expressed doubts about the existence of Lingua Franca, and, when provided with evidence by Prince Louis Lucien Bonaparte, still insisted that "there is no such separate language as Lingua Franca," and that it was no more than imperfect Italian, exactly like "Broken English, which is spoken differently by Frenchmen, Hollanders, Germans, Danes, Spaniards, Italians, Greeks, etc." Prince Bonaparte appears to have had the last word, in terms with which modern creolists would not seriously disagree: "Lingua Franca stands in the same relation to Italian as the Indo-Portuguese and Negro Dutch to the languages of Portugal and Holland," and he went on to specify a set of grammatical rules for Lingua Franca, which he claimed, quite rightly, would not and could not apply in the case of foreigners of different nationalities speaking a second language inadequately and incorrectly. He established, in short, that one of the primary tests of whether a language is a pidgin is that it should have a basic grammaticality which does not derive from what might be supposed to be the target language.

Other red herrings have been introduced into the debate much more recently. No less a figure than the doyen of modern creolists, Robert A. Hall, Jr., has asserted more than once that the so-called Lingua Franca of the nineteenth century was simply pidgin French, that the seventeenth-century Lingua Franca (or *hablar franco*) recorded by Fray Diego de Haedo, was pidgin Spanish, and that neither language had any connection with medieval Lingua Franca, which he claimed was Provençal-based.[9] The primary thesis, the denial of the unity and continuity of Lingua Franca, can be refuted relatively easily: one need do little more than set side by side samples of the extant texts. The proposition that Lingua Franca was based on Provençal, even though it would seem to be historically implausible, demands more complex counterarguments; but most of the phonological coincidences between Provençal and Lingua Franca are accounted for if one bears in mind, first, semi-adjustment to the trivocalic system of Arabic (which accounts for some vowel-raising), second, apocope of final vowels, third, the monophthongization of Italian diphthongs, and fourth, the peculiar characteristics of the Italian dialects, notably Genoese and Venetian, which supplied the bulk of the lexicon of Lingua Franca.[10]

These are fundamental issues, but if we can assume that Lingua Franca is something other than L2 Italian (however we choose to define "pidgin"), that it had a long and continuous history, and that it was Italian-based, we can move on to other and perhaps more subtle points, which are not without importance.

One concerns the time span and the regional variation of Lingua Franca. About Lingua Franca in the modern period there is certainly no shortage of information. The nineteenth century contrasts very markedly with the eighteenth, and it is not hard to see why this should be so. France embarked on the systematic conquest and colonization of Algeria in 1830 (and subsequently of Tunisia and Morocco), while Italy annexed Tripoli and Cyrenaica in 1912; and it was precisely in the old corsair-states of Tripoli, Tunis, and Algiers that Lingua Franca was in the nineteenth century most extensively used. (It is even recorded that Tunis, before the French protectorate, employed Lingua Franca as the language of diplomacy in its dealings with European powers.) The French chose to call the language "Petit mauresque," and produced a full-scale grammar and dictionary of it.[11] The nineteenth century was also, of course, a famous age of linguistic inquiry, and when the great German linguist Hugo Schuchardt turned his attention to Lingua Franca in 1909, he was able to draw on an extensive bibliography. Indeed his article remains the fundamental piece of work on Lingua Franca. But this abundant nineteenth-century information can, by its very abundance, produce a distorted impression.

While Schuchardt was certainly in no doubt about the status of Lingua Franca (or Sabir, or Petit Mauresque), his important study can be faulted in certain details that are not without significance. Although he acknowledges the amazing longevity of Lingua Franca, it could be argued that Schuchardt failed to appreciate the possibility of evolution in a language that extended over at least seven centuries, a span of time that corresponds approximately to the gap between Chaucer and contemporary English. He was also, to be fair, handicapped by the fact that he knew of no text between the strange poem published by Grion and the anonymous Italian farce of 1550. I shall pick up only two details. Schuchardt established a three-tense system for Lingua Franca: the (sometimes apocopated) Italian infinitive for present and imperfect, the simple Italian past participle, which served for perfective aspect, and a construction with *bisogno*, which could be used to indicate future. It seems clear, however, that no such system existed in medieval Lingua Franca. There is no trace of it in the Grion poem, nor in the poem, which Schuchardt did not know, discovered by the late Professor Jones.[12] We must assume that the repair of this defect, if it can be called such, was effected during the Renaissance or later, not inconceivably influenced by the Portuguese pidgin system of tense or aspect markers.[13] Again, as Schuchardt noted, nineteenth-century Lingua Franca uniformly made all object pronouns disjunctive and marked them with *per*: *Mi mirar per ti*, and so on. But earlier texts, such as the Grion poem or the Encina *villancico*, would appear to indicate that medieval Lingua Franca regularly employed the weak enclitic pronoun in its normal Romance position: *Alá ti da bon matín*, etc. The history of the grammar of the language has thus been obscured.

Schuchardt might also be accused of failing to appreciate the vulnerability of pidgin languages to relexification or partial relexification. While relexification as the explanation of the origin of sundry modern pidgins and creoles may still be questioned, we can scarcely doubt the word of Fray Diego de Haedo when he tells us that the massive influx of Portuguese captives into Algiers after the disastrous rout of the Portuguese under Sebastian at Alcazarquivir in 1578 had resulted in a marked increase of Portuguese words in the vocabulary of the Lingua Franca of Algiers.[14] There undoubtedly were, and it is scarcely surprising, local and regional variations of Lingua Franca, none of which could have been so marked as to constitute a barrier to communication. It would seem, indeed, that the different contributory languages produced not merely regional variation but some degree of synonymity: the Arabic-derived *taybo* alongside Romance *bono*, etc. The picture is more complex than it has habitually been painted: regional differentiation occurs in a pidgin that was never creolized.

But to leave these matters for the moment, what of the linguistic context in which Lingua Franca flourished? Although it is possible to glean information from a variety of sources, we have one very detailed description of the context of Lingua Franca in Algiers around 1600. The crucial pages, by Fray Diego de Haedo, have been summarized or partially quoted more than once, and it is no easy matter to reduce to any simple tabulated formula the information that he provides.[15] He distinguishes five linguistic communities, Turks, renegade Christians, Christian captives, Jews, and "moros," but one must think in terms of at least ten. While the captives were predominantly Spanish, Portuguese, French, and Italian, the Christian renegades certainly included Englishmen. Although nominally subject to the Sultan of Constantinople, the three military republics of Algiers, Tunis, and Tripoli enjoyed almost complete independence, and formed a refuge for the scum of Europe. Indeed the success of the corsairs in the early seventeenth century, when within seven years they captured no fewer than four hundred and six English ships (not counting French, Spanish, and Italian), was due largely to the fact that English adventurers and outcasts had taught them how to build better boats. Haedo's "moros" also present something of a problem. Although he has interesting things to say about the mutual incomprehensibility of the Arabic dialects of different groups, and does mention that some groups still spoke their Berber dialects, he fails to distinguish between Arabs and Berbers; and, although one must assume that by 1610 such a distinction no longer held much validity, it is clear that there were both Arabicized Berbers who spoke Arabic as a first language (even though in strange dialectical forms indubitably influenced by the substrate Berber) and Berbers who continued to speak Berber dialects as their first language. There were in addition returned Muslims who had spent several years in Christian captivity. We know also, from stray remarks elsewhere in Haedo's volume, that there was a Greek community engaged primarily in trade and commerce. The population of the Barbary coast in the early seventeenth century consisted, therefore, of Turks, Arabs, Berbers, Western Europeans, whether renegades or captives, of all nationalities (Spaniards, Portuguese, Frenchmen, Italians, Catalans, Englishmen, Provençaux), as well as the ubiquitous Greeks, Armenians, and Jews.

Under his initial five categories Fray Diego lists carefully the languages spoken by each group. The all-important fact that emerges from his analysis is that the only language common to every community was Lingua Franca. Turkish was almost negligible, Arabic was the language of religion and of a large proportion of the Berbers, who spoke it defectively, but the common language of daily intercourse between slaves and masters, captives and gaolers, merchants and traders, Muslims and Christians, was, on the evidence of Fray Diego, Lingua Franca. "Este hablar franco es tan general que no ay casa do no se use. No ay turco ni moro, ni grande ni pequeño, hombre o muger, hasta los niños, que poco o mucho y los más dellos muy bien, no le hablan."[16] ("Lingua Franca is in such general use that one cannot find a house in which it is not spoken. Turks, Arabs, Berbers, great and small, men and women, and even the children, all use it to some extent, but the majority speak it very fluently indeed.")

In the chaotic linguistic situation in Algiers (and other North African ports) it is not at all difficult to understand why a grammatically simple language, lacking any native speakers and possible nationalistic connotations, gained such extraordinary currency. Certainly Lingua Franca is no exception to the general rule that pidgins appear to flourish in multilingual situations. But the language had been in existence for at least three centuries when it became, in vernacular usage, the *lingua franca* of Algiers and Tunis: we have still to confront the problem of its origins. The suggestion has been made that Lingua Franca is itself a development of a simplified trading Latin to which reference is made in some early texts. But we may need to treat this and similar suggestions with some caution.[17]

It has been maintained (by, e.g., Roncaglia [1965, pp. 187-89]) that the earliest reference to Lingua Franca dates from 844-48, in Ibn Khurradādbih's account of the Muslim empire, in which he opposes the language of the Franks (al lugha al-Ifranjiyya) to Arabic, Turkish, Slav languages, Rūmiyya (Greek), and Andalusiyya (Hispanic dialects). The Abbasid Caliphate had at that time trespassed on Romance-speaking territory outside Spain only in a small part of Sicily, and it is clear that Ibn Khurradādbih is referring to the Romance dialects of the Frankish Empire: French, Provençal, Italian, etc. And as Vianello (1955) and Folena (1968-70, esp. pp. 357-58) have noted, "Lingua Franca," a calque

of the Arabic, was the term used by Dalmatians and Slavs to refer
to colonial Venetian, and what we now call Lingua Franca was
formerly distinguished as "Sabir." Furthermore, even though it is
not legitimate to consider the absence of documents in Lingua
Franca as proof of its nonexistence, the extant documents do
provide a rather full picture of a complex linguistic situation that
appears to exclude Lingua Franca.

For the earlier period, when the Mediterranean was divided
among Byzantium, the Frankish Empire, and the Muslims, there is
no satisfactory evidence at all. But it may be illuminating to return
for a moment to the chaotic linguistic situation in Algiers at the
beginning of the seventeenth century. Fray Diego de Haedo
reports that some of the Turks spoke a little Arabic, some of the
Christian renegades spoke a little Turkish, some of the Christian
captives spoke a little Turkish or a little Arabic depending on the
households in which they were kept as slaves, the Jewish
community spoke various Romance languages and sometimes
some Arabic, and the "moros" spoke nothing but mutually
incomprehensible dialects of Arabic. All groups spoke Lingua
Franca. But if Lingua Franca had not existed, one can see that
communication between any two groups with no language in
common could have been established through a member of a third
group, acting as an interpreter.

We must assume that at all stages of East-West contact in
the Mediterranean, there were always individuals available who
could act as interpreters, however imperfect their knowledge of
the languages of the principal parties. A further possibility that we
cannot ignore is that of "silent trade": given a context well
understood by both sides, a simple commercial transaction can be
accomplished by gestures, such as pointing, holding up a certain
number of fingers, indicating refusal or acceptance of the bargain
by shaking or nodding the head, and so forth. How else, one
wonders, did the Phoenicians trade for tin with the ancient
inhabitants of Cornwall? But the quantity and quality of the
communication must have been severely limited, no records
subsist, and when some written legal document was required, a
gestural convention, even highly developed, provides no answer.

If we move on in time, to an epoch when the West was
very much in contact with the East, namely the period of the
Crusades, and go searching for specimens of Lingua Franca, what
we actually find in the surviving documents[18] is a quite different
alternative. These papers are concerned almost exclusively with
commercial and legal affairs: they consist of contracts, receipts,

extracts from account-books, and so on. This is not the place to embark on a detailed linguistic analysis of these documents, but to describe many of them we can only revert to the term "Mixed Languages." It would be arbitrary to insist that the language employed is basically bad medieval Latin or incorrect Venetian dialect, with massive intrusion of lexical borrowings from other languages such as French or Arabic. They are macaronic, but without any comic intent underlying them. Sometimes they are a mixture of French and Italian; sometimes sentences or phrases in bad Latin are followed by paragraphs, sentences or phrases in bad Italian (even allowing for the peculiarities of the Genoese and Venetian dialects). And, except for the recurrence of certain set Latin formulae, the code-switching is apparently arbitrary.

Code-switching, as most modern linguists would prefer to call it, is a universal linguistic phenomenon that deserves, perhaps, more attention than it has received. Apart from macaronic verse, composed as a joke, the sixteenth century (if we can turn for a moment to a later age) has an abundance of perfectly serious prose texts in which a vernacular language alternates with Latin. Sixteenth-century Spanish Jesuit dramas, which, according to the rules of the Order, should have been composed exclusively in Latin, display a mixture of Latin and Spanish.[19] Luther, as is well known, used Latin words and phrases in his German devotional works.[20] The explanations offered in each case are slightly different. Birgit Stolt argues (though I oversimplify her case) that Luther needed his Latin for theological concepts that could not be expressed in German. Nigel Griffin argues that his dramatists lapse into Spanish so that their audiences, less proficient in Latin than the Jesuit authors, would not become hopelessly bored. A rare Italian devotional treatise of the early sixteenth century alternates between Latin and Italian in a manner for which there is no obvious or satisfactory explanation.[21] Nils Hasselmo, in an undeservedly neglected article, examines code-switching among contemporary Swedish immigrants in the United States and explains it (though again I oversimplify) as habitual patterns of interference in certain contexts among bilinguals. But none of these explanations will serve for Richard's or Folena's documents. One possible answer is that, certainly for the contracts, two parties were involved in the drafting, and that each was not only concerned with unequivocal clarity but prepared to accept only terms which both clearly understood, and among these a good handful of Arabic and Greek words.

What is remarkable and significant is that none of these

documents employs anything remotely resembling Lingua Franca. They appear to demonstrate that, even in the thirteenth century, a barbarous medieval Latin was the common language to which speakers of different Romance tongues tended to revert when faced with the more complex problems of communication on legalistic matters. How they communicated with the Saracens is another problem, but the most likely solution is that they consistently employed interpreters: Jews, Armenians, prisoners, and ex-prisoners. Richard (1962) argues that the documented French-Italian jargon of the Crusaders (" 'fritalien', e fritto con olio greco," as Folena calls it) was a "prefiguration" of Lingua Franca. Folena (1968-70, esp. pp. 345-61) vehemently denies this, and the presumption must be that he is right: none of these documents displays the essential grammatical characteristics of Lingua Franca, and it is extremely hard to envisage the processes by which these mixed jargons could have evolved into a pidgin. There would seem to be some difficulty, in short, in placing the origins of Lingua Franca much before the thirteenth century. The cliché that it began with the Crusades cannot be substantiated by the existing evidence.

It may not be legitimate to discard totally the possibility of Lingua Franca's being an imitation of the reported Jewish trading Latin of which we have no specimens extant; but we do know that, once this extraordinarily simple code had achieved some measure of diffusion, it virtually displaced all other alternatives, which are immeasurably clumsier. We could choose to infer that the abundantly documented existence of these clumsy alternatives among Romance-speakers shows that a generally accepted simplified Latin trading code had been long forgotten. Certainly one other plausible hypothesis appears to be supported by the testimony of the extant documents, namely that Lingua Franca did not develop from the contact of Western Europeans of diverse tongues. This is borne out by the Richard and Folena documents, and, possibly, by the fact that the Grion text, the earliest known specimen of Lingua Franca, is a lament placed in the mouth of a Muslim girl captive. This evidence suggests that it arose from the contact of Romance-speakers with non-Romance-speakers. And it may be possible to go further and insist, as I have insisted elsewhere (1971), that it arose, as all pidgins arise, in a multilingual situation, and, specifically, one in which none of the speakers primarily involved in its genesis had Italian (or an Italian dialect) as a first language.

Why it became extinct in the early years of the present

century is a sociolinguistic problem that, while complex in detail, presents no insuperable difficulties of comprehension.[22] The decline of Mediterranean trade, the collapse of the Ottoman Empire, the annexation of the North African littoral by European powers who had other available channels of communication, the disappearance of the more important of the mixed communities, the superior prestige of French, English, and Italian—all these factors, and others, clearly played a part.

But in all this, fascinating as Lingua Franca may be, there is one important point that should draw our attention, and that is that there were and are a variety of modes of communication lying between primary and secondary languages on the one hand, and pidgins and creoles on the other. Linguists have concentrated their attention on codified languages and simple problems of interference. The grammaticalized and semistandardized language, whether a primary language or a pidgin, tends to win out in the end. But pidgins are, in fact, extremely rare, and we ought not to neglect all the other possible and actual modes of communication, linguistic and nonlinguistic. With a handful of exceptions, the now huge bibliography on pidgin and creole languages is the product of the past twenty-odd years. To complete the picture it is time that more linguists turned their attention to other types of marginal language.

NOTES

1. This is an abridged version of a paper published as "The Context and Origins of Lingua Franca" in J. M. Meisel, ed. *Langues en contact— Pidgins—Creoles—Languages in Contact.* Tübingen: Gunter Narr, 1977.

2. See, for instance, Corominas (1948), Whinnom (1966-67 [1969]), Hancock (1973), Milani (1973). In addition, Boyd-Bowman (1976) reports a thesis in progress by Jame J. Pontillo on "Nautical Terms in Sixteenth Century American Spanish" (SUNY, Buffalo) which reveals the role of LF in spreading Mediterranean nautical terms to the New World. It should be noted that the book by Kahane, Kahane, and Tietze (1958) is quite misleadingly entitled, and fails to point to Lingua Franca proper as the channel of transmission of this nautical vocabulary.

3. The thesis that it was LF that might lie at the base of other European-based pidgins was adumbrated by Whinnom (1956, p. 10) and

subsequently elaborated by Thompson (1961), Whinnom (1965), and Hadel (1969).

4. It was Prof. P. E. Russell of Oxford who drew my attention to these well-documented facts. The problem of the origin of Portuguese pidgin is still unsolved, but the various suggestions so far advanced are clearly too simple. For a useful review of the various hypotheses (including the possible influence of LF), see Hancock (1975, esp. pp. 212-18). Prof. Germán de Granda informs me that he has an article in press (in *Revue de Linguistique Romane*) supporting the thesis that LF lies at the base of African Portuguese Creole.

5. 1300: see Grion (1890-92); the MS was written shortly after 1353, but the naming of places that were or were not in Christian hands would seem to place the date of composition of the poem between 1284 and 1304. 1400: although I have not had the opportunity to examine the MSS in question, Prof. L. P. Harvey of London informs me of samples of dialogue in LF in some of the unpublished sermons of St. Vincent Ferrer (1355-1419). 1520: see Harvey, Jones, and Whinnom (1967) and Jones and Lee (1975, pp. 253-55); the poet, Juan del Encina, returned from his trip to Jerusalem in 1520. 1550: this is an anonymous Italian farce, the evidence from which was utilized by Schuchardt (1909). 1610: this is the date of publication of the fundamental work on Algiers by Fray Diego de Haedo. 1680: Molière's *Le Bourgeois Gentilhomme*; it is remarkable that in the "turqueries" with which the play concludes (expanded in the edition of 1682), Molière's "Turkish," carefully copied from Rotrou's *La Soeur,* is almost pure gibberish, but his Lingua Franca is unexceptionable, since Molière consulted his friend the Chevalier d'Arvieux, who spent half a lifetime as an independent traveller and then as French envoy in Tunis, Constantinople, Algiers, and Aleppo. See Labat (1735).

6. See A. C. Wood (1935), from whom I take the quotation, but other sources give the same information. For further bibliography and a more recent account, see Perry (1975, pp. 33-40 and 57-77). There are sundry pieces of supporting evidence for my basic supposition that "Italian" should be construed as "Lingua Franca." Noall (1968), for instance, cit. Coates (1971), tells of the crew of an Algerian ship wrecked near Penzance in 1760 who spoke LF and found an interpreter in Penzance, one Mr. Mitchell, who had been in the Levant trade. Vianello (1955), supported by Folena (1968-70), insists that many early references to LF are to be interpreted only as "italiano parlato," but this is quite a different question, to which I return below.

7. I am indebted to Prof. Ian F. Hancock of Texas for drawing my attention to this correspondence, and indeed for photocopies of it.

8. Clough (1876), esp. pp. 11ff.

9. See Hall (1966, pp. 4, 6, 128), and 1961, and others of his publications referred to therein. Ian F. Hancock, in his invaluable inventory of pidgin and creole languages, published in Hymes (1971, pp. 509-23), separates as item 29 "Pidgin French or 'Petit Mauresque' of North Africa" (which he says is "sometimes wrongly referred to as Sabir") from item 30, "Sabir (or Lingua Franca)." I believe that he is now persuaded that he was in error in doing so. I have not seen his revised list, in Perrot (1977), which is still in press.

10. See Harvey, Jones, and Whinnom (1967, esp. pp. 575-76). There is further discussion of LF vocabulary and its origins in Coates (1971). See also, for a historically well-documented but in some respects linguistically naïve discussion of the problem, Fronzaroli (1955). For the raising of *e* to *i* in early non-metropolitan Venetian texts (*plasir, sabir,* etc.), see also Folena (1968-70, p. 360).

11. This is the famous *Dictionnaire de la Langue Franque ou Petit Mauresque* (Marseille, 1830). The section of useful phrases is reproduced in Coates (1971). Reinecke (1975) is not complimentary about the *Dictionnaire* and says that it was very hastily compiled.

12. See Harvey, Jones, and Whinnom (1967) and Jones and Lee (1975).

13. Thompson (1961), in a very well known and highly influential article, tabulates the durative, perfective, and contingent/future markers in a dozen creole languages, but solely as evidence of their structural affinities. All the older historical evidence appears to indicate that, like LF, these creoles lacked this system of markers. This now almost universal system could well be of African origin, propagated via Portuguese pidgin.

14. Haedo (1612, ff. 23v-24r, or 1927: I, p. 27).

15. Fronzaroli (1955, p. 231) produces a grossly oversimplified tabulated synopsis of Haedo's information.

16. Haedo (1612, f. 24r, or 1927: I, p. 27).

17. Among other authorities Petronius speaks of a dialect of mixed Latin and Greek that became the *lingua franca* of the seaports of the Mediterranean. See Mackail (1895), Schiaffini (1930), Hall (1966, p. 3), and Hancock (this volume).

18. See Richard (1962) and Folena (1968-70). One may add to these Mediterranean documents one from Delhi, 1338-49, in a mixture of Latin and Italian, reproduced by Lopez (1955).

19. See Griffin (1976).

20. See Stolt (1964). I am indebted to Prof. R. E. Keller of Manchester for drawing my attention to this point.

21. *Tractato per vtile & deletabile nominato amatorium acto ad ordinare lo amore humano alli de biti virtu & deuiario de omne illicito amore*

in che solum consiste virtu nouamente exposto da frate Jacobo Maza de Rhegio ad instantia de Dom Ramundo de Cardona, Vice re del regno Neapolitano (Naples, 1517).

22. The date of its total extinction is not easy to determine. Schuchardt (1909) believed that it was on the point of disappearing completely. Rossi (1928) thought that pockets of speakers of LF still existed. It is not even certain that it is yet extinct: Ian F. Hancock informs me that Bruce Rodgers of California claims it is still spoken.

REFERENCES

Boyd-Bowman, Peter. 1976. Review of Milani (1973). *Hispanic Review* XLIV:85-86.

Clough, James Cresswell. 1876. *On the Existence of Mixed Languages: Being an Examination of the Fundamental Axioms of the Foreign School of Modern Philology.* London: Longmans.

Coates, William A. 1971. The Lingua Franca. In *Proceedings of the Fifth Kansas Linguistics Conference,* Frances Ingemann, ed. Lawrence, Ks.: University of Kansas, pp. 25-34.

Corominas, Joan. 1948. The origin of the Spanish *ferreruelo,* Ital. *ferraiuolo,* and the importance of the study of Lingua Franca for Romance etymology. *PMLA* LXIII: 719-26.

Dictionnaire de la Langue Franque ou Petit Mauresque, suivi de quelques dialogues familiers et d'un vocabulaire de mots arabes les plus usuels: à l'usage des Français en Afrique. Marseille, 1830.

Folena, Gianfranco. 1968-70. Introduzione al veneziano "de là da mar." *Bolletino dell'Atlante Linguistico Mediterraneo* X-XII:331-76.

Fronzaroli, Pelio. 1955. Nota sulla formazione della lingua franca. *Atti e Memorie dell'Accademia Toscana di Scienze e Lettere "La Colombaria"* XX:212-52.

Gilbert, Glenn F., ed. 1970. *Texas Studies in Bilingualism.* Berlin: Walter de Gruyter.

Griffin, Nigel. 1976. *Two Jesuit Ahab Dramas.* Exeter Hispanic Texts. Exeter: University of Exeter.

Grion, G. 1890-92. Farmacopea e lingua franca del dugento. *Archivio Glottologico Italiano* XII:181-86.

Hadel, Richard E., S. J. 1969. Modern creoles and Sabir. *Folklore Annual of the University Folklore Association* (Austin, Texas) I:35-43.

Haedo, Fray Diego de. 1612. *Topographia e historia general de Argel*

(Valladolid); repr. 1927, 2 vols. Madrid: Sociedad de Bibliófilos Madrileños.

Hall, Robert A., Jr. 1961. Pidgin. *Encyclopaedia Britannica* XVII:905-07.

―――. 1966. *Pidgin and Creole Languages.* Ithaca: Cornell University Press.

Hancock, Ian F. 1971. A survey of the pidgins and creoles of the world. In Hymes, pp. 509-23.

―――. 1973. Remnants of the Lingua Franca in British slang. *The University of South Florida Language Quarterly* XI:35-36.

―――. 1975. Malacca Creole Portuguese: Asian, African or European? *Anthropological Linguistics* XVII:211-36.

―――. 1977. Liste des langues pidgins et créoles. In Perrot (1977, in press).

Harvey, L. P.; Jones, R. O.; and Whinnom, K. 1967. Lingua franca in a villancico by Encina. *Revue de Littérature Comparée* XLI:572-79.

Hasselmo, Nils. 1970. Code-switching and modes of speaking. In Gilbert, pp. 179-210.

Hymes, Dell, ed. 1971. *Pidginization and Creolization of Languages.* Cambridge: Cambridge University Press; paperback repr. 1975.

Jones, R. O., and Lee, Carolyn R., eds. 1975. Juan del Encina, *Poesía lírica y cancionero musical.* Madrid: Castalia.

Kahane, H.; Kahane, R.; and Tietze, A. 1958. *The Lingua Franca in the Levant. Turkish Nautical Terms of Italian and Greek Origin.* Urbana: University of Illinois Press.

Labat, Jean-Baptiste. 1735. *Mémoires du Chevalier d'Arvieux... recueillis de ses mémoires originaux et mis en ordre avec des réflexions par le R. P....* Paris.

Le Page, R. B., ed. 1961. *Proceedings of the Conference on Creole Language Studies.* London: Macmillan.

Lopez, Roberto S. 1955. Venezia e le grandi linee dell'espansione commerciale nel secolo XIII. In *La civiltà veneziana del secolo di Marco Polo.* Florence: Sansoni, pp. 37-82.

Mackail, John W. 1895. *Latin Literature.* University Extension Manuals. London: John Murray. Frequent reprints up to 1952.

Milani, Virgil I. 1973. *The Written Language of Christopher Columbus.* New York: State University of New York.

Noall, Cyril. 1968. Account of the loss of an Algerine corsair, on the coast of Cornwall (from the Naval Chronicle, 1809). *Old Cornwall,* Autumn: 127-28.

Perrot, J., ed. 1977. *Les Langues du monde,* 3d. ed. (in press).

Perry, Norma. 1975. *Sir Everard Fawkener, Friend and Correspondent of Voltaire.* Studies on Voltaire and the Eighteenth Century, CXXXIII. Banbury: The Voltaire Foundation.

Reinecke, John E., et al. 1975. *A Bibliography of Pidgin and Creole Languages.* Honolulu: University Press of Hawaii.

Richard, J. 1962. *Documents chypriotes des Archives du Vatican (XIVe et XVe siècles).* Paris: Institut Français d'Archéologie de Beyrouth.

Roncaglia, A. 1965. *Storia della letteratura italiana,* I. Milan: Garzanti.

Rossi, E. 1928. La lingua franca in Barberia. *Rivista delle Colonie Italiane* (dated only; no vol. number):143-51.

Schiaffini, A. 1930. Profilo storico della lingua commerciale dai primordi di Roma all'età moderna. I: Roma e i regni romano-barbarici. *Italia Dialettale* VI:1-56. (No sequel to this first installment was ever published.)

Schuchardt, Hugo. 1909. Die Lingua franca. *Zeitschrift für romanische Philologie* XXXIII:441-61. (An English translation is forthcoming in *Journal of Creole Studies* I(2).)

Stolt, Birgit. 1964. *Die Sprachmischung in Luthers Tischreden.* Stockholm: Stockholmer Germanistische Forschungen 4.

Thompson, R. W. 1961. A note on some possible affinities between the creole dialects of the Old World and those of the New. In Le Page, pp. 107-13.

Vianello, N. 1955. "Lingua franca" di Barberia e "lingua franca" di Dalmazia. *Lingua Nostra* XV:67-69.

Whinnom, Keith. 1956. *Spanish Contact Vernaculars in the Philippine Islands.* Hong Kong and Oxford: Hong Kong University Press and Oxford University Press.

————. 1965. The origin of the European-based creoles and pidgins. *Orbis* XIV:509-27.

————. 1966-67 (1969). *Tafanario:* problema etimológico. *Filología* XII: 211-17.

————. 1971. Linguistic hybridization and the "special case" of pidgins and creoles. In Hymes, pp. 91-115.

Wood, A. C. 1935. *A History of the Levant Company.* Oxford: Oxford University Press.

v.

Creoles and Pidgins
and National Development

Creole Languages
and Primary Education

Dennis R. Craig

SOCIOLINGUISTIC CONTEXTS

Creole languages of necessity exist in two broad types of sociolinguistic situation. In one type, one of the base languages of the creole happens to be the official language or one of the official languages of the society. In the other type of situation, the creole has no formal linguistic relationship with the official language or languages. Of the 80 creole-language areas listed in Hancock (1971), over 60 seem to represent the first type of situation, although it is natural to expect that even in the second type the creole will exhibit some lexical borrowings from the language or languages with which it coexists in the society. Some areas that provide examples of the first type of situation are: Haiti and the French West Indies, where the official language is French and the creole is French-based; Sierra Leone and the former British West Indies, where the official language is English and the creoles are English-based. Some examples of the second type of situation are Surinam (Dutch Guiana), where the official language is Dutch and creoles such as Saramaccan and Sraanan are English/African-based; St. Lucia and the Seychelles, where the official language is English and the creoles are French-based. Creole languages that are not European-based, like the Swahili and Lingala pidgin-creoles of Africa, seem also susceptible to this kind of situational classification.

What is significant for education in both of these situations is that the specific societies have to be considered at least bilingual if they are not, owing to their specific circumstances, multilingual. This claim, however, might need some qualification in order to include such cases as those in the English-speaking West Indies, where, instead of a discrete creole, the language of speakers tends to consist of a range of variation between a hypothetical creole basilect and an accepted, standard acrolect. The latter has to be regarded as a special case within the first type of situation, where an original creole existing side by side with one of its base languages has become decreolized; this kind of case has been extensively discussed, as regards its formal characteristics, in Stewart (1962), Bailey (1971), DeCamp (1971), and Bickerton (1972, 1973), for example, and as regards its educational implications in Craig (1966, 1971). Such a case, if not exactly what one could call 'bilingual' is in any event 'biloquial', since the creole-influenced speech form retains its own rules and remains sufficiently distinct from the standard language to be accorded a separate status. Consequently, most of the characteristics of a bilingual situation would still be found to apply here.

BILINGUAL EDUCATIONAL ALTERNATIVES

In considering education, and particularly primary education, in creole-language communities, some attention needs initially to be paid to the nature of the bilingual context in which formal education is supposed to take place. That context tends to be defined by two main sets of factors. One of these sets has to do with relationships, of the kind already referred to, between the linguistic structures of the language forms in the bilingual context, i.e., whether or not the two language forms are structurally related, whether they are linked variationally, and so on; the other set of factors has to do with the speakers' attitudes toward the two language forms.

In general, the sociopolitical history of creole-language situations has resulted in the creole language's being the less valued of the languages in the bilingual context. The fact that the creole is invariably a survival of the language of originally enslaved or colonized people, who at present continue in depressed and low-social-status conditions, is one determinant of this attitude. Another determinant is the lack of utilitarian value in the creole for literate activities at national and international levels. The fact that monolingual creole speakers themselves often have this low estimation of their own language is well understood in many parts of the world. Vincent (1972, oral remarks), for example, comments on the intentional ambiguity of the Nigerian proverb: "Pidgin is no man's language," one of its meanings being that no one likes to admit possession of the low-valued speech form. The same attitude is widely dispersed in Jamaica and Hawaii, and rejection of 'dialect' readers by parents of American nonstandard speakers (see, e.g., Wolfram 1970, p. 29) is no more than a reflection of the same feeling in a situation of decreolization.

It also has to be noted, however, that attitudes toward the creole language in a bilingual situation do not only derive from the sociocultural correlates of that situation, but might also derive directly from the structural relationship or lack of relationship between the two language forms. Stewart (1962, p. 53), for example, points out the favorable attitude toward creole in the Dutch West Indian territories as compared with the relatively unfavorable attitudes in both the French- and English-speaking territories; it would seem that the reason for this contrast is the fact that the structural relationships between creole and the standard languages in the latter territories encouraged officials in the past to treat creole as if it did not exist, or if it did exist, as if it should be eradicated. In the former territories, on the other hand, the traditional attitude has tended to be similar to that of speakers in general toward a foreign language, since, apart from some lexical borrowing, there is little structural relationship between creole and the official language in those territories.

Another consequence of the existence of a structural relationship between two language forms is that where a creole exists side by side with one of its base languages, a potential is automatically created for a particular kind of dynamic bilingual situation. This potential will become realized depending on whether or not sociocultural conditions are favorable. An example may best be seen in the English-speaking Caribbean areas where the original creole/Standard English bilingualism has been affected since the middle of the eighteenth century by a gradual development of English-based education, first promoted by missionary bodies, for the mass of originally creole speakers, and by a concurrently increasing social mobility in which proficiency in English provided an upward thrust. In this kind of dynamic situation, code-switching and diglossia in response to social-situational stimuli were able to develop to an extent that has resulted today in an almost complete decreolization of English in many communities, with only a post-creole language continuum as the survival. By contrast, there has not been a similar realization of this dynamic potential in Haiti and the rest of the French Caribbean, and the reason for this non-realization is to be found in the more conservative kind of social organization and attitudes that exist in those areas, the relative slowness of social mobility for the mass of the population, and the opportunity that has thereby been provided for the original creole to consolidate itself and become 'fossilized' (to use the term as in Selinker 1972). Valdman (1969), however, indicated that in Haiti, at least, code-switching and diglossia frequently occur, although a post-creole continuum, as in the English territories, is not yet in evidence.

The nature of the bilingual context in creole-language situations, and the factors operating in such situations as sketched above, have much to do with determining the educational alternatives that might prove feasible within specific communities. There are several possibilities for education in a bilingual context; Fishman and Lovas (1970), for example, list four main ones:

(1) Transitional bilingualism, in which the home language of the child is used in school only to the extent necessary to allow the child to adjust to school and learn enough of the school language to permit it to become the medium of education.

(2) Monoliterate bilingualism, in which both languages are developed for aural-oral skills, but literacy is aimed at only in the one language that happens to be dominant in the community.

(3) Partial bilingualism, in which aural-oral fluency and literacy are developed in the home language only in relation to certain types of subject-matter that have to do with the immediate society and culture; while aural-oral fluency and literacy in the school language are developed for a wider range of purposes.

(4) Full bilingualism, in which the educational aim is for the child to develop all skills in both languages in all domains.

THE MONOLINGUAL ALTERNATIVE

Apart from the preceding possibilities, there is of course available in creole-language communities a fifth educational alternative, which, by being even less bilingual than (1) above, moves out of the sphere of bilingualism altogether. This is the alternative of completely ignoring the creole in school. In this system, the child, if he/she acquired the school language, could be regarded as bilingual, but the educational program would remain monolingual. This fifth alternative warrants serious discussion, since, in most creole-language communities, it is the one that school systems have traditionally tended to adopt, under the motivation not so much of a carefully thought out educational rationale as of the attitude of low valuation already referred to, by which the status of being a discrete language was rarely accorded to a creole, especially when the latter existed side by side with one of its base languages. There is hardly a creole-language area in the world where at some time in the recent past this alternative has not been the one selected, although more recently, the justice of the alternative began to be questioned. More recently still, fresh evidence in favor of the alternative started to appear.

The question of the rightness of this fifth alternative can be posed in terms of cognitive development, as in the research of Eichorn and Jones (1952) on the adverse cognitive effects suffered by children who grew up in communities where the language of school was not that of the home. Anastasi and Cordova (1953) showed that the restriction of the normal development of the home language in bilingual situations tended to produce a cognitive handicap, although bilingualism under fairer conditions might not itself be a handicap. More recent research, however, such as that of Lambert and Tucker (1972), has tended to show that monolingual school programs in a language different from the home language of the child do not necessarily create any handicap, provided that the monolingual factor is handled as it was in the St. Lambert experiment. Lambert and Tucker (ibid.,p. 6) explain the situation as follows:

> As researchers and evaluators, we had our own concerns about the possible consequences this type of educational program might have on the cognitive development and academic standing of pupils taught in other than their home language. The research literature on the topic is not altogether encouraging. For example, Michael West (1926) reported a large academic handicap for children trained through a foreign language. Cheeseman (quoted in Isidro, 1949) also found that Malay children who enter schools taught in English fall far behind those taught in the home language. And Prator (1950) carefully describes the Iloilo experiment conducted in the Philippines in which one group of pupils took their first year of schooling in the home language, and a matched group studied through English. The achievement standings at the end of grade 1 clearly favoured those instructed in their home

languages. Even though the message of these studies is clear, certain questions arise about the reliability and generalizability of the conclusions. As to reliability, a more recent study conducted in the Philippines, designed as a replication of the Iloilo experiment, had a quite different outcome (Davis, 1967). In this case, Filipino pupils instructed entirely through English performed as well as carefully matched counterparts instructed through Tagalog. Furthermore, on careful reading of the earlier studies one has the impression that the children learning through English may have had to neglect educational content and focus instead on the mastery of a second language apparently taught in a mechanical, routinized manner by non-native speakers of the language. One also wonders about the relevance of English for Indian, Malaysian, or Filipino children who generally leave school and return to rural communities after three or so years. In planning the St Lambert experiment, we tried to take these factors into consideration by making the development of language skills incidental to educational content. In other words, the children were enticed into the mastery of the new language in a natural manner in their daily interaction with teachers who were native speakers.

It would appear, therefore, that a monolingual primary school program in a language other than the home language does not necessarily have adverse effects on the child. However, one factor in relation to monolingual school programs that has to be taken into account in a creole-language situation, but thal would need no special attention in an experiment of the St. Lambert type, is the attitude of the child, the home, and the community in general toward the child's home language. In most creole-language situations, the use in school of a language other than creole reflects and reinforces the stigma that has traditionally been placed on creole. The effect of this attitude is clearly apparent in areas such as the Caribbean, where creole speakers are in the midst of societies with monolingual, standard-language education systems. Because of the high social value of education and, with it, the standard language, creole speech becomes regarded as synonymous with backwardness and unintelligence; creole-speaking children, as well as adults, learn to be fearful of possibly incurring ridicule by venturing to speak in non-casual situations; and this tendency to avoid creole leads to a restriction of its domains— unless, of course, the creole-speaking community has a residual life and culture of its own that could withstand the inroads of monolingual, standard-language education. The problem here referred to in general terms is the same as that discussed relative to Jamaica in Bailey (1964), for example, and in Labov (1964, 1966,

1969) relative to what has to be regarded as a case of decreolization: the nonstandard speech situation in ghetto areas in the United States.

In monolingual, standard-language educational systems such as those just referred to, it could result that the child's normal development in his/her home language, creole, becomes stifled, while at the same time the child fails to acquire native fluency in the language of school, with harmful results such as those suggested, and already referred to, in Anastasi and Cordova (op. cit.). Whether or not such results occur, however, depends, as has been suggested already, on the community strength of the creole language and culture and the ability of the latter to provide a complete affective, cognitive, and linguistic experience for creole speakers. There is no doubt that apart from those creole-language areas in Sub-Saharan Africa and East and Southeast Asia and Oceania, where many creole speakers also possess indigenous languages and cultures that would provide possibilities for complete personal development, there are many creole-language and cultural environments that provide possibilities of a similarly complete development for their monolingual creole speakers, despite the standard-language educational policies of the schools. The latter has historically been or is the case, for example, in Haiti and in the Papiamentu areas of the Dutch West Indies.

Whether, however, a monolingual, standard-language educational program or one of the four Fishman-Lovas bilingual alternatives will be selected for primary education in a community of which creole speakers form a part depends on several factors.

CURRENT PROBLEMS IN THE CHOICE OF ALTERNATIVES

Despite the current worldwide liberalization of educational policies, it seems unlikely that full bilingualism in the sense mentioned earlier will be accepted as the educational policy in creole-language areas. What has been accepted in some areas, and is likely to gain increasing acceptance in others, is the policy that can be defined in the Fishman-Lovas typology as partial bilingualism. In this system, the creole home-language will be used in early and primary education, in many cases with concurrent standard-language programs at least at an upper primary level, but secondary and higher education, with the experiential and cognitive domains that are subsumed within these, will tend to be treated in standard or international languages.

A rationale for this kind of partial bilingualism is not hard to find. The economic cost of fully bilingual educational systems tends to be too great for newly developing, traditionally creole-language areas to bear, especially in view of the fact that there is generally no national or international advantage to be gained by orality and literacy in a creole language over all subject-matter domains; but the integrity of the self-concept and the balanced development of the creole speaker demand that at least the first part of his/her formal education should utilize the home language. However, it seems important to note that this kind of partial bilingualism in education will occur only where the numerical proportion and the cultural traditions of creole speakers are particularly strong and where, at the same time, national educational policies have the commitment and the means to provide an education for all persons. There are relatively few creole-language areas where all the latter conditions concurrently exist, and in most of these areas, partially bilingual education on a national scale still remains a possibility rather than an actuality—only relatively small-scale experimental projects that could later develop into more widely based, partially bilingual national systems are in evidence. In Curaçao, for example, where the climate for this kind of educational development has for a long time been more favorable than it still is in most other creole-language areas, it is only relatively recently that a nationally financed program of early primary education in Papiamentu has been initiated. A similar kind of educational development seems possible for Tok Pisin, which is one of the three official languages of New Guinea, and for Haitian Creole. In Haiti there have been programs for adult literacy in creole, much biblical translation and religious activity in creole, dictionary compilations and grammars of the creole, popular radio and television programs in creole, and even a few missionary and other privately financed, creole-language, primary-school projects. Yet a nationally financed partially bilingual primary-school system continues to be a remote possibility.

The linguistic (as distinct from the social-psychological) difficulties faced by educational programs that could develop into partially bilingual educational systems stem from problems of standardizing creole languages so that they might serve whole national areas, of constructing spelling systems that would relate easily to those of the respective standard languages, and of compiling creole-language school texts and materials quickly enough and in sufficient quantities for large-scale education.

STANDARDIZATION AND SPELLING

The first problem, that of standardizing the creole language over a given national area, is often more difficult than it would seem at first glance. Creole-language areas often consist of a series of relatively small, traditionally self-contained communities and, sometimes, regions that have developed their own peculiarities of phonology, morphology, and lexis within the system of the general creole. These community or regional differences are often found associated with particular attitudes and prejudices; for example, differences between the Northern Region and the west and south of Haiti and between urban and rural creole are known to be correlated with specific attitudes and identifications that have to be taken into account when standardization is attempted in Haiti (Pompilus, e.g., 1973, p. viii; Valdman 1969; Klein n.d.). Urban/rural differences with a similar effect have been noted in the English-based Caribbean and West African creoles, and in Guyana such differences are additionally correlated with racial affiliations that are socially significant; the variation that exists across the Melanesian pidgin-creoles, including those of New Guinea, is well attested (see list and bibliography in Hancock 1971, pp. 72-77).

It is, of course, possible to avoid standardization problems by taking the dialect of each community where an educational program is to be implemented and using it as it is, and this is actually what has happened in many community-based creole-language educational projects. A problem arises only when the production of separate educational materials for relatively small regional groupings of pupils proves uneconomical, as it is currently likely to do. A serious consequence of such a solution, however, is the linguistic fragmentation that would be promoted. Even when standardization problems are overcome, problems that have to do with the choice of an orthography for use in schools are likely to be considerable, especially in situations where, despite lexical affinities, the phonology of the creole diverges significantly from that of the standard language with which it coexists. In such situations, one well-justified aim of education is likely to be that the possession of literacy in either the creole or the standard language ought to be transferable; if it is not transferable, then, for creole speakers, the utility of literacy remains limited and questionable, since being able to read creole is not automatically an aid to the acquisition of the related standard language and the benefits it confers. In some cases, as in Haiti, for example, this question of the transferability of literacy tends to become mixed with questions of maintaining the authenticity of the creole and not distorting it by standard language-remoulding. In a country that is proud of its national past, and where creole is regarded as an important survival of that past, such considerations can be very important. In the long run, it is only the educational aims set by the nation as a whole that can arbitrate questions of this kind.

CURRICULUM MATERIALS AND TEACHING PROGRAMS

When problems of standardization and orthography are solved, there will remain certain strictly educational problems that have to do with the preparation of curriculum materials and teaching programs. Very often, the difficulties of such preparation are not recognized beforehand, and the intended new school program is forced to adopt, with no change other than translation into the new language, programs that in content and methodologies can function effectively only in societies and environments that might be significantly different from the specific creole-language one that is being provided for. The UNESCO program for Anthropology and Language Science in Educational Development took note of this fact in its first report (ALSED 1972), and among other things pointed out that:

> It should be recognized that similar first language programmes often will have varying results in different cultural settings because of . . . sociolinguistic and sociocultural factors. The cultural contact is particularly important in areas where teaching programmes and materials are being prepared in hitherto unwritten languages or in mother tongues being used for the first time in formal education.

However, the efficient preparation of such programs and materials requires an interdisciplinary cooperation among education, linguistics, and the other social sciences, which, so far, has not often materialized.

Problems such as the preceding, together with the residual reluctance in many areas to accept creoles as written, as distinct from oral, languages have contributed to the already mentioned fact that few creole-language educational programs have developed into nationally extensive, fully bilingual or partially bilingual educational systems.

THE INEVITABILITY OF CREOLE

In the absence of nationally extensive programs, most creole speakers, if they receive a formal primary education, tend to do so in school situations that can be expected to vary, sometimes even in the same locality, from monolingual, standard-language education as already described, to transitional bilingualism, to monoliterate bilingualism. The reason for this is that the differences between these three types of possible school situations are not very wide and very often cannot be rigidly maintained; this is easily understood when it is realized that a school program that intends to be monolingual in a standard language can hardly fail to become transitionally bilingual if it is taught by teachers who are native and who themselves can speak the relevant creole—and virtually all primary-school teachers in creole-language areas would be in the latter category. Children and teachers at this level, as long as they possess the creole language in common, are most unlikely to avoid it altogether, even when the school system prohibits it, as was usual in many areas in the past. It is well known, for example, although many formal studies have not been done, that even those teachers who assess themselves as speaking the standard language all the time unconsciously lapse into creole when interacting with children in this situation. This kind of behavior of intendedly standard-speaking teachers has often been noticed in the English- and French-based creole-language areas where the official language is a base of the creole; in other types of creole-language areas, it might not be so easy for the teacher to lapse unconsciously into the creole of the child, and in such areas the foreign-language gap between the child's language and that of school might make a declared policy of monolingualism in the official language more imperative to be followed. But even here, the speech of the native teacher is likely to tend to approach that of the children. Once this happens, a situation of transitional bilingualism would have materialized, but this same situation, if it persists long enough that the creole speaker starts to acquire the school language and literacy in it, would have to be regarded as having developed into monoliterate bilingualism; in other words, the difference between the two situations has to do only with the duration and continuation of creole-language communication between teachers and children.

From what has been said so far, we may generalize about the use of language in primary education in creole-language situations as follows: (a) In all situations, even where the professed educational policy is monolingualism in the standard language, there will be varying degrees of oral usage of creole by children and teachers in schools. (b) There will be literacy in creole at the primary level only in cases where there is a clear educational policy of full or partial bilingualism; such cases are very few. (c) There will be an attempt at orality and literacy in a standard language, at least at an upper primary level, in most cases.

RELEVANCE AND CULTURAL DOMINANCE

Apart from factors that have to do with the use of language, a common element in all cases of primary education in a creole-language context is likely to be the search for an educational content or curriculum that is fully relevant to the sociocultural environment of the creole. This search is the *sine qua non* of primary education in the modern world, and it is assumed that the colonial tradition of the eighteenth and nineteenth centuries that dictated otherwise in newly developing countries has now all but passed away. It is expected everywhere that the content of primary education will be such as would give children adequate concepts of themselves within their own environments, develop in them an intimate knowledge and appreciation of that environment, and equip them with a set of basic skills and attitudes that will make them want to remain in that environment and improve the quality of life in it. But seeking relevance in primary education inevitably impinges again on the language factor. *House* and *maison* do not mean to children in a Nigerian and Haitian village respectively the same that they mean in London and Paris; the images and associations of the words are very different in cultural terms. The implication is that the involvement of a second or standard language in a creole-language educational context must also be understood to involve the creation of cultural correlates that will be associated with that second language. It is to be expected that the second language, where it is not an easy vehicle for the cultural realities of creole-speaking children and native teachers, will become re-moulded by the intrusion of native lexis and idiom, as has happened to some extent, for example, in Caribbean French and Caribbean English. The concerns of the ALSED report relate to these factors.

PRIMARY EDUCATION AND THE STYLE OF
CREOLE-LANGUAGE COMMUNICATION

Continued orality in creole in the primary school means that children become consolidated not merely in the phonological, morphological, and syntactic conventions of creole, but also in the way in which concepts are given lexical form or idiomized in creole. If literacy in creole is also one of the aims of primary education, then this will strongly reinforce the consolidation, but whether or not literacy in creole is an aim, the acquisition of a standard (and particularly a European standard) second language will manifest the influence of a creole-language style of communication. This is not a matter that can be dismissed as one of the incidentals of first-language interference with the learning of a second language. It is a matter that has to do with the specific cognitive orientations of individuals, and that is known to be important for education even in language situations where differences between speakers are of the social-dialect kind, rather than of the type between more disparate language systems. The point is that both types of differences arise out of the close relationship between language and sociocultural conditioning. In its most generalized and at the same time most precise form, the discussion of this factor begins in the work of psychologists who have looked at the structure of cognitive abilities across sociocultural groupings.

Vernon (1955, 1965a, 1965b), for example, has shown that measured intelligence is not necessarily the same as innate ability (whatever the latter is), and that sociocultural environment has a significant influence on factors of measured mental ability; Vernon (1966, 1967), Bruner et al. (1956, 1966), and Goodnow (1968) also show that in culturally different societies factor analyses of test results reveal that subjects differ across cultures in the organization and structure of mental abilities and in relative habituations in the performance of mental tasks, and that the direction of mental growth (Bruner et al.) comes as a reaction to environmental stimuli.

In some research, conclusions that ought to be related to the preceding findings have been misinterpreted. In the early work of Bernstein, for example (Bernstein 1961a, 1961b, 1961c; 1962a, 1962b; 1965, 1966), the impression is given that children growing up in less-favored sociocultural environments (i.e., working-class conditions in Britain) tend to possess a *restricted* linguistic-cognitive code, in contrast with children conditioned in a more favorable sociocultural (i.e., middle-class) environment, who tend to possess an *elaborated* linguistic-cognitive code. The impression is given not that both types of children can perform the same set of linguistic-cognitive operations, each type in its different and characteristic way, but that restricted-code users have an absolute disability in linguistic-cognitive operations, while elaborated-code users have an absolute advantage. Bernstein seems now to have modified his viewpoint as is evidenced, for example, in Bernstein (1972); but, in the interval, misinterpretations of a similar nature led to the development of a set of early-education principles based on the concept of lower social class deprivation, for example, in Corbin et al. (1965), Crow et al. (1966), and Bereiter et al. (1966). However, the work of sociolinguistics and arguments such as in Labov (1969) have now brought such educational principles into question and have revealed the misinterpretations on which they are based.

Creole-language situations, as remarked earlier, are invariably situations of lower social class status, and especially where a continuum has developed between a creole and the standard language, as in the Caribbean, the structure of sociocultural linguistic differences is not unlike that apparent in the situations studied in Bernstein and Labov, respectively. In Craig (1974; Craig and Carter, to appear), I examine evidence to show that habitual Jamaican Creole speakers and speakers of English have different styles of communicating, that these communication differences are similar in kind to those noticed in metropolitan countries between social class extremes, and that there is no reason to assume that users of the contrasting communication styles are not performing fully equivalent cognitive operations on the same given subject matter; I further suggest that each communication style has its advantages for special purposes, but that neither is absolutely superior to the other.

It seems certain that primary education in all types of creole-language contexts would be subject in different ways to the effects of communication differences such as those referred to; and, unless the nature of such differences is understood, educators in creole-language contexts might be led into unfounded assumptions similar to those that underlie the theories of cultural and linguistic deprivation. The fact that communication differences of the relevant kind appear not only between the European-based creoles and their respective standard languages, but also between other creoles and their standard languages, points to the universality of the danger. Heine (1975), for example, points out that African-based pidgin-creoles (like the Swahili and Zulu pidgins, for example) have the following universal characteristics relative to their respective standard African languages: (a) lower type-token ratios; (b) suppression of redundant distinctions of number and gender; (c) fewer noun-class distinctions; (d) fewer distinctions of tense and modality; (e) fewer complex sentences and fewer markers of types of embedding; (f) more conjoining as a means of linking sentences. There is a striking similarity between these characteristics and those of the Bernstein restricted code relative to the elaborated code, nonstandard English relative to Standard English, and European-based creoles relative to their standard languages; the implications for primary education in all cases seem to be exactly the same.

In a Creole-English continuum, characteristics related to those mentioned above might have implications for the theory of language (Craig 1975). What is important for education, and primary education particularly, is that educators must understand that the features of signalling systems (i.e., languages) give speakers many alternatives for the expression of identical sets of meanings. All signalling systems would not necessarily give the same alternatives, but it is wrong to conclude from this that speakers themselves differ in terms of the meanings they can or cannot process in any given, naturally evolving, signalling system, or in terms of their own innate capacities. There is no point, for example, in assuming that the Standard English speaker who says:

(1) He has no sincerity

is doing anything different from the creole-influenced speaker who does not possess the term *sincerity* in his lexicon, but would say instead (in one creole language)

(2) / im neva du   wa   im se/
he never does what he says

of, if *does* is inappropriate for the desired, specific meaning of *sincerity*, substitutes some other more appropriate verb. But many educators, and the theory of linguistic-cultural deprivation in general, would tend to regard the possession of the abstract-noun category, to which *sincerity* belongs, as necessarily indicating a cognitive capacity greater than what would be indicated if that category were absent in the language of the speaker.

The final conclusions from these facts are first, that if the attitudes of the speech community and national convenience permit the use of a creole language in education, there is no reason to believe that the creole language will be in any way inadequate as a vehicle for thought and expression; the human being seems to have a universal capacity to make all languages equivalent in this respect. Second, if creole-speaking children have to acquire a standard language in school, then the style of communication will tend to be a contrastive factor in the same way as phonology, morphology, and syntax could be contrastive factors. Finally, any type of behavior involving the overt or covert use of language could be affected by communication differences of the kind here referred to. This last point deserves a further comment, although an adequate treatment of it cannot be given here.

A special type of behavior that could be affected by communication differences and that has been much used in the theory of linguistic-cultural deprivation is performance in intelligence or mental achievement tests. However, the involvement of language as a factor in such performance has been known ever since the pioneering work in the 1920s by Vygotsky (e.g., 1962), Luria (1961, Luria and Yudovich 1959), and several others. In the latter it is shown that the possession of language for specific items, attributes, or relationships assists in the performance of cognitive operations involving those items, attributes, or relationships. Not much notice has been taken of the fact, however, that the types of performance required in many educational tests of the mental achievement type are exactly those that can be assisted by possession of the lexical categories and relationships that belong to the communication style of standard languages. Craig and Carter (1976) examine an instance of performance in language aptitude and intelligence tests where this factor seems to operate, but much more study needs to be given to this and related questions. What seems certain, however, is that it would be unwise to use the criteria of standard-language-based educational tests in cases where creole-speaking children are to be compared with other children. Furthermore, mere adaptation of such tests by translating their superficial features into specific creole languages would not be sufficient to render them suitable; the very bases of their requirements in terms of how the latter relate to the communication characteristics of creoles would need to be examined.

The field of creole languages in relation to education holds many interesting questions for further study.

REFERENCES

Alatis, J. E., ed. 1969. *Twentieth Round Table Meeting.* Washington, D.C.: Georgetown University School of Languages and Linguistics.

ALSED. 1972. *The Role of Linguistics and Socio-Linguistics in Language Education and Policy.* Document ED/WS/286. Paris: UNESCO.

Anastasi, A., and Cordova, F. A. 1953. Some effects of bilingualism upon the intelligence test performance of Puerto Rican children in New York City. *Journal of Educational Psychology* XLIV:1.

Bailey, B. L. 1964. Some problems in the language teaching situation in Jamaica. In *Social Dialects and Language Learning,* R. W. Shuy, ed., pp. 105-11.

_____. 1971. Jamaican Creole: can dialect boundaries be defined? In *Pidginization and Creolization of Languages,* Dell Hymes, ed. London: Cambridge University Press, pp. 341-48.

Bereiter, C.; Engleman, S.; Osborn, J.; and Reiford, P. A. 1966. An academically oriented pre-school for culturally deprived children. In *Pre-School Education Today,* F. M. Hechinger, ed., pp. 105-37.

Bernstein, B. 1961a. Social structure, language and learning. *Educational Research* 3:163.

_____. 1961b. Social class and linguistic development: A theory of social learning. In *Economy, Education and Society,* A. H. Halsey, J. Floud, and A. Anderson, eds. New York: The Free Press.

_____. 1961c. Aspects of language and learning in the genesis of the social process. *Journal of Child Psychology and Psychiatry* 1:313. Reprint 1964, Hymes, *Language, Culture and Society,* pp. 251-63.

_____. 1962a. Linguistic codes, hesitation phenomena and intelligence. *Language and Speech* 5:31-46.

_____. 1962b. Social class, linguistic codes and grammatical elements. *Language and Speech* 5:221-40.

_____. 1965. A socio-linguistic approach to social learning. In *Social Science Survey,* J. Gould, ed. London: Penguin, pp. 144-68.

_____. 1966. Elaborated and restricted codes. An outline. In *Explorations in Sociolinguistics,* S. Liberson, ed. *Social Enquiry* 36.

_____. 1972. A critique of the concept of compensatory education. In *Functions of Language in the Classroom,* Cazden, John, and Hymes, eds., pp. 135-57.

Bickerton, D. 1972. The structure of polylectal grammars. In *Social Dialects and Language Learning,* Shuy, ed., pp. 17-42.

_____. 1973. On the nature of a creole continuum. *Language* 49:640-69.

Bruner, J. S.; Goodnow, J. J.; and Austin, G. A. 1956. *A Study of Thinking.* London: Chapman and Hall.

Bruner, J. S., and Olver, R. 1966. *Studies in Cognitive Growth.* New York: Wiley.

Cazden, C. B.; John, V. P.; and Hymes, D. 1972. *Functions of Language in the Classroom.* Columbia University: Teachers College Press.

Cheeseman, H. R. 1949. In A. Isidro, *Ang wikang pambasa at ang paarlan.* Manila: Bureau of Printing.

Corbin, R., and Crosby, M. 1965. *Language Programs for the Disadvantaged.* Champaign, Ill.: The National Council of Teachers of English.

Craig, D. R. 1966. Teaching English to Jamaican Creole speakers. *Language Learning* 16(1-2):49-61.

———. 1971. Education and Creole English in the West Indies: Some sociolinguistic factors. In *Pidginization and Creolization of Languages,* Hymes, ed., pp. 371-91.

———. 1974. Developmental and social class differences in language. *Caribbean Journal of Education,* Vol. 1, pp. 5-23. Jamaica, West Indies.

———. 1975. A Creole English continuum and the theory of grammar. Paper presented at the International Conference on Pidgins and Creoles, University of Hawaii. To appear, Hawaii University Press.

Craig, D. R. and Carter, S. 1976. The language learning aptitudes of Jamaican children at the secondary level. *Caribbean Journal of Education,* Vol. 3, No. 1., pp. 1-21.

———. To appear. *Social Class and the Use of Language: A Case Study of Young Jamaican Children.* Arlington, Va.: Center for Applied Linguistics.

Crow, L. D.; Murray, W. I.; and Smythe, H. A. 1966. *Education and the Culturally Disadvantaged Child.* New York: David McKay.

Davis, F. B., ed. 1967. *Philippine Language-Teaching Experiments.* Quezon City, Philippines: Alemar-Phoenix.

DeCamp, D. 1971. Toward a generative analysis of a post-creole speech continuum. In Hymes, ed., pp. 13-42.

Eichorn, D. H., and Jones, H. E. 1952. Bilingualism. Chapter 2 of *Review of Educational Research,* Vol. XXII, 5.

Fishman, J. A., and Lovas, J. 1970. Bilingual education in sociolinguistic perspective. TESOL Quarterly 4:215-22.

Goodnow, J. J. 1968. Cultural variations in cognitive skills. In *Cross Cultural Studies,* D. R. Price-Williams, ed., pp. 246-64.

Hancock, I. F. 1971. A survey of the pidgins and creoles of the world. In Hymes, ed., pp. 509-24.

Hechinger, F. M., ed. 1966. *Pre-School Education Today.* Garden City, N. Y.: Doubleday.

Heine, B. 1975. Some generalizations on African-based pidgins. Paper prepared for the International Conference on Pidgins and Creoles, University of Hawaii.

Hymes, D., ed. 1971. *Pidginization and Creolization of Languages*. London: Cambridge University Press.

Klein, W. n.d. The dialect differences of Haitian Creole. Mimeographed.

Labov, W. 1964. Stages in the acquisition of standard English. In *Social Dialects and Language Learning,* Shuy, ed., pp. 77-103.

———. 1965. A Preliminary Study of the Structure of English Used by Negro and Puerto Rican Speakers in New York City. Cooperative Research Project 3091, Columbia University.

———. 1966. *The Social Stratification of English*. Washington, D. C.: Center for Applied Linguistics.

———. 1969. The logic of non-standard English. In Alatis, ed., pp. 1-43.

Lambert, W. E., and Tucker, G. R. 1972. *Bilingual Education of Children: The St Lambert Experiment.* Rowley, Mass.: Newbury House Publishers, Inc.

Luria, A. R. 1961. *The Role of Speech in the Regulation of Normal and Abnormal Behaviour.* London & New York: Pergamon Press.

Luria, A. R., and Yudovich, I. 1959. *Speech and the Development of Mental Processes in the Child.* London: Staples Press.

Pompilus, P. 1973. *L'Etude comparée du créole et du français.* Port-Au-Prince: Editions Caraibes.

Prator, C. H. 1950. *Language Teaching in the Philippines.* Manila: U.S. Educational Foundation in the Philippines.

Price-Williams, D. R., ed. 1969. *Cross Cultural Studies.* London: Penguin Modern Psychology Readings.

Rice, F. A., ed. 1962. *Study of the Role of Second Languages in Asia, Africa and Latin America.* Arlington, Va.: Center for Applied Linguistics.

Schaedel, R. P., and Rubin, V., eds. 1975. *The Haitian Potential: Research and Resources of Haiti.* New York and London: Teachers College, Columbia University Press.

Selinker, L. 1972. Interlanguage. *International Review of Applied Linguistics in Language Learning* 10:3.

Shuy, R. W., ed. 1964. *Social Dialects and Language Learning.* Champaign, Ill.: The National Council of Teachers of English.

———, ed. 1972. *Proceedings of the Twenty-Third Annual Round Table.* Washington, D. C.: Georgetown University.

Stewart, W. A. 1962. Creole languages in the Caribbean. In Rice, ed., pp. 34-53.

Vernon, P. E. 1955. *The Bearing of Recent Advances in Psychology on Educational Problems.* Studies in Education 7. University of London Institute of Education.

————. 1965a. Environmental handicaps and intellectual development. *British Journal of Educational Psychology* 35:1-12, 117-26.

————. 1965b. Ability factors and environmental influences. *American Psychologist* 20:723-33.

————. 1966. Education and intellectual development among Canadian Indians and Eskimos. *Educational Review* 18:79-91, 186-95.

————. 1967. Abilities and educational attainments in an east African environment. In Price-Williams, ed., pp. 76-91.

Valdman, A. 1969. The language situation in Haiti. In Schaedel and Rubin, eds., pp. 61-82.

Vincent, T. 1972. Pidgin in Nigerian literature. Paper presented at the Conference on Creole Languages and Educational Development, sponsored by the ALSED Programme of UNESCO and the University of the West Indies, Trinidad.

Vygotsky, L. S. 1962. *Thought and Language*. Cambridge, Mass.: MIT Press. Printing of the edition translated by E. Haufmann and G. Vakar.

West, M. 1926. *Bilingualism (With Special Reference to Bengal)*. Calcutta: Government of India Central Publication Branch. Bureau of Education Occasional Reports, No. 13.

Wolfram, W. 1970. Sociolinguistic alternatives in teaching reading to non-standard speakers. *Reading Research Quarterly* VI,1:9-33.

Pidgins, Creoles, Lingue Franche, and National Development

Stephen A. Wurm

1. INTRODUCTION

1.1. *General remarks*

The factors leading to the development of pidgins and creoles have been discussed elsewhere in this volume. Traditionally, such languages occupy clearly definable positions in the linguistic hierarchy of a society that is strongly stratified linguistically and socially, and their functions and role are determined by the class standing of their speakers and the social situations in which they are used within and across class boundaries.

In recent years, there have been fundamental political and social changes in many parts of the world in which pidgins and creoles are spoken. The social positions of the speakers of such languages have, in such areas, undergone radical changes, and this has far-reaching effects upon the standing, functions, and use of these languages. In particular, some languages that until recently carried the stigma of low-caste languages—and continue to do so in the eyes of some members of the new social setups—have suddenly been elevated to much higher social and functional levels than has hitherto been the case.

A typical instance of such a development has been observable in Papua New Guinea, where, of the two widespread pidgin languages, New Guinea Pidgin (formerly also referred to as Neo-Melanesian), particularly, has undergone a considerable reorientation of its status and functional role in recent years. The other pidgin language, Hiri Motu (formerly known as Police Motu), has very recently experienced a similar development after having been rather overshadowed by Pidgin in recent years. Comparable developments are beginning to take shape in the British Solomon Islands with regard to Solomon Islands Pidgin, and it may not be too far-fetched to suggest that Bichelamar (or Pislama), the pidgin language of the New Hebrides, may be heading for a similar change in the not-too-distant future.

1.2. *New Guinea Pidgin in recent times*

New Guinea Pidgin has, in its main sociolectal forms and function (Mühlhäusler 1975b, 1977a), typically become the vehicle of expression of a newly emerging, and in many places already emerged, subculture in Papua New Guinea that replaces the traditional culture, and whose domain lies between this culture (for which the vernacular is the linguistic vehicle) and the superimposed Western culture (whose means of expression is English). For this purpose, New Guinea Pidgin is fully adequate, and the power of expression of Pidgin has remained in step with the gradual evolution and increasing complexity of the subculture. In several areas, Pidgin is beginning to replace or has already replaced the local vernaculars on its way toward creolization.

However, sudden shifts in the role of such languages tend to put them into positions in which their previous ranges of applicability and efficiency are inadequate for the type of communication now required. Recent political developments on the Papua New Guinea scene and the rapid progress of the country toward independence have created a situation in which very sizable groups expect Pidgin to extend its role into areas of expression and communication in which it has not been used previously. Such areas are, for instance, (a) its prevalent use as a debate language in the House of Assembly (the Papua New Guinea Parliament) on issues—often of great political and legal complexity—that traditionally have been referred to in the English language; (b) its increasing use in broadcasting, where it is used to report on world news and for the discussion of political, economic, social, and other concerns that sometimes require quite high levels of complexity of expression; (c) its comparable use in writing in the press; (d) its increasing role in educational matters.

It seems clear that Pidgin, in the forms that it had at the beginning of these developments, was not an adequate tool for uses such as those outlined above, in spite of the fact that, in contrast to other pidgin languages of the world, it was very close to being a fully fledged first language even when used as a second language by its speakers (Todd [1974] uses the term "expanded pidgin" for it). In particular, the size and range of its vocabulary fell far short of being able to satisfy the requirements of expression. While the internal structure of New Guinea Pidgin contains quite powerful means of word formation and creation (Mühlhäusler 1973, 1975a; Wurm, Mühlhäusler, and Laycock 1977), the necessary expansion of its lexicon has unfortunately not taken place to any great extent through internal creation, but through wholesale borrowing from English. In many instances, the newly introduced lexemes violate the rules underlying the lexicon of New Guinea Pidgin and seriously endanger its continued existence as an independent language.

In addition to this problem, the generally unplanned (or if planned, largely amateurish), unsystematic, and haphazard interference with New Guinea Pidgin has to a great extent threatened the previously considerable uniformity that characterized its main sociolectal form, Rural Pidgin (Mühlhäusler 1977a, 1977b, 1977c), and has contributed to the establishment of another main sociolectal form, Urban Pidgin. This has resulted both in a partial breakdown of one of Pidgin's main functions, i.e., to constitute a major lingua franca in Papua New Guinea, and in Pidgin's becoming less and less uniform even within the individual sociolects.

Clearly, a situation has developed regarding New Guinea Pidgin in which concerted language-planning actions are urgently called for, and increasing attention is being paid to this problem in Papua New Guinea.

2. LANGUAGE PLANNING IN GENERAL

Before the question of language planning and New Guinea Pidgin can be discussed in detail, a few general remarks on language planning and on the exceedingly complex linguistic scene in Papua New Guinea and some adjacent areas may be helpful.

One form of language planning constitutes, in essence, a preconceived and systematic interference with the normal dynamic processes to which every language is subject, be it in terms of channelling such processes into a specific direction, artificially accelerating or retarding them, encouraging some of their facets at the expense of others, or even introducing into the languages features that lie outside their rules and setup. A different system of language planning is concerned with artificially interfering with the existing social and functional status of a given language by means of channelling it in certain directions, or in general either broadening and/or elevating its role and standing, or narrowing it to the point of suppresssion. This situation creates a terminological problem: it may seem appropriate to apply the label "language planning" to the latter variety only, and "language engineering" to the former. Alternatively, "language planning" could be used to refer to the stages of deliberation and programmatic planning in preparation for active interference with a language or languages in any form, and "language engineering" to the processes of this active interference itself (Wurm, Mühlhäusler, Laycock 1977). However, for our purposes we shall employ the terms "internal language planning" for the first and "external language planning" for the second of the two possibilities, though there may be some difficulties in establishing a clearcut boundary between the two in all cases.

3. THE LINGUISTIC SCENE IN PAPUA NEW GUINEA AND FURTHER EAST, AND EXTERNAL LANGUAGE PLANNING

As a background to the discussion of facets of language planning, it is necessary to elaborate on the language situation in these areas, particularly in Papua New Guinea.

3.1. *The indigenous languages*

The total number of distinct indigenous languages in Papua New Guinea is about 760, with most of these languages spoken by small to very small speech communities. Relatively few of these languages have more than 10,000 speakers, and the largest language, Enga, has only about 150,000 speakers. In the British Solomon Islands, 87 indigenous languages are found, and in the Banks Islands and New Hebrides 110 indigenous languages have been identified.

3.2. Lingue franche

It is not surprising that, in addition to providing a favorable background for widespread bi- and multilingualism, this exceedingly complex language situation led to the emergence of a number of lingue franche in the area as soon as social situations arose in which there was a need for intercommunication across several language boundaries—especially intercommunication going beyond that with neighboring language communities only (which could adequately be served by bi- and multilingualism). In what is today the area of Papua New Guinea, three distinct situations of this kind occurred, which resulted in the development of three different types of lingue franche, at least two of which owe their emergence directly to the impact of the modern world. In addition to these, English, as a fourth lingua franca, made its appearance as a result of direct external language planning.

3.2.1. Missionary lingue franche. One of these three types is constituted by the missionary lingue franche that resulted from the adoption of certain local languages by various missions for their activities. In most cases, the missions did not give very much consideration to selecting a language in the light of its potential suitability as a lingua franca, i.e., taking into account the number of its speakers in contrast to that of other languages of the area, its close relationship or otherwise to neighboring languages, the potential prestige of the tribe speaking it, etc. Often, when the missions were first established in certain areas, these factors were not known, especially in the early days of missionary activity in what is today Papua New Guinea. The missions were predominantly concerned with the suitability of the locations for the intended missionary activities, and the language of the location chosen was then adopted as the mission language. As a result, some of the missionary lingue franche in Papua New Guinea were the most suitable candidates for adoption in light of the criteria mentioned above; others were not.

With the expansion of the activities of given missions beyond the boundaries of the areas in which the languages adopted were tribally spoken, and the continuing use of these languages by the missions in the linguistically different neighboring areas, the currency of these languages was artificially extended, at least for matters relating to missionary, church, and associated activities. This fact, which constituted acts of external language planning, made these languages regional lingue franche, but their currency was largely restricted to speakers who belonged to a particular social orientation. At the same time, the tribe whose language had been adopted by a mission as the church language and missionary lingua franca, and the language itself, tended to rise in prestige in the eyes of indigenes who were not committed to that particular mission and church (unless they were committed to a different mission using another lingua franca), and such indigenes were sometimes inclined to look toward that tribe, the mastery of the lingua franca, and, as a result, the mission itself, as a source of possible economic and other advantages. Such a situation could lead to the adoption of a missionary lingua franca as a general lingua franca in an area adjacent to that of the tribe whose language had become this lingua franca—Kâte, one of the three church languages used by the New Guinea Lutheran Mission, is a case in point (Wurm 1966).

The adoption of English for primary education in 1953 (see below) brought about a decline in the use of missionary lingue franche, and events in recent years caused them to recede more and more before the onslaught of New Guinea Pidgin, and, to a much lesser extent, of Hiri Motu, and to narrow their functions— mostly as the consequence of deliberate acts of external language planning.

3.2.2. *Hiri Motu.* The second type of lingua franca in Papua New Guinea is represented by Hiri Motu (formerly Police Motu). This language is a native-based pidgin language that came into being, in a form directly ancestral to its present form, as a lingua franca used within and by the native police force in British New Guinea, i.e., Papua, around the turn of the twentieth century (Dutton and Brown 1977). Before that time, i.e., in pre-European times, a special trade language (or languages) was (or were) used by members of the Motu tribe, of the present-day Port Moresby area, on their frequent trading expeditions to the west, to the present Kerema coastal area in the Gulf District, where they bartered clay pots, shell ornaments, and stone axes for sago, canoe logs, and other products. This trade language, of which we have only a few unreliable records, may well have been a simplified Motu (an Austronesian language) with a high lexical content from the Papuan, i.e., non-Austronesian, languages of the Kerema area and some structural modifications reflecting that Papuan influence.

Whether the lingua franca adopted by the police force represented a new development unrelated to the trade language mentioned above or whether it was a continuation of one (or more) of these or a modification of them, is difficult to say in the absence of evidence. Dutton and Brown (1977) mention, however, that it seems likely, in view of the fact that the police force consisted largely of Papuans from outside the area of Motu proper, that some form of the trade language, relexified with Motu vocabulary, formed the basis of the new lingua franca, which is not readily understandable for speakers of Motu proper if they have not previously been exposed to it (Wurm 1964).

Over the years, the language spread as a far-flung, but still regional, lingua franca through most of Papua, and between World Wars I and II, its encouragement as a lingua franca and its use by the police force and administrative officers led to the elimination of Pidgin in Papua—an effective act of external language planning. After the end of World War II, and particularly during the last decade, Police Motu had more or less rapidly been giving up ground to New Guinea Pidgin in Papua and losing its importance in many areas. Not much conscious external language planning was involved in this development, which could be regarded as a consequence of the rapid spread of Pidgin as a lingua franca throughout Papua New Guinea and the influx of Pidgin speakers into areas in which Police Motu used to hold sway. The unwillingness of most expatriate Europeans to learn Police Motu, and their decided preference to use Pidgin, of which most Europeans in Papua New Guinea had at least a rudimentary knowledge, can also be assumed to have aided this development. In recent years, since the rapid progress toward self-government in Papua New Guinea, and independence in 1975, the New Guinea Government carried out, more or less consciously, acts of external language planning that had a bearing on the respective positions of Pidgin and Police Motu—such as the prevalent use of Pidgin as a debate language in the Papua New Guinea House of Assembly, in contrast to Police Motu, which was hardly used, though equally admissible under the rules; the much more extensive use of Pidgin than of Police Motu in the media; the encouragement of the use of Pidgin in primary education; etc. All this seemed to augur badly for the future of Police Motu, but it has, in very recent times, staged a marked recovery. It has, in parts of Papua, been adopted as a symbol of self-identity and chosen as a rallying point for the current separatist movement in Papua—a clear act of external language planning by a political group. As a result, Police Motu—now renamed Hiri Motu—has sharply risen in prestige, and also in the numbers of its speakers: indigenes from Pidgin areas who live in Port Moresby, for instance, and who, for many years, have found it unnecessary to acquire a knowledge of the language, now face social situations in which there is heavy pressure on them to know Hiri Motu, and its knowledge is rapidly spreading among them. Its mastery, or that of Pidgin, is now one of the prerequisites for Papua New Guinea citizenship, and in general the language is treated officially by the Papua New Guinea Government as equivalent to Pidgin, as another major general language—again an act of external language planning.

3.2.3. *New Guinea Pidgin.* The third type of lingua franca in Papua New Guinea is represented by New Guinea Pidgin. Contrary to earlier views (Wurm 1966) that New Guinea Pidgin owed its origin directly to Queensland Plantation Pidgin, itself a descendant of nineteenth-century South Seas Pidgin English, recent research by Mühlhäusler (1975d) has shown that the influence of Queensland Plantation English upon the development of New Guinea Pidgin has been secondary, and more indirect, i.e., more via the main recruiting areas of indentured labor for the South Seas plantations. At the same time, Mühlhäusler could establish that the earliest form of a stable New Guinea Pidgin was found in the area of the Duke of York Islands, to the north of the Gazelle Peninsula of New Britain, around 1882. Mühlhäusler holds the view that the establishment of this earliest form of New Guinea Pidgin owes its origin to the development of a stabilized plantation Pidgin on Samoa. Recruitment for the Samoa plantations was, after 1879, from the Duke of York area, and the first laborers returned there from Samoa in 1882. This is the year in which the first plantations were established in the Blanche Bay area of the Gazelle Peninsula, and on Bulea, with labor from Bougainville and New Ireland, and it seems plausible that experienced ex-Samoan laborers were employed as overseers. The newly stabilized language seems subsequently to have gone through an enrichment of its lexicon with Tolai and German words in the administrative center of Rabaul. With the spread of administrative control and pacification through much of German New Guinea, intercommunication across tribal boundaries became important, and New Guinea Pidgin became nativized, or primarily a linguistic tool for intertribal communication. This resulted in its becoming an expanded pidgin, i.e., very near to the speakers' first language in its range of expression and functions. Little conscious external language planning entered into this development, though the police force and administrative agents were of course highly instrumental in the spread of Pidgin.

When German New Guinea was taken over by the British and Australian forces in 1914, New Guinea Pidgin was firmly established in the area. Its stabilization, nativization, and spread continued thereafter, and regional dialects and distinct sociolects began to develop. Most of these developments were not the result of external language planning. However, acts of internal language planning carried out by the Catholic mission and aimed at the standardization of Pidgin in the fields of orthography, lexicon, and grammar led to the emergence of two distinct dialects (mainland Pidgin versus Islands Pidgin). This differentiation stemmed from the differing views on the standardization of Pidgin held by members of the Catholic missions of Alexishafen near Madang on the mainland and in New Britain. Also, the standardization and description by the Catholic mission tended to lag behind the linguistic developments in spoken Pidgin and resulted in the emergence of a kind of archaic Church Pidgin. At the same time, Pidgin began to spread in the highlands toward the mid-thirties, with its main source the anglicized Pidgin spoken by many patrol officers and other members of the administration.

World War II brought about a fundamental change in the social setup in Papua New Guinea and led to the emergence of new social patterns in which Pidgin was to have new functions (Mühlhäusler 1977b). The importance of Pidgin was suddenly recognized by the Australian authorities, and the prewar social barriers between indigenes and Europeans broke down, especially with regard to members of the armed forces. Pidgin began to function as a means of expressing solidarity among all racial groups in Papua New Guinea. These events can be regarded as more or less deliberate acts of external language planning—but much more deliberate acts were performed in the extensive use of Pidgin in war propaganda, with a view to strong social control. In addition, the large-scale recruiting by the armed forces of natives from many, often remote, areas as carriers and laborers led to an increase in the number of the speakers of Pidgin and resulted in its spread into new areas.

After the end of World War II, Pidgin continued and accelerated its spread through Papua New Guinea, a regional dialect became stabilized and nativized in the highlands, and Pidgin began to make inroads into the realm of Police Motu—the first steps toward this had already taken place during the war years. The breakdown of the social barriers between indigenes and Europeans, initiated during the war, continued and resulted in the gradual change of Pidgin from a caste language to one suited for new roles in the changed Papua New Guinea society.

In the early fifties, an event of fundamental importance took place on the Papua New Guinea sociolinguistic scene: English began, for the first time, to play a major role with regard to the indigenous population, with primary schools switching to English as the main—and in the Government schools the sole—medium of instruction. Indigenes were beginning to be encouraged to learn and use English. At the same time, the United Nations Organizations called upon Australia in 1953 (Hall 1955) to discontinue the use of Pidgin in the then Trust Territory of New Guinea. This was an unrealistic and ill-informed pronouncement, because the Australian administration had no control over the use of what was, at that time, a nativized lingua franca whose main function was to serve intercommunication among the indigenous population. The pronouncement did, however, have the effect of strengthening the pro-English language policies of the administration, though after that time the spread of Pidgin accelerated at an increasing rate, both geographically and with regard to its social functions. A new sociolect of Pidgin, Urban Pidgin, which had previously had only a limited existence, became well established and developed. New styles such as written style, style of radio announcing, etc. emerged. Regional dialect development, especially in the highlands, first reached a peak during the early sixties, with subsequent gradual neutralization of regional variants resulting from the increasing mobility of the population and the widening impact of mass media. English influence on Pidgin steadily increased, particularly in Urban Pidgin. Creolization of Pidgin in some areas began to become a factor, though it had little influence on the form of the language for sociolinguistic reasons: the children who were and are the speakers of creolized Pidgin had to conform to the nativized, extended forms of Pidgin that were already in constant daily use in internative communication situations.

During the seventies, the functional extension of Pidgin accelerated: it became the first and main debate language in the Papua New Guinea House of Assembly, was more and more used in the media, and began to be used again in primary education. As has already been mentioned above in 1.1., it became the means of expression of a new contact culture lying between the traditional and the Western. With the extension and spread of this subculture at the expense of the traditional, the functional and geographical role of Pidgin increased, and Pidgin entered into a diglossic relation with English in urban environments. The sociolects became clearly established, with Rural Pidgin and Urban Pidgin the main variants, and Bush Pidgin and Tok Masta (the broken English spoken by Europeans) as fringe forms (Mühlhäusler 1975b, 1977d). At the same time, stabilization and regional and sociolectal uniformity in given areas and sociolects began to disappear, with fluidity and variability appearing at an increasing rate. This development is largely attributable to the powerful influence of English, and to the fact that because of the lack of insight into the nature of Pidgin and insufficient coordination of language planning, the necessary linguistic elaboration accompanying the functional extensions of Pidgin took place in an ad hoc way (Mühlhäusler 1977f). These factors disrupt the basic underlying rules of Pidgin and threaten its existence as a separate language.[1]

3.2.4. *Solomon Islands Pidgin and Bichelamar.* It may be briefly mentioned that Solomon Islands Pidgin and the New Hebridean Bichelamar (or Pislama), which, according to Mühlhäusler (1977b) can be much more readily accepted as direct descendants of Queensland Plantation English than New Guinea Pidgin, are beginning to move toward an expansion of their functions, especially Solomon Islands Pidgin. Both these languages have functioned as caste languages and internative lingue franche, almost until the present, but with important political changes on the horizon in the Solomon Islands and the indigenous population beginning to take on new social roles, the status and functional range of Solomon Islands Pidgin is beginning to alter fundamentally. Similar developments may well be in the offing for the New Hebrides in the foreseeable future.

To complete the picture, the existence of some missionary lingue franche in parts of the Solomon Islands and the New Hebrides must be briefly mentioned. Of these, especially the Mota language was used widely in earlier days, but its importance has very much declined during the past decades.

3.2.5. *English and French.* When speaking of lingue franche in the area, the two metropolitan languages, English and, in the New Hebrides, also French, have to be briefly mentioned. They differ fundamentally from the languages mentioned so far by being languages introduced into the areas and used by colonial rulers and masters; thus their use as lingue franche was the result of strict external language planning and control.

At the same time, these languages are not in any form subject to internal language planning (if we disregard some limited attempts at the use of Basic English in Papua New Guinea). However, these languages constitute target and lexifying languages for several of the major lingue franche of the region, and the pervading influence, especially of English, has already had a decisive influence on the linguistic structure of at least one of the main sociolects of the largest lingua franca of the area, New Guinea Pidgin.

4. INTERNAL LANGUAGE PLANNING AND NEW GUINEA PIDGIN

What has been said in the above sections constitutes the necessary background to the discussion of internal language planning. New Guinea will be singled out for this purpose.

4.1. *Facets of internal language planning*

As has been pointed out, internal language planning relating to a particular language is concerned with active interference with the form and internal nature of that language. The reasons for such actions, which can be directed at all levels of a language, such as lexicon, grammatical and even phonological structure, style, expression, and discourse patterns and, in written form, orthography, are manifold and can be basically (1) restrictive and (2) creative facets. Restrictive facets would, for instance, be: (a) the standardization of the language through artificial neutralization of its dialectal and sociolectal variations (or, in written form, of its orthographic variations); (b) the elimination of free fluctuation, linked creatively with the introduction of predetermined stablilization (in its written form, this could also refer to the orthography of a language); (c) the artificial stemming of the tide of a foreign influence, which usually manifests itself in vocabulary and can violate established rules of the language, but can potentially also affect various other levels of structure. This can be coupled with the creative act of artificial encouragement of established features and rules of the language that achieve linguistic ends equivalent to those for which the foreign impact is striving; (d) the artificial suppression and elimination of a particular script or alphabet used for a language and, as a creative facet, the invention of a new one and the replacement of the former by it; etc. Creative facets would, for instance, be concerned with (a) the reduction to writing of hitherto unwritten languages through the creation of alphabets; (b) the standardization of the alphabets and/or orthographies of a language for which two or more parallel alphabets and/or orthographies have been in use, through the creation and introduction of a new standard alphabet and/or orthography; (c) the artificial enlargement and expansion of the lexicon of a language, e.g., through means as mentioned above under (c); (d) the artificial introduction of grammatical rules into the standard target form of a language. Such rules may already be found in some varieties of the language and would permit increased differentiation and/or standardization of expression. Some examples from New Guinea Pidgin would be: In some variants, *-wan* is used to form attributive adjectives that permit a formal distinction between adjectives and verbs in the predicate, e.g., *man i strongwan* = "the man is strong," *man i strong* = "the man insists"; in other variants, a distinction is made between *mi laik kaikai* = "I will eat soon" and *mi laik i kaikai* = "I want to eat"; (e) the artificial creation of different styles, forms of expression, discourse, and specialized jargons for given purposes.

4.2. *Reasons for internal language planning*

The reasons for such actions in a given language situation are implicit in the points listed above and can be summed up as: (1) the presence of dialectal and sociolectal differences and/or inherent variability and fluctuation in the language, and the absence of a standard form; (2) conflict, be it social or otherwise, with regard to parallel forms of a language and the question of what constitutes the standard or predominant form, and in what function or functions; (3) temporary shortcomings—usually on the lexical level but also on other structural levels—of a given language, in any of its varieties, that prevent it from adequately fulfilling a given social role at a given point in time. This is the result of the rapid movement of the language into a new and different social function or functions (the language requires time to adapt to such a new situation); (4) the need for special styles or registers as a means of expression for certain new social functions; (5) the overloading of a language, usually as a result of reason (3), with foreign loan elements, predominantly in its lexicon, which violates the rules underlying the lexicon and structure of the language and endangers its continued existence as a separate language.

With special reference to the written form of a language, the reasons for internal language planning can be: (6) in the case of a heretofore unwritten language, the absence of an alphabet for it; (7) the utilization of a script or alphabet for a language that is inadequate and/or unsuitable for graphic-linguistic or social reasons; (8) the absence of a standardized alphabet and/or orthography, or the presence of two or more alphabets and/or orthographies with potential or real conflict between them; etc.

4.3. Background facets and applicability of internal language planning decisions

4.3.1. *General remarks.* Any internal language planning is, like all forms of language planning, based on a number of background considerations, such as the factors affecting the degree of technical applicability of various actions. Internal language planning has two main phases: the conceiving and working out of the steps to be taken to carry out specific acts, and the practical application of such steps.

4.3.2. *Policy matters.* The background considerations referred to above constitute what may be termed philosophical, or in political parlance, policy questions of a general order. For instance, let us say that a particular language, either as a result of natural development or of acts of external language planning, has assumed certain social roles and functions and shows shortcomings such as those listed above as providing reasons for internal language planning. The question may then well arise in the minds of governmental and other authorities whether such acts of internal language planning should be considered and implemented, or whether the situation should officially be left untouched in the hope that it might right itself anyway. Factors influencing such decisions are often political in nature and outside the scope of this chapter. Suffice it to say that in actual situations, the final approaches to such problems tend to be very vague solutions— compromises between the two possible extremes of total planning and total laissez-faire; or the planning action may be vigorous but the implementation of the plans inadequate, or the results nullified either through other, contradictory official actions or the lack of some necessary official action.

4.3.3. *Applicability and implementation of decisions.* Concerning the factors affecting the technical applicability of various facets of internal language planning, it must be pointed out (Wurm 1975a) that standardization and artificial influencing of language forms are very much easier to put into effect with regard to the written form of a language than to its spoken form. The standardized European languages provide ample evidence of this. Standardization of the written language form can apply, in increasing order of difficulty, to orthography, vocabulary, grammar, and style. However, the standardization of orthography may encounter emotional, traditionalistic, and other comparable problems. Applying the same standardization principles to the spoken forms of a language presents greater difficulties: the spoken language is more elusive than the written, less subject to conscious control by the speaker, and, because of the much more spontaneous, transient nature of a spoken discourse compared with a written one, automatic pressures upon the standard forms from nonstandard forms already accepted and normally used by the speaker are much greater. In addition, factors that affect the form and nature of discourse, such as emotional attitudes, are much more strongly present in spoken expression than in written. In the written form of a language, the external form of the expression, i.e., the writing system and orthography, is technically the most easily accessible to control and standardization. In contrast, the external form of the spoken expression, i.e., the phonology (or "pronunciation"), is most difficult to control and standardize. Even in highly standardized European languages such as English and German, traces of nonstandard spoken language (in the form of the "local accent" of speakers of the standard language who come from different parts of the language area) have persisted tenaciously in spite of all standardization efforts through the educational systems and through auditory mass media such as radio and television.

With regard to the question of how standardization can take place, the size, nature, and composition of the community concerned are important factors. With very small speech communities, standardization can come about as a result of mutual consent, but under ordinary circumstances it will have to be a process directed from a focal point and take the form of a teaching and implementation procedure, not uncommonly against considerable resistance that will have to be overcome through various methods.

This teaching and implementation procedure will have to be primarily the concern of education, in particular through the school and training systems present in a community. This will have to be strongly supplemented, and put into practical application, through the mass media, i.e., the press and publication facilities for the written form, and radio and television for the spoken. The success of the standardization process initiated through the school system really depends on the cooperation and effectiveness of these mass media.

However, in addition to these factors, the chances of a widespread, or general, acceptance of a standardized written—and spoken—language form are greatly enhanced if this form is persistently adhered to and used by a prestige group that is regarded as such by the great majority of the community, and especially by the authorities in their dealings with the community on all levels.

Furthermore, the standardized language form is much more likely to gain general acceptance if it carries some prestige value of its own, e.g., if mastery of the standard language leads to economic advantages. So, for instance, one prerequisite for obtaining coveted jobs and positions could be a good mastery of the standard language. Such a situation would result in respect and esteem for the standard language and a good mastery of it.

4.4. *New Guinea Pidgin: internal language planning*

4.4.1. *General remarks.* The present state of Pidgin and the need for urgent language planning action relative to it has been pointed out above in 1.2. It may be added that the present and envisaged future increase in the use of Pidgin for educational pursuits, and its role as a general language on many levels of expression and intercommunication, both spoken and written, make its standardization and enrichment through language planning actions imperative.

Such actions are being considered in various quarters, though decisions on them appear to be slow in coming, mainly, it seems, for political reasons involving questions of the status and role of Hiri Motu, and, to some extent, English. Whatever the decisions, it appears that the following may constitute in brief a probable picture of the language planning situation concerning Pidgin:

One fundamental decision of external language planning needs to be made, i.e., which of the parallel forms and variants of Pidgin should become the standard form—or should the authorities strive for a compromise between such forms?

It seems (Wurm 1975a) that the standardization and enrichment of Pidgin would, in the first place, have to be concerned with its written form—a measure of standardization of its spoken form can be achieved almost as a by-product of the use of a written standard form in education, by the press, publishing agencies, and the authorities, and the adoption of a standard spoken form by the auditory mass media.

Bearing this statement in mind, what standard forms on the various levels of language mentioned in 4.3.3., if any, are already available for New Guinea Pidgin to adopt and build on, and how can this be done?

4.4.2. *Areas of applicability of internal language planning to New Guinea Pidgin.*

4.4.2.1. *Orthography.* One standard orthography is used by two major missionary publishing agencies in Papua New Guinea and has also been employed in some important publications, such as Pidgin teaching textbooks that were published elsewhere (e.g., Dutton 1973). However, it is generally not much used by writers of Pidgin, both indigenous and expatriate, who are outside the two missions referred to, it still seems to lack government sanction, and it is not much used in written expression by government instrumentalities and in the House of Assembly. Instead, a great variety of unsystematic and often inconsistent spellings hold sway.

However, it is essential that a standard orthography be accepted universally. To ensure this, its exclusive adoption in education on all the levels on which Pidgin is to be used is needed. At the same time, it is necessary that the orthography be officially sanctioned by the government and designated as the only admissible one for use in government instrumentalities and agencies. Also, the press and publishers need to be encouraged to use that orthography exclusively for all ordinary purposes. Special bonuses placed on the mastery of that orthography, e.g., making it a prerequisite for obtaining government positions, would enhance its spread considerably.

4.4.2.2. *Vocabulary.* Some core vocabulary is available in a few recently published dictionaries of New Guinea Pidgin, but it is limited, and much of it is not employed by speakers of variants of New Guinea Pidgin that differ from the one on which these dictionaries are based. Unsystematic and haphazard additions to the Pidgin lexicon, mostly direct loans from English, are the order of the day in response to a pressing need, and as has been pointed out above in 1.2., these developments violate the fundamental rules of Pidgin lexicon and word formation and threaten the identity of the language (Mühlhäusler 1975c).

It is in the field of vocabulary that internal language planning would have to play its most vital role in New Guinea Pidgin. This work, which could perhaps best be directed and carried out through some official body or institution, something like a Pidgin Academy, would have two distinct facets: one aimed at collecting and assessing the vocabulary items already in use in the various forms of Pidgin and deciding to accept, or reject, observed new items into an envisaged standard Pidgin vocabulary, and another concerned with the active expansion and enrichment of the vocabulary of New Guinea Pidgin. The language has elaborate rules permitting the formation of new lexemes through composition, affixation, the extension of semantic ranges of bases, etc., and this should make possible the establishment of a large number of new lexical items in New Guinea Pidgin that are consistent with the nature and character of the language. Discussions of these processes are found in literature—in addition to some brief early treatments such as Laycock 1969 there are extensive treatments of the subject such as Wurm, Mühlhäusler, and Laycock 1977, and in even much greater detail, Mühlhäusler 1977f. Recourse to direct loans from English is of course unavoidable, but it should be restricted to those instances in which this appears to be the best approach, and such words should be spelled in accordance with New Guinea Pidgin phonology.

A successful dissemination of the results of the work of such a Pidgin Academy with regard to vocabulary may be best achieved through a combination of (1) official sanctioning of such results by the authorities and the government, and authoritative decrees that declare such forms as those to be used in educational establishments, in government instrumentalities, by the media, etc.; (2) the setting of examples by the agencies mentioned under (1); and (3) the availability of awards in terms of praise, increased job opportunities, and perhaps differential pay rates for those who show good aptitude in this line.

4.4.2.3. *Grammar.* A number of descriptions of Pidgin grammar, of varying approaches and detail, have been compiled in recent years after pioneering efforts such as Hall's (1943), e.g., by Mihalic in his dictionary (Mihalic 1957, 1971), Laycock (1970), Wurm (1971), Dutton in his practical introduction (Dutton 1973), and much more extensively, Mühlhäusler (1977g). These studies are, to some extent, at variance with each other with regard to their descriptions and interpretations of grammatical phenomena because of differences in the underlying Pidgin variants discussed, and also because of the importance attached by some to purely descriptive and by others to prescriptive approaches.

While in general there is much less diversity between the variants of Pidgin on the grammatical level than on that of vocabulary, recent developments have tended to lead to a greater extent of variation and fluidity in grammar than was the case before. As a result, differences in grammar between the two main sociolects of Pidgin, Rural Pidgin and Urban Pidgin, have begun to be more accentuated.

Existing descriptions of Pidgin grammar are largely based on earlier Pidgin varieties uninfluenced by English. The gap between the grammar already studied and the unstable and fluid grammars of some present varieties of the language is widening. Grammar is another important area for internal language planning, and the codification and regularization of the grammatical structure of the language would constitute a proper task for the proposed Pidgin Academy. The present variants of Pidgin contain some complex features whose application has become highly fluid, such as the role and functions of the so-called predicate marker *i*, and at the same time largely lack some features that were present in some variants until recently and that added to the clarity and preciseness of expression. It appears that internal language planning could well ascertain, in an artificial and arbitrary, but carefully considered, fashion, the best rules to govern such phenomena, and could prescriptively determine the use of these grammatical forms (Wurm 1975b) in a standardized form of New Guinea Pidgin.

As has been pointed out in 4.3.3., standardization on the grammatical level is much more difficult to achieve than on the levels of orthography and vocabulary, and it appears that the best method for likely success would be the setting of examples in prestigious written (and to a lesser extent, spoken) materials such as school manuals and other textbooks, governmental and administrative pronouncements, newspapers and the like, with benefits such as praise, better employment opportunities, etc. rewarding the correct use of the prescribed forms.

4.4.2.4. *Discourse patterns and style.* Discourse patterns (i.e., systems of address and reference to persons, styles of expression, composition of written passages, and, in the spoken language, rules determining the forms of conversations) show comparatively little differentiation in the present variants of New Guinea Pidgin. Their successful standardization and the dissemination of standard forms would, even more than that of grammatical forms, employ the means of example and reward, rather than authoritative decree.

4.4.2.5. *Phonology and pronunciation.* The present variants of Pidgin show some marked differences in phonology and pronunciation that reflect (1) varying local substrata and (2) varying degrees of English influence. It seems that a standard pronunciation of Pidgin might well be based on the most widespread version, encountered in Rural Pidgin, with the least possible English influence to ensure that Pidgin remains a language separate from English. In this, it has to be kept in mind that Rural Pidgin, i.e., non-anglicized Pidgin, constitutes a prestigious variety of Pidgin in being generally regarded as "good" Pidgin by the speakers of the varieties of Pidgin. Anglicized pronunciations may be used to enhance the prestige of the speaker, but even the speaker will acknowledge that such a Pidgin is not "good." The use of anglicized pronunciations thus constitutes a social phenomenon, i.e., an individual phenomenon of prestige.

The standardization of pronunciation is of course a long and extremely difficult task that many European countries have not yet fully achieved. The setting of examples is of paramount importance in this matter, and auditory mass media play a decisive role in it.

At the same time, the standardization of pronunciation is of subsidiary importance when compared with that of orthography, vocabulary, grammar and discourse patterns, as long as differences in pronunciation do not reach such a degree that they interfere with intelligibility or reflect decisive foreign influence.

4.4.3. *Dissemination of the results of internal language planning.* A number of remarks have already been made concerning the methods considered best suited for the dissemination of standardized forms and innovations resulting from considerations of internal language planning. To sum up, there seem to be three main ways open for the dissemination of such features: (1) official sanctioning and authoritative decree; (2) the setting of examples; and (3) the promise of benefits for those who use such features correctly. The varied applications of these alternatives with regard to different facets such as orthography, vocabulary, etc. have already been discussed above under these individual headings.

It seems that standardized forms resulting from internal language planning actions would in general have a chance of wide acceptance in the following descending order: orthography; vocabulary; grammar style and discourse patterns; pronunciation. Of the three main dissemination ways mentioned above, that involving benefits is the most likely to lead to success; the method involving the setting of examples would be the next most successful. However, the best results are likely to be achieved by varied combinations of the three facets, as has already been indicated.

5. CREATIVE LITERATURE IN NEW GUINEA PIDGIN

Until recently, most efforts in written Pidgin outside the media belonged to the sphere of translation and prescriptive literature, such as mission publications, handbooks on health, agricultural matters, etc., training and teaching handbooks, and the like. Most of these were written by foreigners and predominantly contained a more or less standardized form of Pidgin. Only recently, New Guinea Pidgin creative literature, written by natives, has started to develop, and it is rapidly gaining momentum. However, the Pidgin used in this literature is nonstandard on all levels, including orthography. It seems vital for the development of this literature that it is not stifled in any way through the imposition of standardization principles upon it, because the language is badly in need of creative spirits to contribute to its development and enrichment. Only the utilization of a standardized orthography may well be suggested for the publication of such literature.

6. OUTLOOK FOR THE FUTURE

In a concise article, Mühlhäusler (1977h) has very ably summed up the likely outlook for the future of New Guinea Pidgin. He points out that, although there has been no official announcement that Pidgin will have the status of a national language in Papua New Guinea, most experts agree that this is a very likely development, with Hiri Motu's being granted a similar status, and English remaining the official language for higher education and special pursuits such as the nation's dealings with the outside world. In any event, Pidgin will remain the majority language and as such provide a viable means of interregional communication. There may even be a possibility that a standardized form of New Guinea Pidgin may become the lingua franca for the Solomon Islands and the New Hebrides as well—at least, collaboration in language planning among the three countries involved could be beneficial to the whole area, seeing that, whatever may happen regarding New Guinea Pidgin's becoming a universal lingua franca there, Solomon Islands Pidgin and New Hebrides Bichelamar (or Pislama) are likely to play a much more important role in the near (for the Solomons) and the foreseeable (for the New Hebrides) future than has hitherto been the case.

With the likely increase of speakers of New Guinea Pidgin and the further expansion of its geographical area, the extension of its functional domains will continue, and there will be more speakers who have Pidgin as their first language. As a result of these developments, Mühlhäusler (1977h) expects that the influence of English in general may increase, the question of standardization will pose itself more vigorously, and new Pidgin varieties, especially creolized ones, will emerge.

Mühlhäusler stresses the fact that, if Pidgin is to become a national language, the necessity of language planning is obvious. Wurm (1977) goes further and takes the view that without the urgently needed standardization of New Guinea Pidgin through internal language planning, the utilization of the language for its envisaged functions in education and for wider national purposes would be difficult, and the results unsatisfactory. Without such a standardization, the now bright future of Pidgin may well become quite dim.

NOTE

1. Examples illustrating the breakdown and restructuring of existing semantic fields through the introduction of new loans from English and the semantic reinterpretation of already established loans in anglicized Urban Pidgin would be as follows:

(a)   *yes* and *nogat* (Mühlhäusler 1977f)
The function of *yes* in Rural Pidgin is to confirm that what was asked in a yes/no question is the case, whether this question is negative or not.

Nogat "no" refers to the opposite cases. The reinterpretation of *yes* and *nogat* in the light of English semantics, however, has led to a situation in which there is complete confusion about the meaning to answers to negative yes/no questions:

New Guinea Pidgin	Interpretation in Rural Pidgin	Interpretation in anglicized Urban Pidgin
Yu no kam asde? Yes.	"Didn't you come yesterday? No, I didn't."	"Didn't you come yesterday? Yes, I did."
Masta i no stap? Nogat.	"Isn't your employer at home? Yes, he is."	"Isn't your employer at home? No, he isn't."

(b)

New Guinea Pidgin	Interpretation in Rural Pidgin	Interpretation in Urban Pidgin
wokim	"to make"	–
mekim	"to do"	"to make"
duim	"to entice, seduce"	"to do"

Violation of word structure convention is another result of strong English influence. The canonical forms of Pidgin words do not exceed three syllables in length: the introduction of English loans such as *konstitusen* "constitution," *andadivelop* "underdeveloped," violates this.

The adoption of the English plural marker -*s* in anglicized Pidgin leads to non-English and non-Pidgin restructuring:

Anglicized Pidgin	Interpretation
ol bratas	"the brothers"
ol gels	"the girls"
ol stafs	"the staff"

REFERENCES

Dutton, T. E. 1973. *Conversational New Guinea Pidgin.* (*Pacific Linguistics*, Series D.12.) Canberra: Australian National University, School of Pacific Studies.

Dutton, T. E., and Brown, H. A. 1977. Hiri Motu: The language itself. In *New Guinea Area Languages and Language Study*, vol. 3, S. A. Wurm, ed., chapter 7.4.3.1. In press.

Fishman, J. A.; Ferguson, C. A.; and Das Gupta, J., eds. 1968. *Language Problems of Developing Nations.* New York: J. Wiley.

Hall, R. A., Jr. 1943. *Melanesian Pidgin English*. Baltimore: Linguistic Society of America.

――――. 1955. *Hands Off Pidgin English!* Sydney: Pacific Publications Pty. Ltd.

Laycock, D. C. 1969. Pidgin's progress. *New Guinea Quarterly* 4/2:8-16.

――――. 1970. *Materials in New Guinea Pidgin (Coastal and Lowlands)*. *(Pacific Linguistics*, Series D.5.) Canberra: Australian National University, School of Pacific Studies.

McElhanon, K. A., ed. 1975. *Tok Pisin i Go We? Kivung* Special Publication Number One.

Mihalic, F. 1957. *Grammar and Dictionary of Neo-Melanesian*. Techny, Ill.: The Mission Press. S.V.D.

――――. 1971. *The Jacaranda Dictionary and Grammar of Melanesian Pidgin*. Milton: Jacaranda Press.

Mühlhäusler, P. 1973. Language planning and the Pidgin lexicon. Paper read at the Annual Meeting of the Linguistic Society of Papua New Guinea, September 1973. Port Moresby. Mimeographed.

――――. 1975a. Reduplication and repetition in New Guinea Pidgin. In McElhanon, ed., pp. 198-214.

――――. 1975b. Sociolects in New Guinea Pidgin. In McElhanon, ed., pp. 59-75.

――――. 1975c. Functional possibilities of lexical bases in New Guinea Pidgin. Paper presented at the International Conference on Pidgins and Creoles, Honolulu, Hawaii, January 1975. Mimeographed. (Selected for publication in the proceedings of the conference.)

――――. 1975d. Samoan plantation pidgin and the origin of New Guinea Pidgin. Paper presented at the Annual Meeting of the Linguistic Society of Australia. Sydney 1975. Mimeographed.

――――. 1977a. New Guinea Pidgin and society: The social role of Pidgin in New Guinea today. In *New Guinea Area Languages and Language Study*, vol. 3, S. A. Wurm, ed., chapter 7.4.1.4.2. In press.

――――. 1977b. History of New Guinea Pidgin: I: The external history. In *Handbook of New Guinea Pidgin*, S. A. Wurm, ed., with P. Mühlhäusler, D. C. Laycock, and T. Dutton. In press.

――――. 1977c. New Guinea Pidgin and society: sociolects in New Guinea Pidgin. In Wurm, ed., chapter 7.4.1.4.3. In press.

――――. 1977d. Variation in New Guinea Pidgin. In *Handbook of New Guinea Pidgin*, S. A. Wurm, ed., with P. Mühlhäusler, D. C. Laycock, and T. Dutton. In press.

――――. 1977e. On regional dialects in New Guinea Pidgin. In Wurm, ed., chapter 7.4.1.3. In press.

――――. 1977f. *Growth and Structure of the Lexicon of New Guinea Pidgin.*

(*Pacific Linguistics*, Series C.52.) Canberra: Australian National University, School of Pacific Studies. In press.

———. 1977g. A grammatical sketch of New Guinea Pidgin. In *Handbook of New Guinea Pidgin*, S. A. Wurm, ed., with P. Mühlhäusler, D. C. Laycock, and T. Dutton. In press.

———. 1977h. Future outlook on pidgin. In Wurm, ed., chapter 7.4.1.4.5.1. In press.

Todd, Loreto. 1974. *Pidgins and Creoles.* Language and Society Series. London and Boston: Routledge and Kegan Paul.

Wurm, S. A. 1964. Motu and Police Motu, a study in typological contrasts. (*Pacific Linguistics*, Series A.4.) Canberra: Australian National University, School of Pacific Studies.

———. 1966. Papua-New Guinea nationhood: The problem of a national language. *Journal of the Papua New Guinea Society* 1/1:7-19. Also in J. A. Fishman, C. A. Ferguson, and J. Das Gupta, eds., 1968, pp. 345-63.

———. 1971. *New Guinea Highlands Pidgin: Course Materials.* (*Pacific Linguistics*, Series D.3.) Canberra: Australian National University, School of Pacific Studies.

———. 1975a. The question of language standardization and pidgin. In McElhanon, ed., pp. 108-17.

———. 1975b. Descriptive and prescriptive grammar in New Guinea Pidgin. Paper presented at the International Conference on Pidgins and Creoles, Honolulu, Hawaii, January 1975. Mimeographed. (Selected for publication in the proceedings of the conference.)

———. 1977. Future outlooks and standardization of pidgin. In Wurm, ed., chapter 7.4.1.6. In press.

Wurm, S. A., ed. 1977. *New Guinea Area Languages and Language Study*, vol. 3: *Language, Culture, Society, and the Modern World.* (*Pacific Linguistics*, Series C.40.) Canberra: Australian National University, School of Pacific Studies. In press.

Wurm, S. A., ed.; with Mühlhäusler, P.; Laycock, D. C.; and Dutton, T. *Handbook of New Guinea Pidgin.* (*Pacific Linguistics*, Series C.48.) Canberra: Australian National University, School of Pacific Studies. In press.

Wurm, S. A.; Mühlhäusler, P.; and Laycock, D. C. 1977. Language planning and engineering. In *Handbook of New Guinea Pidgin*, S. A. Wurm, ed., with P. Mühlhäusler, D. C. Laycock, and T. Dutton.

Summary Bibliography

No attempt has been made to regroup the bibliographies appearing at the end of each contribution under a single comprehensive list. The reader who wishes to refer to a given title can consult the Index, which contains reference to all the works cited in the volume.

The following is a short list of important books and articles that treat problems of pidgin and creole linguistics beyond the scope of this volume or that provide more detailed descriptions of individual pidgin and creole languages.

1. INTRODUCTORY TREATMENTS

The most comprehensive introduction to the field is Robert A. Hall, Jr., *Pidgin and Creole Languages* (Ithaca, N.Y.: Cornell University Press, 1966). Though it deals mostly with English-derived pidgins and creoles, Loreto Todd, *Pidgins and Creoles* (London, Boston: Routledge and Kegan Paul, 1974) is very useful and provides a good summary of recent theories of the genesis and development of these languages.

2. COLLECTIVE VOLUMES

For more in-depth treatment of theoretical issues in pidgin and creole linguistics and for various points of view on the genesis and development of creoles and pidgins, the reader should consult Dell Hymes, ed., *Pidginization and Creolization of Languages* (London: Cambridge University Press, 1971), which contains the proceedings of the Mona (Jamaica) Conference on Pidgin and Creole Languages, 1968. Of particular interest are two sections:

(A) General Conception of Process:
1. Introduction by Dell Hymes (containing, particularly, definitions of the processes of pidginization and creolization);
2. Keith Whinnom, Linguistic hybridization and the 'special case'
   of pidgins and creoles;
3. William J. Samarin, Salient and substantive pidginization;
4. Charles A. Ferguson, Absence of copula and the notion of
   simplicity: a study of normal speech, baby talk, foreigner talk,
   and pidgins;
5. John J. Gumperz and Robert Wilson, Convergence and creolization; a case from the Indo-Aryan/Dravidian border;
6. Mervyn C. Alleyne, Acculturation and the cultural matrix of
   creolization.
(B) Interdisciplinary Perspectives:
1. Allen D. Grimshaw, Some social forces and some social
   functions of pidgin and creole languages;
2. William Labov, The notion of 'system' in creole studies;
3. Henry M. Hoenigswald, Language history and creole studies;
4. Sidney W. Mintz, The socio-historical background to pidginization and creolization.

Other collective volumes are: David DeCamp and Ian F. Hancock,
Pidgins and Creoles: Current Trends and Prospects (Washington, D.C.:
Georgetown University Press, 1973); Robert B. Le Page, ed., *Proceedings of
the Conference on Creole Language Studies,* Mona, Jamaica, 1959 (Creole
Language Studies II) (London: Macmillan, 1961); George Cave, ed., *New
Directions in Creole Studies* (Georgetown, Guyana: University of Guyana,
1976); Derek Bickerton and Richard R. Day, eds., *Proceedings of the
International Conference on Pidgins and Creoles,* Honolulu, 1975 (Honolulu:
University of Hawaii Press, 1977); Jurgen Meisel, ed., *Languages in
Contact—Pidgin, Creoles—Langues en contact* (Tübingen: Gunter Narr, 1976).

3. PIDGINS AND CREOLES AND LANGUAGE VARIATION

Because of their highly variable nature, the study of pidgins and
creoles is linked to the problem of the elaboration of dynamic models for
language description. The most notable references in this area are: Derek
Bickerton, *Dynamics of a Creole System* (London: University of Cambridge
Press, 1975); and in the Hymes volume: Stanley Tsuzaki, Coexistent systems
in language variation: the case of Hawaiian English; David DeCamp, Toward a
generative analysis of a post-creole speech continuum.

4. THE GENESIS AND DEVELOPMENT OF PIDGINS AND CREOLES

For the development of various hypotheses for the genesis and development of pidgins and creoles, and in particular, the relexification hypothesis, one might read, in addition to some of the more readily accessible writings of Hugo Schuchardt (see Meijer and Muysken's contribution): Keith Whinnom, *Spanish Contact Vernaculars in the West Indies* (London and Hong Kong: Hong Kong University Press, 1957); Douglas R. Taylor, Language shift or changing relationship? *International Journal of American Linguistics* 26:155-61 (1960); R.W. Thompson, A note on some possible affinities between the creole dialects of the Old World and those of the New, in Robert B. Le Page, ed., *Proceedings of the Conference on Creole Language Studies*, pp. 107-13; Douglas R. Taylor, The origin of West Indian Creole languages: evidence from grammatical categories, *American Anthropologist* 65:800-14 (1963); Keith Whinnom, The origin of the European-based creoles and pidgins, *Orbis* 14:509-27 (1965); Ian F. Hancock, A domestic origin for the English-derived Atlantic Creoles, *Florida Foreign Language Reporter* 10:7-8, 52 (1972).

5. DESCRIPTIONS OF INDIVIDUAL PIDGINS OR CREOLE LANGUAGES

While no comprehensive description is available for any individual pidgin or creole language, several recent detailed descriptions are available for various pidgins and creoles derived from English or French. For Dutch-, Portuguese- and Spanish-derived creoles, there are few recent studies available in English (see the Repertory of Languages and the bibliography of the Meijer and Muysken contribution for Hesseling's studies published in Dutch). Detailed studies of pidgins and creoles of non-European lexical base are scarce.

5.1. *English-derived*

Frederic G. Cassidy, *Jamaica Talk* (London: Macmillan 1961); Beryl L. Bailey, *Jamaican Creole Syntax: A Transformational Approach* (London: Cambridge University Press, 1966); Frederic G. Cassidy and Robert B. Le Page, *Dictionary of Jamaica English* (London: Cambridge University Press, 1967); Jan Voorhoeve, The verbal system of Sranan, *Lingua* 6:374-96 (1957); Joe L. Dillard, *Black English* (New York: Random House, 1972); Rebecca M. Agheyisi, *West African Pidgin English: Simplification and Simplicity* (Ann Arbor, Mich.: University Microfilms [Stanford University Ph.D. Diss.], 1971); D.C. Laycock, *Materials in New Guinea Pidgin (Coastal and Lowlands). Pacific Linguistics*, Series D.5 (Canberra: Australian National University, School of Pacific Studies, 1970).

5.2. *French-derived*

Albert Valdman, *Le créole: structure, statut et origine* (Paris: Champion, 1977); Morris F. Goodman, *A Comparative Study of Creole French Dialects* (The Hague: Mouton, 1964); Robert A. Hall, Jr., *Haitian Creole: Grammar—Texts—Vocabulary* (Memoir of the American Folklore Society 43) (Baltimore, Md.: Waverly Press, 1953); Phillip Baker, *Kreol: A Description of Mauritian Creole* (London: C. Hurst and Co., 1972); Robert Chaudenson, *Le Lexique du parler créole de la Réunion* (Paris: Champion, 1974).

5.3. *Portuguese-derived*

Marius F. Valkhoff, *Studies in Portuguese and Creole* (Johannesburg: University of Witwatersrand Press, 1966).

5.4. *Non-European-derived*

Bernd Heine, *Status and Use of African Lingua Francas* (Munich: IFO, Institut für Wirtschafts Forschung, 1970); Michael Silverstein, Chinook Jargon: Language contact and the problem of multi-level generative systems, *Language* 48:378-406 (1972).

6. PROBLEMS OF LANGUAGE ACQUISITION

John H. Schumann and Nancy Stenson, eds., *New Frontiers in Second Language Learning* (Rowley, Mass.: Newbury House Publishers, 1974).

7. SOCIOLINGUISTIC STUDIES

Dennis R. Craig, ed., *Proceedings of the Conference on Creole Languages and Educational Development, St. Augustine, Trinidad, 1972* (Paris, UNESCO, 1974); William Labov, *Language in the Inner City: Studies in the Black Vernacular* (Philadelphia: University of Pennsylvania Press); Claire Lefebvre, Discreteness and the linguistic continuum in Martinique, *Anthropological Linguistics* 16(2):47-78 (1974); Robert B. Le Page, et al., Sociolinguistic survey of multilingual communities, Stage I: British Honduras survey. The analysis of sociolinguistic data, *Language in Society* 3:1-32 (1974).

Appendix: Repertory of
Pidgin and Creole Languages

Ian F. Hancock

The following repertory and accompanying maps provide a summary identification of extant pidgin and creole languages as well as some others known to have existed in the course of the last two centuries. Except for well-documented languages, the most recently known bibliographical reference is provided. For well-documented pidgins and creoles, a recent, easily accessible source is sometimes given; for these, the reader may consult John E. Reinecke et al., *Bibliography of Pidgin and Creole Languages* (BPC), Honolulu: University of Hawaii Press, 1975; BPC has been updated for French-based pidgins and creoles in Albert Valdman et al., *Bibliographie des études sur les parlers français-créoles 1971-76*, AUPELF: Montreal and Paris, 1977.

The numbers preceding each entry in the Repertory refer to corresponding keys on the detail maps. Circled numbers on the maps indicate that the particular pidgin(s) or creole(s) is (are) spoken over a wide area. An unkeyed map showing the worldwide distribution of the languages is also provided. To facilitate use of the keyed maps, there follows a list of the languages in consecutive numerical order, cross-referenced to the specific sections of the Repertory in which they are discussed.

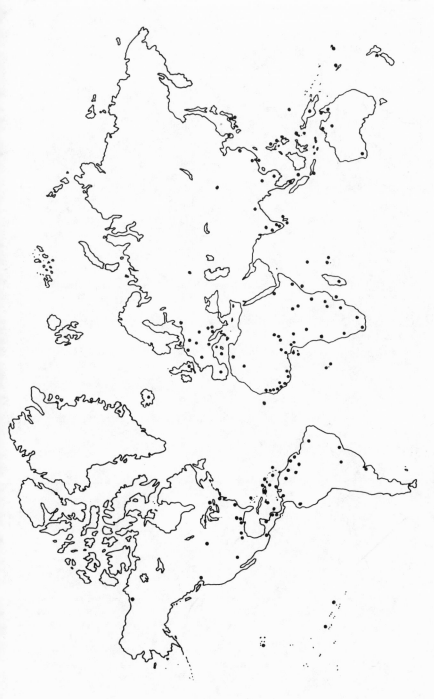

Distribution of Pidgins and Creoles in the World

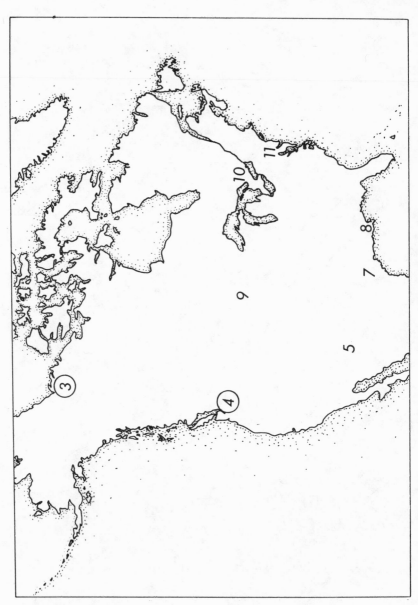

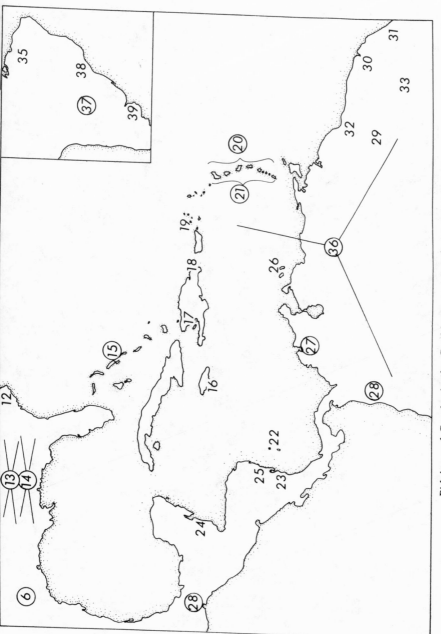

Pidgins and Creoles in the Caribbean and South America (inset)

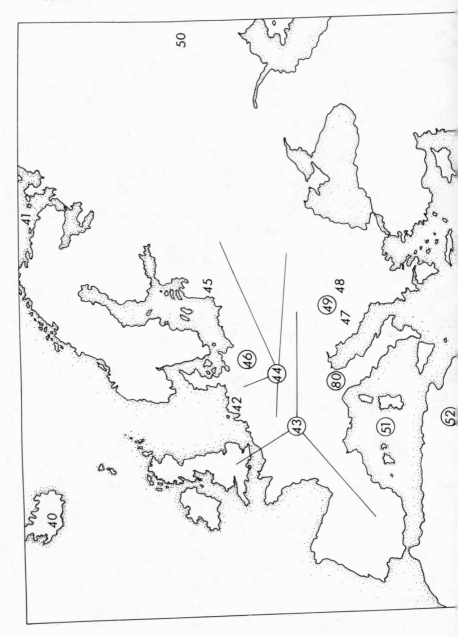

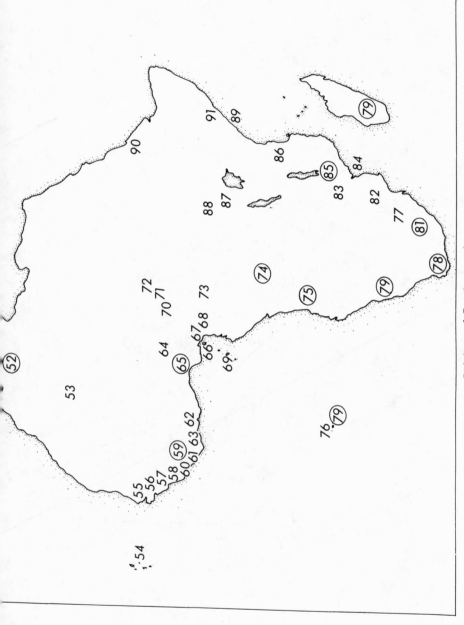

Pidgins and Creoles in Africa

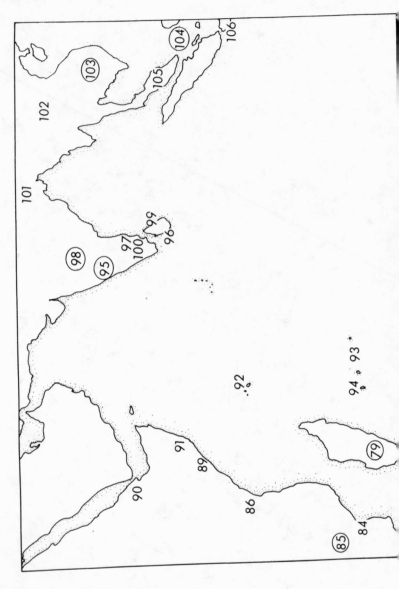

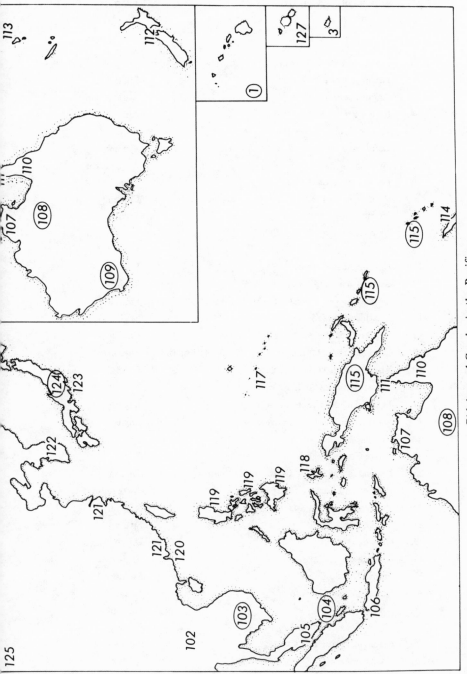

Pidgins and Creoles in the Pacific

MAP   NAME OF LANGUAGE   SECTION REFERENCE

1.	Hawaiian Creole English	English
2.	Pitcairnese Creole English	English
3.	Pidgin Eskimo	Amerindian
4.	Chinook Jargon	Amerindian
5.	Trader Navaho	Amerindian
6.	Pachuco	Spanish
7.	Mobilian	Amerindian
8.	Louisiana Creole French	French
9.	Michif Creole French	French
10.	Souriquoien	French
11.	New Jersey Amerindian Pidgin	Amerindian
12.	Gullah	English
13.	U.S. Black English	English
14.	General Amerindian Pidgin English	English
15.	Bahama and Caicos Islands Creole English	English
16.	Jamaican Creole English	English
17.	Haitian Creole French	French
18.	Cape Samaná, Dominican Republic Creole English	English
19.	Virgin Islands Dutch Creole	Dutch
20.	Lesser Antilles Creole French	French
21.	Lesser Antilles Creole English	English
22.	San Andrés and Providencia, Colombia Creole English	English
23.	Nahuatl-Spanish	Spanish
24.	Belize Creole English	English
25.	Nicaragua's Mosquito Coast Creole English	English
26.	Papiamentu Portuguese/Spanish Creole	Portuguese
27.	Venezuelan Pidgin Spanish	Spanish
28.	Palenquero	Spanish
29.	Guyana Dutch Creole	Dutch
30.	Guyana Creole English	English
31.	Sranan Creole English	English
32.	Guyane French Creole	French
33.	Saramaccan	Portuguese
34.	"Bush Negro" Creole English	English
35.	Brazilian Portuguese Creoles	Portuguese
36.	"Ashanti"	African

37.	Lingoa Gêral	Amerindian
38.	Fazendeiro	Italian
39.	Cocoliche	Spanish
40.	Icelandic French Pidgin	French
41.	Russenorsk	Miscellaneous European
42.	Plat Leewaaders	Dutch
43.	Romani-derived cants	Miscellaneous European
44.	Yiddish	German
45.	Letto-German Pidgin	German
46.	Gastarbeiter Deutsch	German
47.	Yugoslavian German Pidgins	German
48.	Rumanian-Hungarian	Miscellaneous European
49.	Slavo-German	German
50.	Volga German	German
51.	Sabir	Miscellaneous European
52.	North African Pidgin French	French
53.	Kouriya	African
54.	Cape Verde Portuguese Creole	Portuguese
55.	Senegal Creole Portuguese	Portuguese
56.	Banjul Creole English	English
57.	Guiné Creole Portuguese	Portuguese
58.	Séyou, Guiné pidgin French	French
59.	Kaŋgbe	African
60.	Krio	English
61.	Liberian English	English
62.	Ivory Coast Pidgin French	French
63.	Commercial Dyula	African
64.	Western Nigerian Pidgin	English
65.	Ful	African
66.	Fernando Po Creole	English
67.	Cameroon Pidgin English	English
68.	Ewondo Populaire	African
69.	Gulf of Guinea Portuguese Creoles	Portuguese
70.	Barikanchi	African
71.	Galgaliya	Arabic
72.	Tekrur	Arabic
73.	Sango	African
74.	Kituba	African
75.	Contact Portuguese	Portuguese

76.	St. Helena Pidgin English	English
77.	Pidginized Afrikaans	Dutch
78.	Afrikaans	Dutch
79.	Southern African Portuguese Pidgins	Portuguese
80.	Lanzi	Italian
81.	Fanagalo	African
82.	Town Bemba	African
83.	Chikunda	African
84.	Barracoon	African
85.	Ki-Setla	African
86.	Mbugu	Swahili
87.	Sudan Arabic	African
88.	Nubi Sudan Arabic	African
89.	Bojuni Swahili Creole	Swahili
90.	Asmara Pidgin Italian	Italian
91.	Ci-miini	African
92.	Seychelles French Creole	French
93.	Mauritian Creole French	French
94.	Réunion Creole French	French
95.	Diu and Daman Creole Portuguese	Portuguese
96.	Ceylon Creole Portuguese	Portuguese
97.	Hobson-Jobson	English
98.	Hindi Pidgins	Hindi
99.	Vedda	non-European
100.	Paliyan	non-European
101.	Nagamese	non-European
102.	Pidginized Chinese	non-European
103.	Tây-Bồi French Pidgin	French
104.	Pasá Malay	non-European
105.	Malacca Portuguese Creole	Portuguese
106.	Jakarta Portuguese Creole	Portuguese
107.	Bagot Aboriginal Reserve, Australian Creole English	English
108.	Northern Territory Pidgin	English
109.	Neo-Nyungar	English
110.	Australian Pidgin English	English
111.	Jargon English	English
112.	Maori Pidgin English	English
113.	Norfolkese	English
114.	New Caledonia Pidgin French	French

115.	Melanesian Pidgin English	English
116.	Police Motu	non-European
117.	Micronesian Islands	English
118.	Ternateño	Spanish
119.	Chabacano	Spanish
120.	Makista Portuguese Creole	Portuguese
121.	China Coast Pidgin English	English
122.	Korean Pidgin English	English
123.	Japanese Pidgin English	English
124.	Japanese Pidgin	non-European
125.	Sino-Slavic	non-European
126.	Siassi Pidgin	non-European
127.	Parau Tinito	non-European

ENGLISH-BASED

1. Hawaiian Creole English, used in varying stages of decreolization as a first language by many of its ca. 500,000 speakers. English-derived, with possible influence from Chinese, Japanese, Hawaiian, and various Philippine languages: J. E. Reinecke, *Language and Dialect in Hawaii* (Honolulu, 1969). A moribund Japanese Pidgin English is also spoken by immigrant workers in Hawaiian plantations: S. Nagara, *Japanese Pidgin English in Hawaii* (Honolulu, 1972).

2. Pitcairnese Creole English, spoken today by ca. 150 descendants of the mutineers from *H.M.S. Bounty* who settled on the island in 1790. The language appears to have more in common with the English-derived creoles of the Atlantic than with those spoken elsewhere in the Pacific, the common link possibly existing in a pan-oceanic nautical English. Extensive Tahitian influences: A. Ross and A. Moverley, *The Pitcairnese Language* (London, 1964).

12. Gullah, Goolah, Geechee, Geedgee, etc., increasingly being referred to as Sea Island Creole, is an Afro-English-derived creole spoken along the coastal strip and on offshore Sea Islands between northern Florida and South Carolina by some 125,000 Americans of African descent. Gullah may be the source of moribund creolized varieties of English spoken from Florida to Texas: Afro-Seminole (in Florida and Western Texas), Geechee or Ghenna (in Louisiana and eastern Texas): J. L. Dillard, *Black English* (New York, 1972), 150-55; Ian F. Hancock, "Creole features in the Afro-Seminole speech of

Brackettville, Texas," *Society for Caribbean Linguistics Occasional Paper No. 3,* April 1975.

13. U.S. Black English, known variously as Afro-American, Flat, Bad, Country, Bammer, Black Vernacular, etc. Possible origins in a creole used in West Africa: J. L. Dillard, *Perspectives on Black English* (The Hague, 1973). Dillard suggests the existence in the early USA of a creole distinct from the more intelligible Black English.

14. General Amerindian Pidgin English: D. Leechman and R. A. Hall, Jr., "American Indian Pidgin English: attestations and grammatical peculiarities," *American Speech* 30:163-71 (1955). J. L. Dillard, *Black English,* pp. 156-63, suggests a link to a pre-extant Afro-Pidgin.

15. English-derived creole spoken throughout the Bahama and Caicos Islands, in various stages of approximation to (especially U.S.) English: Alison Watt Shilling, "Negation in Bahamian English," in George Cave, ed., *New Directions in Creole Studies* (Georgetown, Guyana, 1976).

16. Jamaican Creole English (Bungo, Quashee, Jagwa-Taak), spoken by most of the country's over one million inhabitants: F. Cassidy, *Jamaica Talk* (London, 1961).

18. English of a community of the descendants of ex-U.S. slaves, with features of creolization/archaic Black English, who settled in Cape Samaná, Dominican Republic, in 1824: C. Benavides, "Orígenes históricos de Samaná," *Español Actual* 25:14-18 (1973).

21. English-derived creole dialects of the Lesser Antilles, spoken in the Virgin Islands, St. Croix, St. Kitts, St. Martin, St. Barts, Nevis, Antigua, Monserrat, Barbuda, Dominica, St. Lucia, St. Vincent, Barbados, the Grenadines, Grenada, Tobago and Trinidad, on some islands alongside creole French. There is a wide range of creolization apparent. The creole of Trinidad (Bouriki, Banana English, Bad/Broad/Broken English) exhibits influence from an earlier variety of Barbadian (Bajan) creole and from Creole French: J. J. Thomas, "Essay on the philology of the creole dialect," *Trübner's American and Oriental Literary Record,* 31st December 1870: 57-58.

22. The creolized English of the Colombian islands of San Andrés and Providencia, known locally as Bendè: J. Edwards, "African influences on the English of San Andrés Island, Colombia," in DeCamp and Hancock, eds.

24. Creole English of Belize (formerly British Honduras), many features in common with Jamaican dialects. The first language of a mainly urban population, rural Belizeans using a variety of languages (Spanish, Mayan, Cariban), with the creole as a lingua franca.

25. A pidginized variety of various Caribbean Creole English dialects is used in ports and coastal settlements along Nicaragua's Mosquito (Moskito, Miskito) Coast and on the Islas del Maïz. Belizean creole influences seem predominant: Ernst Schultze, "Die Sklaven- und Dienersprachen," *Sociologus* 9:377-418 (1933), and for specimens, C. N. Bell, *Tangweera* (London, 1899). Other varieties have been reported in the Canal Zone of Panama and on the Honduras Box Islands.

30. Guyana Créole English (Creolese). Various discernible contributing elements, including the creoles of Barbados and Sierra Leone: D. Bickerton, *The Dynamics of a Creole System* (London, 1975).

31. Sranan, known as Taki-taki, Ningre-tongo, Krioro, etc., is the creolized English of coastal Surinam, spoken by ca. 350,000 persons, often as a second language: J. Voorhoeve and A. Donicie, *Bibliographie du négro-anglais du Surinam* ('s-Gravenhage 1963).

34. The English-derived "Bush Negro" dialects of Surinam and the Guyane bank of the Marowijne and Lawa Rivers consist of three groups, viz., Boni (or Aluku), Djuka (or Aucan), and Saramaccan-Sara Kreek, with a total speaking population of ca. 20,000: J. E. Grimes, ed., *Languages of the Guianas* (Norman, 1972). Djuka is unique among the creoles in that it has developed a syllabic writing system, one having remarkable similarities with the various indigenous scripts of West Africa: D. Dalby, "The indigenous scripts of West Africa and Surinam: their inspiration and design," *African Language Studies* 9:156-97 (1968).

56. Creole English of Banjul (formerly Bathurst), the Gambia, known as Aku, Krio, or Patois, is spoken by some 3,500 Creoles or "Akus," descendants of freed (mainly Yoruba) slaves, and traders from Sierra Leone, as a first language, and as a lingua franca inland along the River Gambia.

60. Krio, the English-derived creole of Freetown and nearby villages in Sierra Leone. Spoken as a first language by an estimated 120,000 people, and used as a lingua franca throughout the country by many thousands more: E. Jones, "Sierra Leone Krio," in J. Spencer, ed., *The English Language in West Africa* (London, 1970). A simplified and anglicized creole English for use by Africans with Europeans, called Talkee-Talkee, is discussed by E. Jones, "Mid-nineteenth century evidences of a Sierra Leone patois," *Sierra Leone Language Review* 1:19-26 (1962). For a discussion of the sources of modern English-based creoles on the Guinea Coast, cf. I. F. Hancock, "A domestic origin for the English-derived Atlantic Creoles," *The Florida FL Reporter* 10 (1-2):7,8,52 (1972), and the same writer's "Lexical expansion within a closed system" in M. Sanches and B. Blount, eds., *Sociocultural Dimensions of Language Change* (New York, 1976), pp. 161-71.

61. Liberian English exists in several varieties, exhibiting features resulting from more or less contact between early nineteenth century US Black English and a preexisting variety of Coast Pidgin. The only mother-tongue variety is spoken by descendants of the liberated American slaves, and is known as Americo-Liberian, Brokes, Kwasai, Waterside, or Water Street English. Liberian Pidgin English is spoken mainly in the interior, by tribal Liberians of different linguistic backgrounds in their dealings with each other, and with Africans and Europeans from the Coast. Kepama or Cape Palmas English has much in common with Americo-Liberian of Monrovia, but originates from more northern US forms of Black English taken to the (now nonexistent) colony of Maryland. Some lexical and phonological influence from Grebo discernible. Kru fishermen, whose tribal home is in Liberia-Ivory Coast, employ a highly conservative form of English-derived creole in their dealings with other African communities along the Guinea Coast. Known as Kru or Kroo English, this speech appears to be most closely related to Freetown Krio: Ian F. Hancock, "Some aspects of English in Liberia" and "Liberian English of Cape Palmas," in J. L. Dillard, ed., *Perspectives on Black English*, pp. 248-71.

64. Western Nigerian Pidgin, often called "Broken": B. Mafeni, "Nigerian Pidgin," in J. Spencer, ed., *The English Language in West Africa*, pp. 95-112. Midwestern Nigerian Pidgin differs from other Nigerian varieties: R. Agheyisi, "West African Pidgin English: simplification and simplicity" (University Microfilms, Ann Arbor, 1971). Pidgin English varieties have also been reported in Ghana.

66. Fernando Po Creole, also known as Poto or Porto Talk, is spoken by ca. 4,000 persons at Santa Isobel and San Carlos. It was imported in 1830 by Sierra Leone and West Indian Maroon settlers: R. P. Mariano de Zarco, *Dialecto inglés-africano o broken-english de la colonia española del Golfo de Guinea: epitome de la gramática seguido del vocabulario española-inglés y inglés-español*, 2d ed., (Turnhout, 1938).

67. Cameroon Pidgin English (Bush English, Broken, West Coast, Cameroons Creole, etc.), spoken in several dialects over a wide area incorporating parts of eastern Nigeria and Fernando Po. It is used in western Cameroon by seventy-five percent of the population as a second language, and in eastern Cameroon by perhaps thirty percent. A creolized variety, possibly the same as that spoken in Fernando Po, is called Krio and is the mother tongue of the descendants of settlers from Freetown, in the city of Victoria. For Western dialects: G. D. Schneider, *West African Pidgin English* (Athens, 1970), and for an Eastern French-influenced variety: C. Gilman, "The comparative structure in French, English and Cameroonian Pidgin English" (University Microfilms, Ann Arbor, 1972).

76. A Pidgin English is reported as once having been spoken on St. Helena by A. Zettersten, *The English of Tristan da Cunha* (Lund, 1969), p. 134.

97. Hobson-Jobson, Babu English or Chhi-Chhi, a rudimentary pidgin employed during the period of British rule in India. Some Hindi influence: H. Schuchardt, "Das Indo-Englische," *Englische Studien* 15:286-305 (1890). Madras Pidgin English, or Butler English, is similar to Hobson-Jobson in form and function, but with strong Dravidian influence: H. Yule and A. Burnell, *Hobson-Jobson* (London, 1903 and 1968), p. 133.

107. A creolized English is spoken on the Bagot Aboriginal Reserve near Darwin, northern Australia. A similar dialect has been described from Arnhem Land by M. Sharpe, "Notes on the Creole-pidgin of Roper River," paper presented at the Conference of the Linguistic Society of Australia, May 1973.

108. Northern Territory Pidgin is the variety of English used by Aborigines throughout north-central Australia: B. Jernudd, "Social change and Aboriginal speech variation in Australia," *Journal of the Linguistic Society of Australia* 1.

109. Neo-Nyungar or Aboriginal English is an English-Nyungar contact language used as the everyday speech of Aborigines in southwestern Australia. A more anglicized version of this is used in communication with white Australians and is called Wetjala, while an intentionally disguised variety called Yeraka is used as a play-language by women: W. Douglas, *The Aboriginal Languages of the South-West of Australia* (Canberra, 1968).

110. Australian Pidgin English is a direct offshoot of a Neo-Melanesian: R. A. Hall, Jr., "Notes on Australian Pidgin English," *Language* 19:283-87 (1943).

111. A creolized English, sometimes called Jargon English and having similarities with New Guinea Pidgin, is spoken in the islands between Cape York and the Papuan coast opposite: T. E. Dutton, "Informal English in the Torres Straits," in W. S. Ramson, ed., *English Transported* (Canberra, 1970), pp. 137-60.

112. Maori Pidgin English, extinct, was current during the early years of colonization. Similar to Neo-Melanesian, Australian Pidgin, etc: S. J. Baker, " 'Pidgin' English in New Zealand," *New Zealand Slang, A Dictionary of Colloquialisms*, Ch. 9 (Christchurch, ca. 1941), pp. 71-92.

113. Norfolkese, an offshoot of Pitcairnese, spoken by the descendants from *H.M.S. Bounty* who settled on the Australian island of Norfolk from Pitcairn in the nineteenth century. Today, only about half of the island's population of around 1,000 is of the original stock and speaks the language: S. Harrison, "Norfolk Island English," unpub. thesis, Macquarie University (Australia), 1972.

115. Melanesian Pidgin English, also known as Neo-Melanesian, Sandalwood English, Bêche-de-Mer, Beach-la-mar, etc., originally an offshoot of China Coast Pidgin English. In Papua-New Guinea, a creolized variety having semi-official status is termed Bisnis-English, Nuginian, Niugini-tok, Tok Pisin, etc. All Pidgin English varieties throughout the southwestern Pacific are closely related and have well in excess of a million speakers: R. A. Hall, Jr., *Melanesian Pidgin English: Grammar, Texts, Vocabulary* (Baltimore, 1944); D. C. Laycock, "Pidgin English in New Guinea," in W. S. Ramson, ed., *English Transported* (Canberra, 1970), pp. 137-60. Pidgin English is also used in the New Hebrides, where it is known as Bichlamar or Bislama, and in the Solomon Islands: P. Laveau, *Apprenons le bichlamar* (Port-Vila, 1973).

117. A now extinct English-derived pidgin was spoken in the Micronesian Islands in the nineteenth century: R. A. Hall, Jr., "English loanwords in Micronesian languages," *Language* 21:214-19 (1945).

121. China Coast Pidgin English, Business English, or just "Pidgin." Developed during the eighteenth century and at one time in extensive use along the China coast. Now no longer used in Communist China, where it is remembered by only a few old people in Shanghai and other seaport communities, and giving way to metropolitan English in Hong Kong: R. A. Hall, Jr., "Chinese Pidgin English: Grammar and texts," *Journal of the American Oriental Society* 64:95-113 (1944).

122. Korean Pidgin English, or "Bamboo English," gained maximum currency during the Korean War in the 1950s: J. T. Algeo, "Korean Bamboo English," *American Speech* 35:117-23 (1960), and G. Webster, "Korean Bamboo English once more," *American Speech* 35:261-65 (1960).

123. During the period of American occupation a variety of Japanese Pidgin English also known as "Bamboo English" came into existence in the Hamamatsu area. It may have provided the impetus for pidginized varieties of English used in Thailand and Vietnam: cf. J. S. Goodman, "The development of a dialect of English-Japanese Pidgin," *Anthropological Linguistics* 9(6):43-55 (1967).

FRENCH-BASED

8. Louisiana Creole French, known as Neg (Nègue), Gumbo, Français nègre, etc., is spoken by a dwindling population in eastern Louisiana and parts of east Texas, as well as by a small community in Sacramento, California, principally by blacks: R. Morgan, "Structural sketch of St. Martin Creole," *Anthropological Linguistics* I(8):20-24 (1959), and Dorice Tentchoff, "Cajun French and French Creole," in S. L. Del Sesto and J. L.

Gibson, eds., *The Culture of Acadiana: Tradition and Change in South Louisiana* (Lafayette, 1975).

10. Souriquoien, now extinct, was at one time used between French fishermen and natives of Nova Scotia: Lescarbot, *Histoire de la Nouvelle France* (1916), p. 694; another Franco-Amerindian contact vernacular is reported to have been used in and around Montréal ca. 1630: J. H. Trumbull, "Words derived from the Indian languages of North America," *Transactions of the American Philosophical Society* (1870), p. 20.

9. A French-Cree contact language called Michif is reported in use in North Dakota. It may be related to a reduced variety of French still surviving in the section of Alberta that corresponded to the Métis nation.

17. Haitian Creole French, spoken in three main dialects by ca. five million Haitians (including ca. 200,000 in New York City): R. A. Hall, Jr., *Haitian Creole: Grammar, Texts, Vocabulary* (Washington, 1953).

20. French-based creole dialects of the Lesser Antilles, spoken in St. Thomas, Guadaloupe, Desirade, Marie Galante, Les Saintes, St. Martin, St. Barts, Dominica, Martinique, St. Lucia, and, though disappearing, in St. Vincent, Grenada, the Grenadines, Trinidad.

32. The French Creole of Guyane (French Guiana) spoken by ca. 40,000 persons, is closely related to Lesser Antilles varieties. Three geographical varieties have been identified: M. St.-Jacques-Fauqenoy, *Analyse structurale du créole guyanais* (Paris, 1972).

40. A French pidgin is mentioned in an article in Vol. XXIV of the 1911 edition of the *Encyclopaedia Britannica*, "Scandinavian languages," by A. Noreen, who states, "as a matter of curiosity it may be noted that on the western and eastern coasts [of Iceland] traces are found of a French-Icelandic language, which arose from the long sojourn of French fishermen there."

52. Pidgin French or "Petit Mauresque" of North Africa, sometimes wrongly referred to as Petit Nègre or Sabir, although possibly a relexification of the latter: A. Lanly, *Le français d'Afrique du Nord*, 2d ed. (Paris, 1970), pp. 38-40; A. Tabouret-Keller, "La motivation des emprunts: un exemple pris sur le vif de l'apparition d'un sabir," *La Linguistique* 1:25-60 (1960).

58. Use of a pidginized French structured on the local Portuguese creole was reported in Séyou, Guiné by M. Bertrand-Bocande, "Notes sur la Guinée portugaise ou Sénégambie méridionale," *Bull. de la Soc. de Géographie de Paris* 12 (1849):75.

62. Pidgin French, Français-Tirailleur, Petit-Nègre, etc., spoken in the Ivory Coast and other former French possessions on the Guinea Coast: M. Delafosse, *Vocabulaires comparatifs* (Paris, 1904), pp. 843-44; *Langues du*

Monde (Paris, 1952), 843-44. A pidginized variety of French of uncertain origins, termed français populaire d'Abidjan, is in use in the Abidjan area.

92. Seychelles French Creole, or Seychellois. Spoken by over 40,000 people in the Seychelle Islands, and in Chagos, Tromelin, and Agalega: A. Bollée, *Etude descriptive du créole Seychellois* (Tübingen: Niemeyer, 1977).

93. Mauritian Creole French, Mauricien, Kreol, etc., spoken by most of the population of ca. 800,000 in Mauritius: P. Baker, *Kreol: A Description of Mauritian Creole* (London, 1972). Rodrigues Creole French appears to be similar to the Mauritian dialect, and is spoken by ca. 17,000 people.

94. Réunion Creole French, Réunionnais, or (formerly) Bourbonnais, spoken by over 500,000 people, is highly variable and undergoing gallicization: R. Chaudenson, *Le lexique du parler créole de la Réunion* (Paris, 1974).

103. Tây Bòi, Franco-Annamite or Indo-French Pidgin, now practically extinct, but widely used in Tonkin, Haiphong, and most of coastal Annam during the period of French control: J. S. Phillips, *Vietnamese Contact French: Variation in a Contact Situation* (University Microfilms, 1975).

114. New Caledonia Pidgin French or Bichelamar: K. J. Hollyman, "L'ancien pidgin français parlé en Nouvelle Caléndonie," *Journal de la Societé des Océanistes* 20:57-64 (1964).

PORTUGUESE-BASED

26. Papiamentu (Papiam, Papiaments, Papiamento, Curaçoleño, Curassese), a lexically Spanish-related creole deriving possibly from an earlier Portuguese-based pidgin spoken in three main dialects by upwards of 200,000 people in Curaçao, Bonaire, and Aruba. Influenced lexically by Dutch, and to a lesser degree by English. Extensively documented.

33. Saramaccan and Matuari, Portuguese-derived "Bush Negro" creoles have a high English-derived lexical content, probably via Sranan. They also appear to have retained a far higher proportion of African (especially KiKóongo)-derived words than any other Surinam creole: A. Donicie and J. Voorhoeve, *De Saramakaanse woordenschat* (Amsterdam, 1962).

35. Varieties of Portuguese having undergone creolization by the influence of African languages have been reported in Brazil: M. J. Valkhoff, *Studies in Portuguese and Creole,* ch. I and II (Johannesburg, 1966); H. Jeroslow, "Creole characteristics in rural Brazilian speech," International Congress on Pidgins and Creoles, Honolulu, January 1975.

54. The Portuguese-derived creole of the Cape Verde Islands, spoken in two

principal dialects, Sotavento and Barlavento, and considerably decreolized: B. Lopes da Silva, *O dialecto crioulo de Cabo Verde* (Lisbon, 1957). It is spoken by a community of Afro-Americans near New Bedford, Massachusetts, descended from nineteenth-century immigrants and known locally as "Bravas": M. L. Nunes, "The phonologies of Cape Verdean dialects of Portuguese," *Boletim de Filologia* 7:56 (1963).

55. Senegal Creole Portuguese, or Kryôl, apparently closer to the Gulf of Guinea creoles than to the geographically closer varieties of Cape Verde and Guiné, is spoken by ca. 60,000 speakers: A. Chataigner, "Le créole portugais du Sénégal," *Journal of African Languages* 2(1):44-71 (1962).

57. Guiné Creole Portuguese, similar to that of Cape Verde, is employed as a lingua franca by much of the country's population of 500,000: W. A. A. Wilson, *The Crioulo of Guiné* (Johannesburg, 1962).

69. The Gulf of Guinea Portuguese creoles, spoken on the islands of Annobon, Sao Tomé, and Principe, the last highly lusitanized: Luiz Ferraz, "The origin and development of four creoles in the Gulf of Guinea," *African Studies* 35(1):33-38 (1976), W. Günther, *Das portugiesische Kreolisch der Ilha do Principe* (Marburg a/L, 1973).

75. "Broken Portuguese," Pequeno Portugues, Pretoguês or "Blackigiese" is spoken in the larger towns of Angola: G. Moser, "African literature in Portuguese: the first written, the last discovered," *African Forum* 2(4):78-96 (1969).

79. Pidginized contact forms of Portuguese are reported to have been spoken widely on the coast of southern Africa, as well as on St. Helena island, in the nineteenth century, near Fort Dauphin in southern Madagascar in the sixteenth and seventeenth centuries. It survived as recently as the twentieth century in Cape Town; according to M. Valkhoff, op. cit., the latter was instrumental in the early partial creolization of Afrikaans. For a structural comparison between Afrikaans and Creole Portuguese, see Ian F. Hancock, "Malacca Creole Portuguese: Asian, African or European?" *Anthropological Linguistics* 17(5):211-36 (1975).

95. Creole Portuguese of Diu and Daman (Damão), both possibly extinct. With Salsette Creole, these constitute the Norteiro group of Indo-Portuguese or Lusoindian dialects. Creole Portuguese was formerly spoken in many ports along the Indian littoral: H. Schuchardt, "Allgemeineres über das Indoportugiesische (Asioportugiesisches)," *Zeit. für Romanische Philologie* 13:476-516 (1889), M. M. Lopes, "Notas sobre o crioulo português de Damão," unpub. diss., University of Lisbon, 1969-70.

96. Ceylon Creole Portuguese, spoken (or formerly spoken) by Indo-Portuguese Christians settled at Mannar, Negumbo, Colombo, Calaturey, Galle,

Batticaloa, Trincomalee and Jaffna (Schuchardt, op. cit.). Recent investigations have confirmed the presence of several hundred creole-speaking families in several towns, e.g., in Uppordai, near Batticaloa.

105. Malacca Portuguese Creole, also known as Papia Kristang, Serani, Malaqueiro, Malaquense, Malaquenho, Bahasa Geragau, Portugues Basu, etc., is still the first language of about 3,000 people in Western Malaysia: Ian F. Hancock, "Malacca Creole Portuguese," *Te Reo* 16:23-44 (1973). A related variety is spoken in Singapore by a creole community centered around St. Joseph's church.

106. The Portuguese Creole of Jakarta (formerly Batavia), probably almost extinct, together with the Malacca and Singapore dialects, forms the Malayo-Portuguese group, other dialects of which are (or were) spoken in Sumatra, Borneo, Flores, Timor, Ceram, the Moluccas, the Celebes, and Macao, Hong Kong, and Shanghai (China Coast): H. Schuchardt, op. cit., and "Über das malaioportugiesische von Batavia und Tugu," *Sitzungberichte der Phil. -hist. Classe der K. Akademie der Wissenschaften in Wien* 122:1-256 (1890).

120. Makista or Macauenho, the Portuguese-derived creole of Macao: G. N. Batalha, "Estado actual do dialecto macaense," *Revista portuguesa da filologia* 9:177-213 (1959); a more conservative form of Makista has been retained by ca. 2,000 Creoles who settled in Hong Kong: R. W. Thompson, "O dialecto português de Hong Kong," *Boletim da filologia* 19:289-93 (1960).

SPANISH-BASED PIDGINS AND CREOLES

6. Pachuco or Pochismo and Tiriloneño or Caló, Spanish-English hybrid languages spoken by youths of Mexican ancestry in the U.S. Southwest and southern California exhibit some features of pidginization, especially in the formation of their lexicon: L. Coltharp, *The Tongue of the Tirilones* (University of Alabama Press, 1965).

27. Pidgin Spanish, used principally by two Amerindian tribes inhabiting western Venezuela, in their dealings with traders in the area: O. L. Riley, "Trade Spanish of the Piñaguero Panare," *Studies in Linguistics* 2 (1):6-11 (1952).

23. A creolized Nahuatl-Spanish was established in Nicaragua during the sixteenth century, but is now probably extinct: A. M. Elliott, "The Nahuatl-Spanish dialect of Nicaragua," *American Journal of Philology* 5 (1):54-67 (1884).

28. Afro- and Amerindian-influenced creolized forms of Spanish have been reported throughout northwestern South America and even in Mexico. Descriptions are available for Palenquero, spoken by two or three thousand Bush Negroes at San Basilio de Palenque, Colombia: D. Bickerton and A. Escalente, "Palenquero: A Spanish-based creole of northern Colombia," *Lingua* 24:254 -67 (1970), and Chocó on the Atlantic coast of Colombia: L. Flórez, "El habla del Chocó," *Thesaurus* 17:446-56 (1962); cf. also Germán de Granda, "Sobre el estudio de las hablas 'criollas' en el area hispanica," *Thesaurus* 6:110-16 (1962).

39. Cocoliche (Rioplatense), an italianized Spanish in use in the Buenos Aires area by Italian immigrants; rudimentarily pidginized, but lacking the degree of formalization necessary to qualify it as a true pidgin: G. M. Zilio, *El 'cocoliche' rioplatense* (Santiago de Chile, 1964). Analogous to Cocoliche is Fragnol: A. Rigaud, "Le fragnol," *Vie et Langage* (1959):96-99.

118. Ternateño, once spoken in Ternate in the Moluccas. The progenitor of the Philippine creoles, this language developed out of contact between Spanish/Mexican soldiers and the local Portuguese Creole-speaking community. Two hundred families from Ternate settled in Manila in 1659: K. Whinnom, *Spanish contact vernaculars in the Philippine Islands* (Hong Kong, 1956).

119. Chabacano (Chavacano, Chabakano) subsumes all Spanish-based Philippine creoles. Three dialects—Caviteño, Ermiteño, and Ternateño—are spoken in the Manila area. Zamboangueño, spoken in Zamboanga City and originating mainly from Caviteño, with strong influences from Tagalog and Cebuano, has offshoots at Cotabato and perhaps at Davao: C. O. Frake, "Lexical origins and semantic structure in Philippine Creole Spanish," in D. Hymes, ed., pp. 223-42; M. I. Riego de Dios, "The Cotabato Chabacano verb," paper presented at the International Conference on Pidgins and Creoles. A pidgin known as "Bamboo Spanish" is reportedly in use in parts of the Philippines by the older generation of Chinese shopkeepers: Whinnom, op. cit., pp. 16-17.

OTHER EUROPEAN-BASED PIDGINS AND CREOLES

Dutch

19. Virgin Islands Dutch Creole (Negerhollands, Creol), now virtually extinct, but at one time having sufficient speakers to warrant a New Testament translation (1818): D. C. Hesseling, *Het Negerhollands der Deense Antillen* (Leiden, 1905). The current situation is discussed in Gilbert

Sprauve, "Dutch Creole: Written-oral discontinuity, and towards complex structures," in G. Cave, op. cit.

29. Dutch Creole survives in two, possibly more, distinct dialects in the interior of Guyana, spoken by a mainly mixed (Afro-Amerindian) population: I. Robertson, "Guyana Dutch: its history and implications for Creole studies," in G. Cave, op. cit.

42. A creolized Dutch, known as Plat Leewadders, is spoken by Jews in the Friesian capital of Ljouwert: G. B. Droege in his review of S. de Jong's *Joods leven in de Friese hoofdstad,* in *Friesian News Items* 29(4) (May 1973).

77. Pidginized Afrikaans, employed by Hottentots and Afrikaners in the Namaland region: J. H. Rademeyer, *Kleurling-Afrikaans, die taal van die Griekwas en Rehoboth-Basters* (Amsterdam, 1938).

78. Afrikaans, Taal, "Baby Hollands," "Kindertaaltje," or Cape Dutch may be said to be a rudimentary creole, its formation involving only partial creolization away from the metropolitan dialects. On Afrikaans as a creole: M. Valkhoff, *New Light on Afrikaans and 'Malayo-Portuguese'* (Louvain, 1972).

Italian

38. A rudimentary creole known as Fazendeiro exists in São Paulo and is spoken by some Brazilians of mixed Italian and African ancestry: A. Nardo Gibele, "Alcune parole usate dalla popolazione mista italiana e negra nelle fazende di Sao Paulo nel Brasile," *Archivio per lo Studio delle Tradizione Popolari* 19:18-24 (1900).

80. A sixteenth-century German-Italian pidgin known as Lanzi or Lanzichenecchi has been described by W. A. Coates, "The German Pidgin-Italian of the sixteenth century," *Papers from the Fourth Annual Kansas Linguistics Conference* (1969):66-74.

90. Asmara Pidgin Italian was originally developed while Eritrea was in Italian hands, and is still spoken in parts of Ethiopia.

German

47. Two pidgins, one German- and one Slavic-derived, used in Bosnia-Herzegovina (Yugoslavia) before World War I: P. Mitrović: "Deux sabirs balkaniques," *Linguistique* 8 (1):137-40 (1972).

49. Slavo-German as it developed during the time of the Austro-Hungarian Empire showed features of pidginization: H. Schuchardt, *Slawo-Deutsches und Slawo-Italienisches* (Graz, 1884); reprinted (Munich, 1971).

50. A highly reduced and Slavicized offshoot of the Volga German dialects survives in Chkalov (Orenburg) Province in the eastern part of the Russian S.S.R.: E. Schultze, op. cit.

45. Letto-German Pidgin, a variety of German once spoken in Latvia with Yiddish and Plattdeutsch elements and a phonology heavily influenced by Latvian: "Das 'Halbdeutsch der Esten," *Zeitschrift für Deutsche Mundarten* 16-17:160-72 (1921-22).

44. Yiddish (Jüdisch, Judaeo-German, etc.) appears to have some features of creolization such as simplified morphology and eclectic lexicon: J. Fishman, "The phenomenological and linguistic pilgrimage of Yiddish," in D. Craig, ed., op. cit. Other Jewish contact languages (Judaeo-Greek, Judaeo-Italian, Judaeo-Spanish, Judaeo-Persian, Judaeo-Arabic) are discussed in C. Adler et al., eds., *The Jewish Encyclopaedia* (London, 1904).

46. Gastarbeiter Deutsch, spoken by immigrant laborers in Germany, and showing features found in such earlier forms of German as those used in prisoner-of-war, concentration, and displaced-person camps, appears to be more a foreigner talk than a stable pidgin: "Heidelberger Forschungsprojekt 'Pidgin Deutsch'," *Sprache und Kommunikation ausländischer Arbeiter* (Kronberg/Ts., 1975).

Slavic

125. A Sino-Slavic contact language came into use in some northern Manchurian cities (such as Harbin and A-szu-ho), where Russians, Poles, and others settled at the beginning of the twentieth century in connection with the construction of the Eastern Chinese Railway: A. Jablonska, "The Sino-Russian mixed language in Manchuria," *Working Papers in Linguistics:* 135-64 (Hawaii, 1969). A similar Russian-Chinese contact language is found in the Soviet town of Kyakhta on the Mongolian border: Neumann, "Zur Chinesich-russischen Behelfssprache von Kjachta," *Sprache* 12:237-51 (1966).

Miscellaneous

51. Of the numerous varieties of European languages showing admixture and morphosyntactic restructuring, the best known are Russenorsk and Sabir. The now-extinct Sabir (Sabeir, Lingua Franca, langue franque) was widely used in the Mediterranean basin: H. Schuchardt, "Die Lingua Franca," *Z. für Romanische Philologie* 33:441-61 (1909) and K. Whinnom, this volume.

41. Russenorsk or Russonorsk, the Russian-Norwegian contact language now extinct, was in frequent use among Scandinavian, Lappish, and Russian fishermen in the Barents and Norwegian Seas toward the end of the nineteenth century: G. Neumann, "Russenorwegisch und Pidginenglisch," *Nachrichten der Giessener Hochschulgesellschaft* 34:219-34 (1965).

43. Sabir and, particularly, Romani appear to have contributed to numerous coded varieties of European languages used by various social groups for a number of special functions; Yiddish has also exerted strong influence. Among the labels used to refer to these speech varieties: in England, Ziph, Cant, Green Language, Flash, Gammy, Peddler's French, St. Giles Greek, Pogado Jib, Broken Talk, Posh-ta-Posh, Half and Half (the latter are varieties of Anglo-Romani); in Holland, Bargoens; in Norway, Rodi or Fantespråk; in Germany, Rotwelsch, Gaunersprache, Jenisch; in France, Manouche or Sinti, Blesquiu, Argot, Argouche, Jobelin, Langue Verte; in Portugal, Caláo, Vasconco, and Giria; in Spain, Caló, Chipé Parabadi, Zincalo, Zingaro, Gitano; in Italy, Gergo, Fourbesque or Fourbesca; in Czechoslovakia, Hantyrka; in Turkey, Kataphiani. Shelta, an Anglo-Irish pidgin known also as Sheldru, Shelru, Bog Latin, Minkyers' or Minklers' Tari, Gammon, Gammoch, Tinker's Cant, Bawconi Jib, and Hinditemeskri Jib, was used primarily by Irish tinkers. Descendants of Shelta have been reported in the U.S. and eastern Canada, notably Béarla Lagair na Saor used by masons in New England: I. F. Hancock, "Shelta: A problem of classification," in D. DeCamp and I. F. Hancock, eds., pp. 130-37; "Pidginization and the Development of Anglo-Romani," in G. Cave, op. cit., p. 21. For a discussion of Jenisch, see Michael E. Bennett, "Aspects of Jenisch: a stratificational study," *Michigan Linguistic Society Papers* 2:1-8 (1976).

48. The linguistic results of Rumanian-Hungarian contact have been discussed by H. Schuchardt, "Romano-Magyarisches," *Romanische Philologie* 15:88-123 (1891).

AMERINDIAN-BASED

3. Pidgin Eskimo, a number of varying Eskimo pidgins used in trading with whites, and a quite different Eskimo pidgin used in trading with Athabascan Amerindians: V. Stefánsson, "The Eskimo trade jargon of Herschel Island," *American Anthropologist* 11:217-32 (1909).

4. Chinook Jargon, more usually called Wawa by its speakers, based mainly on Chinook proper but with considerable lexicon from Nootka, French, English, and Salishan languages, gained maximum currency in the Pacific Northwest during the late nineteenth century, being spoken by an estimated 100,000 people between southern Oregon and Alaska. Thought to have been creolized in some areas; well documented.

5. Trader Navaho, a name applied to forms of Navaho in Arizona, is spoken only by traders to Navahos and not vice-versa: O. Werner, *A typological comparison of four Trader Navaho speakers* (Bloomington, Indiana, 1963).

7. Mobilian, an Amerindian-derived pidgin, based mainly upon Choctaw, was used in earlier times by all tribes along the Gulf coast and the Mississippi as far as the Ohio River. This and other Amerindian-derived contact languages are described in M. Silverstein, "Dynamics of recent linguistic contact," in I. Goddard, ed., *Handbook of North American Indian Languages* 16 (1975).

11. New Jersey Amerindian Pidgin, now extinct, based lexically on the Munsee, Unami, and Unalachtigo (Delaware Algonkian) dialects of that region, and with a grammatical structure resembling English. Used between the local population and visiting English and Dutch traders: J. D. Prince, "An ancient New Jersey Indian jargon," *American Anthropologist* 14:508-24 (1912).

37. Lingoa Gêral (Lingua Geral) occasionally known as Ava'-neé or Tupï-haïa, is a rudimentary pidgin based on the Tupi-Guarani languages of South America, at one time in extensive use in coastal and inland Brazil: P. Ayrosa, *Apontamentos para a bibliografia da lingua tupí-guaraní* (São Paulo, 1943); F. G. Edelweiss, *Estudos tupis e tupi-guaranis* (Rio de Janeiro, 1969).

AFRICAN-BASED

36. Surviving African languages (Ashanti, Koromanti, Yoruba, KiKóongo, etc.) containing heavy admixture from European languages have been reported in the Caribbean and the northwest coast of South America, from the Guianas to Brazil; many of these languages are associated with religious cults, cf., for example: D. Olmstead, "Comparative notes on Yoruba and Lucumí," *Language* 29:157-64 (1953); M. A. Nazario, "Notas sobre el habla del negro en Puerto Rico durante el siglo XIX," *Revista del Instituto de Cultura Puertorriqueña* 2:43-48 (1959).

53. "A variety of mongrel Sudanese dialects," now almost extinct, and known as Kouriya, is spoken by slaves and their descendants at Gourara near Touat: L. C. Briggs, *The Living Races of the Sahara* (Cambridge, Mass., 1958), p. 75.

59. Over a wide area of Manding-speaking West Africa, a vehicular dialect

called Kaŋbɛ, i.e., "clear language," is in use between speakers of various Manding languages such as Mandinka and Bambara: D. Dalby, "Language distribution in Sierra Leone: 1961-1962," *Sierra Leone Language Review* 1:62-67 (1962), p. 63.

63. Commercial Dyula, a pidginized variety, is used in towns in the Ivory Coast: G. Partmann, *Le dioula véhiculaire en côte d'Ivoire* (Ann Arbor University Microfilms, 1973).

65. A reduced Ful is spoken at various places in Cameroon and Nigeria, P. F. Lacroix, "Observations sur la 'koinè' peule de Nguoundéré," *Travaux de l'Institut de Linguistique* 4:57-71 (1959).

68. Ewondo Populaire, also known as Bulu des Chauffeurs, Bulu Bediliva, and Pidgin A70, an African-derived lingua franca, is in use over a large area of eastern Cameroon: P. Alexandre, "Aperçu sommaire sur le pidgin A70 du Cameroun," *Symposium on Multilingualism* (Brazzaville, 1964), 251-56.

70. A Pidgin Hausa, called Barikanchi, grew up around the European barracks in northern Nigeria and was used as a lingua franca in the armed forces, sometimes being taught by English speakers to speakers of diverse Nigerian languages. For Hausa as a second language: C. Gouffé, "La langue haoussa," *Description linguistique du Monde* (Paris: CNRS 1977).

71. Galgalïya, a pidgin Arabic used by the Kalamáfi people in northeastern Nigeria: F. W. Taylor, *Fulani-English Dictionary* (Oxford, 1932), p. 62.

72. Tekrur, Tourkol, Shuwa, or Pidgin Arabic, employed as a lingua franca over a wide area to the east of Lake Chad, and in the Bodélé region: G. Muraz, *Vocabulaire du patois arabe tchadien ou "tourkou"* (Paris, 1931).

73. Sango, a pidginized variety of the Ngbandi language, itself also known as Sango. Extensively used in the Central African Republic (Oubangui-Chari), as well as in some areas of Cameroon and Chad: W. Samarin, *A Grammar of Sango* (The Hague, 1967).

74. Several pidginized forms of indigenous African languages are current in the Congo-Zaïre area, including Kituba (also known as Kibulamatadi, Munukutuba, Kisodi, Fiote, Ikeleve, Kileta, Commercial Kikongo, Commercial Kikwango, etc.), derived from KiKóongo and in use by perhaps 2,000,000 speakers as a second language; Ngbandi or pidginized Swahili, spoken in the eastern part of Zaïre; Pidgin Chiluba, employed extensively in Kasai Province; and Bangala or Lingala, a pidginized Ngala used in and around Kinshasa: E. Nida, "Tribal and trade languages," *African Studies* 15:155-58 (1955); J. Berry, "Pidgins and creoles in Africa," *Symposium on multilingualism* (London, 1962), 219-25; W. Samarin, "Lingua francas, with special reference to Africa," in F. Rice, ed., *Study of the Role of Second Languages* *in Asia, Africa and Latin America* (Washington, 1962), pp. 54-64; and B. Heine, *Status and Use of African Lingua Francas* (Munich 1970); E. Polomé, "Lubumbashi Swahili," *Journal of African Languages* 7:14-25 (1968).

81. Fanagalo, also called Isikula, Silunguboi, Isilololo, Chilapalapa, Isipiki, Chikabanga, Mine Kaffir, Kitchen Kaffir, Basic Bantu, etc., is a pidginized Zulu employed by migrant African mine workers around Johannesburg, and also in parts of southern Rhodesia on the Zambian copperbelt: D. T. Cole, "Fanagalo and the Bantu languages in South Africa," *African Studies* 12:1-9 (1953).

82. Several simplified indigenous African languages are in use in the Zambian copperbelt area, the most widespread being Town Bemba (or Chikopabeluti): L. Epstein, "Linguistic innovation . . . on the Copperbelt, Northern Rhodesia," *Southwestern Journal of Anthropology* 15:235-53 (1959), and I. Richardson, "Linguistic change in Africa, with special reference to the Bemba-speaking area of Northern Rhodesia," *Symposium on Multilingualism* (London, 1962):189-96.

83. A "mongrel dialect" called Chikunda, spoken by the descendants of a slave community on the lower Zambesi, is mentioned by H. Johnson, *British Central Africa* (New York, 1897), p. 391.

84. Barracoon, a contact vernacular in use during the nineteenth century in the Mozambique ports, and consisting of elements from Arabic, Swahili, Portuguese, Malagasy, Makua, and Hinzua: I. Richardson, "Evolutionary factors in Mauritian Creole," *Journal of African Languages* 2:2-14 (1963).

85. Swahili, itself the result of Arab-Bantu contact and intermarriage, has given rise to various pidginized forms widely spoken in eastern Africa. Perhaps the most aberrant variety is the so-called Ki-Setla (Settler) spoken in Kenya between Europeans and Africans: W. Whiteley, *Swahili, the Rise of a National Language* (London, 1969); cf. also B. Heine, op. cit., and E. Polomé, op. cit.

86. Some languages in the Tanzania-Kenya border region in East Africa, such as Mbugu and Beja, appear to have a Bantu-derived structure with a non-Bantu lexicon: M. Goodman, "The strange case of Mbugu," in D. Hymes, ed., pp. 243-54.

87. Sudan Arabic, Southern Arabic, Ki-nubi, Juba Arabic, Mongallese, Bimbashi Arabic, etc., flourished in the southern provinces of the then Anglo-Egyptian Sudan from about 1870 to 1920: A. A. J. Nhial, "Ki-nubi and Juba Arabic," paper presented at the International Conference on Pidgins and Creoles.

88. The pidginized military Sudan Arabic was carried into Uganda ca. 1891, where it adopted further lexical items from Luo, Bari, Swahili, and Lendu and became the mother tongue of a Muslim community called the Nubi: H. Thomas and R. Scott, *Uganda* (London, 1935), p. 88.

89. A Swahili-derived and reportedly creolized language is spoken in the Bajuni Islands in the Somali-Kenya coastal border area. Its speakers are also know as Bajuni.

91. A very similar language to Ki-Tiku, known as Ci-miini (Kilambizi, Chilambuzi, etc.), is spoken by a mixed and inbred population in Brava (Miini, Barawa) on the Somali coast. Its speakers believe that Ci-miini is a mixture of Portuguese and Swahili: W. Whiteley, "Notes on the Ci-miini dialect of Swahili," *African Language Studies* 6:67-71 (1965).

MISCELLANEOUS NON-EUROPEAN-BASED

98. Several pidginized or otherwise reduced varieties of Hindi have been reported, cf., for example: K. Abbas, "A link language for the common man," *Language and Society in India* (1969), pp. 31-33; S. K. Chatterji, "Calcutta Hindustani: a study of a jargon dialect," *Indian Linguistics* 1 (2-4):1-57 (1931); for other contact situations in India, cf. J. J. Gumperz and R. Wilson, "Convergence and creolization: a case from the Indo-Aryan-Dravidian border," and F. Southworth, "Detecting prior creolization," in D. Hymes, ed., pp. 151-68, 255-74. There are numerous languages in India showing admixture and possible pidginization and/or creolization, but most of which have not been described, notably: Nahili, of Mounda, Dravidian, and Indo-Aryan sources, used in the Satpura and Mahadeo mountains; Kharia, Mounda-Aryan spoken in Chota Nagpur; Koch, a mixture of Bodo and Assamese spoken in the northern part of Mymensingh; Horolia Jhagar, a Moundari-Gond language of Ranchi; Khetran, a mixture of Lahnda and Dard spoken in the Laghari mountains; Halabi or Bastari, a Marathi-Oriya mixed language; Tharui, a form of Bhojpuri; Sādan or Sādrī, a hybrid of Bhojpuri and Mundari, spoken in Bihar; Hajong or Haijong, containing elements of Bengali and Tibeto-Burman, employed in the state of Manipur; Jharwa, a pidginized Assamese with Garo elements in the Garo hills of Assam, Bengal, and Garo; Nimadi, a Rajasthani-Malwi language; Pendhari, of Hindi-Marathi-Rajasthani provenance of the Dharwar and Belgaum districts, and Desiya, a hybrid of Onya and Kui, spoken in Orissa, cf. G. A. Grierson, *Linguistic Survey of India*, vol. 1 (Calcutta, 1927), esp. Introduction; B. K. Roy Burman, "Languages of the tribal communities of India and their use in primary education," in *Language and Society in India* (Simla, 1969), pp. 251-59.

99. Vedda, spoken by about 400 speakers of an Austro-Mongaloid and Sinhalese creole in the Polonnaruwa and Dambulla districts of Sri Lanka: K. N. O. Dharmadasa, "The creolization of an aboriginal language: the case of Vedda in Sri Lanka (Ceylon)," *Anthropological Linguistics* 16:79-106 (1974).

100. The language of the Paliyans, a hill tribe in southern India, is described as being an "unintelligible Tamil jargon" with "deformed and limited vocabulary": F. Dahman, "The Paliyans, a hill-tribe of the Palni Hills (south India)," *Anthropos* 3:19-31 (1908).

101. Several miles northeast of Garo territory, Nagamese (Naga-Assamese, Pidgin or Broken Assamese, Pidgin Naga) is spoken throughout the entire state of Nagaland as a lingua franca: M. V. Sreedhar, "Nagamese," *Working Papers in Linguistics* 4 (8):65-66 (1972).

104. Pasá or Bazaar Malay, a pidginized variety of High Malay in widespread use throughout Malaysia and Indonesia: R. B. Le Page, "Multilingualism in Malaya," *Symposium on Multilingualism* (London, 1962):133-46. Compared with High Malay, Afrikaans, and Creole Portuguese in Ian F. Hancock, "Malacca Creole Portuguese: Asian, African or European?" *Anthropological Linguistics* 17(5):211-36 (1975).

102. A pidginized Chinese is reported to be in use as a contact language on the northwest frontiers of Laos and Vietnam in K. Whinnom, op. cit., viii, n.5.

124. A nineteenth-century Japanese-based pidgin is described in F. J. Daniels, "Vocabulary of the Japanese Ports Lingo," *Bulletin of the School of Oriental and African Studies* 12(3/4):805-23 (1948).

116. Police Motu or Hiri Motu, a pidginized variety of Hanuabada Motu with considerable lexical adoption from the coexistent Pidgin English, is used extensively in the Port Moresby area: S. Wurm and J. Harris, *Police Motu, an Introduction to the Trade Language of Papua* (Canberra, 1963).

126. Use of a pidginized form of the Siassi language as a lingua franca in the Astrolabe Bay area: T. Harding, *Voyagers of the Vitiaz Strait* (Seattle, 1967), p. 203.

127. Parau Tinito or Prao Tinto, a pidginized Tahitian, is spoken by older Chinese merchants in Papeete, Tahiti.

Index

PM
7802
P48   Pidgin and creole
         linguistics

DATE			

61-160·770